Footsteps in the Dark

Footsteps in the Dark

The Hidden Histories
of Popular Music

George Lipsitz

University of Minnesota Press   Minneapolis / London

An earlier version of chapter 3 was published as "'Home Is Where the Hatred Is': Work, Music, and the Transnational Economy," in *Home, Exile, Homeland: Film, Media, and the Politics of Place,* ed. Hamid Naficy (New York: Routledge, 1999). An excerpt of chapter 4 was published as "Songs of the Unsung: The Darby Hicks History of Jazz," in *Uptown Conversation: The New Jazz Studies,* ed. Robert G. O'Meally, Brent Hayes Edwards, and Farah Jasmine Griffin (New York: Columbia University Press, 2004). An earlier version of chapter 5 was published as "Like a Weed in a Vacant Lot," in *Decomposition: Post-Disciplinary Performance,* ed. Sue-Ellen Chase, Philip Brett, and Susan Leigh Foster (Bloomington: Indiana University Press, 2000). An earlier version of chapter 6 was published as "Their America and Ours: Intercultural Communication in the Context of 'Our America,'" in *José Martí's Our America: From National to Hemispheric Cultural Studies,* ed. Jeffrey Belnap and Raul Fernandez (Durham: Duke University Press, 1998). An earlier version of chapter 7 was published as "The Hip Hop Hearings," in *Generations of Youth: Youth Cultures and History in Twentieth-Century America,* ed. Joe Austin and Michael Willard (New York: New York University Press, 1998). Portions of chapter 8 were previously published as "Noises in the Blood," in *Crossing Lines: Race and Mixed Race across the Divide,* ed. Marc Coronado et al. (Lanham, Md.: Alta Mira Press, 2005), 19–44.

Published by the University of Minnesota Press
111 Third Avenue South, Suite 290
Minneapolis, MN 55401-2520
http://www.upress.umn.edu

Library of Congress Cataloging-in-Publication Data

Lipsitz, George.
    Footsteps in the dark : the hidden histories of popular music / George Lipsitz.
      p.   cm.
    Includes bibliographical references and index.
    ISBN-13: 978-0-8166-5019-4 (hc : alk. paper)
    ISBN-10: 0-8166-5019-5 (hc: alk. paper)
    ISBN-13: 978-0-8166-5020-0 (pb : alk. paper)
    ISBN-10: 0-8166-5020-9 (pb: alk. paper)
    1. Popular music—Social aspects. I. Title.
    ML3918.P67L56 2007
    781.6409—dc22

                                   2007003817

Printed in the United States of America on acid-free paper

The University of Minnesota is an equal-opportunity educator and employer.

12 11 10 09 08 07   10 9 8 7 6 5 4 3 2 1

Contents

Introduction: The Long Fetch of History;
or, Why Music Matters   **vii**

1. Pop Stars: The Hidden History of Digital Capitalism   **1**

2. Crossing Over: The Hidden History of Diaspora   **26**

3. Banda: The Hidden History of Greater Mexico   **54**

4. Jazz: The Hidden History of Nationalist Multiculturalism   **79**

5. Weeds in a Vacant Lot: The Hidden History of Urban
Renewal   **107**

6. Merengue: The Hidden History of Dominican
Migration   **133**

7. The Hip Hop Hearings: The Hidden History
of Deindustrialization   **154**

8. Masquerades and Mixtures: The Hidden History
of Passing   **184**

9. Salsa: The Hidden History of Colonialism   **211**

10. Techno: The Hidden History of Automation   **238**

Epilogue: Long Waves after 9/11   **263**

Acknowledgments   **279**
Notes   **281**
Index   **319**

Introduction

The Long Fetch of History;

or, Why Music Matters

We have songs of confusion and trial, burden and tribulation. Then we have songs of peace and a brighter day. We have songs of promise. We have songs of God and destiny. We have songs of life and death. So that any message that you really want to get over, you can get it over in a song. Isn't it so?

— C. L. Franklin, *Give Me This Mountain*

In places where the ocean meets the beach, most waves rise, crest, and fall in the space of a few yards. They are visible to the eye for only a few seconds. The life of a wave seems to be short, both spatially and temporally. Yet these waves can have enormous power. Under the right circumstances, they can erode rocky coastlines, pull sand from the shore back out to sea, crash through windows and walls to destroy buildings, and even wash up on shore miles inland. Scientists know that the short life of waves is an illusion. Ocean waves begin their journey thousands of miles out at sea. Their form, size, and shape come from the speed of prevailing winds in the atmosphere, the power of currents hidden beneath the sea, and their "long fetch"—the distance between a wave's point of origin and its point of arrival. Waves appear abruptly and immediately, but they have a long hidden history before the human eye notices them.

Marcus Reddiker and Peter Linebaugh compare history to those waves. The force and fury of history come from its long fetch.

Events that seem to appear in the present from out of nowhere in actuality have a long history behind them. An eruption of hatred, an outbreak of violence, or the overthrowing of an entire social order can shock us by its surprising force and fury, but the surprise comes largely because its long fetch remains hidden from view. The purpose of studying history is to train ourselves to look for its fetch, to realize that things that appear suddenly in our lives have a past, and to appreciate that part of what things are is how they came to be. Historical knowledge reveals that events that we perceive as immediate and proximate have causes and consequences that span great distances.

This is a book about hidden histories and long fetches. It delineates the ways in which popular music during the 1990s and early 2000s reflected both continuities and ruptures in history. I contend that many of the musical expressions that became popular during this period reflected and shaped important historical realities, even though their creators for the most part never intended them to be heard in that way. Of course, recorded music functions within commercial culture as a commodity produced to procure monetary returns for investors. It makes no pretense of presenting historical events with accuracy. Yet when read critically and symptomatically, popular music, like all forms of commercial culture from any era, registers change over time in important ways and serves as a vitally important repository for collective memory.

It was the long fetch of history that produced part of the force and fervor of "Footsteps in the Dark," a 1977 rhythm-and-blues recording by the Isley Brothers. In that song, the Isleys sing about being torn between wanting to know the truth and being afraid to know it. The lyrics of their haunting, mysterious, and moody ballad air the anxiety of someone fearful of being left behind by a lover but thinking about leaving, too. The footsteps in the dark might be the partner walking away, another lover approaching, or a projection of the singer's plan to slip away. Although the song's last verse pleads for reconciliation and proposes that the couple stop "walking around" because there's "love lost to be found," "Footsteps in the Dark" never reaches narrative or harmonic closure, conveying instead a gnawing, throbbing anxiety that cannot be eased.

"Footsteps in the Dark" may be one of the least sentimental love songs ever to have become popular. It airs fears, doubts, and desires generally suppressed by the obligatory cheerfulness or contradictory self-pity that permeates popular ballads. The Isley Brothers' song worries about the past and the present. It expresses doubt about the future. It tries to face the facts honestly, pleading urgently, "Let's look at what's been happening and try to be more aware." Yet the song's social significance extends far beyond the literal meaning of its lyrics.

Released on the *Go for Your Guns* album in 1977, "Footsteps in the Dark" has lingered as a faint yet powerful presence within popular music for nearly three decades. Disco diva Evelyn "Champagne" King and funk–soul singer Kipper Jones covered the song in their own distinctive styles in the 1980s and 1990s. Hip hop group Compton's Most Wanted used the track as a sample on its early 1990s hit "Can I Kill It?" Gangsta rap virtuoso Ice Cube made the song's chord progressions the center of his song "It Was a Good Day" in a particularly effective way. Ice Cube juxtaposed the dread, anxiety, and fear conveyed by the music with diametrically opposed lyrics celebrating an idyllic day of release from tension in the hood.[1]

"Footsteps in the Dark" seems to me an emblematic song for our time. Its lyrics center on something unseen, on sounds only vaguely heard or perhaps even imagined. It is a song that presumes that it is difficult to know the truth. Its relentlessly repetitive structure offers listeners an affect of anxiety to inhabit but no resolution. Accentuated by the brilliant phrasing of lead singer Ron Isley's haunting falsetto voice, the song simultaneously conveys contemplation, curiosity, desire, and resignation. It is suffused with sadness and weariness, yet holds out a hope that everything will still turn out all right. It conveys a profound ambivalence about whether it is better *not* to know the truth and only fear the worst or to *know* the truth and possibly have our fears confirmed.

Like other Isley Brothers songs from the 1960s and 1970s, "Footsteps in the Dark" fused private personal concerns with public and political issues. The Isleys started as a gospel group in the 1950s, enjoying sporadic subsequent successes as a rhythm-and-blues and soul act for the better part of two decades. They embarked on a new direction in 1969, starting with "It's Your Thing" and continuing in the 1970s with "Freedom" (1971), "Fight the Power" (1975), "Harvest for the World" (1976), and "Climbing Up the Ladder," "The Pride," and "Go for Your Guns" (1977). With these recordings, the Isleys seemed to capture the tenor of their time, addressing many of the social conditions faced by their core target audience of African Americans coded through lyrics that were sufficiently personal to secure airplay on mainstream radio, yet adequately figurative, poetic, evocative, and allusive to enable listeners to read shared social concerns and experiences into them.

At a time when the bright promise of the civil rights movement was starting to become eclipsed by the grim realities of economic restructuring, deindustrialization, the failure to enforce newly passed civil rights laws, and the deliberate abandonment of inner cities and their most vulnerable inhabitants, the Isley Brothers' songs sensitively registered changes taking place. The devastation enacted on Black communities by the white backlash against the civil rights movement, economic restructuring, deindustrialization, and the racially targeted policies of the Nixon, Ford, Carter, and Reagan presidencies has never been chronicled fully by journalists or historians. It appears powerfully, however, in the forms of Black popular culture that emerged in that era—in "blaxploitation" films and break dancing, in street styles of dress and spoken word poetry, in graffiti writing, and in rhythm and blues.[2] Because they serve as one of the few repositories of the memory of this period of rupture, African American cultural productions of the 1970s, including the songs of the Isley Brothers, have taken on iconic status for subsequent generations of consumers. The sights, sounds, and themes of that decade's popular culture have continued to permeate popular music, film, and fiction in the 1980s, 1990s, and 2000s. Much more than the culture of the more celebrated 1960s, the popular culture of the 1970s has become a foundational source and an informative archive for succeeding generations, because, even in its excesses, it registered the effects of a historical turning point. The progress made by Blacks in narrowing the wage, income, and asset gaps that separated them from whites reached a peak in 1974, but the gaps widened substantially after that. Capital flight to low-wage countries, computer-based automation, budget cuts that slashed social programs, tax breaks for the rich, and white determination to resist the mandates of civil rights laws damaged minority communities in the United States with devastating consequences. Drugs imported from overseas flooded Black neighborhoods, while urban renewal and redevelopment schemes destroyed entire communities, displaced their inhabitants, and diminished their political power.

The music of artists like the Isley Brothers and Curtis Mayfield, blaxploitation films like *Superfly* and *Shaft*, and even mainstream motion pictures like Berry Gordy's *Mahogany* and Sidney Poitier's *Buck and the Preacher* portrayed Black America as a community under a state of siege.

As far as we can know, the Isley Brothers did not intend to be historians of these changes or even to create a historical record of them with their music. They never chose to present an empirical accounting of events organized in chronological order, nor did their songs speak directly about politics, laws, or leaders. The Isley Brothers did not do research in traditional archives filled with government documents, personal records, or diaries of famous people. Yet they displayed extraordinary familiarity with and knowledge of what we might call the alternative archives of history, the shared memories, experiences, and aspirations of ordinary people, whose perspectives rarely appear in formal historical archival collections.

Many of the songs made by the Isley Brothers in the 1970s treated the present as history, sensitively registering changes that take place over time. Their lyrics often presumed that "what things are" stems from "how they came to be." The musical forms they deployed had credibility with audiences, because they referenced a long history of rhythms, chords, melodies, harmonies, and performance styles honed *over* time in work songs, field hollers, blues, gospel, jazz, rhythm and blues, and rock 'n' roll. The lyrics of their songs evoked responses, because they focused on people *in* time, on the changes in outlook and perception taking place in contemporary everyday life, changes caused by history but only rarely connected to recognized historical narratives.

As entertainers whose livelihood depended on purchases by the public, the Isley Brothers (and many other musicians like them) mined the memories, experiences, and aspirations of their audiences to build engagement and investment in the music they made. Their music was dialogic in the sense delineated by literary theorist Mikhail Bakhtin. He argues that no monologue exists in culture, that all utterances answer something that was said before, that the word (or the note, the chord, the harmony, the melody, the pitch, the timbre, and the rhythm) is "always half someone else's." Popular music is not history, but it can be read historically, dialogically, and symptomatically to produce valuable evidence about change over time. Popular music can mark the present as history, helping us understand where we have been and where we are going.

The enduring presence of "Footsteps in the Dark" in contemporary culture exemplifies how popular songs about personal issues can provide evidence about change over time in public life. The political and economic problems facing Black communities in the 1970s had profound ramifications for the everyday lives of their inhabitants. As Tricia Rose points out in her insightful and generative work on Black women and sexuality, suppression of social justice throughout society has important and deadly ramifications for justice in the intimate arenas of everyday personal life. Relations between romantic partners take place in a context. In Black communities in the United States in the 1970s, discrimination and disinvestment on the macrosocial level put pressure on immediate and intimate relations on the microsocial level. They intensified antagonisms between generations and genders, disrupted relations between romantic partners, and exacerbated differences between parents and their children. The evisceration of the social wage and massive disinvestment in Black communities exacted costs on the private, personal, and intimate lives of Black people in incalculable ways.

Cultural expressions like "Footsteps in the Dark" emerged under these conditions as a repository of collective memory and a vehicle for collective witness. Aggrieved communities are always susceptible to radical divisiveness. People in them compete with one another for scarce resources. In times of transition and change, tensions among neighbors and within families can be aggravated. The collective solidarity enacted by the race-based social movements and pro-Black cultural affirmations of the 1960s and 1970s provided alternatives to that divisiveness. "Footsteps in the Dark" both reflected and shaped that solidarity. It succeeded as art, at least in part because it served as a dialogic nexus bringing together personal and public as well as past and present parts of people's lives, because it used Black idioms to explore the problems facing Black people.

Ice Cube's use of "Footsteps in the Dark" on his 1992 song "It Was a Good Day" makes explicit the implicit link in the Isley Brothers' song between the personal experiences of everyday life and the collective reckoning with the hurts of history. Ice Cube's lyrics link the personal problems about romance delineated in the lyrics of "Footsteps in the Dark" to larger public issues: to racism, police surveillance, and the radical divisiveness of ghetto life, to a feeling that happiness in this society is precarious, that small moments of private pleasure may be precious largely because they provide a welcome distraction from a broader social crisis that we are powerless to prevent. Ice Cube recognized that the Isley Brothers' song enacted the emotional state to which it alluded, and he deployed that affective power by using the chord progressions, rhythm, and timbre of the original recording to provide a stunning musical counterpoint to lyrics about a day of good food, friendly recreation, sensual pleasure, and peace of mind. Yet the music in "It Was a Good Day" completely undercuts the words. Even as rendered in Ice Cube's reassuring baritone, his descriptions of happiness take on a melancholy sadness juxtaposed to the sounds of the Isley Brothers' song. The recording sounds as if even the speaker cannot believe that today's good times will last. The foreboding menace conveyed by the song's chord progressions provides perfect accompaniment to lyrics that describe "a good day" as one of temporary respite rather than permanent peace, as a day when the narrator wonders if he will live to see another twenty-four (hours), but at least "I didn't have to use my AK" and "nobody I know got killed in South Central LA."

The promotional video for Ice Cube's "It Was a Good Day" explains and augments the paranoid affect underlying the song's tale of precarious satisfaction. After following Ice Cube through all the activities celebrated in "It Was a Good Day," the camera pans back from his house to reveal police helicopters and a SWAT team waiting to ambush him on his return. On the album *The Predator,* Ice Cube added another layer to the dialectical tension in "It Was a Good Day." When the song concludes, we hear a southern politician (perhaps Birmingham's Eugene "Bull" Connor or President Lyndon B. Johnson) extolling the virtues of peace, quiet, and good order, followed by news reports of the Los Angeles riots of April 29–May 1, 1992. Another voice follows, reporting the acquittal of the four police officers whose brutal beating of Rodney King captured on videotape was not enough to convince a suburban Simi Valley jury to convict them. Ice Cube then segues into "We Had to Tear This ____ Up," his song explaining and justifying the riots.

One section of the "acknowledgments" in the liner notes of *The Predator* album speaks bitterly and directly about wanting to know and being afraid to know. It reads:

> Ice Cube wishes to acknowledge the failure of the public school system to teach all of its students about the major contributions made by our African American scientists, inventors, artists, scholars, and leaders (with all due respect for your lectures on the planet). Without its role in the conspiracy, the Predator album might not have been made.[3]

The enduring and lingering (if peripheral) presence of "Footsteps in the Dark" in contemporary culture adds an additional layer of meaning to the Isley Brothers' song. In a society where advertising, entertainment, public relations, and political communications perpetually promise fulfillment, happiness, and security, the truth can be hard to find. Newspapers, motion pictures, and even history textbooks tend to tell the story of society from the perspective of its rulers. Uncomfortable and inconvenient evidence about the past disappears from public view. The people whose life circumstances compel them to ask questions about the dominant story—to ask with the Isleys, "Am I sure?" or "Do I really care?"—can be made to feel uneasy, out of step, unsure, and insecure. They seek to read between the lines to search for signs about the truth, to "look at what's happening and try to be more aware." They wonder about what might have been. They ask whether they should continue in the same direction or turn back. They listen for the footsteps in the dark.

In a world in which war, disease, hatred, hunger, environmental destruction, and so many other forms of calculated cruelty pervade the present, faith in the future can be hard to sustain. The confident optimism that prevailed in U.S. culture in the first half of the twentieth century now seems exhausted and obsolete. The peace, prosperity, and security perpetually promised to the populace by elite decision makers and technocrats alike have not materialized. As Hannah Arendt noted years ago, feelings of paranoid isolation and loneliness that at one time stemmed largely from idiosyncratic and personal catastrophes, accidents, and illnesses now constitute common experiences for a large part of the world's population. They make it difficult even to imagine what it would be like to live in a just or loving community. Arendt argues ominously that the origins of totalitarianism lie in such loneliness.[4]

Popular music takes on significance in relation to these issues, because most people in today's world do not have the opportunity to express their political opinions or to participate meaningfully in the decisions that shape their lives. Despite the expansion of the number of nations that purport to be democracies, control over electoral politics by the rich and monopoly control over media outlets preclude meaningful public dialogue about political issues. Severe and growing economic inequality provides the "haves" with permanent advantages over the "have nots." Decades of free market fundamentalism have concentrated enormous power in very few hands, undermining the legitimacy of public institutions, dispersing and disaggregating aggrieved populations, and promoting a consumer notion of citizenship that encourages each individual and each subunit of government to make gains at the expense of others. This system feeds the desire and greed of investors and owners while suppressing the responsibilities and obligations of citizens.

Yet people continue to long for better and more meaningful lives in the arenas open to them and with the tools they have available. Precisely because consumption plays such a central part in the activities of everyday life in today's society, the products of popular culture often become focal points for the expression of desires suppressed in other spheres—desires for connections to others, for meaningful work, for a culture not based on lies.

This is a book about popular music as social history, as an archive of past and present realities and future possibilities, as one place where we may hear footsteps in the dark. I argue that historical changes that are only remotely registered in history books, newspapers, or the pronouncements of politicians can appear in vivid relief and full complexity within products of the popular music industry—if we learn how to read them correctly. I examine different forms of music that became popular during the 1990s and early 2000s, in order to reveal the hidden histories of the present and the recent past.

On the pages of this book I argue that the popularity of the singing group Eden's Crush and the emergence of the techno music subculture in Detroit represent contradictory manifestations of the emergence of digital capitalism, an economic and social system that produces distinctly new kinds of people in order to meet the needs of new forms of production, distribution, and consumption. In these chapters, I am especially interested in the ways in which new consumer practices disturb traditional understandings of gender, race, and place.

I examine Afro-diasporic and Asian diasporic identities in popular music as indices and registers of the transnational movements of people, products, capital, and culture. My readings of banda, merengue, and salsa music argue that these old forms gained new prominence in the 1990s, not only because of their artistic and affective dimensions but also as registers and reflections of changes in Mexican, Dominican, and Puerto Rican nationalisms, alterations in gender relations within transnational communities, and transformations in the nature of life and labor in the United States.

I discuss how the PBS television series *Jazz* framed the history of the nation's greatest indigenous art form directly in response to the politics of the 1990s, not so much to give us a better understanding of jazz music as to give us a way of advancing a celebratory U.S. nationalism that would render obsolete the civil rights era's critiques of racial inequality. My chapters on the campaigns to censor hip hop music and on the relationships linking urban spatial relations to the Black Arts movement and to millennial folk memories of the mid-twentieth century enable me to connect musical creations to the intergenerational effects of deindustrialization and urban renewal. A chapter on racial imposters and masqueraders in music enables me to address how racial norms are influenced by ideas about racial passing, mixed-race identities, and performativity. My hope is that reading popular music as history and interpreting history through popular music will help us to hear the footsteps in the dark, to see how history happens and why music matters.

Of course, popular music can be deceptive. It is not meant to be interpreted literally. The musician known as St. Louis Jimmy inexplicably hailed from Detroit. Memphis Minnie was not originally named Minnie and did not come from Memphis. Neither member of the duet Don and Juan was named either Don or Juan. The Thompson Twins were not twins, were not named Thompson, and there were three of them. Tex Williams was from Illinois, but

Illinois Jacquet hailed from Texas. The group called the Detroit Emeralds came from Little Rock, Arkansas. The Manhattans came from Jersey City. The musician known as Jhimmy the Hawaiian hailed from Brazzaville in the Congo.[5] Perhaps most egregiously, the group called 10,000 Maniacs was never as large an ensemble as its name indicated.

More seriously, deception is part of the work that popular music performs. All entertainers assume personas onstage, but commercial culture offers particular monetary inducements to successful masqueraders. Working musicians sometimes learn to fabricate stories about where they live, because they fear being taken for granted (and being paid less) as a local act. In chapter 8, I detail the commercial imperatives that led African American musicians John Redd and Lee Brown to pose successfully as an Asian Indian and a Mexican American, but less spectacular acts of imposture are actually routine in the music industry. New Orleans pianist and singer Mac Rebennack has performed under the pseudonym Dr. John throughout his career, but when as a young musician he feared that club owners were becoming suspicious of his band's ability to continue to attract crowds, he secured jobs for them all over town under different names. On any given night, the same ensemble might be called Mac Rebennack and the Skyliners, Frankie Ford and the Thunderbirds, Jerry Byrnes and the Loafers, Leonard James and the Night Trains, or the Shadows.[6] Rebennack did not feel remorseful about his disguise, in part because he knew that the local duo Sugar and Sweet routinely passed themselves off as the more successful Shirley and Lee, that Ricky Ricardo got jobs by claiming he was Frankie Ford, and even the incomparable James Booker gained commercial value by billing himself and his band as Huey Smith and the Clowns.[7]

Some disguises, however, do more harm than others. Centuries of orientalism, tropicalism, and primitivism in Europe and North America have produced a series of stereotypes encapsulated into sound cues in symphonies, motion picture scores, and popular songs. Gongs and specific string instruments signal "Asia," trumpets, congas, and maracas suggest "South America," and tom-toms, vibrato, and familiar chord progressions simulate Native American "Indian" territory. These stereotypes have almost no relationship to actual Asian, South American, or indigenous music; they are more a caricature of what such music sounds like to provincial

Western listeners. The market category of "world music" makes a single genre out of Nigerian juju, Siberian–Mongolian throat singing, and Native American Tohono O'odham *waila* music by treating all forms of music outside Euro-American pop conventions as exotic and interchangeable.

The repetition of these cultural fictions, moreover, sometimes turns them into social facts. They circulate so widely as representations that they sometimes become self-stereotyped, taken up by aggrieved populations as the price of entry onto the world stage. Members of aggrieved groups perform caricatures of their own cultures in television advertisements promoting tourism and in musical compositions that seem "exotic" and therefore palatable to popular audiences. Yet at the same time, popular music sometimes provides inversions, subversions, and alternatives to orientalist, tropicalist, and primitivist stereotypes. The indigenous Australian band Coloured Stone blends Anglo-American rock and pop with traditional tribal harmonies that convey clearly both the specific cultural politics of Aboriginal Australians and their connections to transnational commercial culture. Algerian *rai* and Peruvian *chicha* brilliantly encapsulate the complex cultural collisions and confluences in the port of Oran and in the hillside settlements near Lima and Arequipa.[8]

It takes research, evidence, interpretation, and argument to find the truths hidden by surface appearances in popular music. Yet when analyzed correctly, popular music can be a valuable source of evidence about social history. Clyde Woods, for example, astutely connects the origins of blues music in Mississippi to the removal of Union troops and the end of Reconstruction in 1877. For a decade after the Civil War, federal troops, known colloquially as the blues (because of the color of their uniforms), protected newly freed Blacks from white vigilante violence. Blacks formed chapters of the Loyalty and Union League, made alliances with poor whites in state politics, and elected two African Americans to the U.S. Senate. The withdrawal of federal troops, however, left Black people at the mercy of their unrepentant former owners, who moved quickly to reduce them to debt peonage through sharecropping. Jim Crow segregation made Blacks second-class citizens while new laws punishing vagrancy and debt criminalized their poverty. Ultimately, the state of Mississippi disenfranchised almost the entire Black population of the state through the Mississippi Constitution of 1890. Woods notes, however, that when the blues (the soldiers) departed, the blues (the music) arrived. His analysis reveals that the blues served serious social functions, that it served as an ethnoracial and an ethnospatial epistemology, a repository of collective memory, a source of moral instruction, and a symbol of shared social conditions.[9] Made up of more than mere musical forms, figures, and devices, blues music as a social institution played a crucial role in creating ways of knowing and ways of being vital to African American people. It did so, however, in coded and disguised form, largely hidden from the sight and surveillance of those who held political and economic power.

The long fetch of history sometimes makes its presence felt in unlikely places and in unexpected ways. Links between expressive culture and collective history have permeated the history of popular music in the United States. For example, in 1961, Gary Anderson gained extraordinary commercial success with his song "A Quarter to Three." Recorded in Norfolk, Virginia, under the name Gary U.S. Bonds, the song was the number-one best-seller in the nation, staying on the charts for fifteen weeks. In the lyrics that he wrote for the song, Anderson mentions the musicians accompanying him on the recording, Daddy G and the Church Street Five, and for good reason.

The melody of "A Quarter to Three" had already been used by Gene Barge (who called himself Daddy G) and his band, the Church Street Five, on their unsuccessful commercial release *A Night with Daddy G*. Anderson and Barge recorded at the same studio in Norfolk, and U.S. Bonds wrote lyrics for the song in the hope of helping his friend get a hit with the tune. Barge called himself Daddy G in part because his first name was Gene but also because, like many Blacks in Norfolk, he had grown up worshipping at a church founded by a charismatic Black Cape Verdean immigrant railway worker who called himself Daddy Grace, hence Daddy G.

Marcelino Manoel de Graca changed his name to Charles Manuel Grace when he came to the United States near the turn of the century. Working as a cook for the Southern Railway, he came into contact with Pentecostal and holiness preachers in the

South. Inspired by their ecstatic forms of worship, Grace founded the United House of Prayer for All People in West Wareham, Massachusetts, in 1919, and from there it spread across the country. He taught his parishioners that the verse in Psalm 150 that commands praise to the Lord with the sounds of the trumpet, the psaltery, and the harp, with timbrel and dance, and with stringed instruments and organs required them to play music in church. Daddy Grace favored bands that emphasized the sound of trombones, and to this day his church continues to produce all-trombone bands playing sacred music.

The raucous, sprightly, and cacophonous sounds of the band on "A Quarter to Three" originated in the church services, baptisms, and weddings for which Barge and his fellow musicians performed in Norfolk in the church founded by Sweet Daddy Grace. Most listeners had no idea of the religious origins of the music they heard on "A Quarter to Three," but Barge and the Church Street Five knew that a long history of Portuguese colonialism, Cape Verdean immigration, African American labor organization, collective self-help, and holiness religious teaching infused the sounds that secured them commercial success. These same sounds subsequently permeated the music of other rhythm-and-blues singers, including Solomon Burke, who served as a minister in the United House of Prayer for All People Church and was the godson of Daddy Grace. Similarly, Bobby Womack remembers, "I sang at every church in Cleveland. I worked with Sweet Daddy Grace, Father Divine, all those people."[10]

Another kind of history permeated Dion DiMucci's hit record "The Wanderer" in 1961. A rock 'n' roll song built around the boasts of a man who loves many women but refuses to be tied down to any one of them, "The Wanderer" was written by Ernie Maresca. It reached the number-two spot on the best-seller charts in the winter of 1961–62. Born in the Bronx, New York, in 1939, DiMucci grew up in an Italian American neighborhood. He belonged to a gang called the Fordham Baldies, a name derived by combining nearby Fordham Road with the neighborhood's Garibaldi fraternal and social club named after the Italian patriot Giuseppe Garibaldi. Nurturing secret passions for the country music of Hank Williams and pop standards sung by Al Jolson, DiMucci made very different kinds of best-selling rock 'n' roll records between 1958 and 1960 as the lead singer of Dion and the Belmonts (named after Belmont

Avenue in the Bronx). "The Wanderer" was the sixth record he released as a solo act, using only his first name, Dion. Maresca claims that in writing the song he was inspired by "I'm a Man," by blues musician Bo Diddley, and the lyrics certainly show an affinity between the two songs.

The infectious beat of "The Wanderer," however, comes from the tarantella, the traditional Italian dance frequently played at weddings and other festive social occasions. Pietro di Donato's Depression-era novel *Christ in Concrete,* published the year Dion DiMucci was born, uses the tarantella as the key symbol of continuity in Italian life, as a part of the Italian past that persists within Italian immigrant communities. In Philip Kaufman's 1979 film *The Wanderers,* about urban street gangs (including one called the Baldies), a scene depicts guests at a wedding dancing the tarantella to Dion's recording of "The Wanderer."[11] In the 1990s, several rap artists in Italy incorporated words from regional dialects and tarantella dancing into their performances. Ethnomusicologists Piero Fumarola and George Lapassade organized festivals and performances that blended hip hop with frenzied tarantella music orchestrated for *taburello,* violin, guitar, and accordion.[12]

Another ethnic festive moment provides the hidden history behind Parliament's 1978 song "Flash Light." In a 1993 discussion with Parliament's founder and guiding spirit, George Clinton, rock guitarist Vernon Reid suggested that the "chant" in "Flash Light" seemed to have come from an opera. Clinton corrected him, however, by relating a story about how he had moved north with his family as a child, from his birthplace in Kannapolis, North Carolina, to reside in Plainfield, New Jersey. Clinton explained that when he was in grade school he attended the bar mitzvah of one of his friends, Aaron Myron. He took the "hook" for "Flash Light" from the synagogue chanting that he heard that day. Explaining that he could not get the melody out of his mind and that he played it over and over, Clinton eventually zeroed in on the part that went "Da da da *dee da* da da," leaving out the rest. Then he added the words "You turn me on," because they seemed to fit. His composition became "Flash Light."[13]

The connection that made little Aaron Myron's bar mitzvah chant from the 1950s a staple of Black culture in the 1970s came from that time after World War II when some Blacks and Jews in the Northeast shared the same neighborhoods, the same networks, and the same schools. It was a link that would be broken by subsidized white flight to the suburbs and by the backlash against school desegregation attendant to it. By 1978, when "Flash Light" sold well throughout the country, Blacks and Jews occupied very different, and frequently antagonistic, places in U.S. society. Yet an earlier moment when they experienced much in common lived on in Clinton's song.

Another festive occasion provoked a similar case of cultural coalescence in two 1973 songs, "Blow Your Whistle" and "Sound Your Funky Horn." In the early 1970s, Harry Casey and Rick Finch were working as white producers at TK Records in Miami, a label that featured music by Black artists. Session musician Clarence Reid, later successful as the salacious rapper Blowfly, invited Casey and Finch to his wedding reception. There, they encountered a Bahamian band playing "junkanoo" carnival music. The ensemble accented its songs with cowbells, whistle flutes, and steel drums. Excited by the sounds they heard, Casey and Finch incorporated those instruments into their compositions "Blow Your Whistle" and "Sound Your Funky Horn." They recorded this new music with a group of session musicians under the name KC and the Sunshine Junkanoo Band. When their compositions unexpectedly became hits in the United Kingdom, Casey changed the group's name to KC and the Sunshine Band. The group placed nine songs on the top forty best-seller charts between 1975 and 1979, and its success played a major role in fueling the popularity of the music known as disco.[14]

The processes that enabled Harry Casey to combine rhythm and blues, junkanoo, and then disco music were quite complex. His white Pentecostal mother loved the doo-wop harmonies of Zeke Carey and the Flamingos, a 1950s African American group whose unusual harmonies were rooted in contemporary Black and white Pentecostalism, born of the interracial Azusa Street Revival in Los Angeles, which took place at the beginning of the century. In addition to the Pentecostal influence was the ethnoreligious influence of the Sunshine Band percussionist Fermin Goytisolo, who was part of Miami's large Cuban American population and an heir to the sacred Santería drumming traditions of that island, which produce what Robert Farris Thompson aptly describes as "medicine, coded as music."[15] Listeners to the disco songs performed by KC and the Sunshine Band or the filthy raps that Clarence Reid recorded as

Blowfly could scarcely suspect the sacred and ceremonial origins of their music, but their songs would not have come into existence had it not been for the histories of European empires in the Caribbean, of slavery and labor migration, of street revivals, sacred wedding vows, carnival celebrations, and Santería ceremonies.

The origins of pop songs in church services at the United House of Prayer for All People in Norfolk, Virginia; at Aaron Myron's bar mitzvah in Plainfield, New Jersey; in dancing the tarantella at Italian weddings in the Bronx; and in junkanoo music at Clarence Reid's wedding in Miami reveal one hidden history within popular music: that musicians hone and refine their art where they get paid to play, that before they make a living playing music in nightclubs or as recording artists, they play at churches, synagogues, and halls hosting wedding receptions and other ritual occasions. But recorded music also has its own dialogic currents, its own hidden histories of affiliation and identification, its own long fetch that connects it to other kinds of histories, as the saga of KC and the Sunshine Band further illustrates.

The lascivious rap songs recorded by Blowfly and the percussion and bass-heavy rhythms recorded at TK studios continued to permeate popular music in Miami for decades. The hip hop group 2 Live Crew drew on both traditions in recording their controversial 1990 album *As Nasty as They Wanna Be*.[16] (See chapters 2 and 7.) Even after Luther Campbell dissolved 2 Live Crew, the influence and appeal of Miami bass became the main source for the first big hit of the new millennium, the Baha Men's "Who Let the Dogs Out?" in 2000.

The Baha Men had recorded a song titled "Going Back to the Island" in 1992. Built around the junkanoo parade beat of Bahamian carnival, the song and its promotional video told the triumphant tale of an expatriate in the United States longing to return home. The Bahamas tourist bureau used the song in its advertisements, but the recording had little impact outside the island. Then the group added three rappers to front the band, blended their junkanoo rhythms with a Miami bass sound borrowed from 2 Live Crew, and recorded with producer Steve Greenberg of S-Curve Records, the producer and arranger of *Funky Town* for the group Lipps, Inc. in 1980. Greenberg persuaded the Baha Men to record a song written for carnival in Trinidad in 1996, "Who Let the Dogs Out?"

Multiple histories permeated the Baha Men's recording "Who Let the Dogs Out?" The Bahamians who recorded it in 2000 could look back to their own upbringing in the Caribbean as well as to the junkanoo sounds that Harry Casey and Rick Finch had heard at Clarence Reid's wedding in 1973. The rap songs that Clarence Reid performed as Blowfly and the rhythms of the Sunshine Band shaped the music of 2 Live Crew, clearly the main hip hop influence in "Who Let the Dogs Out?" It might have been easy for the Baha Men to understand how to interpret a song written for carnival in Trinidad because of the similarities between Trinidadian and Bahamian junkanoo, but they may not have known that "Who Let the Dogs Out?" was written not in Trinidad-Tobago but rather in Whitby, Ontario, where its lyricist, Anselm Douglas, and its composer, Ossie Gurley, lived as expatriates from Trinidad-Tobago.

"Who Let the Dogs Out?" could be claimed as a Trinidadian song, a Bahamian song, a south Florida song, and a Canadian song all at once. It became the theme song of the U.S. women's basketball team in the 2000 Olympics, appeared in a commercial for Honda automobiles and in the movie *The Rugrats,* and served as a rallying cry for New York Mets fans when the team broadcast the song through the loudspeakers in Shea Stadium during the 2000 World Series.

Thus, even seemingly apolitical songs such as "Who Let the Dogs Out?" "Sound Your Funky Horn," "The Wanderer," and "A Quarter to Three" have complicated political and social histories. They demonstrate the dialogic nature of culture, the ongoing conversation with the past that guarantees that every utterance enters a dialogue already in progress. These songs are surface manifestations of long, and largely unrecorded, histories. They do not tell those histories in and by themselves, but, like footsteps in the dark, they alert us to be aware, to be on the lookout for things that may be all around us but not yet seen.

In his autobiography, New Orleans guitarist and pianist Mac Rebennack (Dr. John, the Night Tripper) points out the ways in which popular music serves as a repository for culture from other realms—both secular and sacred. He notes that when musicians call a job a "gig" or when they refer to an instrument as an "axe," they are borrowing terms from gamblers and numbers runners. A *gig* originally referred to a bet (a dime gig would be a dime bet). When gamblers wanted to destroy rival establishments, they traditionally carried axes, using them to chop up the wooden tables and chairs. When in later years they destroyed rivals with guns, they preserved the term *axe* as a way of disguising their plans from eavesdroppers.[17] Proximity to gamblers led musicians to refer to their instruments, especially guitars, as their axes. When gamblers collected a bet, they declared it was "in the bag." Musicians borrowed that term to describe a contained and secure musical groove or style. Moreover, as free jazz virtuoso Ornette Coleman often complained, popular music has never completely disassociated itself from these origins, often serving as a way to enhance atmospheres in establishments designed to get people to buy more drinks, pay for sex, or gamble.[18]

Yet the same musicians who get their slang from gangsters and their jobs from industries devoted to vice also draw on sacred sounds that they learned in religious centers. Drummer Earl Palmer established the definitive cadences of many rhythm-and-blues, rock 'n' roll, and soul records by drawing on the traditions of sanctified church drumming brought into rhythm-and-blues music in his native New Orleans by Melvin and David Lastie, whose father played drums in church.[19] As Dr. John explains:

> In New Orleans, everything—food, music, religion, even the way people talk and act—has deep, deep roots; and like the tangled veins of cypress roots that meander this way and that in the swamps, everything in New Orleans is interrelated, wrapped around itself in ways that aren't always obvious.[20]

A popular song may seem to have a short life. It appears suddenly. It catches on and seems to be everywhere all at once. Then, it disappears. Like an ocean wave at the beach, it appears to be ephemeral and transient. Yet both ocean waves and the sonic waves that produce popular songs have long fetches. The interpretations I present in this book of jazz, pop, techno, banda, salsa, merengue, hip hop, and rock music focus on both the sudden arrival of new cultural forms in the United States and the long fetch of history that brought them into being. My hope is that these inquiries will help us answer questions about our world that are not asked often enough and that they will help us see why culture counts and how history happens. As the Isley Brothers plead in "Footsteps in the Dark," "Let's look at what's been happening, and try to be more aware."

1. Pop Stars

The Hidden History of Digital Capitalism

One of the illusions created by modern social science is that the commodity relations which exist among us today constitute the normal, natural, primordial, way in which society was always organized.
—Walter Rodney

A container ship known as the *Hansa Carrier* encountered a severe storm in the North Pacific one day in 1990. Rough seas and strong winds shook up the vessel, causing twenty-one intermodal containers to fall overboard. Four broke open, releasing sixty-one thousand pairs of Nike running shoes to float in the currents of the Pacific Ocean. Months later, beachcombers on the west coast of North America, from Oregon to Alaska, started coming across individual shoes washing ashore. They set up swap meets to match right and left shoes of the same size so that they could be worn or sold.[1]

A similar episode in 1992 dispersed some thirty thousand plastic bath toys onto the waters of the Pacific between Hong Kong and Tacoma. Thousands of plastic green frogs, yellow ducks, red beavers, and blue turtles "escaped" from a container washed overboard from another ship during a storm. Fortunately, as oceanographer Curtis Ebbesmeyer notes wryly, these animals were all good swimmers. Ten months after the spill, most of these bath toys "landed" on the beaches near Sitka, Alaska. Prevailing winds propelled the high-floating bath toys on a course different from the low-floating shoes, whose movements had been determined more by the gyre of ocean currents than by the winds. Some of the bath toys that did not reach shore spent the winter of 1992–93 frozen in the ice of the Bering Sea, only to be released in the spring. Some of them floated back into the North Pacific, while others drifted around the Arctic Ocean until they made their way to the North Atlantic.[2] Although they once sailed on the same waves, the running shoes and the plastic bath toys reached different destinations because of wind and water currents and differential depths and weights.

The unexpected trajectories of running shoes and plastic bath toys through ocean waters produced unanticipated evidence for oceanographers. These spills enabled them to learn things about ocean currents that had previously been occluded from their purview. Yet, when ships do not sink and containers do not crack open, the routine commercial patterns of worldwide distribution and circulation of products such as shoes and bath toys are hidden from view for most of us. The linked and integrated production and distribution system that containerization entails is not just a way of shipping goods from one place to another; it also structures an entire way of life with profound ramifications for how we experience identities, places, and races.

The use of automated cranes and interchangeable containers for shipping creates a totally integrated freight transport system based on transfers from ships to trucks and trains. Metal boxes that are forty feet long, eight feet high, and eight feet wide serve as the universal mechanism for cargo shipments. The interchangeability and flexibility that containerization facilitates ensure high profits for manufacturers and shipping lines alike, but they also dramatically transform the practices and processes of production, distribution, and consumption for people all over the globe.

Like most forms of automation, containerization in theory could serve vital human needs. Used in the right way, it could eliminate dangerous and difficult jobs, increase productivity, and bring people from far-flung corners of the earth closer together. Under current conditions, however, containerization is controlled by an oligopoly of predatory transnational corporations and financial institutions. In our world, containerization conditions humans to serve the machines instead of the other way around. Patterns of consumption, production, and popular culture come into being not as a result of human desires but because they fit the mold created for the convenience of profit-making commercial interests. The mechanisms of containerized production and distribution produce patterns of containerized consumption.

Very few consumers recognize the ways in which containerization influences their lives, but music listeners and television viewers in the late 1990s and early 2000s could not help but notice one of containerization's logical outcomes: the growth of prefabricated musical acts. Containerization exerted a powerful, albeit secret, influence on the production, distribution, and reception of popular music ranging from new "boy bands" and the "girl bands" that emerged in response to them to the growth of reality television shows like *Making the Band* and *American Idol*.

Boy bands generally get very little respect, but they make a lot of money. From the era of New Edition to the emergence of New Kids on the Block to the popularity of 'N Sync, Menudo, and Backstreet Boys, succeeding cohorts of preteen girls have shared generational experiences built around identification with all-male pop-singing groups. The boy bands sell out arenas around the world, create records that reach the top of the best-seller charts, and become important markers in the experiences of their generation. Their youthful exuberance, coordinated choreography, tight harmonies, skilled studio production, and carefully crafted public images play an important role in introducing young girls to popular music and its related practices of fandom and consumption.

Yet the boy bands generally draw derision from authors of books about music, from journalists, and from fans of other musical genres. In the eyes of their detractors, the success of the boy bands proves only the gullibility and poor taste of that part of the public that likes them. Boy bands are generally marketed more as objects of romantic desire than as admired singers or musicians. Their commercial viability often owes less to the sales of their recordings than to the marketing of magazines, fan club memberships, school notebooks, clothing, and accessories bearing their names and images. Boy bands do not build a loyal following through extensive apprenticeships in music, playing in small clubs for years, and gradually developing their musical skills. Instead, they appear on the scene rapidly, attract enormous attention for a few years, and then fade from view. Part of their popularity stems from their function as the fad of the moment, from their ability to mark a particular moment in time. Their celebrity status constitutes an event in itself: to ignore them is to be out of the loop.

The pubescent middle-class and wealthy girls who make up the core target market for boy bands constitute a desired market segment for advertisers. Because they have disposable income and have not yet established fixed patterns of consumption, they serve as a logical target for novelty marketing initiatives. Yet while marketers respect young girls for their purchasing power, their tastes, identifications, and interests are relentlessly subjected to scorn. The favorite bands of adolescent girls are often derided as silly, sentimental, and unserious. Girls' romantic attraction to teen idols is ridiculed as inappropriate, excessive, and even dangerous. Young women grow up in a society that allocates enormous amounts of money, energy, and media time enticing them to become consumers but then condemning them for their gullibility when they do.

Of course there are plenty of reasons to dislike the boy bands. Every aspect of their identities—from the physical features of group members to the songs they sing to the answers they give in interviews—is scripted and carefully coordinated on the basis of market research. They are never original, innovative, or unpredictable. In their stage personas and song lyrics, the boy bands succeed because they hint at the provocation of erotic desire only to contain it by presenting themselves ultimately as adolescent, innocent, wholesome, and cute, simply longing for longing rather than for love or lust. Their celebrity status seems to reduce the dignity of their fans, enlisting them as spectators and admirers of boys they do not know, apparently for the simple reason that other girls have focused on the band members as objects of desire.

Boy bands prey on the contradictions endemic to sexism and consumption in this society. On the one hand, an endless barrage of media messages pressures women to make themselves attractive to men, to seek security and status in romantic heterosexual love. Nearly every motion picture, television program, book, song, and advertisement endorses this scenario, punishing female characters who fail to conform to it. On the other hand, the women at whom these messages are directed find themselves dismissed as frivolous, foolish, vain, and shallow for consuming the images and ideas that have been thrust at them. The boy bands add to the insecurities of young girls by having them focus on young men as objects of admiration, by encouraging them to inhabit a state of romantic longing as an end in itself, and by suggesting that erotic and romantic desire can be fulfilled by purchasing the appropriate commodity.

Becoming fans of boy bands, however, can also enable young women to negotiate these contradictions. The practices of fandom permit them to develop intimacies with other girls, which may well be more important to them than their identification with the boys in the band. The bonding with other girls that takes place through fandom enacts relationships that are exuberantly homosocial, that depend on intimacy, excitement, and enthusiasm shared with others of the same gender. At a time when young girls might be most insecure about their own changing bodies, focusing on boy bands turns their gaze away from themselves and onto males. Perhaps most important, the shy vulnerability and dreamy romanticism exuded by the boy bands can offer a welcome respite from the aggressive vulgarity and calculated cruelty promoted in popular culture products marketed mainly to boys, such as professional wrestling, action-adventure movies, and violent video games.

The innovative cultural criticism of Gayle Wald and Judith Halberstam enables us to see how and why the boy bands might loom so large in the lives of young girls.[3] These scholars do not portray the popularity of the boy bands as socially progressive, nor do they make claims for the value of the music these bands play. Wald and Halberstam do, however, read the popularity of the boy bands symptomatically and critically as important evidence about the complexities of gender and sexuality in this society.

Halberstam explains that the dominant reigning model of "youth" presumes a normative life course rooted in gradual progression from a presexual childhood to an adulthood defined by heterosexual marriage, procreation, and parenting. Each life stage is designated by age- and status-appropriate commodities and consumption practices. Properly managed pubescent fandom can be permitted as a temporary step along this path, but it cannot be allowed to become so appealing that it serves as an end in itself. A moment of pleasure with other women unrelated to the goal of marriage, procreation, and parenting might undermine the logic of the heterosexual gender system. The emphasis that boy bands place on the singers as "boys" fixes them in youth, establishing their identity as a stage to be transcended as the fan grows up. The boy bands thus provoke, but then manage, homosocial and homosexual possibilities by rendering them "only" temporary.

Wald points out that boy bands themselves perform a "girlish masculinity" that speaks to the anxieties and interests of young women discovering their sexualities. The archetypes that appeal to young girls are often androgynous. Boy bands usually feature lean young men who do not yet shave, whose voices sometimes have not yet changed, whose choreographed movements and close relations to one another encode queer desires and looks as much as heterosexual ones. Contempt for boy bands can be a covert form of homophobia, as well as a punishment meted out to young women and men for not yet mastering the codes of heterosexism.

The emphatic ridicule directed at the "stage" of pubescent fandom betrays fears that the stage may not be temporary. It also originates in the things that distinguish girl culture from boy culture. Halberstam notes that motion pictures and television programs aimed at teenage males also offer the promise of an extended adolescence, which in turn raises fears about homosociality and homosexuality. The motion pictures and television programs targeted to teenage males manage these anxieties through recurrent and even obsessive displays of misogyny and homophobia. By encouraging hatred of women and queers, these forms of commercial culture enable putatively heterosexual men to repress the homosociality of their own extended adolescence. In this society, men are not punished for maintaining an extended adolescence. On the contrary, both popular culture and politics do much to promote it. Much of talk radio depends on it. Yet the investment in extended adolescence that heterosexual men manifest through misogyny and homophobia forces women and queers to come up with their own versions of extended adolescence that sometimes challenge the hegemony of the dominant chronology: the life course that women are supposed to follow from presexual adolescence to marriage and parenting. Cultural forms that appeal to girls and women sometimes challenge the ideal of masculinity as only paternal, protective, and patriarchal.

What Halberstam calls "queer time" threatens the normative life-cycle chronology that permeates popular culture. Sustained participation in "adolescent" subcultures interrupts the progression to adulthood. For queers this may mean voluntary immersion in subcultures as a way of living outside the temporality of family time. Queer fandom, in Halberstam's account, may mimic but nonetheless reformulates adolescent fandom. It offers the possibility of a temporality of "not yet," of roles for women that "are not absolutely predictive of either heterosexual or lesbian adulthoods; rather, the desires, the play, and the anguish they access allow us to theorize other relations to identity."[4] Halberstam's analysis enables us to see that the boy bands may not permanently manage the anxieties they provoke, that the investment in condemning boy bands stems as much from defensive heterosexism as it does from aesthetic conviction. Her work also enables us to see the logic of the girl bands that started to appear in popular music as a result of staged competitions in reality shows at the start of the twenty-first century.

In the wake of *Making the Band*, a reality show that created and marketed a new boy band, market logic combined with the affective power of female fandom to bring into being a new reality show built around the construction of a girl band. In 2001, *Pop Stars*, an unscripted "reality" television show staging a competition among young women to be part of a new band, appeared on the WB network. Although it enjoyed only modest success in the ratings—attracting an average audience of 4.1 million viewers, far below the network's most popular program, *Seventh Heaven*, which attracted 7.5 million viewers per episode—the preponderance of females between the ages of twelve and thirty-four among the viewers of *Pop Stars* constituted a ready-made niche market coveted by advertisers.

Time Warner executives signed the members of Eden's Crush, the band created on the show, to an exclusive recording contract, enabling the conglomerate to market the band's music through the company's subsidiary Warner Music Group. At the same time, computer server America Online, also owned by Warner, promoted the television show and the group's forthcoming compact disc extensively to its customers through an exclusive window, allowing (and encouraging) fans to download the first single of Eden's Crush. The continuing episodes of the television program also promoted the group's first concert at the Palace Theatre in Hollywood, which was taped for showing on the WB network. In addition, members of Eden's Crush, both a real band and a fictional entity from a television show, appeared on the WB-owned talk show *Live with Regis and Kelly* and in an episode of the network's prime-time situation comedy *Sabrina, the Teenage Witch,* both slated for airing during the week the group's album was to be released. Members of Eden's Crush also appeared on additional news and variety programs on the network, and they conducted a "chat" with fans on the company's AOL server.

Viewers were encouraged to develop identifications with the various members of the featured group, making all of their appearances part of an extended commercial for their subsequent recorded compact discs, tours, T-shirts, and other licensed material. The value added to the group's first recording by all this cross-promotion is impossible to calculate. Rather than advertising a single product, these efforts colonized entertainment content (the television program's plot, the group's music) as part of an exercise in corporate synergy, all in order to generate mutually reinforcing profits for different divisions of a single conglomerate. WB chairman Jamie Kellner explained that *Pop Stars* was an effort to get producers to stop thinking solely about the products they marketed in their own divisions and to start thinking about how they could work together to give AOL Time Warner shareholders higher returns on their investments.[5]

Eden's Crush Web sites and links constituted a particularly important venue for the program. They enabled AOL Time Warner to reach affluent consumers, to compile information about them, and to lead them through a series of opportunities to translate their interest in Eden's Crush into commercial purchases of concert tickets, photographs, fan club memberships, downloaded music, and other commodities. AOL Time Warner owned both EMI and Warner Music, making the company the world's largest merchandiser of music, a corporation accounting for one of every four units of recorded music purchased in the United States. As more and more music sales came from recordings downloaded from the Internet, the company's ownership of AOL placed it in a privileged position to profit from what might seem like a competitor medium under other circumstances. Yet even this synergy formed just the tip of an iceberg.

In addition to surveilling and shaping the buying habits of teenage music consumers, AOL Time Warner's *Pop Stars* Web site provided the company with access to information about the show's fans' tastes in clothes, makeup, books, and even pornography.[6]

This information could be used to shape "personalized" advertising appeals, sold to other e-marketers, or stored for future AOL Time Warner promotional activities. *Pop Stars* was such a fully linked and integrated system of marketing that it is possible to think of it as devoid of content, an empty container. Music connoisseurs especially might wonder what happens to musical quality once this kind of marketing and publicity power can be generated on behalf of a group that did not even exist before the show aired.[7] Fans of television drama might be concerned about a program that is, in effect, simply one long commercial. Parents and teachers interested in helping young people to locate themselves within the world might be horrified by the reach and scope of commercial mass media, by its ability to stimulate such intense empathy, investment, and engagement from children who may appear routinely bored, alienated, and disinterested in school, family, or community activities.

Yet the content of the program was neither random nor arbitrary. It was shaped in every detail by the logic of the historical moment in which it was created. At a time when sophisticated marketing strategies permeated every aspect of social life in the United States—education and evangelism and politics as well as popular culture—*Pop Stars* emerged as part of a well-coordinated social pedagogy training viewers to become the kinds of consumers that marketers desire them to become. In the manner that rodeos served as the favored form of recreation for western cowhands in the agrarian era or the way romance novels and soap operas provided a fictional focus for the real-life family and relationship issues confronting housewives in the industrial era, *Pop Stars* provided viewers with an "escape" that perfectly reflected the "work" they do as shoppers in the era of postindustrial digital capitalism.

The core dynamics of *Pop Stars* promoted the "violent competition and impersonal appetite" that Raymond Williams identifies as popular culture's key dynamic in a capitalist society.[8] The show staged a competition among dozens of female aspirants to stardom. Yet only five of them could be chosen to become members of the group. To the camera, contestants confided their desires to become successful entertainers through a seemingly endless series of statements that almost always began with some variant of "I want . . . ," "I wish . . . ," "I've always wanted . . . ," or "I dream of . . ." Emotional expressions of fear, anxiety, and self-doubt took center stage when viewers were encouraged to strategize along with the aspirants, to speculate along with them about which forms of self-presentation would prove most effective with the judges.

Although beauty and talent clearly mattered in this competition, success ultimately emanated from candidates' mastery over the discourses of liberal individualism and self-making. *Pop Stars* demonstrated that one must seem to be virtuous as well as fortunate in order to win, but that virtue can be best demonstrated by both yearning for success and then muting that very ambition by acting in a "sisterly" fashion toward one's rivals. The competition required contestants to display mastery of the self-help apparatuses (exercise, makeup, clothing, and choreography) that might provide the crucial edge in the competition. Much like the beauty pageant contestants analyzed so brilliantly in Sarah Banet-Weiser's wonderfully perceptive book, *The Most Beautiful Girl in the World,* the participants on *Pop Stars* faced the dilemma of proving that they were special, different, unique, completely individual by proving their mastery of exactly the same shared social codes that construct each of them as interchangeable parts of a mass market.[9]

Fans logging on to the Eden's Crush official Web site could have questions answered by members of the families of band members. The answers revealed a distinct social pedagogy at work in respect to liberal individualism, a pedagogy that echoes the discourse of beauty pageants. For example, a fan asked "Ivette's Dad" if Ivette is rich. He answered, "It all depends on what you mean by 'rich.' She has a family that loves her unconditionally, and supports her completely. She is talented, intelligent, beautiful, and a very caring person. She has a strong belief in God, and has had the courage to follow her dreams no matter where they may take her. I would certainly call that rich."[10]

Ivette's dad switched the question from the material to the moral sphere, enabling himself and his daughter to disavow any interest in money, to portray participation in the group as a courageous way of pursuing one's dreams wherever they may lead, if even to the WB network. The possibility of gaining sudden wealth, however, played an indispensable part in the lure of *Pop Stars.* The inclusion of this question on the Web site even contributed to the construction of that expectation. Yet the required performative social pedagogy is to "misunderstand" the question, to be so worthy of wealth that you pretend not even to notice it when it appears. Fans could still root for Ivette as she climbed from respectability to riches (her father is a drama teacher in a suburban New Jersey high school), without ever getting to the point of resenting her when she became one of the haves.

A similar tension is arbitrated in the answer that Ivette's dad offered when asked, "Don't you think it's a little odd that all the girls in Eden's Crush are skinny, dark-haired, and tan? It seems sad that this is the group they picked, and there's no hope for other girls." Like the obligatory question about feminism in beauty pageants that is always answered by defining feminism as following one's dreams, this question speaks directly to an issue that might have become a problem for the program. It is raised in order to be knocked down, to contain and co-opt any possible oppositional reading.

Ivette's dad had the right answer. "In all honesty," he wrote, "I really do not understand this question. I believe that these girls were picked based on their talent and professionalism. I'm sure that the people in charge had an image in mind as they entered this selection process *(Pop Stars)*. I also believe that the people in charge of the process, being well-known figures in the music industry, were looking for the best combination of individuals to ensure the success of this group. There is always hope for people—just because someone was not selected for *PopStars [sic]* does NOT mean they cannot go on to fulfill their dreams through other venues. I guess I have a question—why is it that some people feel the need to try to always find something negative about other people's success?"

Evidently Ivette's dad never suspected that women might be judged on their looks anywhere in U.S. society, even in the entertainment industry. He apparently had no inkling that his daughter might have been selected for the group because satisfying the male gaze and fulfilling the standards of the beauty system are an important part of contemporary marketing. In fact, he purported to be so surprised by the question that he could only conclude that the questioner was belittling his own daughter's talent and professionalism out of laziness ("just because someone was not selected for *PopStars* does NOT mean they cannot go on to fulfill their dreams through other venues") or out of a perverse desire simply to find something negative in another person's success. Of course, this too was all a performance. The show's innate contradiction—that anyone can be a star and be special, even though viewers are constantly encouraged to judge themselves as inadequate, not special, not stars, and not ever likely to become stars, because that is the best way to keep them hungry for more products and more images of successful beauties—was both named and contained by this exchange.

The insouciance that Ivette's dad displayed about her appearance notwithstanding, the appearance of the women in Eden's Crush was a tremendously important part of their market value. Donald Lowe describes the "technologies of the look" and the "relay of juxtaposed images and signs" as the center of sexualization of commodities in our society. Part of the purpose of this is to increase the areas of the body accessible to marketability, to produce new sites to be accessorized, salted, soaped, shaved, and sculpted. "We currently present ourselves, and see ourselves and others, as sexual persons who exude the allure and power of the sexualized commodities we consume," Lowe explains.[11] The practices Lowe describes serve not so much to make bodies sexier by applying commodities to them as to sexualize the commodities by associating them with the human bodies presented to us as desirable and beautiful.

Sexuality in the mass media is almost never about intimacy, love, caressing, pleasure, or trust, but rather about attraction, power, domination, and possession. Media representations of sexuality rarely focus on private intimacy but frequently revolve around public performance and display. They depict very few actual sex acts but direct our gaze again and again to commercial transactions with purported "sexual" content as exemplified in the seemingly endless succession of good-hearted hookers, strippers, and supermodels in television programs and motion pictures.

Lowe connects the sexualization of commodities to the sociopathology of anorexia nervosa, the obsessive desire for thinness. Seen in this light, the fan's question to Ivette's dad on the Eden's Crush Web site raises issues more profound than petty jealousy about the success of someone else. Archetypes of beauty vary across societies and time periods, but emphasis on thin women in the "technologies of the look and the relay of juxtaposed images and signs" that condition our reception of Pop Stars does not express an aesthetic preference so much as it performs a disciplinary practice.[12] The driving force behind the contemporary culture of consumption is the stimulation of appetites, not just the impersonal kind identified by Raymond Williams as the core of commercial culture evident in most forms of advertising and entertainment, which promote desire for more power, more recognition, and more products, but also the very personal appetite and body issues the people face, such as bulimia, anorexia nervosa, and crash diets on the one hand and pumping iron and taking steroids on the other.

It should be no surprise in a society permeated with so many messages to eat *and* to lose weight, to spend *and* to save, to accumulate goods *and* to invest, that so much entertainment, advertising, and even news programming revolve around the incitement and containment of appetites.[13] Moreover, the body itself changes under these circumstances, as Lowe points out. Cyclical regimes of dieting and exercise often leave individuals with memories of the many different bodily sizes and shapes "their" body has experienced.[14]

The slender bodies of the members of Eden's Crush conformed to the standards mandated by the technologies of the look and the relay of juxtaposed images and signs at the center of contemporary commodity culture. As a media creation and a simulation as well as an actual pop group, Eden's Crush became more credible, or at least more bankable, because its members looked like the other images circulated within commodity culture.

Their thoughts had to conform to this system as well. On their Web site, messages from each member of Eden's Crush unintentionally highlighted the group's similarities, the homogeneous character of their individual differences. "I find inspiration from my family," claimed Maile Misajon, age twenty-four. Nicole Scherzinger, age twenty-two, confided, "Every day I get support from my family members. I talk to my mom and family every day or every other day." Twenty-four-year-old Ivette Sosa declared, "My family inspires me," while Rosanna Tavarez, also twenty-four, told her fans, "My family always encouraged me to dance and sing." Twenty-two-year-old Ana Marie Lombo was described as someone who "has spent her whole life traveling the world and performing music with her parents and two sisters."[15]

Yet complete sameness would not have worked as a marketing tool. Capitalism requires change, or at least the appearance of change, in order to promote product differentiation. Consequently, Eden's Crush did display differences. The members of the group were all "tan," in part because three of them were Latinas, and the other two claimed part Asian, Pacific island, or indigenous ancestry. Rosanna Tavarez was born in New York and raised in Miami, but her parents came to the United States from the Dominican Republic. Ana Maria Lombo was born in Medellín, Colombia. Ivette Sosa hailed from New Jersey but was of Puerto Rican descent. Nicole Scherzinger was born in Hawai'i, where her mother was "the lead hula dancer in a big Hawai'ian family." Maile Misajon, from Long Beach, California, claimed Irish, Filipino, and Hawai'ian ancestry.

As "mixed race" but not Black (at least by generally understood U.S. norms), the members of Eden's Crush brought a safe degree of "difference" to the fore, yet not so much that they might have raised the issues of racialization, oppression, and exclusion associated with the history of race within U.S. culture. No doubt the ascendant popularity of Jennifer Lopez and perhaps even Christina Aguilera positioned the members of the group as potentially marketable to a broad range of audiences, including the huge hemispheric market that now links North American rock to *roq en español*.

Like López and Aguilera, the members of Eden's Crush made music that sounds very much like the music made by whites imitating Blacks, especially the boy bands 'N Sync, the Backstreet Boys, and 98 Degrees. "Latinas" like Lopez, Aguilera, and 60 percent of Eden's Crush can take center stage with this kind of music, as long as they have the appropriate faces, bodies, and hair. This was not a space, however, open to Celia Cruz, a Latina generally acknowledged as one of the greatest singers ever, because Cruz's monolingual Spanish lyrics, musical grounding in Afro-Cuban styles, dark skin, and husky body disqualified her from becoming one of the interchangeable parts in the linked chain of production and distribution of the music–television–Internet industry.

The Latina, Asian, and indigenous elements in the backgrounds of the members of Eden's Crush served simply as differences that do not make a difference, as elements of identity that are not really bounded in space or time, as interchangeable parts in a larger system characterized by the logic of containerization. Group members affirmed their allegiance to their heritage as a personal matter. "It just means so much to me to sing Spanish lyrics in a song," one maintained but brought no broader history to the fore. The group's Puerto Rican grew up in New Jersey, the Dominican in Miami, and the two who were part Hawai'ian grew up in Louisville, Kentucky, and Long Beach, California. The group's racial differences served market ends, but their connections to racial histories had to be muted for commercial purposes, because too much particularity might have inhibited their suitability as role models for their target audience of affluent, young, white teenage girls.

Pop Stars was a pure product of a particular moment in the history of marketing and technological change. In part, it emanated from the 1996 Telecommunications Act, passed by a Republican Congress and signed by a Democratic president. This law encouraged consolidation of the ownership of media outlets into fewer and fewer hands. Giant conglomerates used the bill to acquire control over hundreds of radio and television stations. By 2003, ten firms controlled two-thirds of radio revenues and listeners. The two largest companies, Clear Channel and Viacom, received 45 percent of industry revenues from programs heard by 42 percent of the medium's listeners.[16] The economies of scale that made sense with this kind of consolidation favored mass distribution of the same safe sounds to the largest possible audience. The music of the Backstreet Boys and 'N Sync fit this format perfectly. Both groups came out of Orlando, Florida, and, like their counterpart Britney Spears, had histories with predictable corporate commercial culture, thanks to their work at Disney World and on the Disney Channel's *Mickey Mouse Club*. Yet by the end of the 1990s, these economies of scale needed to accommodate themselves to economies of scope as well.[17]

In the emerging era of digital capitalism, integrated computer networks make it possible to rationalize and maximize the profitability of consumption in much the same way that containerization transformed the social relations of production, distribution, and reception in the industrial era. New technologies loom large in these transformations, but they do not cause them. As Raymond Williams explains, "Virtually all technical study and experiment are undertaken within already existing social relations and cultural forms, typically for purposes that are already in general foreseen."[18] The technologies of radio and television could have been adapted for many different kinds of educational and entertainment uses, but the commercial model of selling audiences to advertisers won out because business and government leaders used their influence to secure favored treatment for the development of the technologies most suited for business uses. Similarly, containerization and the digital technologies that flow from it could have been developed for many different kinds of social uses. In this society, however, the adaptation of new technologies for the expansion of market sites and the generation of new sources of profit has received favored treatment (and funding) from the government agencies whose research and development resources have brought the new technologies into existence in the first place.[19]

The commercial culture of containerization and digital capitalism follows the well-worn pattern produced in previous periods of capitalist growth and technological transformation. Confronted with declining rates of profit and working-class resistance at the point of production, business leaders seek access to new markets and new ways of reducing labor costs. They pressure governments to develop new technologies that can be appropriated for private purposes. Containerization and digital capitalism enable entrepreneurs to transcend political, cultural, and commercial boundaries, to secure new markets, to create new points of sale, to turn previously noncommercial social activities into for-profit transactions, and to force others to pay the social costs and suffer the social consequences of the disruptions caused by the new economy.[20]

Culture itself changes under these conditions. Production becomes more homogeneous, because products need to become more interchangeable to be marketed effectively. Corporate interests so dominate cultural production that previously independent sites of cultural creation become dependent on the patronage and favors of big business for their survival.[21] The state no longer serves as a site of countervailing power against business. Instead, it functions as an agent of capitalist transformation and change. The most widely circulated cultural creations under these circumstances reflect the ideas and values of the capitalists who sponsor them. They emphasize the emotions and ideas most valuable to marketers, privileging the needy narcissistic self of consumer desire over the intersubjective and interactive social subject. The resulting culture of "capitalist realism" relies on a limited repertoire of themes over and over again, themes that Williams eloquently characterizes as *alienation* and *dislocation,* the former fueled by "a violent competition and impersonal appetite" and the latter by "arbitrariness and human disability."[22]

Violent competition and impersonal appetite provide the raison d'être for low-budget "reality" television programs like *Pop Stars, Survivor, Big Brother, The Real World,* and *American Idol.* Arbitrariness and human disability constitute the core of the voyeuristic pleasures offered by *Cops, America's Most Wanted, The Jerry Springer Show,* and *The Howard Stern Show.* The transformation of television news into a series of sensational scandals and soap opera–like serial narratives and the linked systems of hypercommercialism that transform teenage infatuation and attraction to pop music stars into fully integrated marketing opportunities testify vividly to the character of the culture of containerization. Under this system, alienation and dislocation are not obstacles to be overcome but rather opportunities for titillation, transgression, and sadomasochistic cathexis.[23]

These dynamics produce new cultural forms that make it increasingly difficult to distinguish between programming and advertising. A music video, for example, sells cable television audiences to advertisers, but it also functions as advertising for the purchase of recorded compact discs and tapes, for music to be downloaded from the Internet, for forthcoming concerts starring the featured artist, and for the T-shirts and other paraphernalia marketed in support of tours, which then serve also as ads for music channels on cable television! Of course, products in previous eras sometimes blurred the line between art and advertisement too. Martin Denny's album *Exotica* in 1959 reached the top of the best-seller charts in part because its innovative use of stereophonic separation, reverberation, and acoustic delay were so well-suited for showing off the capacities of new kinds of stereo equipment.[24] In the early days of stereo, percussion recordings were particularly popular, because they showed off the properties of the new medium advantageously. In that era, Buddy Rich, Gene Krupa, Art Blakey, and Max Roach recorded albums on which they played drums without accompaniment.[25] Similarly, Les Baxter's *Perfume Set to Music* album was both a commercial recording and a promotional device for the Corday perfume company.[26] In the early 1980s, the CBS television series *Fame* secured only modest ratings and advertising dollars, but "soundtrack" record albums and tapes of music by the program's featured stars more than made up for the meager returns on investment from the show itself.[27] The congruence between advertising and art in contemporary culture has progressed to the extent that, as Raymond Williams's deft phrase explains, "the tail wags the dog so vigorously that the tail is rapidly becoming the definition of any useful dog."[28]

Donald Lowe argues that the triumph of cybernetic systems generates "a new currency of power." The cognitive mapping of the spaces of the globe that characterized the age of discovery from the sixteenth century through the eighteenth and the sense of temporal development and succession that dominated the historical thinking of the nineteenth and twentieth centuries have been superseded by what Lowe describes as a new synchronic order "unbounded by absolute space or time, since space and time have themselves become elements of a system." Individual components of this system are interchangeable, and none has intrinsic value by itself outside the system.[29] Understanding this epistemic shift can help us theorize how the new economy is generating new social subjects in the process of generating new spaces for the consumption of commodities as well as new spaces for their production.

During the industrial era producers of commodities sought to broaden their markets by expanding absolute space. They wanted to sell more commodities to more people, and consequently they encouraged domestic consumers to spend more money. They sought augmented access to overseas markets.[30] Precisely for the purpose of expanding markets for U.S. goods, the U.S. Department of Defense collaborated with labor leaders and executives from the shipping industry to develop and implement containerization technologies during the 1950s. These taxpayer-subsidized collaborations shaped new technologies for maximum corporate profit and maximum expansion of private consumer spending rather than designs to reduce arduous labor or involve workers in making production decisions. Similarly, the Department of Defense supervised the development of Internet technologies in ways that privileged the commercial applications of the new medium over its educational or social possibilities.[31]

During the present postindustrial era of flexible accumulation and containerization, however, commodity producers aim not so much at expanding the market as at deepening it, replacing mass economies of scale with targeted economies of scope. Deepening the market requires the expansion of relative space by selling more specialized products to targeted audiences to secure higher profits. Under this regime, MCI directs its advertising toward "the top third of the consumer market," while AT&T focuses on "the 20 percent of people who account for 80 percent of the company's $6 billion in annual profit."[32]

Massive government subsidies shaped the technology of containerization and influenced government efforts to develop "standards" for digital high definition and Web access to television–computer links. These subsidies have been crafted to channel the most advanced technologies toward the generation of new spaces for profit, most notably in building a digital marketplace geared toward private profits. Although celebrated as a "free market" approach, the development of compatible systems among different manufacturers actually required incessant orchestration and intervention by government agencies, financed by taxpayers.

Containerization came into being by breaking the skill monopolies and control over working conditions by dockworkers in the shipping industry. Today's digital capitalism depends on relegating production to low-wage countries, such as Mexico (where some ten million color television sets adaptable to high-capacity computer networks are produced every year), in order to create a fully integrated global system of marketing, merchandising, and sales that will cause the boundaries of the shopping mall to become fluid and flexible, to extend into the home via the personal computer. High-capacity computer networks will stimulate new levels of consumption by the affluent while completely bypassing low-income neighborhoods, and perhaps even low-wage countries, entirely.[33] "Public" spaces for consumption can be allowed to decay into shopping sites of last resort for the parts of the population without access to the digital market.

The biggest problem facing marketers during the age when radio and television reigned supreme was that these electronic media created no direct points of sale. Unlike books, newspapers, theatrical performances, and motion pictures, radio and television depended on future purchases, on spending by audiences whose time and attention had been "sold" to advertisers.[34] Consumers paid directly for television sets and radio receivers. Indirectly, they financed the advertising industry, because product prices included the costs of advertising and because corporations deducted advertising expenses from tax liabilities as business expenses. The profits made from radio and television, however, remained dependent on consumer purchases to be made in the future dispersed sites.

The age of digital capitalism establishes the home computer as a privileged new site for direct sales. Corporate marketers can use computers to gain access to information about each of their customers, to keep track of individual financial transactions, spending habits, tastes, interests, and desires. Marketers armed with this information can target individual buyers, anticipate what they will buy and how much they will spend. In turn, these companies can then sell the record of their transactions to bankers, stockbrokers, and insurance agents in search of customers who fit very specific profiles. People whose incomes (or thrifty habits) mark them as less active consumers can be marginalized altogether by these systems. Affluent consumers who make plenty of purchases will receive inside information about bargains and specialized services. Low-income and low-volume shoppers will pay higher prices and receive inferior services. Company personnel will know that complaints and inquiries coming from poor people need not be answered.[35]

Digital television and radio receivers will layer consumer opportunities on top of one another. They will turn the physical space of the home into a shopping mall while bringing entertainment and consumption ever closer together as centers of the social world. Broadcast outlets are likely to give way to narrow-casting and Internet downloading, television sales will eclipse telemarketing or "live" shopping, and public performance and recreation spaces will dwindle as affluent consumers inside gated and locked communities carry on collective transactions in atomized fashion, sitting in front of separate computer monitors at the same moment.

The technologies of digital capitalism have the potential to expand consumer access to a broad range of cultural expressions, but powerful oligopolies in every major entertainment field will make every effort to create the lingua franca of global commercial culture out of only a very small number of blockbuster action/adventure films, a very small number of songs with Anglo-American melodies and chord progressions, and a very small number of television programs owned by an even smaller group of producers.

Digital capitalism also threatens to transform the meaning of the subcultural spaces that emerged among consumers during the era of Fordist production and consumption. In the age of mass production and mass marketing, small subgroups resisted the tyranny of the market in creative ways. They developed "subversive" uses for standardized products by customizing cars or wearing "work" clothes such as denim jeans as leisure wear. They embraced art-ists not validated by the market system, according great prestige to folk singers and craft practitioners who seemed to do their work independently of market considerations. These rebellions went against the logic of the market and carved out oppositional sub-cultural spaces within market relations.

In an age of flexible accumulation, economies of scope, and increasingly differentiated markets, however, the creation of new spaces simply allows more opportunities for niche marketing while training consumers to desire difference and distance from the tastes of others. Part of this entails a proliferation of products that can be marketed as new. The Gillette Company seeks to secure 40 percent of its sales every five years from entirely new products, and more than 30 percent of Toshiba's products in 1987 had reached the market within the previous three years.[36] Thus, even subcultural spaces may become a de facto part of the research and develop-ment apparatuses of niche marketers.

Commercial culture is not without its own contradictions, how-ever. Its very hegemonic force sometimes puts people in situations that encourage them to try to produce new cultural forms with very different presuppositions and purposes. In the 1920s, the comfort-ably middle-class parents of Leon "Bix" Beiderbecke in Davenport, Iowa, fretted about what they thought of as their son's unhealthy interest in the jazz music played on riverboats in their town. So they sent him away to prep school in a Chicago suburb. He soon discovered he had even better access to the jazz played in the slums and vice districts of the metropolis there than he had back home in Iowa. In the 1950s, Los Angeles city authorities disapproved of the racially mixed Black and white crowds attending band leader Johnny Otis's rock 'n' roll shows, so they devised a series of ordi-nances that made it too risky for social halls and nightclubs in the city to host these performances. Closing off the city to rock 'n' roll shows, however, drove them to the unincorporated areas of Los Angeles County, where Otis and other impresarios discovered a large number of local Chicano and Asian American teens eager to dance and socialize with the whites and Blacks who ventured out from the city. British censors banned Peter Ford's "Chikki Chikki Ahh Ahh" in 1988, because they interpreted the words "disco me to ecstasy" as an invitation to use the drug known as ecstasy. Ford had no such intention, but by banning the song the censors made it more interesting to people who actually were interested in drugs, making the recording a huge hit. The same revolutionary transformations of culture and space that have given capitalist culture a new hegemony in the age of containerization are also generating what Raymond Williams calls "a long march to alternative institutions, which have to be raised from the resources of surviving and potential in-place communities."[37]

Pop Stars did not invent the intersection of pubescent sexuality and sophisticated marketing. In Boston in the early 1980s, African American producer Maurice Starr discovered and molded the boy band New Edition and guided them to stardom. Starr took four Black teenagers who had begun singing together, doing covers of Jackson 5 songs in elementary school, and shaped them into teen idols with three major hits by 1983. When their success attracted the attention of a major label, New Edition left Starr's Streetwise label and went on to even greater success under the guidance of legendary producers Jimmy Jam and Terry Lewis.

Embittered by his experience with New Edition, Maurice Starr assembled a new boy band, New Kids on the Block, a group made up of five young suburban white males. Following the formula of romantic ballads, bouncy rhythm and blues, and mild funk that worked with New Edition, Starr guided the New Kids on the Block to superstar status, selling millions of records, tapes, and compact discs between 1986 and 1990. As had happened so many times before in the history of U.S. popular music, the blend of white phenotypes with Black musical styles proved especially lucrative.

In the mid-1990s, white producer Louis Pearlman imitated Starr's successful New Kids on the Block with the Backstreet Boys. Blending a modicum of hip hop into the New Kids on the Block/ New Edition format of rhythm and blues, ballads, and funk, the Orlando, Florida–based Backstreet Boys became the dominant boy band of their era. Their success paved the way for 'N Sync, a band also based in Orlando, also composed of five young white males, also featuring a singing style in the tradition of New Kids on the Block, New Edition, and the Jackson 5. It was these successes that paved the way for *Pop Stars*.

The formation of Eden's Crush differed significantly from the pattern established by the boy bands. As the pure product of corporate synergy, Eden's Crush was created so that the group could not do to Time Warner what New Edition had done to Maurice Starr (leave for another label) or what the Backstreet Boys had done to their management team (sue them over royalties). As a corporate creation, Eden's Crush resembled the boy bands less than it did previous so-called groups based in studios—the Cuff Links, the Archies, and the Monkees.

The Cuff Links had a top ten hit with "Tracy" in 1969, even though the group did not actually exist. Session musician Ron Dante recorded himself singing "Tracy" in different voices and put the dubs together as a recording by a group called the Cuff Links.[38] The Archies did not exist either, even though they had six songs among the top one hundred in 1968 and 1969, including the best-selling "Sugar Sugar." Their lead vocalist, too, was the seemingly ubiquitous Ron Dante, this time providing his voice to accompany television cartoon characters.[39] The link between the cartoon show and the recordings served as an early exercise in the kind of cross-marketing that came to fruition in *Pop Stars*. The producer of the Archies music and television show was Don Kirshner, who turned to cartoon characters because of his experience with a real-life group that actually existed, or at least sort of existed—the Monkees.

Kirshner created the Monkees for a fictional television program about a pop music group like the Beatles. For the lead roles, he hired four actors who could sing, but he prohibited the group from playing their own instruments or selecting their own songs. Dr. John played piano on several recordings by the Monkees, but he never met any of them.[40] As producer, Kirshner assigned himself 15 percent of the royalties on each recording the Monkees sold while limiting the four members of the group to 1.5 percent apiece. Group member Michael Nesmith, an accomplished songwriter and guitarist, protested against these arrangements, becoming particularly vociferous when the producer asked the group to sing "Sugar Sugar." When the Monkees fired Kirshner to gain control of the production of their songs, Kirshner "took" "Sugar Sugar" to the Archies, a made-up group that could not rebel against his direction, since they were cartoon characters.[41]

The producers of *Pop Stars* designed Eden's Crush also to be the kind of group that could not rebel against its creators. As the brilliant work of Matthew Stahl reminds us, control over the costs of labor remains a central goal of all capitalists, especially those in the music industry.[42] Labor costs rather than aesthetic preferences explain the heavily produced standardized sounds of Eden's Crush, their own version of the kinds of arrangements that had been successful for New Edition, New Kids on the Block, the Backstreet Boys, and 'N Sync, their vocal timbre and pitch signifying adolescent longing that the boy bands had borrowed from Michael Jackson and the Jackson 5, who had taken it from Diana Ross, who got it from Frankie Lymon. The women in Eden's Crush might well have been distinctive vocalists, innovative writers, or even competent instrumentalists, but the format in which they performed made any display of those talents impossible. Their interchangeability and personal anonymity made them fit into the fully integrated system of production, distribution, and consumption that the age of containerization and economies of scope required.

Eden's Crush did not survive as a group. *Pop Stars* did not survive as a television program. The kinds of corporate synergy that Time Warner sought from this project did not quite come to fruition for that conglomerate. Yet none of that matters in this kind of market. Time-specific products such as Eden's Crush and the popularity of the Spice Girls, Pokemon cards, and Beanie Babies do not have to last. They turn products into events, manufacture an intense and artificially inflated demand that marks a particular time, but senesce before they become too expensive for their owners to maintain and before their popularity inhibits the development of similar new products.

The rise of the boy bands and the girl bands created to answer them, however, cannot be confined to a marketing event. For the young women who followed the group avidly, the social pedagogy of marketing taught by *Pop Stars* might ultimately be less significant than their exposure to images of women having fun working together, receiving the kinds of attention generally given to the other gender, and displaying more ethnic and racial diversity (however tame and limited) than any of their predecessor boy bands had ever been able to represent. From the perspective of Halberstam's queer temporality, viewers of all sexual preferences and affiliations might have benefited from the band's interruption (however timid) of life trajectories focused exclusively on marriage, procreation, and family. The eclipse of economies of scale by economies of scope is a significant historical event, one with terribly detrimental implications in a society in which things are more highly valued than people. Nonetheless, every act of cultural creation, distribution, and consumption depends on unpredictable interactions between and among thinking subjects who (unlike the Archies) always hold the capacity to step out of character and exceed the roles allotted to them. The ability of contemporary marketing to raise and to contain deep personal and collective contradictions simultaneously helps account for the prominence and power of consumer purchases in this society. The dynamics of this system, however, always runs the risk of opening up the very wounds it aims to salve, of producing the very nonnormativity it seeks to prevent.

2. Crossing Over

The Hidden History of Diaspora

The thunder I have known, that I have fled with all my soul and now return to, humbled, is nothing more than the light contained in the distant murmurings of an unforgotten land.

—Myriam Chancy, *Spirit of Haiti*

Long waves of history and long journeys over ocean waves contributed equally to the creation of *The Score*, a hip hop album released by the Fugees in 1996. The recording rapidly became one of the most successful hip hop albums of all time, selling more than seventeen million units worldwide. U.S.-born Lauryn Hill, along with Haitian immigrant friends Wyclef Jean and Pras Michel, started singing together as teenagers in New Jersey in the late 1980s. They began as the Tranzlator Crew, but by the time they reached their early twenties, they renamed themselves the Fugees to acknowledge and honor Haitian refugees. Their name for their group turned the negative slang term used to demean refugees into a mark of positive self-definition.

The Score features an innovative blend of hip hop, soul, salsa, Jamaican reggae, and Haitian rara that accentuates the transnational and panethnic dimensions of African American identity. On this album, Lauryn Hill and Wyclef Jean display especially stunning gifts as songwriters, rappers, and singers. Many of *The Score*'s songs contain memorable, compelling, and socially conscious lyrics. The group celebrates the rich textures of everyday life in the inner city, documenting the lives of people who, although often broke, have not yet been broken. They rap about police brutality, racism, and sexism, yet manage to affirm an indomitable collective determination to live meaningful lives nonetheless.

Like much of 1980s and 1990s hip hop, *The Score* features rap artists in their midtwenties performing significant cover versions of songs that were first popular in the 1970s, during the years when these artists were children. Just as Ice Cube turned to the Isley Brothers' "Footsteps in the Dark" as the basis for his "It Was a Good Day," Lauryn Hill covered Roberta Flack's 1973 hit, "Killing Me Softly with His Song" on *The Score*. This effort became a best-selling single and helped prepare audiences for the solo career that Hill began two years later with her superb album *The Miseducation of Lauryn Hill*.[1] Similarly, Wyclef Jean's cover (with Stephen Marley) of Bob Marley's "No Woman, No Cry," from the Jamaican's 1974 album *Natty Dread,* reached back to the past to situate the moral and political concerns of the Fugees in the long fetch of history and to display their spatial and racial affiliations to a pan-African and pan-Caribbean framework.

The Fugees recorded *The Score* at a time when nearly one-quarter of the African Americans in the New York City area hailed from the Caribbean. During the early 1990s, the ranks of refugees and emigrants in the world were increasing by more than two million people every year. The disruptions of war and economic structural adjustment policies mandated by the World Bank and the International Monetary Fund dispersed more than one hundred million people outside their nations of birth or citizenship. At a time when these realities remained largely absent from mainstream media messages, the Fugees responded by introducing their version of "No Woman, No Cry" with a spoken "dedication to all the refugees worldwide."

As Stephen Marley and Wyclef Jean start to sing the melody of "No Woman, No Cry," they change the lyrics to reflect Wyclef Jean's personal life history. Jean first came to the United States in 1981 as a nine-year-old immigrant from Croix-des-Bouquets, Haiti. He grew up in Brooklyn and New Jersey. The version of "No Woman, No Cry" on *The Score* alters Bob Marley's lyrics about sitting in "the government yard in Trenchtown" (the Kingston neighborhood that Marley moved to from the Jamaican countryside) to "a government yard in Brooklyn," referring to the Marlborough

Projects in that borough, where Wyclef Jean's family lived after their arrival from Haiti. In the next verse, Jean changes the words to "a project yard in Jersey," detailing the autobiographical progression that he has described elsewhere as moving from "Haiti, to NYC, to Jersey."

One of the most cited and sampled lines from Bob Marley's version of "No Woman, No Cry" pays tribute to "the good friends we've lost along the way" and asserts "in this great future you can't forget your past." On *The Score,* Wyclef Jean talks about "my peeps [people] who passed away," a reference that could mean people killed in the United States by gang violence, police brutality, or AIDS but could also refer to the Haitians killed by political violence in their home country or on the high seas while trying to flee to the United States in rafts and boats. On *The Score,* Wyclef Jean has the younger Marley repeat the line "in this great future you can't forget your past," but the verse takes on new meaning in a rap song by a twenty-four-year-old immigrant from Haiti invoking the words of Bob Marley some fifteen years after the Jamaican singer's death. Marley himself has now become part of the past that cannot be forgotten in this great future. Yet the Fugees' version of the song speaks as well to the painful experiences of exile and refuge in the United States, about "the pain of losing family," and about "the gunman in the house tonight." In the place where Marley's song details "logwood burnin' through the nights," Wyclef Jean sings it "as stolen cars passed through the night."

The Fugees' cover of "No Woman, No Cry" drew attention from journalists and fans, because it fused hip hop and reggae, two seemingly incommensurable musical genres sold to two distinct market segments. The novelty of a group composed of two Haitian immigrants and a U.S.-born African American who attended Columbia University saluting the acknowledged hero of reggae also seemed to differentiate the Fugees from other artists in hip hop. This impression grew stronger when Lauryn Hill began dating (and had a child with) Rohan Marley, another son of the late reggae singer and a former college football player at Miami University.

The album's link between hip hop and reggae, however, hardly broke new ground. Bridges between the two were already well established, especially in New York and Miami. But the long-standing connections between Caribbean- and U.S.-born Blacks have increased rapidly in recent years. Several prominent performers in hip hop have been Caribbean immigrants or the children of immigrants, even if they have been perceived as "only" Black in the United States. Fused forms such as reggaeton and dancehall rap have emerged in the Caribbean in dialogue with hip hop and its relationship to interethnic coalitions and conflicts in North American cities.[2]

The forces that led the dreadlocked Wyclef Jean to the music of Bob Marley stemmed both from Jean's widespread musical tastes as a consumer and from his history as a Haitian immigrant to the United States. Bob Marley's prominence resonated powerfully throughout Haiti in the 1970s and 1980s, when Jean was a child. Many Haitians embraced the Jamaican singer's music and his persona not only because he was a great musician who wrote politically charged pro-Black lyrics but also because he was a Caribbean worker who labored for a short time in the United States, a believer in an Afrocentric religion that recognizes no official church hierarchy, and a successful Black man who spoke up politically on behalf of the poor and against colonialism.

Although he wears his hair in dreadlocks, Wyclef Jean is not a Rastafarian. His father was a Pentecostal minister who guided a congregation in Newark, New Jersey, a history that Wyclef would document fully in his subsequent autobiographical solo album, *The Preacher's Son*. Pentecostalism's embrace of emotion, music, and the personal courage to live in exile from earthly rewards permeates Wyclef Jean's lyrics in unmistakable, if indirect, form. Yet his dreadlocks are nonetheless meaningful. Haitians sometimes describe long strands of braided hair worn by men as *cheve Simbi* (the hair of Simbi, a *l'wa*, or spirit, connected to freshwater springs and snakes and a deity well known to practitioners of vodou). In the days when Haiti was ruled by François (Papa Doc) Duvalier and his son Jean-Claude (Baby Doc), the government jailed men who wore their hair long. When Baby Doc fled to France in 1986 after his regime was overthrown in the wake of popular protests, some Haitians celebrated their new freedom by wearing their hair *cheve Simbi*.[3]

At about the same time that the Tranzlator Crew became the Fugees, two of Haiti's most popular compas bands released songs about refugees and political struggle. The song "Pou Yo" (For Them), by Tabou Combo, laments the fate of different groups of Haitians overseas. The lyrics salute refugees imprisoned at the Guantanamo Bay Naval Base in Cuba for trying to enter the United States illegally, migrants working for subsistence wages in the fields of the Dominican Republic, and refugees drowned when the small crafts carrying them break up in the rough waters of the Caribbean.[4] Another popular Haitian compas band, Phantoms, recorded "Cowboy," a song written by their lead singer, King Kino. "Cowboy" condemns the long history of repression and brutality by the Duvalier dictatorships and by the then-current U.S.-backed military coup that overthrew the democratically elected government of Jean-Bertrand Aristide in 1991.

In those same years, the Haitian band Boukman Eksperyans blended rara, rock 'n' roll music, and highly political lyrics supporting Aristide's Lavalas movement and condemning the U.S.-backed military regimes that ruled the nation. Lolo Beaubrun of Boukman Eksperyans credited Bob Marley's music as a key source of inspiration for his group. "When I heard Bob Marley sometime around 1987," Beaubrun recalled, "I decided that if he could do something like that in Jamaica, we could do that with vodou in Haiti."[5] Haitian rara bands also borrow the language of Rastafarians when signaling one another about the presence of the police, alerting listeners to the danger by saying "Babylon is here."[6]

In the politicized climate in Haiti and its diaspora during the years when Wyclef Jean came of age, interactions between diasporic Haitians and diasporic Jamaicans provided important spaces for the development of socially conscious music. Haitian and Jamaican migrant workers encountered one another laboring side by side in the fields in southern Florida. Immigrants from both nations shared neighborhoods in New York City with Puerto Ricans and Dominicans. Haitian DJs and rappers performed frequently in Roberto Clemente Park in the Bronx and in venues in Brooklyn in the late 1980s and early 1990s. Charles Dorismond, a Haitian who interacted daily with Jamaicans in the Flatbush section of Brooklyn, where he lived, achieved some commercial success rapping in Jamaican English patois and Haitian Kreyòl under the name Bigga Haitian.[7]

Yet the route to reggae and rap for Haitians also included the rara music of their homeland. A music that roaming ensembles perform during Haiti's postcarnival period, rara shares many affinities with hip hop. Rooted in performative orality, rara lyrics move rapidly from solemn to silly, from serious to salacious. Rara bands pull listeners and spectators into their performances, playing for different groups of people as they march along, dissolving distinctions between artists and audiences. They make special efforts to salute sacred places that might not seem special to the uninitiated, stopping for special ceremonies at intersections, bridges, and cemeteries—all places where worlds collide. Rara lyrics express social criticisms in coded forms, meaningful to insiders but impenetrable by outsiders. In Haiti, rara bands fight the military for the right to occupy and traverse public space. Ethnographer, ethnomusicologist, and cultural critic Elizabeth McAlister identifies rara as a key repository of collective memory in Haiti, as a way of expressing and preserving the many histories of conquest, colonialism, and exploitation left out of the officially validated histories of Haiti.[8]

Rara groups began performing in Central Park in Manhattan and in Prospect Park in Brooklyn as early as 1990. Wyclef Jean and Pras Michel grew up in a community in which rara performances were widely available. *The Score* and subsequent recordings by members of the Fugees clearly express the aesthetics, intentions, and insights of rara through the generic conventions of hip hop. Deft displays of eloquent analysis punctuate comic and dramatic skits. Lyrics celebrate sites such as housing projects, stores, and city streets as if they were sacred shrines. "The Beast" and other songs on *The Score* directly confront the police and the practices used to control ghetto spaces in North America. The music made by the members of the Fugees serves as an extraordinary repository of collective memories encompassing the consumer memories encoded in song samples, the "waves" of fashion and style produced within commercial culture, and the political histories of terrible anti-Black racism but also resolute interracial antiracism in the New York metropolitan area and around the world.

The history of social consciousness permeating Haitian compas and rara music appears emphatically in the lyrics of the Fugees. Urban conditions and concerns in the New York–New Jersey area hold center stage in all of the songs on *The Score,* including "No Woman, No Cry." That song in particular enables the Fugees to fuse the history of Haitian immigrants with the history of deindustrialization and economic restructuring in urban ghettos in the United States, through an intertextual reference to another popular hip hop song. In 1991, Naughty by Nature (a hip hop group from

East Orange, New Jersey) had used a sample of "No Woman, No Cry" as an ironic counterpoint in their hit song "Ghetto Bastard." The song's lyrics describe the brutality and hopelessness of ghetto life with unadorned and unsentimental frankness. The refrain "everything's gonna be all right" from "No Woman, No Cry" plays in between the verses. The point of the song is that everything is *not* going to be all right, so the sample from "No Woman, No Cry" bitterly references an earlier time when it still might have made sense to harbor hope. To add yet another layer, Naughty by Nature did not sample the original Bob Marley and the Wailers' version of "No Woman, No Cry" but instead sampled the version by Boney M, a German Eurodisco group whose expatriate members came from Jamaica, Aruba, and Montserrat.

The bitter sarcasm in Naughty by Nature's use of "No Woman, No Cry" set the stage for its use as a multiply accented intertextual reference by the Fugees. On *The Score,* it not only references Bob Marley's song but also Naughty by Nature's cover of Boney M's cover of the Marley original. *The Score* also gestures toward Naughty by Nature's ruthless documentary honesty about the problems facing inner-city youth. In the song "The Beast," the Fugees draw on Rastafarian wordplay to condemn "poli-trickcians," a clear reference to the Rasta slogan that poli-tricks is the white man's plot and the Black man's lot. Echoes of Naughty by Nature's sarcasm also appear in the middle of "The Beast," where Jean invokes "The Star-Spangled Banner" to ask, "Say, can't you see, cops more crooked than we?"

At the time when *The Score* soared to the top of the best-seller lists, Haitian immigrant Abner Louima frequented the Club Rendez-Vous in Brooklyn on weekend nights. He particularly enjoyed the compas music of Phantoms and their lead singer King Kino, especially the song "Cowboy." Louima, born in Thomassin, Haiti, was sympathetic to Aristide's Lavalas (the cleansing flood) movement in Haiti, and he admired Kino's frankness in decrying the brutality of right-wing forces in that country. On August 9, 1997, Louima encountered equivalent violence in the United States. While he was engaged in conversation outside the club after it had closed, police officers attempted to disperse the Haitians lingering on the sidewalks. They arrested Louima and took him to the Seventieth Precinct police station. At the station, officers beat and tortured Louima, shoving a wooden stick up his rectum and into his mouth. During the protests that Haitian immigrant activists and their allies staged against this treatment, King Kino added another verse to his 1992 song "Cowboy," connecting the police brutality in Brooklyn to the brutality of U.S.-backed paramilitary forces in Haiti.[9]

Wyclef Jean reiterated both his Haitian identity and his political concerns about the treatment of inner-city youths in the solo albums he made after the Fugees' success with *The Score*. He recorded songs rapped entirely in Kreyòl, released some music independently to Haitian radio stations in Port-au-Prince, and played concerts in Haitian cities. Just as the dancehall and rap music of El General, a Black Panamanian, reflects the histories and cultural contradictions of the descendants of Jamaicans who left their homeland to work on the Panama Canal, Wyclef Jean's Kreyòl recordings map part of the experiences of the Haitian diaspora in Brooklyn, Boston, Montreal, and Paris. His music demonstrates that these sites functioned as a part of Haiti located far from home—as *le dixième département* (tenth state), the name Jean-Bertrand Aristide gave it in hopes of having overseas Haitians play constructive roles in homeland politics. Exile from Haiti also awakened and activated different kinds of interethnic and international identities and identifications.

Near the beginning of *The Score,* the Fugees sample "Gypsy Woman" by Joe Bataan. Although it contains English-language lyrics sung by an Afro-Filipino, this version of Curtis Mayfield's composition serves as an icon of Nuyorican identity and collective memory from the era of Latin bugalu.[10] Referencing the song in *The Score* enabled the Fugees to ground themselves in a history that includes a fusion among African American, Afro-Asian, and Afro-Latino identities, that recalls the bilingualism of Latin bugalu as a forerunner of the English–Spanish and English–Kreyòl bilingualism of contemporary Latinos and Haitians in New York, as well as the Kreyòl–Spanish hybridity vital to communication between Dominicans and Haitians on the island of Hispaniola and among Haitians, Puerto Ricans, Dominicans, and Mexicans in New York.

On his solo album *The Carnival*, Wyclef samples Cuban patriot José Marti's "Guantanamera," sung by the great Celia Cruz as the core sound behind an original composition with English-language lyrics. On *Welcome to Haiti: Creole 101* he sings a version of "La bamba," a Spanish-language song from Mexico popularized by Ritchie Valens and Los Lobos but originally a *son jarocho* from Veracruz. These songs exemplify and highlight affiliations linking Haitians, Puerto Ricans, Cubans, and Mexicans in the Caribbean and in the United States, but they also present Afro-Caribbean people and culture as the key points of commonality among speakers of different languages in the Caribbean and its diasporas. The embodied blackness of Wyclef Jean, Joe Bataan, and Celia Cruz establishes this in one way, but the origins of "La bamba" in Veracruz, the most Caribbean and most Black part of Mexico, emphasize how the common African presence takes different forms in these very different, yet still similar, Caribbean countries.

Mexican-born Carlos Santana made the same point in a different way early in his career in his 1973 album *Lotus*. Santana moved with his family to San Diego and then San Francisco as a child. He immersed himself in blues music and eventually married the daughter of Saunders King, an important African American blues and jazz musician in the San Francisco Bay Area. Santana's fusions of blues and Afro-Caribbean rhythms, lyrics, and melodies proved extremely successful. He brought Tito Puente's "Oye como va" into the mainstream of popular rock music and established himself as one of the few musicians capable of securing consistently high sales among anglophone audiences with music that contains Spanish-language lyrics. Although a Mexican, Santana displayed extensive understanding of and commitment to pan-African and pan-Caribbean politics. On the *Lotus* album, he included two songs paying tribute to Toussaint L'Ouverture, Haiti's late eighteenth- and early nineteenth-century revolutionary hero: "Incident at Neshabur" and "Toussaint L'Ouverture."[11]

Santana's tribute to Toussaint touches on the long history of intercultural contact within and among islands in the Caribbean. Both Kreyòl-speaking Haitians and English-speaking Jamaicans labored in sugarcane fields under the supervision of Spanish and English speakers in Cuba and the Dominican Republic. The famous massacre of Haitian workers in the Dominican Republic in 1937 took place, in part, because the U.S.-backed Machado dictatorship expelled Haitian sugarcane workers from Cuba, forcing them to seek work in the Dominican Republic, where the U.S.-backed Trujillo regime ordered them slaughtered. Yet Santana's songs about Toussaint and the battle at Neshabur also draw on a long tradition of Haitian influence in African American music.

Douglas Henry Daniels notes that Jelly Roll Morton attributed his earliest musical education to his Haitian godmother, Eulalia Echo, and that his musical tributes to other artists, such as "King Porter Stomp" and "Mamie's Blues" in honor of trumpeter Porter King and blues singer Mamie Desdoumes, and his habanera rhythms and "stomps" resonate with the vocabulary and grammar of Afro-Caribbean musical forms. Similarly, Daniels suggests that Lester Young's music contains various vodou influences that he gleaned during his years growing up in New Orleans, from his belief that ordinary events contain signs and messages from spirits to his propensity to give songs titles that reflect Afro-Caribbean dance styles emphasizing upward movement off the earth, such as "Lester Leaps In" and "Jump Lester Jump."[12]

Wyclef Jean draws on these rich traditions in his collaborations with the Fugees and on his solo albums. On *The Eclectic,* he cites a popular political slogan that had formed the core of a song by Boukman Eksperyans in defiance of the military dictatorship in 1991, "Kem pa sote" (My Heart Does Not Leap, I Am Not Afraid).[13] Jean remained concerned about racial issues in the metropolis as well. The album *2 Sides II a Book,* released in 2000, contains a song condemning the February 4, 1999, killing of African immigrant Amadou Diallo by New York City police officers. Diallo had committed no crime and had no weapon. Fumbling for his keys in his own doorway, Diallo was shot at by the officers forty-one times. Nineteen of the bullets riddled his body. In the song, Jean quotes Peter Tosh's reggae song "Equal Rights" and compares Diallo to Steven Biko, the founder of the Black Consciousness Movement in South Africa, who was murdered by the security police in that country in 1977.

On March 17, 2000, a New York City undercover police officer, Anderson Moran, approached Patrick Dorismond, a twenty-six-year-old Haitian immigrant security guard, entreating him to buy some drugs. Dorismond yelled "get out of my face" and pushed Moran away. Moran pushed back. As the two grappled, Moran's partner, undercover detective Anthony Vasquez, shot Dorismond in the chest and killed him. The incident was the third shooting of an unarmed "suspect" by New York City police officers in a thirteen-month period. It occurred one month after the acquittal of the four officers who had killed Amadou Diallo. Journalists reported that Moran and Vasquez formed one of the New York City Police Department's "buy and bust" teams, special units under orders to make at least five arrests on each tour of duty. The resulting arrests played an important role in bolstering the crime-fighting reputation and the personal ambitions for higher office of the New York mayor at the time, Rudolph Giuliani.[14] Lieutenant Eric Adams, leader of the One Hundred Blacks in Law Enforcement organization, noted bitterly that Patrick Dorismond had become the first Black man in history to die simply because he decided to "just say no to drugs."[15]

Patrick Dorismond was the son of Andre Dorismond, distinguished Haitian compas and rampa singer. The slain security guard's brother, Charles Dorismond, is the rap artist known as Bigga Haitian. Marie Rose Dorismond, the mother of Charles and Patrick, is the cousin of So Anne (Annette Auguste), a professional singer and a Lavalas activist in Haiti. The events, patterns, and networks that link Patrick Dorismond, Bigga Haitian, Boukman Eksperyans, Naughty by Nature, Tabou Combo, Wyclef Jean, and the Fugees to Bob Marley have the long fetch of history behind them.

It is not just the contemporary pressures, displacements, and oppressions of transnational capitalism that subjected Amadou Diallo and Patrick Dorismond to the homicidal tactics of the New York City Police Department or that made the Fugees' complaints about the police credible to hip hop audiences. These connections are overdetermined by long waves from the past. Wyclef Jean hails from a country with a long history of both repression and resistance, of nationalist fervor and transnational pan-African pride, of serial colonization and resolute anticolonialism. This history haunts his music, even when he does not directly reference it.

Haiti has suffered from dictatorships and foreign interventions throughout its history, but Haitians have also been resolute fighters for freedom. The half of the island of Hispaniola occupied by Haiti has endured colonization by Spain and France, attacks from the Dominican Republic, and occupation by military forces from Germany, England, and the United States. Several Haitian leaders have ruled largely because of support from foreign powers.

U.S. warships entered the waters within Haiti's jurisdiction at least twenty-five times between 1849 and 1915.[16]

In 1791 in the wake of the French Revolution, Haitian slaves launched the most successful slave revolt in history. Their actions set off a wider war that ultimately led to an alliance among slaves, free Blacks, and some whites that dealt the armies of Napoleon Bonaparte their first defeat ever. The popular rebellion secured Haiti's independence from France and established a free republic— the second of only two republics in the Western Hemisphere (after the United States) and the first republic in this hemisphere to be free of slavery.

The new nation adopted a red and blue flag, deleting the color white from the French tricolor. The nation's first constitution barred "whites" from owning land while granting citizenship to all persons of African or Indian descent. Yet these color categories involved politics as much as biology. The same constitution that barred whites from owning land also made *all* Haitians who had supported independence legally Black, regardless of the color of their skin. Thus, the German, Polish, and French immigrants who had fought for Haitian independence alongside Toussaint L'Ouverture became "Black," while all who had opposed freedom, including those with dark skin, became designated as *blanc* (white).[17]

Haiti's successful slave revolt, its flexible racial categories, and its affirmations of blackness terrified slave owners in North America. At the same time, however, investors cast a covetous eye toward Hispaniola's natural resources, markets, and labor. For most of the nineteenth and twentieth centuries, U.S. diplomats tried to extend North American economic influence over the island while seeking to prevent what Secretary of State John C. Calhoun in 1844 diplomatically termed "the further spread of Negro influence in the West Indies."[18] The "Negro influence" in the West Indies feared by elected officials in the United States was the spread of the movement to abolish slavery. As early as 1802, Thomas Jefferson's postmaster general justified excluding free Blacks from jobs as postal riders by pointing to the dangers of "plans and conspiracies" like those that had generated the slave revolt in Santo Domingo.[19] Throughout the nineteenth century, the U.S. government collaborated with France and other European powers to keep Haiti dependent and in debt.

White supremacist fear of Haiti was not completely unfounded. In truth, many Haitians were offended by North America's slave system and did wish to hasten its demise. Haitians also looked to North America for allies against white supremacy. Haiti's leaders named a street after John Brown after the white abolitionist's execution by the U.S. government in 1859. A century later, another street in Port-au-Prince, one that bisects John Brown Avenue, was renamed Martin Luther King Avenue.[20] The African Americans who challenged Jim Crow segregation in the 1896 Supreme Court case *Plessy v. Ferguson* had originally come from Haiti. To humiliate them and add insult to injury, the Supreme Court issued its ruling on behalf of the segregationist "separate but equal" doctrine on May 18, Haitian Flag Day.

U.S. troops directly occupied Haiti continuously between 1915 and 1934,[21] training the local constabulary and protecting U.S. control of Haitian custom houses and all of its governmental expenditures. By 1922, a New York bank "owned" the national treasury and the national bank of Haiti. The United States supported the dictatorship of François (Papa Doc) Duvalier between 1957 and 1971. Supported by the Haitian army and by U.S. citizens with economic power and influence in the country, Duvalier secured the presidency through an election in which his most popular opponent was excluded from the ballot. In that contest, election judges on the island of La Tortué gave Duvalier seventy-five hundred votes in a precinct that contained nine hundred registered voters.[22]

Papa Doc spared no extreme in maintaining power. He banned entire orders of Catholic priests and even outlawed the Boy Scouts, because he feared that they might mobilize against him. Duvalier pressured the national parliament to name him "president for life" and to lower the required age of the presidency from forty to eighteen so that at his death his son could be installed as the nation's leader. He did submit that change to popular approval in a referendum, but the results were called into question when Duvalier reported that the Haitian people had "elected" his son to succeed him by a vote of 2,392,916 in favor, and *none* opposed.[23]

At one point, Duvalier and his favored associates actually made money by selling the blood of Haitians to blood banks in the United States. The dictator's associates organized the company Hemo-Caribbean, which arranged with Miami stockbroker Joseph

Gorinstein to pay impoverished Haitians three to five dollars per liter of plasma. The company then sold it at seven times its cost to U.S. hemophiliacs in need of coagulant VIII, which was distilled from the plasma. Biochemist Werner A. Thrill supervised the technical side of this operation for laboratories owned by U.S. firms: Dow Chemical, Dade Regent, Armour Pharmaceutical, and Cutter Laboratories. The scientist defended this trade in Haitian blood with a rhetorical question: "If the Haitians don't sell their blood, what do you want them to do with it?"[24]

When democratic forces in Haiti succeeded in establishing duly elected leaders after the overthrow of Baby Doc in 1986, the United States intervened again. The administration of President George H. W. Bush supported the overthrow of the democratically elected government of Jean-Bertrand Aristide in 1991. As a condition of his return to power in 1993, the Clinton administration compelled Aristide to abandon his progressive land reform policies and to place his security in the hands of private armed forces from the United States rather than in the Haitian military. In 2004, the administration of President George W. Bush helped engineer a coup by thugs under the supervision of Guy Philippe while the U.S. private security firm stood by idly, once again overthrowing a democratically elected Aristide administration.

Despite centuries of colonization, corruption, and control by outside forces, Haiti has developed an irrepressible, self-active, and democratic popular culture through years of struggle. The Lavalas movement headed by Aristide was built on vodou traditions in much the same way that Bob Marley used Rastafarianism as an ethical code sanctioning rebellion against privilege and power in this world. The music made by Tabou Combo, Phantoms, Boukman Eksperyans, and many other bands have tapped into peasant customs, dress, dances, and popular speech to forge oppositional practices and performances. The processions and music of the folk form known as rara, with its politically and sexually tinged lyrics and collective performance styles similar to hip hop, have informed a broad range of popular practices. Even the Kreyòl language has served as a rich source of opposition with its subversive homonyms and puns that use the same pronunciations to describe the state and a bully *(l'etat)* and the same sounds to describe both the law and the spirit presence of ancestors *(loi* and *l'wa)*.[25] The popular motto of the Lavalas movement encapsulates the principles of collectivity for Haitians: Yon sel nou feb, ansanm nou fo, asanm nou se lavalas (Alone we are weak, together we are strong, together we are a cleansing flood).

Haitians have also been bequeathed a legacy of pan-Caribbean and diasporic intimacy. Haitian cane cutters have traveled routinely to Cuba, the Dominican Republic, and the United States. The *tipico* guitar and the troubadour tradition came to Haiti from Cuba. The influence of Dominican merengue permeated the music of the bands that Andre Dorismond performed with, ensembles led by Nemours Jean-Baptiste and Weber Sicot.[26] The rara group Boukman Eksperyans has been greatly influenced by Latin American liberation theology. The name of their ensemble pays tribute to U.S. Black rock guitarist Jimi Hendrix (whose group was called the Jimi Hendrix Experience) and to Boukman Jetty, the Jamaican-born Haitian vodou practitioner and Catholic priest whose visions sparked the Haitian slave rebellion of 1791.[27] The Kreyòl word *lakou* refers to a place for collective gathering and serves the same function as *yard* in Jamaican patois, the same "yard" in Trenchtown, Brooklyn, and Jersey that appears in the Fugees version of "No Woman, No Cry."[28]

The long history of U.S. intervention in Haiti serves as the main impetus for Haitian immigration to the United States. By the early 1990s, only Jamaica sent more Black immigrants to the United States than Haiti, and the nation had become the fifth largest source of immigration to New York City over all, behind the Dominican Republic, Jamaica, China, and Guyana.[29]

Although born in the United States, Lauryn Hill has still been able to draw on her own experiences in fusing a pan-African persona for herself. As exemplified in her song "Every Ghetto, Every City," Hill presents herself as a person nurtured by the plurality and diversity of Afro-diasporic life in the cities and suburbs of the United States and around the world. When *The Score* became successful in 1996, Hill started the Refugee Project, a program for young people, designed to promote courage, peace, discipline, faith, strength, determination, wisdom, excellence, service, knowledge, and love. She raised money for Haitian refugees, funded projects designed to provide clean well water for communities in Kenya and Uganda, and financed efforts to help at-risk inner-city children. Hill also appeared at rallies promoting voter registration.

Several of the songs on *The Miseducation of Lauryn Hill* were recorded at the Bob Marley Studio in Kingston, Jamaica, including "Lost Ones," which contains a verse in which Hill sings, "I know all the tricks from Bricks to Kingston." *Bricks* refers to Brick City, a hip hop nickname for Newark, New Jersey. A clothing line has also been named Brick City. In February 2005, Hill performed before an audience of three hundred thousand people in Addis Ababa, Ethiopia, at the Africa Unite conference, commemorating what would have been the sixtieth birthday of Bob Marley. Also on the bill were Marley's mother, widow, and five of his sons.

Perhaps the most important political work performed by Lauryn Hill has been done in the terrains of gender and sexuality. In *The Score* she ridicules the misogyny of male rappers "trying to be Al Capone" by attaching herself to the lineage of politically conscious Black women, proclaiming her alternative in rhyme: "I'll be Nina Simone." On *The Miseducation of Lauryn Hill,* a title indebted to Carter G. Woodson's classic book *The Miseducation of the Negro,* Hill presents sex-affirmative but antisexist lyrics, blending religious devotion and moral critique with rich descriptions of Black life in "every city, every ghetto, and every suburb." She insisted on producing all the tracks on *The Miseducation of Lauryn Hill,* not just singing on them. Asked to sing Christmas carols at a concert in the Vatican in Rome, Hill shocked an audience of seventy-five hundred by reading a statement that criticized church officials for tolerating and covering up the abuse of children by pedophile priests.

Part of the critical edge presented by the Fugees in *The Score* came from their lives at the intersection of experiences as raced subjects in the United States and as refugees and exiles from Haiti. Wyclef Jean helped mobilize entertainers LL Cool J, Jay-Z, Alicia Keys, Erykah Badu, and P. Diddy to speak and perform at a demonstration that drew twenty thousand people in New York in 2002 to protest cuts in school funding. Jean was one of ten people at the rally arrested for disorderly conduct. Yet the Fugees also inherited the contradictions of each of those sites.

The Fugees are a commercial act, not a political organization. Wyclef Jean and Lauryn Hill are famous entertainers, not political leaders. Their conscious lyrics serve important progressive purposes, but they also have a cash value in the market. Principled political positions differentiate them from other entertainers, giving their "brand" a unique status in the market. Yet, the more successful they become, the less likely they are to share the experiences and perspectives of most of their audience. As aspiring musicians, they felt compelled to observe their communities closely, to find something in them that could be turned into commercially viable entertainment. As celebrities, however, their whims, feuds, anxieties, and personal problems help sell tabloid newspapers and music magazines. The political and historical ramifications of the music of the Fugees are important because of what it says about the communities from which they come and toward which they direct their work, but their music and lyrics should not be read as political manifestos or even necessarily as guides to the actual political stances and beliefs of the artists who create them.

Moreover, three individuals cannot represent the full range of experiences in Black communities or reconcile the contradictions of those experiences. Many of the lyrics in *The Score* and *The Miseducation of Lauryn Hill* deploy pro-Black sentiments to craft a clever alliance between Black people who live in suburbs and come from professional backgrounds and the poorest of the poor in the inner city. "The Fugees is a unique situation," proclaims Wyclef Jean, "the real marriage of the hood and the suburbs together."[30] This strategy has important positive effects. It discourages educated and successful Blacks from abandoning those in the inner city while offering pro-Black unity to the ghetto poor as a potential response to the radical divisiveness and self-hatred that so often emerge as consequences of discrimination and deprivation. Yet this unity suppresses real antagonisms and differences based on class tensions within Black communities.[31]

Some of the very things that have positioned Wyclef Jean and Lauryn Hill to emerge as spokespersons for certain political positions also contain contradictions that constrain them. Wyclef Jean called for Aristide to step down before the 2004 coup, arguing that the chaos in the country had to be contained. Yet he did not acknowledge that it was mercenaries backed by the United States who instigated almost all of the violence. The same experiences that make Wyclef Jean progressive in the United States can render him reactionary in Haiti. U.S. society has its own contradictions as well. The political lyrics of *The Score* propelled the members of the Fugees, while they were still in their twenties, into prominence as unelected spokespersons for masses of inner-city youths. The centrality of entertainment in the commercial media in the United States means that entertainers' views on political issues are more likely to be reported than the views of knowledgeable experts. When Janeane Garofalo or Sean Penn opposes the war in Iraq, when Susan Sarandon speaks out against the death penalty, when Bill Cosby or Oprah Winfrey opines on the behavior of Black people, their views are disseminated more widely than the views of scholars and activists with far more knowledge about those issues, such as Noam Chomsky, Sister Helen Prejean, Melvin Oliver, and Dorothy Roberts.

Wyclef Jean and Lauryn Hill have made impressive efforts to acquit themselves honorably in this role, but little in the direct experience of entertainers qualifies them to speak for masses of disenfranchised and disaffected people. Their very prominence gives them public personas with cash value to protect, acting careers and ambitions in the music industry that could be squelched if they offend the wrong people. As Lauryn Hill advanced her acting career with roles in television soap operas and motion pictures, as she retreated into her family life and increasingly turned to religious fervor as a way of coping with the pressures on her as a celebrity, the social activism she championed earlier seemed to recede in importance. The site for her Refugee Project disappeared from the Web at about the time that rumors circulated that she had terminated her involvement with the charity. It was the pan-African world from which they emerged that made the Fugees progressive, not their individual personalities or perceptions. The more removed they have become from that world, the less they have to say about the issues that concern it.

The pan-African world that produced the Fugees, furthermore, also has its own contradictions. On the basis of solidarities of sameness, of the belief that the things that unite Black people are more important than the things that divide them, that world produces a strategic essentialism that can easily be misinterpreted, even by its adherents, as a belief that race is a real and foundational entity. The limits of this analysis appear clearly when contrasted with the real-life circumstances of the person whose image and reputation are most often summoned to support it—Bob Marley.

Marley earned his status as a Black icon through his art and his activism. He is, however, an unusual choice to serve as an exemplar of an unproblematic Black Jamaican identity. Marley's father was a white man from England. His mother-in-law was a Cuban, and his wife, Rita Marley, was born in Cuba.[32] The reggae music

Marley came to exemplify emerged out of Rastafarianism and Ethiopianism in Black religious life in Jamaica, to be sure, but it also was a product of Jamaican migration to South Africa, New Jersey, and Panama, as well as of the multiethnic nature of Jamaican society.[33] Marley has been adopted as a spiritual ancestor by Native Americans in Kykotsmovi, Arizona, by the Australian Aboriginal band No Fixed Address, and by Algerian-French *rai* virtuoso Cheb Khaled, who employed Marley's back-up singers, the I-Threes, on his 1996 album *Sahra*.[34]

The presence of Asian immigrants in the Caribbean played a major role in Marley's career and in the emergence of reggae music. One of the key entrepreneurs in starting the dancehall sound systems in Jamaica in the 1960s was Tom "the Great Sebastien," really Thomas Wong, a Chinese Jamaican hardware merchant. Jo Jo Hoo Kim led a band of session musicians called the Revolutionaries and produced reggae songs at the famous Channel One studios in Kingston. Dickie Wong owned the Tit for Tat Club on Red Hills Road in Kingston, where Sly Dunbar attracted crowds with his innovative reggae drumming.[35] Vincent "Randy" Chin ran a popular music shop and produced sessions recorded by Lord Creator, Alton Ellis, John Holt, and Jackie Opel.[36] Chin's brothers, Leonard and Clive, worked as producers and musicians with Augustus Pablo, Horace Andy, Gregory Isaacs, Carroll Thompson, and Jean Ademambo.[37]

One of the first musicians to play reggae in carnival settings on that island was also a Chinese Jamaican, Byron Lee. Successful as a performer, band leader, promoter, and producer, Lee started in calypso and ska before turning to reggae with his band the Dragonaires.[38] He eventually went on to his greatest success as a soca musician, but he played an important role in establishing reggae music as a viable commercial form. Some journalists credit Lee with being the first Jamaican to popularize electric bass and to use a bass amplifier, an innovation crucial to the development of the reggae sound.[39] Famed producer and later prime minister of Jamaica, Edward Seaga (a Lebanese Jamaican) selected Lee to organize the session band backing up performers singing ska songs at the 1964 World's Fair in New York in an effort to promote tourism to Jamaica.[40]

Herman Chin Loy and Clive Chin played key roles in formulating Augustus Pablo's "Far East" sound, a style fashioned through the use of minor chords, accompaniment on the clavinet or melodica, and titles invoking Asia, as in the song "Java."[41] Leslie Kong, a Chinese Jamaican, played a key role in producing reggae recordings. Much of his business acumen came from running a combined record shop, restaurant, and ice cream parlor named Beverly's, in Kingston.[42] He produced hits by the Maytals, the Melodians, Desmond Dekker, and Derrick Morgan.[43] Even the Jamaican slang term for marijuana, the herb that proved so central to Marley's religious beliefs, came from Asia. The term *ganja* entered the Caribbean from India.[44]

Yet it would be a mistake to portray Black–Asian relations in Jamaica as completely cordial.[45] Anti-Chinese riots erupted in 1966, and anti-Asian sentiment led Byron Lee to eschew reggae for calypso and soca. Prince Buster recorded a series of songs chiding Derrick Morgan for stealing Buster's songs and recording them for the "Chiney man," Leslie Kong. Bob Marley is reputed to have placed a curse on Kong, a threat given significance, since Kong died suddenly when only thirty-one years old. Another story claims that Bunny Wailer warned Kong not to release the album *The Best of the Wailers,* because Wailer believed it needed more work before commercial release. He relates, "He went ahead anyways and the album came out. A month afterward Kong fell ill in the studio and went home—*and he died*. He was tryin' to kill us and it bounced back on 'im!"[46]

Reggae would not have emerged on the world scene had it not been for the Asian presence in Jamaica. That presence in Jamaica and other Caribbean islands stemmed from long histories of European imperialism in Asia, contract labor under brutal conditions in the Caribbean, and elite manipulation of tensions between Afro-Caribbeans and Asian Caribbeans to lower labor costs and retain European influence on politics. These histories are especially significant given the tensions between Asian Americans and African Americans in New York, Los Angeles, and other U.S. cities, tensions that are reflected in some of the vignettes included by the Fugees on *The Score,* which contains indefensibly racist characterizations of Asian store owners.[47] The presence of Asians in Jamaican reggae is part of a larger picture that suggests that the pan-African world and the pan-Asian world have deep and long-established connections. Afro-Caribbeans, Indo-Caribbeans, and Chinese Caribbeans have a long history of interaction in Trinidad,

Guyana, Jamaica, Panama, and Cuba but also as doubly diasporic immigrants to the United States and the United Kingdom. Yet this shared heritage hardly guarantees harmonious relations between diasporic Asians and diasporic Africans.

Africa itself has an Asian history. Chinese expeditions reached the east coast of the continent as early as the fifteenth century. The fair-skinned people who inhabit the coastal regions of Kenya call themselves *bajuni*, the Chinese word for a long robe. The population of Madagascar shows signs of intermarriage between Indonesians and Africans centuries ago. South Asians who crossed the Indian Ocean to settle all over southern and eastern Africa sometimes became *dukwallas*, the Swahili word for shopkeepers. The name of the Swahili language itself stems from the Arabic word for coast, *sawahil*. Swahili contains many technical maritime terms that come from Farsi, and part of the population of Africa's east coast celebrates the Persian New Year and follows the Persian calendar.

Links between Asians and Africans have also been important throughout the Americas. Just as Asia has played a role in the history of Africa, diasporic Africans have found a fertile field for musical expression in Asia, especially through jazz. In the 1920s, California bands led by Sonny Clay, Jack Carter, Earl Whaley, Bob Hill, and Frank Shievers performed frequently in Asia. Bill Powers, Gene Powers, and Buck Campbell played jazz in Yokohama, Japan, while pianist Bill Hegamin and dancer Freddie McWilliams secured gigs in China.[48] Sid LeProtti and Reb Spikes traveled from San Francisco to play jazz in Hawai'i, while scat singer "Bo Diddley" (the original) performed in Japan. Sonny Clay and his orchestra toured Australia.[49]

Teddy Weatherford first traveled to Asia as a member of Jack Carter's band, and he remained in Shanghai, China, for years. Weatherford played professional engagements in Singapore as well as China, recruiting trumpet player Buck Clayton to China to play with his group in 1934. Later, Weatherford worked in Calcutta, India.[50] He trained musicians who became important jazz players in Japan, including drummer Yamaguchi "Shanghai" Toyosaburo and trumpeter Nanri Fumio.[51] In the 1960s and 1970s, rhythm-and-blues singer Laverne Baker kept her career alive by performing in Manila nightclubs.

Asian influence has also been pronounced in the Caribbean.

The group La Anacoana emerged as one of the most popular bands in Cuba during the 1930s. Its name came from the indigenous woman leader of resistance against the Spanish conquest of Haiti. The historical Anacoana extended the hand of friendship to the European invaders, only to be tortured and killed by them. She became a symbol of resistance, pride, and independence throughout the Caribbean, an early icon of Black Power in the region. The members of the musical aggregation La Anacoana, however, were not simply Black and Cuban; they were women of mixed Afro-Cuban and Asian Cuban origins. The Castro Sisters, sometimes referred to as the Lee Sisters, formed the core of the band. Their father was a Chinese immigrant shopkeeper who married a mixed-race Cuban woman. His name in China had been Li, but when he decided to remain in Cuba and raise his family there, he changed the name "Li" to "Castro," so the Lee Sisters became the Castro Sisters.[52]

The complex and global nature of the Asian diaspora has placed Asians in many unexpected places in world music. Mexican ranchera singer Ana Gabriel was born in Gaumuchli in Sinaloa, Mexico, but her maternal grandparents came from China.[53] Salsa musician, producer, and promoter Chino Rodriguez is a Chinese Puerto Rican born in New York in 1954. The late Chinese Jewish Canadian ethnomusicologist and pianist Lise Waxer performed in women's salsa ensembles in Cali, Colombia, in the 1990s.[54] Jazz bass virtuoso Charles Mingus came from a multiracial background that included a Chinese grandmother. Filipino American Neal McCoy became a sensation in country music during the 1990s, flaunting his mixed-race heritage as a "Texapino."

The flamboyant lead singer of the heavy metal group Queen, Freddie Mercury, changed his name from Farrokh Bulsara. He was a Parsi born in Zanzibar and had lived in India before he migrated to England at the age of sixteen.[55] A hip hop and "bhangra-muffin" recording artist calling himself Apache Indian secured extensive sales in the Caribbean, North America, Europe, and South Asia in the 1990s. Only a few of his fans knew that Apache Indian was really Steve Kapur, the son of Punjabi immigrants to Birmingham, England. The Brooklyn-born artist who calls herself Foxy Brown (Inga Marchand) is known to hip hop fans around the world as an African American, but her ancestry is also Filipino and Trinidadian.

Musicians from the Philippines have been especially versatile, appearing in virtually every genre of popular music around the word. Rhythm-and-blues audiences in the 1950s and 1960s generally thought of Sugar Pie DeSanto as a Black woman. The singer who placed several songs on the best-selling soul charts and dazzled audiences with her energetic stage shows, however, was really an Afro-Filipina who grew up speaking both English and Tagalog at home and who jokingly referred to her mixed ancestry by designating herself a "Spook-a-pina." Bandleader Johnny Otis named her Sugar Pie DeSanto because he feared that Umpeylia Marasema Balinton would be a hard name for audiences to master. DeSanto's father was a Filipino merchant seaman who met her African American piano-playing mother in Philadelphia. Similarly, Joe Bataan, whose version of "Gypsy Woman" is sampled by the Fugees near the start of *The Score,* became a treasured icon of Puerto Rican identity and pride with his 1970s Latin rock and salsa songs, even though he, too, was Afro-Filipino. Bataan made recordings while still a teenager just out of prison. The urgency of his lyrics seemed to complement his (then) unpolished skills as a musician. He became a favorite among Puerto Ricans, because his songs resonated with the slang, spirit, and subjectivity of the street.

Hawaiian-born Eleanor Academia grew up in San Diego, the daughter of an Ilocano father from Zambales and a Pangasinan mother from Bimalay. A star solo violinist and concert master for school and community orchestras, she also played rhythm and blues, rock-fusion, and blues music.[56] Academia spent some time as musical director for the Quincy Jones jazz workshops, toured the world as the keyboard player in rhythm-and-blues star Ray Parker Junior's ensemble, and conducted the orchestra for an off-Broadway play. Her song "Adventure" topped Billboard's International Dance charts in the 1980s, but she never considered herself solely part of the "dance" genre. "The perception of labeling in itself, to me, comes from a marketing or advertising base," she says, "and also, labeling something, to me, constricts the vision and the scope of an artist, what they want to convey."[57]

Academia developed her mastery over diverse genres as a struggling student, taking jobs in music to pay her tuition and expenses at the University of Southern California. She conducted orchestras, accompanied stand-up comedians, played keyboards at nightclubs, copied and arranged music, and worked as a studio session musician. At one particularly unglamorous job, a stray bullet careened across the room and went right though her synthesizer, but she continued playing.[58]

Academia's 2002 album *Oracle of the Black Swan* displays a consummate mastery over the genre of dance music but also features traces of heavy metal, jazz, rock, and Filipino folk music. She founded the World Kulintang Institute in Reseda, California, an organization dedicated to the preservation of traditional music and martial arts from the southern Philippines. Academia combines her career as a highly respected commercial musician with work at the institute, reminding her students of the social dimensions of the culture they study. Kulintang may be understood as an important folk form of music, but it also has a revolutionary history in the southern Philippines, originating as music designed to disguise martial arts training as dance in order to fool the Spanish colonizers of the Philippine Islands. Academia's students learn music at the institute, but in to order to understand the full context from which the music emerged, they must also understand Filipino history, global politics, and diverse spiritual traditions.[59]

The 1990s and early 2000s witnessed a marked increase in the number of Asian Americans and Pacific Islanders prominent in global popular music. Yet very few of them played anything that might be considered primarily Asian music. Vijay Iyer, Jon Jang, Anthony Brown, and Francis Wong distinguished themselves as jazz musicians, while James Iha from Smashing Pumpkins and Jeff Lin from Harvey Danger rose to prominence in rock. The Japanese band Shonen Knife secured acclaim for its pop-punk music, while expatriate Japanese musicians Yuka Honda and Miho Hatori declared their electronica and "hip pop" group Cibo Matto to be "an American band run by Asian people."[60] Pacific Islanders and Asian Americans in the Boo Yaa Tribe, Jamez Chang, the Mountain Brothers, Key Kool, DJ Rhetmattic, and the Seoul Brothers made contributions to hip hop, while the emergence of Hmong American pop and rock bands Paradise, High Voltage, and the Whyteshadows signaled a new relationship to U.S. culture for members of that refugee and émigré group. Filipina American Jocelyn Enriquez secured success as a Latin dance artist. New York's South Asian American DJ Rekha and San Francisco's Filipino American Q-Bert achieved fame among DJs and turntablists.

The long fetch of history shapes musical production throughout

Asia and the Asian diaspora. East Asia has become a major center for producing musicians trained in the performance traditions of classical art music from Europe as well as for pop groups that play the styles and genres dominant in the West. Colonialism, imperialism, orientalism, and Anglo-American domination of global media all influence the opportunities available to musicians perceived as Asian in the West. Rehan Hyder's excellent study of "Asian" bands in Britain reveals the difficult struggles waged by the members of Asian Dub Foundation, Cornershop, Fun-da-mental, and Voodoo Queens in blending bhangra, hip hop, and rock into fusions that could secure commercial validation and yet still express the cultural contradictions they experienced because of their national origins and racial identifications.[61] These bands used different combinations of South Asian instruments and lyrics to bring something new to many of their listeners, yet that very strategy made them vulnerable to being interpreted through racist and orientalist frameworks that reduced their complex cultural fusions to exotic novelties.

The prominence of anticommunist ideologues among Vietnamese refugees in Southern California severely constrains the popular music that can be produced, distributed, and consumed there. Yet those limits also impelled the great Vietnamese composer Pham Duy to create compositions and CD-ROMs that produce a "virtual Vietnam" to replace the one that the anticommunists have lost in real life.[62] For the gatekeepers who control the economic, cultural, and political institutions of the community, however, the music that used to be popular in Vietnam between 1954 and 1975 expresses a national identity that many of them feel they have lost because of the Communist victory in the Vietnam War. Thus, they privilege the music of the past over current compositions and try to ban completely the music made in contemporary Vietnam. The music from Vietnam between 1954 and 1975, however, reflects not so much Vietnamese nationalism as serial colonization—by the French, the Japanese, and the United States. It contains elements of the tango, cha-cha, and bolero that were played in the Saigon nightclubs patronized by the corrupt comprador elite that benefited most from, and identified most strongly with, French colonialism and U.S. domination. Yet the same long fetch of history that propelled these Vietnamese people into exile in Orange County and other locations in Southern California has brought them to an area with a long history of immigration from Mexico and Central America and a long history of mastery over musical forms such as the tango, the cha-cha, and the bolero. The powerful "Latin" elements in contemporary Vietnamese American musical production echo their presence in Saigon at midcentury but also stem from the accomplished local Latino music producers and studio musicians who play on recordings of popular Vietnamese music in Southern California.[63]

Asian Latino interactions in the United States are not always as idiosyncratic as the ones that place Latino musicians prominently within contemporary Vietnamese popular music. Six hundred thousand Asian Americans are also Latinos, some of them products of secondary migration to the United States from Brazil, Peru, Panama, Argentina, Jamaica, and other countries more open to immigration from Asia than the United States. Moreover, the patterns of residential segregation in the United States have often relegated Asians and Latinos to the same neighborhoods, such as El Monte, Montebello, and Monterey Park in Los Angeles and lower Manhattan and Flushing, Queens, in New York. John Esaki's great film *Maceo: Demon Drummer of East LA* recounts the multicultural experiences that have made Macao Hernandez Delgado a *taiko* virtuoso. Evidence of this proximity permeates the history of popular music, from Japanese American saxophonist Walter Takaki's presence in Chicano rock 'n' roller Ritchie Valens's first band to the lyrics of Don Tosti's "Chinito chinito." During the 1950s and 1960s, Ronnie Spector, an Afro–Puerto Rican–Anglo–Native American, unintentionally wound up looking Chinese to many of her fans because of her eye makeup, even though she was attempting to imitate the look of "Spanish" and "half-breed" girls she admired in her East Harlem neighborhood.[64]

The Asian disapora has also been profoundly affected by interactions with the African diaspora, as evidenced by Bob Marley's important interactions with Asian cultures in Jamaica. Asian American youths such as Filipino American turntablist Q-Bert (who grew up as Robert Quitevis in San Francisco's Excelsior District) and Korean American rapper Jamez Chang (who grew up as James Chang in Los Angeles) came to music as nonwhite raced subjects who have been surrounded by the prestige of African American musical forms in their immediate environments their whole lives.

Jamez sees his involvement in hip hop as part of what he calls the "Azian/Pacific Renaissance." He blends Korean *poongmul* drum beats, the oral traditions of Korean *pansori* music, and other Korean folk forms with recognizable hip hop styles. His tribute to the IRT 7 subway line from Manhattan to Flushing, Queens (the same line that provoked baseball player John Rocker to express revulsion and disgust at New York's multiracial population), expresses Jamez's delight at living in a neighborhood where Korean, Chinese, Jamaican, and Haitian people interact daily. He struggles to avoid tokenism in his art by taking the Korean elements seriously, studiously immersing himself in the broader cultural patterns that have produced *pansori* and *poongmul* in order to make them more than a novelty in his performances. Yet he also expresses his debts to role models steeped in Afro-Asian dialogue, such as Fred Ho, a Chinese American jazz saxophonist who heads an Afro-Asian jazz ensemble and once belonged to the Nation of Islam, and to Bob Marley, whose politics and aesthetics provide Jamez with his guiding mission, which he traces to the Jamaican's "Redemption Song"—to emancipate ourselves from "mental slavery."[65]

At the same time that Asian American musicians find a point of entry for themselves into U.S. popular culture through Afro-diasporic forms, African Americans evidence a new interest in and respect for Asian culture. Stimulated in part by the popularity that Hong Kong cinema enjoys with Black audiences yet always susceptible to a dangerous exoticism and orientalism, hip hop artists have turned to Asian martial arts and philosophical traditions to arm themselves against a racism that they perceive to be both national and global in scope. The members of the hip hop group Dead Prez, who call themselves Mutulu Olugbala and Knm Olugbala, have studied the theory and practice of kung fu martial arts and the enigmatic book of divination the *I Ching*. They quote the late kung fu action motion picture star Bruce Lee on their Web site.[66]

Music making by diasporic Africans and diasporic Asians emerges out of both profound attachments to place and powerful experiences with displacement. Inequalities among continents, nations, and cultural producers compel diasporic musicians to attach themselves to the cultures of their oppressors, to convey their own traditions through communications controlled by their enemies. Yet these unfair and unjust imperatives produce new forms of cognitive mapping that contain critical insights about how power actually works in the world. Discrete local and national mappings no longer account adequately for the complex relationships that conflate cultures and places.

The old geographies do not disappear, however. National boundaries and municipal borders still matter a great deal, even at a time of tremendous transformation and change in spatial and social relations. But diasporic imaginaries demonstrate ways of speaking to both local and global conditions at the same time. They draw some of their determinate force by riding the long waves of history, by turning the power of the long fetch of history to their own advantage. In the process, they promote new ways of thinking about the things that unite us and the things that divide us.

3. Banda

The Hidden History of Greater Mexico

> Although banda music had been left out by those who wrote history, it was always remembered by the people. . . . The history that was kept silent by the official discourse has been and continues to be narrated by the music itself.
>
> —**Helena Simonett,** *Banda: Mexican Musical Life across Borders*

Late in his life, the great Louis Armstrong developed a standard response to younger musicians who asked him how he was doing. "Well," the great virtuoso would reply slowly, "white folks still on top." Armstrong's answer seemed to imply that small changes in the lives of individuals could hardly alter the big picture, that the pervasive white supremacy that plagued the music industry—and all of U.S. society—remained constant, even when his personal fortunes waxed and waned. Although he reacted to it with a wry quip, this situation did not make Armstrong happy. As Eric Taylor has observed, as Armstrong got older, his smile seemed bigger and bigger, but his eyes appeared sadder and sadder.[1]

For most people most of the time, the long waves of history seem far away. Needed historical changes seem to proceed at the glacial pace alluded to in Armstrong's deliberate "misunderstanding" of polite questions about his well-being. Historical time seems monumental and slow, characterized more by the continuities that we recognize across time in social institutions, social relations, and the arts than by ruptures and transformations.

Yet there are some moments when historical change is evident, immediate, and palpable. A sense of transformative possibility often manifests itself in cultural expressions long before it becomes fused into a political force. New signs and symbols spring up, new forms of speech emerge, new styles of dress become popular, and new kinds of songs take root, because the old ones no longer seem to suffice. Revivals of traditional songs and renewed emphasis on French-language lyrics preceded mass mobilizations in the 1970s calling for Quebec's secession from Canada. The popularity of French-lyric songs by Robert Charlebois and Gilles Vigneault (among others) encouraged François Guy to transform his anglophone rock band the Sinners into a francophone ensemble called La Révolution Française (The French Revolution), whose anthemic song "Quebecois" became an important source of unity and inspiration for Quebecois nationalists in the years that followed.[2]

Similarly, in Los Angeles in 1966, keyboardist Bobby Espinosa left a racially mixed band known as Mickey and the Invaders to form the VIPs, a Chicano band that soon attracted a strong local following among Chicano, Black, Anglo, and Asian youths. They recorded a version of "Viva tirado," jazz artist Gerald Wilson's tribute to a famous Mexican bullfighter, under the band's new name, El Chicano. The song and the band soon became emblematic objects of pride for the Chicano movement in Southern California.[3] In the early 1960s, Joe Hernandez from Temple, Texas, sought fame and remuneration as the leader of a band called Little Joe and the Latinaires. His group specialized in Spanish-language cover versions of anglophone rock, blues, and country hit songs. After visiting California in the early 1970s, however, he changed the name of his band, first, to Jose Maria DeLeon Hernandez y la Familia and, then, to the interlingual Little Joe y la Familia. His group's recording of "Las nubes," a Mexican standard, did for the Chicano movement in Texas what "Quebecois" did for the nationalist separatism movement in Quebec.[4]

The popularity of banda music in Los Angeles in the early 1990s signaled one of the historical moments when new social relations generated new cultural forms speaking to new social identities. The change caught many residents of Los Angeles by surprise. For them, the emergence of something new first became evident in 1992, when a local Spanish-language radio station known as La Equis (KLAX 97.9) astonished its competitors by becoming the station rated number one in the nation's most lucrative market.

Programming a steady rotation of banda music, a seemingly obscure regional music made by urban immigrants from rural Mexico, KLAX enjoyed an unprecedented level of commercial success for a broadcast outlet aimed at the Latino market. After having been invisible in the ratings for years, the station started programming a steady rotation of banda songs. It attracted a market share of 5.3 percent during the fall 1992 ratings period, 7.2 percent during the winter of 1993, 5.7 percent during the spring of 1993, 6.6 percent during the summer of 1993, and 7.0 percent during the fall of 1993.[5] Astounded by losing the number-one position in the ratings and even more insulted to be eclipsed by a station playing a music he had never heard and intended for an audience he seemed to despise, nationally syndicated radio personality Howard Stern charged that the ratings agencies had made a mistake, that the ratings credited to KLAX really measured the audience Stern attracted through daily broadcasts on a Los Angeles station with similar call letters, KLSX. But Stern was wrong. La Equis attracted an average of 1,114,500 listeners at any given time, making the station one of the most listened-to radio outlets of all time. In fact, given the biases in radio survey methods, which tend to overrepresent wealthy Anglo listeners and undercount the numbers of working-class and poor Latino listeners, it seems very likely that La Equis was even more popular than the ratings indicated.

Because of banda music, advertising revenues at KLAX grew from four million dollars in 1990 to twenty million in 1993. While these amounts remained far lower than the sums advertisers paid to reach smaller numbers of listeners from Los Angeles's more affluent Anglo communities, they did reflect growing awareness and acknowledgment of the economic implications of dramatic demographic changes.

KLAX rose from number twenty to number one among Los Angeles radio stations, with its format of the banda music that originated in the rural regions of the states along Mexico's Pacific coast. At a time when talk formats emphasized the right-wing politics of "angry white males" and when music stations featured playlists stressing pop or rock music, KLAX rose to the top playing music that contained strong traces of the polka and parade music that European immigrants helped bring to Mexico and Central America in the nineteenth century.[6]

In the Northern California metropolis of San Jose, banda programming in 1992 enabled station KLOK to increase its ratings share from 1.2 to 2.3.[7] Actual sales of banda cassettes and compact discs were hard to track, because so many of them were sold outside the stores in suburban malls that provide the basis for the music industry's Scantron accounting system, but the album *Casimira* by Banda Machos quickly sold at least three hundred thousand units in North America in 1992, an astounding total in the U.S. market for music from Mexico with Spanish-language lyrics.[8]

The sudden and unexpected popularity of banda might seem like simply the latest postmodern hybrid, a story about music with a long history in one location succeeding as a novelty in another. One could use the popularity of banda to argue for the increasing irrelevance of place. Today a significant part of daily life in Los Angeles reflects the rhythms of rural Mexico, and a defining moment in Mexican culture draws its power and force from what happens in California. Yet like Dominican merengue in New York, Andean *chicha* in Peru's largest cities, and the Afro-Cuban music called salsa, played largely by Puerto Ricans in Venezuela, Colombia, and other countries throughout the hemisphere, banda music emerged as a subtle and significant register of the social dislocations engendered by the rapid mobility of capital and the mass migrations of low-wage workers across national borders in an age of hypermobile transnational capital. More than merely about music, the banda phenomenon served as the center of complex dynamics wherein identities appropriate to dramatically new political, economic, and social realities were in the process of being developed and deployed.

Banda music and the practices attendant to it signaled a new cultural moment, one that challenged traditional categories of citizenship and culture on both sides of the U.S.–Mexico border. New demographic and economic realities threw forth distinctive forms of social organization and style, of dance and dress, that spoke to the unique and singular conditions facing migrant low-wage workers in the United States. The 1992 "banda boom" appeared to emerge suddenly from out of nowhere, but it actually represented the long fetch of history, the culmination of long-established policies on both sides of the border that encouraged Mexican migration to the United States. Economic crises in Mexico coupled with the increasing significance of low-wage labor in labor-intensive service industries in the United States propelled the size of the Mexican-origin population north of the border from fewer than five million people in 1970 to more than seventeen million by 1997. Remittances sent back to Mexico from the United States assumed major importance within the Mexican economy, totaling close to six billion dollars per year by 1996, an amount equal to the sum the Mexican economy derived from all its exports and nearly equal to the sum secured through total tourism revenues. By 1998, 68 percent of the students in the Los Angeles Unified School District were Latinos. In the city's southeast suburbs, Latinos made up 98 percent of the school population.[9]

The huge audiences attracted to KLAX conformed to a larger pattern of media reception in Los Angeles. Between 1981 and 1998, the circulation of the Spanish-language newspaper *La Opinión* increased by 155 percent, enabling a 600 percent boost in advertising revenue. Only six Los Angeles radio stations featured Spanish-language programs in 1986, but that number grew to seventeen by 1997.[10] The rapid rise of KLAX drew investors and entrepreneurs to the lucrative Latino market. The Liberman Broadcasting Corporation lured disc jockey Fidel Fausto away from La Equis and made him program director at KBUE-FM, where he enjoyed tremendous commercial success programming banda and ranchera music. Televisa, a media conglomerate centered in Mexico City, cashed in on the popularity of banda by launching *Furia musical,* a biweekly fan magazine for U.S. Latinos that soon attained a circulation of more than three hundred thousand readers each week.[11]

Though important as a commercial trend, the popularity of banda music in Los Angeles in the early 1990s was even more significant as a collective community response to the social disapproval Mexicans experienced in the United States. Banda enabled them to celebrate their origins and flaunt their identities in the face of hate crimes and harsh policing, low-wage labor and unsafe working conditions. At the very moment when opportunistic politicians led by California governor Pete Wilson attempted to make Mexican immigrants scapegoats for the state's economic recession, banda offered an arena where Mexicanidad was honored, cherished, and prized.

KLAX's highest-rated program in 1992, the morning "drive time" show, featured not only banda music but also the humor and social commentary of Juan Carlos Hidalgo and Jesus Garcia. According to published accounts, Hidalgo initially entered the United States illegally from Michoacán, Mexico, in 1984, hidden in the spare tire compartment of a station wagon.[12] He worked picking strawberries in the fields near Oxnard before enrolling in a Spanish-language broadcasting school that prepared him for a career in radio. Garcia, who played Juan Carlos's comic sidekick "El Peladillo," also came from Michoacán. Garcia has been quoted as remembering that during both of his first two attempts to cross the border illegally, he was caught and returned to Mexico. But desperate economic conditions in Michoacán motivated him to keep trying. On his third effort he made it across the border, securing employment picking avocados and working part-time at a Thrifty Drug Store before being pulled into a radio career as a result of a chance meeting with Hidalgo at a Halloween party.[13]

Garcia adopted the broadcast name "El Peladillo" (the little rascal) in tribute to a well-known character from the comedy routines of the legendary Mexican comic Mario Moreno, professionally known as Cantinflas. In their banter each morning, Juan Carlos and El Peladillo addressed controversial issues from the perspectives of their largely immigrant and working-class listeners. "When there are problems in the community, like in the case of Governor Wilson attacking immigrants, we don't have, as we say, hair on our tongues keeping us from telling the truth," Hidalgo explained.[14] At one point a representative of the governor's office asked for the opportunity to respond to the pair's incessant needling of his boss. He wanted to come on the program and "talk about all the good things that Wilson has done for Mexican Americans," but Hidalgo and Garcia declined the offer, explaining politely that there were no good things to talk about. "He's using immigration like a political campaign for publicity," Hidalgo said about Pete Wilson. "How can the Governor talk about these people when they provide the food on his table? They're humble, but they pay taxes like everyone else."[15]

Through their morning broadcasts, Juan Carlos and El Peladillo provided a common frame of reference for working-class Mexicans and other Latinos in Los Angeles. In a city characterized by dispersed development and inadequate public transportation, most workers drive to their jobs in automobiles, making morning and afternoon radio broadcasts particularly important to the social construction of civic life. The KLAX on-air personalities delivered audiences to advertisers by entertaining listeners with comedy routines and banda music, but they also shaped and reflected the consciousness of a community coming into being under pressure, stress, and duress.

They drew on a long tradition in doing so. During the 1930s, former longshoreman Pedro González provided entertainment and important information about social issues and employment opportunities to the largely Mexican immigrant audience that listened to his four to six o'clock morning broadcasts on KELW, in Burbank. The early-morning hours generally constituted "dead" and unprofitable air time for English-language broadcasters, but the long hours worked by low-wage Mexican laborers made González's program prime time for his audience, offering them broadcasts as they were getting up in the morning and preparing for work. González's radical politics and mass popularity so worried Anglo elected officials that they tried to have him removed from the air. Los Angeles district attorney Burton Fitts believed that English should be the only language spoken on radio broadcasts in the United States. When the FCC refused to support that position, Fitts arrested González, harassed him off the air, and railroaded him into prison in 1934 on what are now recognized to have been trumped up charges.[16] González was paroled and deported to Mexico in 1940, where he stayed until he was allowed to return to the United States in 1971.[17]

Radio remained an important force in Mexican American community life in L.A. throughout the twentieth century. Throughout the 1930s, labor organizers from the Congress of Industrial Organizations broadcast appeals to Mexican American workers in Spanish and in English on a twice-weekly Spanish radio hour, and during the 1940s and 1950s English-language disc jockeys Hunter Hancock, Johnny Otis, Art Laboe, and Dick Hugg played important roles in shaping Mexicano and Chicano culture in L.A. with programs broadcasting rhythm and blues, soul, and rock music.[18]

Banda music itself also emerged from a long history, originating in the nineteenth century. It had been popular consistently in some Mexican states, especially Sinaloa, Nayarit, Jalisco, and Michoacán. Traditional ensembles in those regions played instrumentals exclusively. Early on, snare and bass drums produced banda's rhythms, and tubas provided bass lines for the dominant brass and woodwind instruments.[19] The *banda sinaloense* appeared in Mexican popular music as early as the 1940s, but it was not until the late 1980s and even the 1990s that banda songs began to attain broad popularity in Mexico. Techno banda music became popular in the 1980s, when bands started to feature vocals, replace the tuba and bass drum with the electric bass, modern drum sets, and timbales, and add the sounds of a synthesizer, which made it possible to scale down the size of banda groups from sixteen to six or seven. These changes allowed for the development of a new style, combining elements of rock 'n' roll with traditional banda practices, such as playing all the instruments simultaneously at strategic points in songs to generate energy and excitement.[20] In an odd reversal of progressive historical development, it was the success of techno banda recordings in Jalisco in the mid-1980s that led to the commercial revival of the earlier acoustic banda sounds in Sinaloa and elsewhere.

The lyrics of the banda songs that became popular in L.A. in the early 1990s only rarely addressed political or social issues. On their best-selling album *Casimira,* however, Banda Machos (a twelve-member ensemble from Jalisco) did feature the song "Un Indio quiere llorar" (The Indian Wants to Cry), about a man rejected by his lover's wealthy and non-Indian family because of his humble background.[21] The band's next album featured the song "Sangre de Indio" (Blood of an Indian), detailing the struggles of indigenous people, who make up a large proportion of the people in poverty in Mexico. Many banda groups (including Banda Machos) have more members with dark faces (and Indian faces) than generally appear in popular music groups from Mexico. The politics of banda, however, has stemmed less from its lyrics and the identities of its stars than from the social world and social relations that it has both reflected and shaped.

Starting in the early 1990s, banda dances in Southern California drew large crowds of working-class immigrants and native-born Mexican Americans. They danced the *quebradita,* the "little break," named after the dip that the dancers perform at dramatic moments in the music. Couples execute the "little break" in most cases by having the male partner dip the woman backward almost to the floor and then guide her back up quickly. This athletic move requires physical strength and flexibility. It depends on timing and demands coordination and cooperation. Many dancers during *quebradita*'s heyday could not actually do this dance, because it was difficult and dangerous. Some who had the skill to execute its moves did not wish to do so. As a result, dancing banda in practice meant performing other dances in addition to the *quebradita,* such as *el zapateado* (a heel and toe stepping dance), the *brinquito* or *caballito* (a dance that imitates the movements of horses when they trot), as well as cumbias, polkas, and waltzes.[22] The *quebradita* emerged as the definitive icon of that particular historical moment, however, as a physical gesture that encapsulated complex social relations.

In Los Angeles alone, more than thirty thousand enthusiasts belonged to more than eight hundred *quebradita* social clubs in 1992. They staged parties and dances every weekend at private homes, union halls, warehouses, and parking lots all over the metropolitan area.[23] The members of these voluntary social organizations forged collective identities by naming their clubs after their favorite songs, after singing groups, and after their places of origin in Mexico. They designed their own club logos and costumes, raising and dispensing money, engaging in rivalries with other clubs, and planning, promoting, and supervising social gatherings. They appropriated private spaces for public purposes and produced a new cognitive map of Mexicano Los Angeles, one no longer centered solely in the East Los Angeles barrio neighborhoods, but dispersed throughout South Gate, Cudahy, Maywood, Huntington Park, Bell, and other south, central, and southeast urban and suburban neighborhoods that housed many new migrants.

The friendly rivalries and festive gatherings facilitated by banda clubs in the early 1990s encouraged physical movement across neighborhood boundaries, making visible and immediate the potential social and political unity that might one day be forged from diverse elements in the community. Physical movement across spaces—so often constrained in Los Angeles by police surveillance, the physical isolation of poor neighborhoods, the deficiencies of public transportation, and violent rivalries among competing gangs—became more feasible because of banda.

The social world called into being by banda created discursive as well as physical spaces, especially through dress and performance. Banda artists and audiences favored *vaquero* (cowboy) styles: Stetson hats (called Tejanos), fringed jackets, leather boots, and jeans. This clothing displayed, even flaunted, the foreign and rural origins of many immigrants, turning what might have once seemed like a source of shame into a point of pride. The titles of instrumental numbers and the lyrics of vocals in banda songs often referred to the rodeo or to life on a ranch. Dancers frequently carried a *cuarto,* a small horsewhip. Women generally wore tight-fitting jeans or western skirts, belts with big buckles, black stretch tops, and cowboy boots. Men characteristically dressed in button-fly jeans, fringed leather vests, straw or felt cowboy hats, and shiny boots. *Quebradita* dancers draped their rear pockets with *correas* (leather straps) engraved with the name of their home state in Mexico, initially most often Michoacán, Colima, Zacatecas, or Jalisco, and then later Oaxaca, Guerrero, Sinaloa, and Puebla. Those who could not afford *correas* used folded white bandannas with their state's name embroidered on them in green and orange to simulate the colors of the Mexican flag.

These practices affirmed an intense affiliation with regional identities and Mexican cultural nationalism, which previously had relatively little meaning in Mexico (although they were becoming more important there too) but which had become tremendously important to migrants living in the United States. Using the names of Mexican states registered the massive displacements in that country's national life, caused by economic crises that followed the 1982 peso devaluation and subsequent structural adjustment policies, by the collapse of Mexican financial markets in 1987, and eventually by the adoption of NAFTA in 1994 and its ruinous consequences for Mexican agriculture thereafter. Driven into exile by desperate conditions in their native land, Mexican migrants to Los Angeles performed arduous low-wage labor that sustained the prosperity of California's middle-class and wealthy residents. Yet they found themselves reviled and despised by politicians and media commentators. In a country that did nearly everything it could to let them know that being Mexican was a mark of shame, the immigrants proudly flaunted rather than hid their national origin, seeking solidarity in numbers and catharsis through aggressive festivity.

"It's almost like a response, a backlash, if you want to call it, against the anti-immigration rhetoric," explained Steven Loza, a distinguished ethnomusicologist from UCLA, who for years has carefully chronicled the entire history of music made in Los

Angeles by people of Mexican origin.[24] A *quebradita* dancer identifying herself as "Veronica" asked an interviewer, "Have you noticed that the more that things turn against the immigrants and the more laws they make against the immigrants, the more they come out, they dress more expressively, they like to turn up their car radios more? They're proud of who they are; they are not intimidated any longer. The *banda* movement helped young people to address the issue of being Mexican. To tell who they are or to fight against injustice and discrimination."[25]

The sixteen-year-old president of Club Dos Amantes, an East Los Angeles *quebradita* organization, told a reporter in 1993 that previously she had listened mostly to music by pop star Michael Bolton and rap artists such as Ice Cube, but she had become converted to banda after discovering Banda Machos, Banda Superbandidos, and Banda R-15. "I used to be embarrassed by my heritage," Sully Camarillo explained. "If someone played a Spanish song, I'd be like 'Take that off.' But now? I never listen to English music. All I listen to is Spanish, Spanish, Spanish. Banda. And that's about it."[26] One aspect of KLAX's popularity that surprised media watchers in Los Angeles came from the station's success in winning young listeners like Camarillo away from stations programming rock music and hip hop.

Mexican American life and culture in the United States have been characterized by tensions between citizens and immigrants for ninety years, by conflicts between desires for assimilation into the United States and insistent loyalty to Mexico, by choices between strategies that have stressed political activism and voting in the United States and strategies based on the idea of exile, which have stressed participation in Mexican politics or advanced conceptions of the southwestern United States and Mexico as one unified region, a place artificially divided by the imposition of national borders.[27] The identification with the Spanish language, with Mexican culture and imagery, and with Mexican music expressed in banda by U.S. citizens of Mexican origin represents a powerful rejection of assimilation or at least a recognition of the need for unity and solidarity among Mexicans and Mexican Americans in the face of a cultural and political system and an economy that work inexorably against the interests of both.

The advent of *quebradita* clubs in the 1990s reflected emergent as well as residual realities. Their activities referenced life in Mexico lovingly but did so in order to speak to the concerns of Mexicans living in the United States. For example, the lettering on T-shirts proclaiming the identity of clubs named after banda songs such as "Vaqueros norteños," "Casimira," and "La herradura" followed the style of graffiti lettering dominant among Chicano wall writers in Los Angeles.[28] The music played at banda dances usually included more than banda. Especially in Los Angeles, techno, house, rock, merengue, bolero, ranchera, and cumbia music often coexisted with banda. These mixtures exemplified Juan Flores's concept of "branching out," a fusion of cultures and styles that has little to do with assimilation into an Anglo center.[29] For Griselda Mariscal, a Chicana activist born in L.A. and educated at Belmont High School and Occidental College, the *quebradita* fused Chicano and Mexicano identities. She danced banda with a *pañuelo* celebrating the state of Nayarit, where her father was born. "*Quebradita* is a way of showing you can be into your culture," she explained. "To me it's a way of holding your head up high. It says that I am in college because of the strength of my culture, because of the sacrifice of *mis papis, mis abuelitos.*"[30]

Banda helped create new social spaces, rituals, networks, and practices. Like all distinctively ethnic forms of dance music, it served as a site for collectivity and mutuality. Through common costumes and collective synchronized motion, it transformed individuals into a community. Spanish-language lyrics and horn-heavy instrumentation evoked the sounds of Mexico, eclipsing the attention formerly given to U.S. songs sung in English and accompanied mainly by electric guitars. Tight clothes and close dancing encouraged erotic desire while demonstrating physical and emotional control. Banda performances exuded a sense of unity and power, with performers onstage waving their instruments back and forth in time to the music, jumping up and down in unison causing the leather fringes on their jackets to fly about, and playing music surrounded by "smoke" generated by dry ice. References to regions of origin in Mexico underscored the heterogeneity of the group's histories and at the same time marked their newfound collectivity as something exceptional and unprecedented. The recognition of different regions allowed a unity with diversity. It used traditional symbols and historical memories to unite people with different backgrounds, who nonetheless felt a strong commonality about what they faced together in the present.

Many banda dances conformed to José Limón's description of Chicano dancing in Texas (building on the work of Frank Manning), involving popular working-class dance practices as "an intensive, concrete, but temporary assertion of various kinship ties" in the face of continuing kinship stress and breakdown, as well as a "symbolic statement of wholeness and integrity in the face of external threats."[31] Banda bore the burden of making sense out of terrifying changes. It arbitrated the tensions created by the disruptions of life in rural Mexico brought on by peso devaluation, structural adjustment policies, and free trade. It spoke to the stress in relations across genders and generations created by the imperatives of migration, resettlement, and low-wage labor. It offered symbolic solutions to real problems and provided rituals for repairing ruptures in the social fabric.

For workers engaged in desperate competition for jobs, for young people often drawn into violent conflicts over urban territory and turf, for laborers who must move from place to place constantly, banda created a significant site of solidarity. *Quebradita* clubs engaged in playful rituals, such as "baptizing" members of another club by pouring champagne on them at parties, an act meant to symbolize friendship between two groups. For some young people, banda dances provided an alternative to gang fighting. "I've been shot in the chest and leg, and I've lost a lot of friends to gang fights," related eighteen-year-old Sergio Castellanos, president of the *quebradita* club Orgullo Maldito. "So when I moved to Huntington Park, I didn't want to be in anything gang-related. Instead of being out on the streets killing people, a lot of gang members are now in clubs having fun, meeting people and dancing."[32] Imelda Flores of the Club Invasion Musical recruited several members of her club from gangs, telling them, "In a way it's the same thing: we act like a big family, we take care of each other. The difference is that they won't always have to be watching their backs."[33]

Quebradita dancing soothed ruptures across generations as well as within them. In the United States, where advertisers and media programmers routinely divide family members into separate markets segmented by age and gender, the mixed-age demographics for banda portrayed an intergenerational affinity that is rare within North American commercial culture. At age nineteen, Imelda Flores attended banda dances with her forty-year-old mother and her three-year-old sister.[34] La Equis secured its number-one rating in the Los Angeles radio market first by scoring among adults aged twenty-five to fifty-four but also by securing status as the second most popular station among teenagers.[35] KLAX drew listeners away from "Latin pop" and other formats on Spanish-language stations but also made significant inroads among young listeners who had previously preferred "top forty" rock music or hip hop.[36]

Yet while banda created new forms of unity, it also played a part in perpetuating and preserving old divisions. Lyrics to banda songs were often misogynistic. Female musicians played only a minimal role in the genre, both because playing brass instruments was traditionally a male activity and because the music developed in spaces proscribed to "respectable" women, such as taverns and brothels. Graciela Beltrán brought her usual fervor to banda songs, and ranchera singer Carmen Jara also recorded banda albums. Vocalist Angélica María sang songs accompanied by banda music, and Rosalva secured success in Los Angeles with a novelty hit composed by male musician Celso Torres about a part of a woman's body prominently displayed by tight jeans, "La chica de las caderas" (The Girl with the Hips). The overwhelmingly male composition of banda ensembles, the self-pitying romanticism and outright sexism of the lyrics of many banda songs, the dangers that women face from the open eroticism of *quebradita* dancing, and the gender politics of the dance floor raise serious questions about the distribution of banda's benefits across genders.

In his studies of Texas–Mexican popular music, José Limón has cautioned us to notice the gender hierarchies of popular music, not just in the lyrics of songs and the identities of artists, but also in what it means for women when a community's most important social site mixes dancing with drinking, sexual cruising, and the fighting that frequently occurs when a man decides to take "the race and class war within oneself, perniciously transform it into 'manhood,' and sometimes inflict it upon other men—perhaps on the slight pretext of a bump on the dance floor or a prolonged stare at one's woman." Limón observes, "In the sudden violence of a fight, we see the ultimate disarray, the sometimes too final fragmentation, in the continually fragmented lives of these people."[37] In the face of urban austerity, disintegrating social networks, increases in opportunities for female workers, and the stagnation and decline of male wages in many parts of the world, working-class musics in many places express increased disparagement of women.

From North American hip hop to Dominican *bachata,* male bragging about violence, illicit sex, and substance abuse has been an increasing feature of the lyrics of popular songs.[38]

For some women fans of banda, however, the dance floor provides an opportunity to demonstrate mastery of cultural codes and style hierarchies. In her thoroughly researched and elegantly argued ethnography of banda, Helena Simonett reports that one interviewee liked songs with multiple rhythm changes, because it enabled her to perform many different kinds of dance steps within one song.[39] Another explained that dancing the *quebradita* and other banda-oriented dances diminished rather than increased the dangers of sexual assault and violence. "Of course, dance is about sexuality," explained the woman identified as Elena. "That doesn't mean you're going there to be picked up. The dance expresses feelings. You can't really separate them. To dance also means to explore your body and to explore your partner's body (in couple dances). It's beautiful to feel another warm body that moves to the same rhythm. On the dance floor you feel secure. The touching has no consequences."[40]

Banda contained its share of sexist practices, images, and ideas, but it also had facets and dimensions that countered sexism. The location of banda events in backyards, business parking lots, and private homes combatted the exclusionary nature of clubs with high admission prices and put less emphasis on consuming alcohol than is the case in commercial clubs. The presence of people of all ages and the emphasis on representing one's region honorably undermined tensions that might otherwise have led to fights. But most important, the need for community solidarity in the face of external brutality and contempt worked to build an extraordinary sense of collectivity that escaped the worst features of other forms of popular festivity and celebration.

Although rooted in the musical traditions and social conditions of rural Mexico, the banda music played in the United States was not a revival of folk forms but more an adaptation of them to new circumstances. The unexpected and sudden commercial success of banda music in the United States led acoustic banda musicians to adopt some of techno banda's features, to replace tubas with bass guitars, add techno elements and effects, emphasize vocals (in what has traditionally been largely an instrumental music), and fuse banda styles with popular North American melodies and lyrics in songs such as "Pretty Woman," "Land of a Thousand Dances," "The Night Chicago Died," and (for better or worse) "Itsy Bitsy Teenie Weenie Yellow Polka Dot Bikini." A hybrid music fusing Mexican and U.S. cultural memories, banda helped its listeners negotiate new identities by fusing them in symbolic form in culture. As twelve-year-old Karen Velasquez, an immigrant from Colima, explained to a Los Angeles reporter, "I like dancing *quebradita* because it reminds me of Mexico and this is the dance of Mexico and Los Angeles. It's a combination of the two. When I'm dancing, it makes me feel happy."[41]

Velasquez's comment underscores an important aspect of banda: its identity as a diasporic product that only later became popular in its country of origin. Of course, Mexican bands were playing banda in the 1980s, but the popularity of techno banda, the *quebradita,* and their attendant subcultural practices happened first in the United States and then in Mexico. Banda's presence on Mexican television and its success in music sales in that country represented unusual developments, given monopoly control over Mexican media and that nation's traditional antipathy (bordering on contempt) for the cultural creations of people who leave Mexico and migrate to the United States. When techno banda appears now in Mexico, however, it is widely recognized as a form from the United States, albeit from the Mexican population there.

When people of Mexican ancestry in Los Angeles started to listen and dance to banda music in large numbers, they deployed shared memories of their former home to help themselves feel at home in a country that has historically wanted their labor but largely despised them and their culture. The emergence of banda music in Los Angeles in the 1990s was a direct consequence of the transnational economy and its mechanisms, especially the imposition of austerity on millions of workers around the world in order to create unparalleled luxury for a privileged few. This unjust order does not serve the long-term interests of even many of those who profit in the short run from the exploitation of immigrant labor, because it creates so much instability everywhere. Yet, precisely because the transnational economy can bring only stagnation and constrained life chances to the majority of the population, it needs to foment a sense of moral panic about the immigration situation that its own policies systematically create. As is so often the case when it comes to moral panics, societies produce the very nonnormativity they purport to police. Not only do Mexican migrants to California face the alienations and indignities of low-wage labor, but also they find themselves demonized for the actions of the economic order that causes their own suffering. In 1992, banda was one of the ways they fought back.

A brand of economic fundamentalism favoring "free" markets, low wages, high unemployment, slow growth, high interest rates, and devastating declines in social spending on health, housing, and education has forced people from their homes all around the globe. The "structural adjustment" policies of the World Bank, the International Monetary Fund, and economic elites everywhere have produced unprecedented concentrations of wealth and power for transnational corporations while relegating the vast majority of the world's people to a future marked by ever-increasing disruption, disorder, and social disintegration.

Under these conditions, migration makes sense. As Walden Bello argues, "Migrants are not obsessed nomads seeking the emerald cities, . . . they are refugees fleeing the wasteland that has been created by the economic equivalent of a scorched earth strategy."[42] The basic contours of this process have been in place for a long time. The creation of homelands and homesteads in industrialized countries has always depended on the exploitation of displaced and dispossessed workers from somewhere else. Romances of patriarchy and patriotism promising secure, stable, and homogeneous homes and homelands have drawn their cultural power as much from the necessity of hiding the heartlessness on which both hearth and *heimat* have been built as from any explanatory or liberatory power of their own.

Economic fundamentalism and the austerity it imposes on workers around the world destabilize and disrupt traditional economic, political, and social relations. During the 1980s, real wages in Mexico fell by 50 percent, and the share of that nation's income earned by working people declined from about 50 percent in 1981 to less than 30 percent in 1990. By 1997, the twenty-four richest Mexican families owned more wealth than the twenty-four million poorest Mexicans.[43] Structural adjustment policies suggested, structured, and supervised by the International Monetary Fund and the World Bank forced Mexico to make drastic cuts in its wage and welfare systems in hopes of attracting foreign capital. Capital did flow into the country, but Mexico's much lauded "economic miracle" turned out to be a fraud. A small group of speculators and swindlers made fortunes at the expense of the vast majority of the population. The North American Free Trade Agreement turned out to be a disaster for Mexican agriculture, while *maquiladora* zones made huge profits for multinationals but brought only low wages, unsafe working conditions, and health hazards to its largely female work force.

Confronted with the failure of their own policies, international financiers placed the blame on others: first on the Zapatista Uprising in Chiapas in 1994, and then on the pervasive corruption within the Salinas regime, an administration that had previously received universal acclaim from these same sources. Ultimately, the U.S. government and international finance sponsored yet another peso devaluation and demanded even more austerity from the Mexican people as the price for restructuring the debt that had brought them these severe problems in the first place. In the context of these conditions, the historic migration of low-wage workers from Mexico to the United States took on new significance and new meaning.

Ever since the Mexican Revolution of 1910, U.S. business leaders have encouraged and profited from the migration of low-wage labor from Mexico to the United States.[44] Contempt for Mexican culture, the Spanish language, and the rights guaranteed by the 1848 Treaty of Guadalupe-Hidalgo to people of Mexican origin in the United States is deeply ingrained in the history and culture of the United States. Violent repression by the Border Patrol and the Immigration and Naturalization Service, as well as by state and municipal law enforcement agencies, has imposed a consistent reign of terror against people of Mexican origin in the United States. Workers crossing the border without documentation or those overstaying their work permits are dismissed as "illegal aliens," but private businesses and public agencies in the United States routinely condone and even celebrate violations of law involving the employment of migrant workers, that is, violations of laws that mandate minimum wages, safe working conditions, and environmental protection. One of the most important points of entry for undocumented workers from Mexico into the U.S. economy is the suburban home, where they work as domestics. Suburban voters and vigilantes alike condemn the people who clean their houses, take care of their children, build their dwellings, and landscape their grounds as "illegal aliens," when in fact most who take this stance are actually illegal employers, violating state and federal labor laws every day.

Changes in the global economy, the stagnation of real wages, and the pervasiveness of recreational hate and racial scapegoating in U.S. politics have turned the traditional tensions along the U.S.–Mexico border into a prominent public issue. The militarization of the border by the U.S. government through a conscious strategy of low-intensity conflict, along with repeated attempts to amend U.S. immigration law, has proceeded from a perception that ties the migration of low-wage Mexican workers in the United States to a broad range of social problems, including low wages, high taxes, welfare costs, terrorism, drug dealing, disease, and violent crime.[45]

During the 1992 Los Angeles riots, more than four hundred out of a total of one thousand federal law enforcement agents sent to quell the rebellion came from the Border Patrol. These agents poured into neighborhoods inhabited by recent immigrants and rounded up more than one thousand undocumented workers, designating them for deportation whether they had been involved in the riots or not. The large numbers of Latinos among those arrested enabled opponents of immigration to place part of the blame for the insurrection on "illegal aliens." Two years later, California governor Pete Wilson overcame extremely low voter approval ratings of his performance in office by connecting his campaign for reelection to Proposition 187, a ballot initiative designed to deny medical care and education to undocumented immigrants and their children and to require schoolteachers and nurses to turn in "suspected" illegal immigrants to the government. Wilson's success at making immigrants scapegoats for California's economic and social problems encouraged other politicians to advocate even greater repression and suppression of the migrant population. Yet Wilson vetoed a bill that would have made retailers responsible for selling products obtained from illegal sweatshop labor. His administration refused to enforce laws regulating wages, hours, and working conditions by the employers who take advantage of immigrant labor. He consistently opposed efforts to raise and enforce the minimum wage, which would have taken away the incentive that employers have for hiring undocumented workers.

The power and greed of big business interests in Mexico and

the United States stand behind the migration of low-wage labor to California. Displaced from their homes by structural adjustment policies, NAFTA, and peso devaluation, Mexican migrants to California find hatred both at home and in exile. But it is also important to acknowledge that some people have the homes they do precisely because others are forced to live far from home. In California, for example, the immigrants demonized and derided as parasites by the successful 1994 campaign to pass Proposition 187 actually do much of the hard work on which California's standard of living depends. These low-wage workers clean yards, pools, offices, hotel rooms, and homes. They plant, trim, and clear trees. They tile, drywall, and plaster new homes, and they lift, move, and haul heavy objects on construction crews. They plant, harvest, prepare, and serve food. They care for other people's children. They find themselves hated for their hard work, made scapegoats for the harm done to life chances in California by the transnational economy, even though that economy victimizes them much more than it does the middle-class or wealthy employers whose standard of living largely depends on the low-wage labor of immigrants.[46]

The new realities of migration and low-wage labor have been imperfectly represented in the political culture of California, but they appear in vivid relief in popular culture. One of the most visible and important registers of demographic, economic, and political change has been registered in the popularity of banda music in sections of the state most settled by new migrants from Mexico. We cannot understand the production, circulation, and reception of banda in isolation from the ways in which the new transnational economy and the migration of low-wage labor have refigured the meanings of neighborhood and nation, of the local and the global, of culture and class. Banda music is no longer the music of rural Mexico, but it uses the cultural fusions of nineteenth-century Central America to speak eloquently to conditions created by transnational capital at the end of the twentieth century.

Banda music may have been the last major musical craze of the twentieth century or part of the first wave of musical innovation in the twenty-first century. Either way, its emergence had everything to do with the historical moment in which it came to the fore. Banda groups such as Banda Machos, whose members have worked on both sides of the border, come from the communities to whom and for whom they sing.[47] The Mexican identity invoked in banda and evident in student demonstrations against Proposition 187 and in the 1992 Southern California drywall strikes focused on being Mexican in the United States. This identity has asked nothing of the Mexican government and has had no real corollary within Mexico. It is not so much a nationalism connected to a nation-state as an icon of national identity that has become all the more important as an active social force at a moment when nation-states appear powerless to combat the imperatives of transnational capital and when the categories of national citizenship can do nothing to protect the rights of low-wage laborers.

In the wake of the banda boom, low-wage immigrant Mexican workers and their allies have mobilized themselves politically as well as culturally. Nonunion janitors, maids, garment workers, and restaurant employees have taken direct action to secure improvements in wages and working conditions. Students, workers, and church groups have staged demonstrations against anti-immigrant ballot propositions, police brutality, and hate crimes. Pete Wilson's demagoguery compelled thousands of legal residents and new immigrants to pursue citizenship, and voter registration drives continue to give Chicanos unprecedented importance in statewide elections. Perhaps most important, undocumented drywall workers in San Diego, Orange, and Los Angeles counties won concessions from employers in the construction industry through a disciplined, sustained, and sometimes violent strike in 1992 and 1993.

California's contractors and builders reaped a bonanza during the 1980s construction boom in the state, in part because they used nonunion immigrant labor to drive down the costs of building. Wages for drywall workers, for example, fell from nine cents per square foot in the 1970s to four and a half cents per square foot in the 1990s. One in four Southern California drywall workers was a Mexican when the job was unionized and high paying, but when contractors broke the union and lowered wages, Mexicans accounted for nine out of ten drywall workers.[48] By the early 1990s, drywall workers earned only $250 to $300 for a six-day week of heavy and hard work, with no medical benefits, no retirement benefits, and no vacation pay. Because many of the workers were undocumented migrants, cash pay predominated in the industry, allowing employers to pocket collectively as much as two billion dollars a year in income taxes, social security, and worker's compensation payments. In addition, knowing that workers who could be deported are in no position to complain about violations of minimum-wage and hour laws or environmental regulations, employers regularly mistreated drywall workers, sometimes even refusing to pay them for work they had already performed.[49]

More than a thousand drywall workers went on strike in May 1992. They had no union to represent them and could not avail themselves of National Labor Relations Board protections. Many of them were not even citizens. Yet they drew on regional and family connections (hundreds of them came from one village, El Maguey, in Guanajuato) to fuse an impressive sense of solidarity. They displayed the Mexican flag in picket lines, turning the stigma attached to their nationality into an emblem of pride (just as high school students protesting Proposition 187 later used the Mexican flag as an icon of shared identity in 1994). Through aggressive picket lines at suburban construction sites, imaginative disruptions of traffic by driving slowly on crowded freeways, and individual and collective acts of violence to enforce picket lines and stop production, they created a crisis for the Southern California housing industry, for law enforcement officials, and even for commuters. Their solidarity attracted attention and allies. Grass roots pressure from their memberships drew previously uninterested third parties (such as the leaders of construction unions and the Catholic Church) into the fray on the side of the strikers.

In August 1992 attorneys for the strikers filed suit in federal court, publicizing a fact well-known among workers: that subcontractors had skipped out on legally mandated overtime payments to hundreds of drywallers. This move exposed employers to the direct financial threat of having to pay workers millions of dollars in back pay, but it also provided a great equalizer in the war of words. Journalists had previously framed the dispute as a battle between tax-paying "American" businesses and unruly "illegal aliens." But the August 1992 federal court filing threatened to invert these icons, to expose the employers as tax-evading "illegals" profiting from the vulnerability of hard-working people seeking a decent life for themselves and for their families. Faced with negative publicity and with the prospect of having to open their books and run the risk of revealing other violations of federal and state laws and confronted with potentially escalating picket line violence and vandalism, building industry officials granted the strikers union recognition (through the carpenters' union) and medical benefits. Even though subsequent actions by both organized labor and management, as well as specially targeted harassment from the Immigration and Naturalization Service, threatened to undermine the victory they won, the drywall workers had forged a collectivity that resulted in an important victory in a tactical situation in which a common culture and class solidarity constituted two of the very few resources at their disposal.[50]

In their reliance on regional identities and their strategic deployment of the Mexican flag, which both flaunted their marginality in the United States and turned it into a strength, the drywall workers drew on many of the same cultural dynamics informing banda music. Fred Lonidier's documentary film about the strike, *Los drywaleros,* even includes a scene showing couples dancing the *quebradita.* Looking for neither a return to an idyllic homeland nor a deracinated assimilation into a society hostile to them and their culture, they nonetheless fabricated a social world capable of transforming their lives.

In the midst of yet another wave of anti-Mexican and anti-immigrant hysteria in 2003, two brothers from South Central Los Angeles turned to banda to create yet another powerful cultural expression of new immigrant identity. As children in the 1980s, Francisco and Sergio Gómez came to Los Angeles from their native Michoacán, Mexico. Living in a neighborhood with both Black and Mexican residents led them to form Juvenile Style, a band that performed West Coast hip hop with English lyrics. As they started to blend more Mexican music and Spanish-language lyrics into their performances, the Gómez Brothers transformed themselves into Akwid, releasing the album *Proyecto Akwid.* Their song "No hay manera" (There's No Way) became a surprise hit during the summer of 2003, on the strength of its deft blend of U.S. hip hop and samples from Mexican banda. As Josh Kun points out in his brilliant analysis of the song, "No hay manera" blends lyrical rhymes—*"un nuevo sonido"* (a new sound) that is *"como un corrido"* (like a ballad)—with a sample of Banda el Recodo's song "Te lo pido por favor" (I Beg of You).[51] The banda sample brings tubas and tight horn arrangements into a hip hop song, but it also establishes a distinct historical lineage.

Banda el Recodo took "Te lo pido por favor" from the great Mexican mariachi singer Juan Gabriel, who is a national icon in Mexico and was also born in Michoacán. Gabriel began his singing career in the border spaces of nightclubs in Ciudad Juárez, directly across the international border from El Paso, Texas. The musicians in Banda el Recodo, a band with a fifty-year history, had proven themselves masters of recombination, making banda music out of nonbanda songs such as Afro-Cuban singer Benny More's "La culebra." Akwid's "No hay manera" thus marks an innovative moment of rupture and recombination (of banda and hip hop) with a distinctly historical inflection that pays tribute to the transnational circuits of Mexican migration encoded within the sounds of mariachi, banda, and hip hop. Rupture and continuity alike also accompanied their success. *Proyecto Akwid* sold so well in the United States that it went platinum on the Billboard charts. Yet less than a month after its release, security guards at the Saddle Ranch restaurant at Los Angeles's Universal City Walk denied Francisco and Sergio Gómez entrance to the restaurant and pushed them around because of their appearance. As "No hay manera" climbed the charts in 2003, the Gómez brothers filed a civil suit against the restaurant.[52]

In December 2005, the House of Representatives passed House Resolution 4437. This punitive legislation sought to turn immigrants' minor offenses into major crimes, proposed to treat as a smuggler anyone who drove an undocumented worker to a church or a health clinic, and demanded that spouses and children of undocumented immigrants be charged with "aiding aliens." This effort to criminalize eleven million people as well as their families, friends, teachers, attorneys, and religious leaders would likely have passed the Senate, too, were it not for the mass mobilization of immigrants and their supporters in the streets of U.S. cities. Politicians and journalists were caught completely by surprise by this massive demand for dignity by humble low-wage workers, but listeners to Spanish-language radio stations and regional Mexican music were not surprised at all. As in the resolution of the drywall strike in 1992, preparation for the battle against H.R. 4437 was well under way within popular culture before it assumed public political form.

In 1971, rhythm-and-blues singer Esther Phillips recorded "Home Is Where the Hatred Is," a song by Gil Scott-Heron detailing the anguish of a heroin addict ashamed and afraid to go home. The song's lyrics transformed the iconic meaning of "home" from the place "where the heart is" to the place "where the hatred is."

Phillips sang the piece with conviction, perhaps in part because she had a history of heroin addiction in her own life, which filled her experiences at home with conflict, deception, and pain. Yet perhaps the song also became popular because Scott-Heron's lyrics said openly what many people know privately: that the idealized depictions of home that permeate politics and popular culture often contrast markedly with the homes in which people actually live. What might have seemed like a largely personal, exceptional, or tragic experience when Esther Phillips recorded "Home Is Where the Hatred Is" thirty-five years ago has become a generalized condition today. Millions of people around the world no longer feel "at home" in their homelands; they flee the hatred at home to seek a better life someplace else, making displacement, exile, and homelessness common experiences.

In their aggressive festivity and their insistence on celebrating a recombinant Mexican identity inside the United States, banda enthusiasts expressed on the terrain of culture the slogan that Mexican immigrants chanted in mass mobilizations against Proposition 187 and other anti-immigrant measures: "Aquí estamos, y no nos vamos" (We're here, and we're not going away). Unfortunately, the same is true for the transnational economy that frames the circumstances in which they find themselves. It remains to be seen how soon the rest of us will learn what the banda enthusiasts seemed to have learned well: that the transnational economy and the people who profit most from it are creating a world in which no one can feel at home, because the hatred is everywhere.

4. Jazz

The Hidden History of Nationalist Multiculturalism

Nobody agrees on anything about jazz (except that it survived beautifully and blossomed), but everybody thinks they know all about it, anywhere in the world. There is an interesting ownership of jazz.

—**Toni Morrison**

New members of Harlan Leonard's "territory" jazz band in the 1940s began to hear about Darby Hicks as soon as they were hired. None of them recognized his name, but the people they played with in their new band seemed to know him well. If a musician failed to hit the right note or adjust to a difficult key change, someone would always say, "Darby Hicks would have nailed that." Even worse, Darby Hicks seemed to know every new band member. "Oh yes, I heard about you," a band veteran would say on being introduced to a new recruit. "Darby Hicks told me that you can't play a lick." Senior members of the band would pull newcomers aside and confide to them, "Darby Hicks was talking about you last night, man. He was saying some terrible things about you. He even talked about your sister, and about your mother, and even about your grandmother!" At this point the initiate often reached the breaking point, exploding in anger and vowing to settle things directly with Darby Hicks by challenging him to a fight.

Darby Hicks, however, did not exist. The musicians made up a name they could use to tease newcomers, to initiate them into the band with an "in joke." Eventually the new band members would become insiders themselves and play the same trick on those who joined the aggregation after them. The "Darby Hicks" story worked, because musicians are competitive, proud, and sensitive to peer pressure, because reputations have professional and personal consequences. The story served a disciplinary function for the band as well, placing newcomers on notice that they were being watched, evaluated, and judged. Whatever the new band members thought of their own talent when they entered the band, they soon learned that they had not measured up to the standards of Darby Hicks. Whatever music they were about to play could never be as good as the music that Darby Hicks had already played.[1]

Historical narratives sometimes have a lot of Darby Hicks stories in them. Instead of identifying the long waves of history accurately, chronological stories about the past built around golden age narratives of heroic origins function to make the present, even its unjust power relations, seem predestined. These long waves construct a past that makes the present seem inevitable, portraying it as the only possible outcome of previous events. History in these accounts is something that happens to people, not something created by them. It concerns itself mainly with sanctifying what has already happened, not with changing what might yet happen. This kind of past looms large and makes most people feel small, as if Darby Hicks has already done everything worth doing.

Much can be learned from these linear developmental narratives, but it is important to remember that they represent a way of thinking that is itself a historical creation; thinking about the past in this fashion is a creation of people in the modern era, an approach designed to serve particular purposes. It treats the past as little more than a simpler, more innocent, and less complex version of the present, valuable largely as the point of origin for contemporary institutions and practices. In this kind of history, national destiny, human progress, and the growing complexity of science and society give a kind of inevitability to the present, as if everything that has happened had to have happened, as if everything that did not happen could not have happened. In school textbooks, television and film productions, novels, and the official narratives of nation-states, we often find the Darby Hicks version of history. It minimizes our ability to act and understand by maximizing what has already been done, said, written, and recorded by others.

Ken Burns's nine-part film *Jazz* has a lot of Darby Hicks in it.

First broadcast on public television stations throughout the country in January 2001, it presents the public with a distinct way of understanding the national history and national culture of the United States. The film has secured extraordinary critical acclaim and extensive commercial exposure, but its ultimate achievement comes from its success in creating an accessible, enjoyable, and convincing story about national identity, progress, and heroic artistic achievement. Not just a film *about* history, this production *makes* history by condensing the complex and conflicted history of jazz music into an allegory of national identity.

The series asserts a crucial connection between the artistry of individual musicians and the national character, between the achievements, practices, and institutions of jazz music and the history of the nation-state and the American people. It makes its claims by organizing the history of jazz and the history of the United States around a focus on American space, modernist time, and individual heroism. This approach entails glaring omissions and grievous distortions of the historical record. It transforms a history of exploitation, appropriation, conflict, and struggle into a fairy tale about cooperation, consent, and consensus.

Yet the film succeeds, because its story conforms so clearly to the ruling ideas of its time, to the need of elites to recruit the populace to their political projects of triumphant nationalism and managerial multiculturalism. The message of *Jazz* echoes the insistence in elite circles at the start of the new millennium about the exceptional (and even divine) character of the U.S. nation-state and its mission in the world, about the obsolescence of the antiracist and egalitarian struggles of the mid-twentieth century, and about a new model of civic life that hides from the persistence of racial inequality by celebrating the incorporation of exemplary individuals from diverse backgrounds into the ranks of those who rule. It is a film for its time and about its time, yet it secures credibility by purporting to be a disinterested and true account of the past.

By emphasizing the U.S. nation as unique, exceptional, and extraordinary, *Jazz* obscures the history of the nation's role in the world and the presence of the whole world within the nation. By acknowledging the importance of racial difference in the nation, yet minimizing the significance of racial inequality, *Jazz* offers inspiring images of Black–white unity, images that mark both groups as insiders, without honestly facing the differences between them, much less inquiring about what this axis of insider/outsider means for members of other aggrieved racial groups inside the nation and for people around the world relegated to roles as eternal outsiders in the U.S. national story.

Ken Burns's representation of the magnitude of Black achievement in the United States is accurate and inspiring, yet his emphasis on the inclusion of African Americans within the history of cultural nationalism covers over their systematic exclusion from equal access to power and property in both the past and present. As James Kyung-Jin Lee argues perceptively, this kind of managerial multiculturalism favors a modest redistribution of recognition and representation in U.S. society while abandoning the struggle for the redistribution of resources and rights.[2]

As a means of staking a claim by Blacks for inclusion in the celebratory nationalism of a nation that has routinely excluded them, the narrative strategy of *Jazz* makes sense. It urges white nationalists to acknowledge the importance of Black people to the U.S. national project while allowing Blacks to see themselves as key contributors to something in which all Americans presumably take pride. Moreover, for all its flaws, *Jazz* does pay homage to artists who very much deserve to be honored while recounting a history that very much needs to be told. Yet by telling the story as a narrative about modern time and American space, the film necessarily, and regrettably, occludes other temporal and spatial dimensions of jazz that also need to be illuminated. It paralyzes the present by locating all worthy achievement in the past. In an increasingly cosmopolitan world, it mourns nostalgically for a previous provincial nationalism. It minimizes the collective accomplishments of communities in order to magnify the reputations of heroic individual virtuosos.

The opening and establishing visual sequence in *Jazz* presents the skyscrapers of New York City illuminated at night during the 1920s. In the distance, viewers hear the sounds of automobile horns morphing into the sounds of the brass horns of a jazz ensemble. This opening serves to prefigure a connection between Black music and modernity as a central focus of the series. A second connection becomes evident immediately when Wynton Marsalis's voice provides a sound bridge to a close-up of his face. Marsalis declares, "Jazz objectifies America," explaining that jazz music is something that can tell us who "we" are. The trumpet virtuoso identifies collective improvisation as jazz's core concept and key achievement. He notes that Bach improvised while playing his own compositions on the keyboard, but Marsalis relegates that accomplishment to a secondary status, because Bach did not improvise with other musicians as jazz artists must do. Thus, in rapid order, in its first three scenes, *Jazz* (the film and television series) links "jazz" (the music) to three key signifiers: modernity, America, and heroic artistic genius.

The opening scenes of *Jazz* skillfully compress much of what follows during more than twenty hours of film stretched over nine episodes. Burns and his fellow filmmakers reduce the infinitely diverse and plural practices that make up the world of jazz into one time, modernity; into one place, "America"; and into one subjectivity, the heroic artist who turns adversity and alienation into aesthetic triumph. As the opening shots of the New York skyline suggest, the film depicts jazz as the quintessential creation of modernity, as an art form shaped by the technological and social complexities of the twentieth-century city. A linear developmental narrative traces the journey of jazz across time and space, from its origins in the rural areas of the southern United States and the hinterlands of Europe before 1920 to the racially mixed and ethnically diverse cities of the twentieth century.

The same developmental narrative governs the growth of jazz's key styles. The film follows the presumably foundational ensemble style pioneered by "Dixieland" innovators in New Orleans during the 1910s and 1920s to the sophisticated section playing, the written arrangements, and the compelling rhythms of "swing" bands in Kansas City, Chicago, and New York during the 1930s, and on to the ultimate fulfillment in the sophisticated styles of bebop players in New York and Los Angeles in the 1940s and 1950s. The film presents jazz as an art form that emerged out of urbanization and industrialization, fused folk forms with modern improvisation, and responded to the upheavals of modernity with artistry oriented around originality and innovation. In this narrative, jazz has a beginning, a middle, and an end.

In addition to its designated proper time in this film, jazz also occupies a discrete physical space: the juridical and geographic boundaries of the United States of America. Jazz music's significance in this film comes from its identity as the most important art form to originate in the United States, from its value as a metaphorical representation of the tensions between diversity and unity that so often characterize "American" society. When Wynton Marsalis begins the film by proclaiming that jazz objectifies America and that it can tell us who "we" are, the audience is being interpellated as national subjects, as "Americans." As *Jazz* proceeds, however, we see that Marsalis's comments mean even more. In this film, jazz has metonymic rather than merely metaphorical significance. It not only reflects the nation; it somehow constitutes it. The story of jazz is exactly the story of America, according to this film. The ability of Black and white jazz musicians to blend European and African musical traditions into a new synthesis despite the rigidly racist and segregated nature of the nation's social institutions is what makes the creation of jazz music a quintessentially American achievement.

The privileged time of modernity and the privileged space of America come together in *Jazz* to draw attention to one privileged social subject: the heroic creative artist. Louis Armstrong serves as the anchor of this project, the prototypical genius who played better (louder, higher, longer) than anyone else, whose creative innovations enabled him to influence and surpass everyone. Armstrong deserves this degree of praise, of course, but his innovations extend far beyond his remarkable physical abilities. They encompass his success in changing the language of jazz, in compelling others to respond to his playing in their own artistry. The film's narrative voices make the word *genius* the key category again and again, linking Louis Armstrong, Duke Ellington, and Charlie Parker to the canonical geniuses of European art music, to J. S. Bach, Wolfgang Amadeus Mozart, and Ludwig van Beethoven. The esteem this demonstrates for Armstrong, Ellington, and Parker is not wrong; in fact, it is fully justified and long overdue in popular discourse. This narrative strategy, however, expresses an approach to the history of jazz this is at odds with the social processes inherent in the music. Armstrong, Ellington, and Parker played in, and with, groups. Their virtuosity depended on dialogic relationships with other musicians, on their responses, additions, and augmentations to the music being played around them and to the music that preceded them. Isolating their artistry from these contexts obscures more about their achievements than it reveals.

In Ken Burns's formulation, each instrument has its own history and its own exemplary performer. Louis Armstrong perfects the possibilities of the trumpet, and Lester Young and Charlie Parker define the apex of artistry on the tenor and alto saxophones. Multi-instrumentalism can be only a footnote to this story. Yet the actual history of jazz tells a more interesting story. In the lives of individual musicians, moving from one instrument to another often led to innovations that would not have occurred had they stuck to a single instrument. Lionel Hampton and Lester Young explored scales extensively when they took up melodic instruments (vibraphone and saxophone), precisely because they started out as drummers who had not been required to think very much about harmony and melody. Under the tutelage of his father, Young had already learned to play clarinet, piano, flute, and piccolo. The unique sounds that he coaxed out of the tenor owed much to his previous playing on the C melody and alto saxophone.[3] Young's friend Mutt Carey brought his experiences as a drummer to bear on his cornet and trumpet playing.[4] Hamiet Bluiett felt he developed special skills as a baritone saxophone player precisely because most bands wanted an alto or tenor saxophonist instead. "I had to learn to play in all registers," he remembers, recounting his experiences in playing parts written for the alto or the tenor on his baritone.[5]

The film's emphasis on individual instruments and instrumentalists relegates the complex textures of Black experience and white supremacy in the United States to little more than dramatic background for the emergence of individuals who, the film tells us, cheerfully turn adversity into aesthetic perfection. Wynton Marsalis describes the overcoming of obstacles in the lives of Armstrong and the other geniuses of jazz as part of a universal process that takes place in all societies. For Marsalis, racism's relationship to jazz is incidental, only the historically specific obstacle to genius that these artists faced. "It happened to be racism," Marsalis observes, "but it is always something."

The narrative strategies deployed by the producers of *Jazz* are understandable, logical, and part of a long tradition. They reflect efforts by Houston Baker and Paul Gilroy to claim a central place for African Americans in the history of modernism. They echo the insistence of Albert Murray on "the inescapably mulatto" character of "American" culture and on the inalienable contributions by Blacks to the national narrative. They advance the arguments made by Billy Taylor, Grover Sales, Reginald Buckner, and many others for the canonization of jazz as "America's classical music." Yet, like any historical narrative, the evidence and arguments advanced in *Jazz* are partial, perspectival, and interested. In telling its own truths about time, place, and subjectivity, the film directs our attention away from the many other temporalities, spaces, and subject positions that are central to the story of jazz. It falls into the pitfalls identified by Vijay Iyer, himself a virtuoso jazz player and composer who warns, "Beware of the prevailing view of 'jazz' as some kind of history lesson that you have to sit through because it's good for you. . . . Understand that this is a living art form whose most esteemed practitioners are continually evolving and engaging with the world around them."[6]

It is not incorrect to view jazz as an exemplary modernist creation of the twentieth-century city, but doing so suppresses other temporalities and spaces equally responsible for the art. The migrant to the city who fashions a new art out of alienation is a recurrent story in the history of modernism, but to tell the story that way privileges the communities that the migrants come *to* in the city over the communities of shared historical experience that they depart *from* in order to become urban. Yet the two are not so easily separated. Musicians seeking work opportunities moved among different modern cities and between urban locations and the countryside. Music that originated in New Orleans, for example, did not just travel up the Mississippi to Chicago and then go eastward to New York. It developed significantly on the West Coast, circulated nationwide through theatre circuits, returned to New Orleans, and then branched out again.[7]

When Lee Young moved to Los Angeles from New Orleans, Mutt Carey took him into his band without an audition because of the relationship he had enjoyed with the Young family back in New Orleans. Carey remembered helping walk Lee Young to his grade school when they both lived in the Crescent City, and he felt that he should continue that guardianship in Los Angeles.[8] When Lee's brother Lester reached the height of his talents, he resided in New York. Yet he carried in his music many of the things that he had learned on the road as an itinerant musician in the seemingly out-of-the-way cities of Minneapolis and Albuquerque, as well as in the major metropolitan jazz centers of New Orleans, Los Angeles, and Kansas City.

String bass player Bill Johnson brought a New Orleans jazz band to San Francisco's Barbary Coast as early as 1908. A few years later, new arrivals from New Orleans secured jobs in Los

Angeles performing in Wayside Park, where they would play music while cooking buckets of red beans and rice on the job.[9] The first published reference to jazz music *ever* appeared in a San Francisco newspaper in 1913. Freddie Keppard brought his New Orleans band to the West Coast the next year, and Kid Ory began a six-year stay in Los Angeles and Oakland in 1919.[10] The first sound recording of New Orleans "Dixieland" jazz by Black musicians anywhere in the world took place in 1922 in the Sunshine Records studios in Santa Monica, California.[11]

New Orleans piano virtuoso Jelly Roll Morton came to the West Coast often, playing professional engagements in both San Francisco and Los Angeles. In 1917, he invited musicians Buddy Petit, Wade Waley, and Frank Dusen to leave Louisiana and join his band in Los Angeles. Yet while Morton wanted them to bring New Orleans music with them, he was less certain that New Orleans clothing styles and work habits would succeed on the West Coast. When the three got off the train wearing box coats and tight pants, Morton took them directly to a tailor to purchase outfits more in keeping with the look on the West Coast. In addition, he scolded them for bringing a bucket of red beans and rice to work and cooking it on the job. Appalled by Morton's transformation into a Californian, Petit, Whaley, and Dusen immediately returned to New Orleans in disgust, unwilling to trade the values and culture of their native city for life in the modern metropolis.[12]

Morton remained on the West Coast, however. He sometimes performed in Tijuana, Mexico, at an establishment named the Kansas City Bar, a club owned by Jack Lanes, a light-skinned African American millionaire whom Morton had befriended years earlier in Muskogee, Oklahoma.[13] Despite occasional forays to other cities, Morton returned to Los Angeles in the 1930s, dying there in 1941. As an artist, he played dance-oriented stomps, evocative blues, classically tinged compositions, and contemporary jazz all in the same period of time. Rather than following the unidirectional trajectory of progress that *Jazz* ascribes to the music, Morton moved back and forth, across regions and nations, among cities and states, and inside and outside musical forms from the past as well as the present.

In the version of modernity described in Burns's film, jazz music becomes a specialized and autonomous activity detached from the plural traditions from which it emerged: from tent shows, brass band performances, drum and bugle corps playing, vaudeville and variety performances, work songs, field hollers, and dances. In this version, jazz appears to be the creation of alienated individuals rather than historical communities. The jazz represented here conforms to the hierarchies of modernist aesthetics, which place more value in the created object than in the creative act and elevate musical compositions and performances over the broad social roles, relations, processes, and practices that music sets in motion. Modernist aesthetics privilege abstract musical techniques over performative expressions like dancing, singing, and comedy. In this tradition, the aestheticization of alienation is seen as an end in itself, as an episode in the history of art, rather than as a manifestation of individual and collective agency for living better in the world by calling new realities into being through performance.

This celebration of modernism grievously occludes the creative tensions in Black culture between modernity and tradition. As Farah Jasmine Griffin explains in her brilliant analysis of the Black "migration narrative," Black artists' enthusiasm for modernity has often been tempered by the pull of the past, by the power of "talkative ancestors" warning against conceptions of freedom based on detachment from tradition. It is understandable that the honor and esteem that elite white artists and critics reserve for high modernism would generate a compensatory desire to celebrate the dynamic presence of African Americans within modernism. But this prestige comes at a high price. It diverts attention from the even more impressive African American tradition of refusing to be absorbed completely by either tradition or modernity, but instead fashioning a dynamic fusion built on a dialectical relationship between the past and the present.[14] Saxophone player and composer Julius Hemphill once observed, "Well, you often hear people nowadays talking about the tradition, tradition, tradition. But they have tunnel vision in this tradition. Because tradition in African American music is as wide as all outdoors."[15]

It is not at all implausible to do what Burns's film does: to view jazz as a quintessential expression of U.S. national identity, as a magnificent art form that emerged from contacts between European and African musical traditions on the North American continent. Yet the added prestige that jazz seems to acquire from its association with celebratory nationalism comes at the expense of appreciating jazz's capacity to create identities far more fluid and flexible than the citizen-subject of the nation-state. Even the music itself becomes represented poorly through this strategy. As feminist musicologist Susan McClary explains cogently, "Instead of searching vainly for continuous 'authentic' traditions, we need to pay attention to the kinds of ferment located in boundaries, to fusions of unpredictable sorts that continually give rise to new genres and modes of expression."[16]

Duke Ellington may be a quintessential "American" to Wynton Marsalis and Ken Burns, but when the expatriate South African pianist Abdullah Ibrahim started playing with Ellington's band in Switzerland, he did not think of his boss as a citizen of any particular nation but thought of him instead as "the wise old man in the village—the extended village."[17] Ellington expressed delight at finally arriving in Africa to play at the Dakar Festival in 1966, because he felt that he had been playing "African music" for thirty-five years.[18] Charlie Parker and Dizzy Gillespie invoked Africa as well as America when they performed with dancer Asadata Dafora and an assortment of Cuban and African drummers at New York benefits for the African Academy of Arts and Research in the 1940s. Mary Lou Williams and Dafora staged a two-day Carnegie Hall show in 1945, structured around the links between African and Western forms of music and dance.[19] Dafora proved to be a natural ally in these efforts because of his own complicated history. Born in Sierra Leone, his great-grandfather had been a slave in Nova Scotia but later returned to Africa to live out his life in freedom. Dafora received classical training in opera in Germany and Italy, served in the British army in World War I, and turned to "traditional" African dance in the late 1920s while pursuing a career in opera in New York City.

The story of jazz as the binary creation of Black and white Americans does little to help us understand how light-skinned Puerto Ricans such as Louis "King" Garcia and Miguel Ángel Duchesne wound up playing for the white bandleaders Benny Goodman, Tommy Dorsey, and Paul Whiteman while dark-skinned Puerto Ricans played with bands led by Fletcher Henderson and Noble Sissle. It leaves little room for the stories of Latino, Asian American, and mixed-race musicians. The celebratory equation between jazz and "America" cannot lead us to a productive understanding of how Rafael Hernández came to play in James Reese Europe's African American 369th Infantry "Hellfighters" Band in

France during World War I but with the Trio Borinquen (made up of two Puerto Ricans and a Dominican) in Cuba, Mexico, New York, and San Juan in the succeeding decades. It does not help us understand why Europe went to the Caribbean to recruit clarinetists for his New York–based Hell Fighters Orchestra.[20]

Was it something about "America" that led John Coltrane to name his son after Indian sitar genius Ravi Shankar?[21] Are we still dealing with "American" culture when Sidney Bechet moves to France, Albert Nicholas to Egypt, Buck Clayton to China, Randy Weston to Morocco, Art Blakey to Kenya, Budd Johnson to Haiti, Hampton Hawes to Japan, and Teddy Weatherford to India? Did Django Reinhardt cease being Romany or Belgian by playing jazz? Did Toshiko Ayoshi cease being Japanese? Does music made in America (the continent) by Machito, Tito Puente, Mongo Santamaría, or Carlos "Patato" Valdes count as jazz in America (the country)? Was Mario Bauza making Latin American music when he served as musical director for Chick Webb? How central was the geography of the United States to jazz when the great Argentinean swing guitarist Oscar Aleman moved to the center of the musical world in Paris to conduct Josephine Baker's back-up band, the Baker Boys?[22]

The national chauvinism that pervades Ken Burns's film occludes the internationalism that has informed the art of so many jazz musicians. Randy Weston toured Africa for the State Department in 1967 but thought of his mission in international terms. Raised in a Garveyite household committed to pan-African ideals and where he learned to think of himself as an African born in America, Weston traced his ancestry on his father's side to Jamaica, Panama, and Costa Rica. He remains best known in Africa for his 1960 tribute to independence movements on that continent, "Uhuru Africa."[23]

The celebratory America of *Jazz* does not prepare us adequately for the Charles Mingus compositions "They Trespass the Land of the Sacred Sioux," "Remember Rockefeller at Attica," and "Once There Was a Holding Corporation Called Old America." The integrationist nationalism of *Jazz* cannot account for Dizzy Gillespie's suite *Burning Spear,* composed in honor of Kenyan independence fighter Jomo Kenyatta, a piece that blends South American, African, and African American elements. Gillespie called it "an international piece" because he considered Kenyatta an international figure.[24] *Jazz* does not help us understand why Dizzy Gillespie refused to attend a briefing arranged for him by the State Department while playing a government-sponsored tour overseas. Officials from the diplomatic corps offered to help Gillespie explain race relations in the United States. The trumpeter noted acerbically, "I've got three hundred years of briefing. I know what they've done to us and I'm not going to make any excuses."[25]

It is not totally incorrect to view jazz as Ken Burns does, as a crucible of heroic artistry forged by the contradictions of life in the United States and its connections to the rest of the world. Jazz musicians have discursively transcoded the hard facts of slavery, migration, industrialization, and urbanization in U.S. history into aesthetically rich and complex creations. Their harmonious balance between individual solos and collective improvisation provides a metaphorical solution to one of the recurrent dilemmas of social life in the United States: how to encourage individuality without selfishness and how to encourage collective consciousness without totalitarianism. The formal complexities of jazz composition, the risks and rewards of collective improvisation, and the artistic virtuosity demonstrated by its most accomplished performers make jazz a logical and suitable site for the exploration of art as transcendence and existential fulfillment.

Yet this emphasis on the heroic individual depends on hierarchies that are not universally, or perhaps even widely, accepted among jazz artists and audiences. The history of Western culture is replete with linear developmental narratives that attach art forms to celebratory nationalisms and to canons of great works and artists. Yet it does not necessarily follow that placing jazz within that pantheon elevates, or even helps explain, its artistry. The emphasis on immediacy, on involvement, and on engagement in jazz playing encourages a sensibility entirely at odds with the romanticization of the alienated artist that has been so central to the Western tradition since the beginning of the nineteenth century. The jazz tradition prizes connection rather than canonization; it finds value in the social relations that playing and listening create rather than in the notes and chords and rhythms all by themselves. New Orleans drummer Baby Dodds emphasized how social connection rather than social alienation permeated the spirit of the New Orleans jazz bands in which he played. "When the leader of an orchestra would hire a new man," Dodds recalled, "there was no jealousy in the gang. Everybody took him in as a brother, and he was treated accordingly. If a fellow came to work with anything, even a sandwich or an orange, the new man would be offered a piece of it. That's the way they were. They believed in harmony."[26]

Some musicians even left successful orchestras to return to communities that offered them a greater sense of social connection. That sensibility is what informed Horace Tapscott's decision to leave the Lionel Hampton Band in 1961 and to devote the remaining forty years of his life to playing and teaching in community-based music, theatre, art, and dance collectives. Tapscott's kindred spirit, Sun Ra, summarized this school of thought eloquently when he explained, "Musicians often play wonderful things, bring together wonderful sounds, but it doesn't mean a thing. Not for themselves, not for other people. Everyone says that's wonderful, that's the work of a great musician. Of course, that's true, but what's the significance of it? People don't get better because of the music even though they certainly need help. I believe that every artist should realize that. That his work has no meaning whatsoever unless he helps people with it."[27]

The story of jazz artists as heroic individualists also overlooks the unequal and exploitative gender relations that structured entry into the world of playing jazz for a living. Women musicians Melba Liston, Clora Bryant, and Mary Lou Williams can be only minor supporting players in Ken Burns's drama of heroic male artistry. Bessie Smith is revered as an interpreter and icon but not acknowledged for her expressly musical contributions. Abbey Lincoln, Sarah Vaughan, and Betty Carter evidently do not qualify for admission into the pantheon. While *Jazz* acknowledges the roles played by supportive wives and partners in the success of individual male musicians, the broader structures of power that segregated women into "girl" bands, that relegated women players to local rather than national exposure, that defined the music of Nina Simone and Dinah Washington as somehow outside the world of jazz are never systematically addressed in the film. *Jazz* gives us no analysis of the practices and processes that obscure the important contributions made to music by women, to pick just a few examples, by keyboard artists Beryl Booker, Patty Bowen, Hazel Scott, and Valerie Capers.[28]

Moreover, the separation of music from other art forms obscures the broader creative activities that engaged the energies of many of the very artists celebrated in *Jazz*. The creation of new social relations through art took many forms for jazz musicians, not all of them limited to playing music. Charlie Mingus worked with Max Roach and Jo Jones in the early 1960s on plans to open a "school of arts, music, and gymnastics" in New York.[29] Reed player Roscoe Mitchell, trombonist Lester Lashley, and trumpeter Bobby Bradford were accomplished painters as well as musicians, while painter–collagist Romare Bearden composed songs, including "Seabreeze," which he wrote with Billy Eckstine.[30]

Max Roach attributed part of his virtuosity on the drums to his "conversations" with dancer Earl Basie, better known by his stage name "Groundhog." Roach maintained, "I learned a lot listening to Hog's feet." The multiple tones and variations in pitch that Roach produced on the drums were simulations of how Groundhog dropped his heels and stamped his feet. For his part, Groundhog claimed, "Max taught me how to drum paradiddles when he was working with Benny Carter. I lie in bed and listen to a metronome for two hours every night, inventing new combinations. I don't like to repeat a step unless it's necessary to help the audience catch on."[31]

Even the mingling among members of different races celebrated in *Jazz* took place with much more difficulty than the series acknowledges. In Oklahoma City, interracial dances did not take place until the Young Communist League deliberately crossed the color line in 1932 by promoting an interracial dance featuring the Blue Devils in that city's Forest Park.[32] In 1940, Los Angeles Police Department officials shut down a performance by the Benny Goodman Orchestra at the Shrine Auditorium because they feared the interracial dancing likely to take place among the band's white, Filipino, Black, and Mexican fans.[33] Black musicians in Los Angeles routinely faced having to accept "escorts" back to Black neighborhoods by police officers unwilling to let them remain in the white neighborhoods, where the best paying musical venues tended to be located.[34] Los Angeles police officers routinely harassed and intimidated interracial couples along Central Avenue. A police officer once arrested African American trumpet player Howard McGhee and his blond wife, Dorothy, for sitting side by side at a showing of a James Cagney motion picture in downtown Los Angeles, claiming than an interracial couple that looked as they did had to be a prostitute and a pimp.[35]

Trumpet player Clora Bryant remembers that "Central Avenue

closed up when they found out how much money was being dropped over there and City Hall started sending the cops out there to heckle the white people."[36] She recalled roadblocks, traffic stops, and sidewalk arrests. According to the memories of pianist Hampton Hawes, on any weekend night, mixed-race couples would be "frogmarched" from Central Avenue to the Newton Street police station for "inspection."[37]

The kind of linear historical narrative presented in *Jazz* leaves little room for the nonlinear thinkers and the nonnormative behavior central to much of the history of the music. For example, both tenor saxophonist Lester Young and clarinetist Wilton Crawley found speaking English inadequate for their purposes. So they invented their own languages. One day Crawley accidentally boarded a train filled with mental patients. He communicated in his language with them so successfully that the authorities took him to the sanitarium too. Young's wordplay, on the other hand, complemented the originality of his artistry on the saxophone. He referred to a chorus as a "lung," called a woman's vagina her "hat," and insisted on the term *edis* for marijuana. Just as he shouted "George Washington" to signal other musicians to go to the "bridge" of a song, he used the expression "I feel a draft" to indicate that he was picking up bad vibrations and indicated a conversation was over by saying "doom." Young also used different fingerings and variations in density and tone to make his playing mimic the sounds of vernacular speech.[38]

The linguistic ingenuity embodied in the secret languages of Lester Young and Wilton Crawley has a long history in African American communities. Horace Tapscott's sister, Robbie Tapscott Byrd, learned a secret language called "tut" from their mother, Mary Lou Malone Tapscott. Byrd describes tut as "a patois that evolved among the slaves, when they didn't want the masters to know what they were talking about."[39] The female members of the family passed along the knowledge of how to speak tut to one another. Robbie learned it from Mary Lou, who learned it from her mother, Pearlina, who traced it to her mother, Amanda, a woman who began life as a slave. Lester Young's transfer of the sounds of speech to his instrument influenced the playing of Eric Dolphy, Bubber Miley, and Ornette Coleman.[40] Julius Hemphill found great significance in the link between the saxophone and speech. "The saxophone has always struck me as a vocal instrument," he noted.

"The very fact that it's difficult to play in tune suggests properties similar to a voice."[41]

The virtuosity of the artistic innovators celebrated in *Jazz* emerged out of a performance tradition that often privileged participation and sensation over cerebral virtuosity. Fess Manetta played piano in Papa Celestin's Original Tuxedo Jazz Orchestra, as well as trombone, saxophone, and violin. He frequently entertained audiences and his fellow musicians by playing the trombone and the trumpet at the same time and in harmony.[42] Wilton Crawley would frequently disassemble his clarinet during choruses and juggle all five pieces in the air while tap dancing.[43] Charley Siegals entertained audiences at Langford's nightspot in Minneapolis in 1927 by playing the trumpet in the style of Louis Armstrong with one hand while mimicking the style of Earl Hines on piano with the other hand.[44] Before he became part of the duo Slim and Slam (with Slam Stewart), Slim Gaillard secured jobs in which he played the guitar and tap danced simultaneously.[45] Rahsaan Roland Kirk regularly marked time by stepping on a hi-hat cymbal with his foot while playing two saxophones at once.

Lester Young delighted carnival audiences by dancing the Charleston while he played the saxophone. Young often amazed his band mates during the days he played with Count Basie's orchestra by turning the mouthpiece of the saxophone upside down and playing the instrument while holding it over his head, as if he were smoking a pipe. At one recording session in 1947, the assembled musicians watched Young's antics in amazement. He sat calmly across the room from them on the other side of the studio during fifteen bars of the sixteen-bar introduction they devised for "East of the Sun." Then halfway through the sixteenth bar, the saxophonist jumped into the air "like a gazelle," ran over to the microphone, and started to play an amazing solo.[46] No one listening to the record they made that day could possibly know how truly amazing Young's solo was, but those present never forgot his feat.

Ornette Coleman found he could produce unique and interesting sounds from a white plastic alto saxophone. Don Cherry emphasized his stylistic departure from the heroic (and implicitly virile) tone of trumpet playing by coaxing thin and wavering sounds from a miniature pocket trumpet.[47] New Orleans piano virtuoso Professor Longhair brought a tap dancer's sense of rhythm to his music, frequently kicking the baseboard of an upright piano to accompany his own playing. He also used unusual fingerings on his chords, largely adaptations of necessity, because he practiced on an abandoned piano with several missing and inoperable keys. Professor Longhair would also make up his own musical terms, ordering his ensembles to play in the key of "e-minus" or to "frolic presto" (which meant playing while inebriated).[48]

Even within music, jazz never existed in a vacuum isolated from other musical genres. Jelly Roll Morton turned Verdi's "Miserere" from *Il trovatore* into a ragtime song.[49] The great gospel singer Mahalia Jackson borrowed stylistic innovations from Ma Rainey and Bessie Smith, and gospel great Rebert Harris admired Blind Lemon Jefferson and Leroy Carr.[50] During Horace Tapscott's early childhood in Houston, his neighbors included rhythm-and-blues musicians Floyd Dixon, Amos Milburn, and Johnny Guitar Watson.[51] Tapscott worked with Preston Love (who had played lead alto in the Count Basie Orchestra in the 1940s) in the West Coast Motown band that accompanied Diana Ross, the Temptations, the Four Tops, and other Motown acts when they toured California, Oregon, and Washington during the 1960s and 1970s.[52] The dancing performed by the Motown acts on these tours was choreographed by the famous tap dancer Cholly Atkins under the supervision of stage manager Maurice King, a former jazz saxophone player who first met Preston Love backstage at the Apollo Theatre in New York in 1944, when Love played alto saxophone for the Lucky Millinder Orchestra and King managed the interracial and all-female International Sweethearts of Rhythm.[53]

Lester Young's work with Johnny Otis and others in small combos after World War II developed the core musical features of rhythm and blues, yet Young also insisted repeatedly that he admired the singing of pop performers, including Frank Sinatra and Jo Stafford.[54] John Coltrane played in bands backing rhythm-and-blues singer Big Maybelle, and he toured with Earl Bostic and Eddie "Cleanhead" Vinson. Because Vinson already played alto saxophone, Coltrane turned to tenor saxophone, the instrument on which he would become a supreme virtuoso.[55] Trumpeter Phil Cohran played in Jay McShann's band when that group was the house band for Don Robey's Duke and Peacock rhythm-and-blues record labels, but he also played behind blues singer Walter Brown. Cohran later worked with jazz composer Oliver Nelson, played trumpet in Sun Ra's Arkestra, and founded the Afro Arts Theatre in Chicago to produce plays, poetry, films, performance art, dance, and music. The Artistic Heritage Ensemble started by Cohran later became the Pharaohs. Their members provided the nucleus of the rhythm-and-blues jazz fusion group Earth, Wind, and Fire. Cohran invented an amplified version of the *mbira* (a Zimbabwean instrument), which he called the "frankiphone" (named after his mother, "Frankie" Cohran). Earth, Wind, and Fire's Maurice White never played music with Cohran, but he heard him play many times and became skilled on the electric thumb piano because of his admiration for Cohran's playing.[56]

The grand narrative of modernity, nationalism, and alienated artistry presented by *Jazz* is understandable and plausible, but incomplete. Its perspectival partiality is not random, however, but rather a way of looking at the world that serves a pernicious set of interests. The film purports to honor modernist innovation, struggle, and artistic indifference to popular success, yet its own form is calculatedly conservative and commercial. This history of jazz interpellates viewers as consumers rather than as creators. The important history of jazz has already happened, it tells us. The genre's consummate artists are already known, and their artistry has already been incorporated into the glory of the nation-state. There is nothing left for viewers to do but to honor—and more important, to purchase—relics and souvenirs of an art greater than themselves. The film is a spectator's story aimed at generating a canon to be consumed. Viewers are not encouraged to make jazz music themselves, to support contemporary jazz artists, or even to advocate jazz education. They are, on the other hand, urged to buy the nine-part home video version of *Jazz* that is produced and distributed by Time Warner AOL, the nearly twenty albums of recorded music on Columbia/Sony promoting the show's artists and "greatest hits," and the book published by Knopf as a companion to the broadcast of the television program, which was underwritten by General Motors.

Thus, a film honoring modernist innovation promotes nostalgic satisfaction. A film celebrating the centrality of African Americans to the national experience voices no demands for either rights or recognition on behalf of contemporary African American people. A film venerating the struggles of alienated artists to rise above the formulaic patterns of commercial culture comes into existence and enjoys wide exposure only because it fits so well within the commercial reach and scope of a fully integrated marketing campaign linking "educational" public television to media conglomerates.

The "reconciliation" of otherwise antagonistic social groups through a unified celebration of "America" that holds center stage in *Jazz* is ultimately a false reconciliation. The "Americans" united through shared vicarious appreciation of *Jazz* live in very different kinds of neighborhoods, experience very different relationships with the police and the courts, breathe different air, drink different water, and die from environmental hazards at very different rates. In fact, the very reconciliation promised by *Jazz* actually depends on these inequalities; without them, there would be no meaningful gaps to transcend.

Horace Tapscott's autobiography, *Songs of the Unsung*, offers an alternative to the Ken Burns's history of jazz. Even their titles reflect the profound difference between the two works: *Jazz* is encyclopedic, comprehensive, and canonical, while *Songs of the Unsung* searches for the occluded, the underappreciated, and the as-yet unknown. Tapscott's opening sentences do not reference the New York skyline of *Jazz* but instead start his story in the segregated hospital named after Confederate president Jefferson Davis in Houston, Texas, where Tapscott was born. His memoir does not identify the modernist city of immigrant and exiled artists meeting one another through their work as the key crucible of jazz but instead details the ways in which his neighbors in the Houston ghetto (and later in Los Angeles) nurtured and sustained a dynamic, lively, and shared musical culture. The film *Jazz* opens with Wynton Marsalis claiming that "jazz objectifies America," while *Songs of the Unsung* starts with Tapscott telling us that from the second of his birth he "was locked here on this earth." While *Jazz* delivers a story about heroic individuals, Tapscott's autobiography delineates a collective world "where everyone was family," where the goal was to "gain some respect as a whole people," where "we had to learn things in groups," and where "how many mentors you'd have in a day was impossible to count."[57]

Songs of the Unsung presents jazz as the conscious product of collective activity in decidedly local community spaces. The significance of the modernist city and the nation pale in Tapscott's account in comparison to the home, the neighborhood, and the community. Physical spaces far more specific than the "city" shaped his encounter with music, and these spaces had meaning because they were connected to a supportive community network. Tapscott remembers his mother placing the piano inside the front door of the family's home in Houston, "so when you came in my house, you had to play the piano to get to the couch."[58]

The Tapscott family moved to Los Angeles in 1943, when Horace was nine. As soon as they disembarked from the train at Union Station, his mother hailed a cab and told the driver to take them to the corner of Fifty-second and Central to meet Horace's new music teacher, Harry Southard, a barber. "We hadn't gotten to the house yet," Tapscott recalls in wonder. "I don't know where I live. And before we get there I'm introduced to my music teacher."[59] Like many of his fellow musicians, Tapscott drew inspiration from the city itself, not from downtown skyscrapers, but from the sights and sounds on Central Avenue, the ghetto's main thoroughfare in those days. For one thing, he discovered a network of neighborhood musicians who had played together in high school bands and orchestras and then became employed in Central Avenue clubs. But beyond that, the very streets of the city pulsated with jazz, with the sounds of rehearsals and practices, with the rhythms of people as they walked along the sidewalks, and with the songs emanating from jukeboxes, radios, and churches.

Buddy Collette tells a story that underscores the musicality of Black Los Angeles in those years. Collette lived on Ninety-sixth Street. His friend Charles Mingus lived on 108th Street. As high school students they often rehearsed with bands downtown, Mingus carrying his enormous stand-up string bass on his back to the Pacific Electric Interurban Red Car stop at 103rd Street. Collette recalls, "Mingus was so excited about playing, he'd get on the car and zip the cover off his bass, and we'd start jamming on the streetcar. . . . He was always a very open guy with his thoughts: 'Let's play! Are we gonna play today?' And I'd say 'Well, OK,' and get the alto out, and the conductor and the motorman would wave—they didn't mind."[60]

Like so many of the artists described in *Jazz*, Horace Tapscott immigrated to a big city and found fellowship within a community of like-minded musicians. The subject position he developed from those experiences, however, was the polar opposite of the isolated heroic individual artist celebrated in *Jazz*. Tapscott learned to think of himself as a responsible part of a larger collectivity. After he graduated from high school, his mother and sister told him that they had saved up enough money to send him to the prestigious Juilliard School of Music in New York, his sister's share coming from the money she had been saving for her own college education. Even though Julliard accepted him as a student, Tapscott turned down his family's offer, because he felt he would be giving up too much by leaving his community. "No thank you," he remembers telling them. "I appreciate it. I love you. But I have the best right here. You already put me in the best atmosphere, and I can't leave. It was SWU, 'Sidewalk University,' because these cats would be on your case all the time."[61]

Tapscott's sense of the links between place and people influenced the most important decision of his life. On tour with the Lionel Hampton Band, surrounded by great musicians and hearing them play perfectly every night, making more money than he had ever made before, he realized he was nonetheless miserable. Tapscott felt that audiences didn't really listen to the music that the band played, that the musicians were wasting their talents playing only the things that would bring them another recording date or another tour. He decided to get off the road, to go home to Los Angeles, and to set up a new kind of space capable of giving rise to a new kind of subjectivity.

Back in Los Angeles, Tapscott started the Pan Afrikan People's Arkestra, or as he called it, the Ark (short for Arkestra, a spelling he borrowed from Sun Ra). The Ark was a locally based group set up to preserve, teach, show, and perform the music of Black Americans and pan-African music, "to preserve it by playing it and writing it and taking it to the community."[62] The members of the Ark taught music, theatre, poetry, art, and dance to their neighbors in South Central Los Angeles. They performed concerts in the parks, in auditoriums, and in their own rehearsal spaces. They played every day, rarely for money, but somehow they supported themselves. "Everybody became part of the scene," Tapscott recalls. "No one was left out, and everyone felt like they were a part of it. There were people who had a lot to say and didn't have anyplace to say it."[63]

The Ark revolved around the arts, but it advanced a particular understanding of them, one that embedded artistic excellence in the everyday life of the community. At some performances, Tapscott's group set the admission charge as a can of beans. Ark members would personally deliver the food they had collected, "and somebody else would be happy because they'd have something to eat that day."[64] Professional artists with global reputations donated their services to the Ark, including actors William Marshall and Marla Gibbs, and saxophonist Rahsaan Roland Kirk. Famous for his breathing exercises that enabled him to play two saxophones at once, Kirk told Tapscott what his mission in life had become: to see to it that every kid in Tapscott's neighborhood learned to play two horns at once.

Tapscott claims he did not realize that the Ark was a success until one day when the group did not have its usual noisy rehearsal. A wino on Central Avenue stopped him and asked, "Hey man, where's our band?" Tapscott remarks that the man said "our band," not "your band." The derelict's expression of the community's sense of ownership of the Ark convinced Tapscott that the group had succeeded.[65]

Eager to expand their activities beyond the Ark, Tapscott and his group started calling themselves the Underground Musicians Association (UGMA) and, later, the Union of God's Musicians and Artists Ascension (UGMAA). They recognized that their pro-Black and pro-Africa sentiments made them unwelcome in white supremacist America. "Because we played and talked about being black, about Africa, about preserving our culture, it scared them," he recalls.[66] But it was not just race consciousness that made the UGMA seem subversive. It was also the group members' distance from the heroic individualism so celebrated in *Jazz*. Tapscott observes, "In those early days, UGMA became a very dangerous commodity to the community, because of our comradeship and because of what we were saying about what was happening in the community. People started caring about each other and that was dangerous. We watched each other's back and took care of each other as a group. That became intimidating, to the point where we were called a gang or a 'perversion against the country.' Everywhere we went, the whole group would be with me. We'd be in cars, four or five of us, all the time, and we'd go to places together, not only to play but also to listen."[67] The sense of collectivity that UGMA cultivated was more than just physical, however. The group ran classes for children in reading, writing, and spelling, as well as offering instruction in playing instruments, singing, and drawing. While rooted in a local community in modern "America," they developed a global perspective. Newspapers from all over the world appeared at the UGMA house. Visiting speakers provided firsthand reports of struggles by oppressed people around the globe. "Our concern was our particular area and black people," Tapscott recalls, "but we sympathized with people's struggles around the world."[68]

Saying that "jazz objectifies America," as Wynton Marsalis did, would not necessarily be a compliment to jazz from Tapscott's perspective. In his account, America becomes the local point of entry into a wider world. Remembering concerts that he played with pianist Andrew Hill in Oakland, California, Tapscott recalls "this young Chinese kid sitting up front and bowing to me . . . he said his name was Jon Jang."[69] Tapscott relates that moment as the start of his friendship with Jang, now a well-known modernist composer. Tapscott and Jang collaborated at the 1998 Asian American Jazz Festival, featuring an original Tapscott composition, "The Two Shades of Soul." Tapscott claims, "Chinese music has never been foreign to me, because I can hear a lot of things within it." By way of elaboration, he then makes a social point, remembering, "When I was growing up in Houston, there was a Chinese guy who used to run the local food store across the street from us and who would let us have food when we needed it just by signing a piece of paper. He was the first Asian I'd seen in my life. I've never forgotten that and have always felt a kind of kinship with the Chinese people."[70]

The new spaces created by the Ark encouraged the formation of new subject positions. Tapscott did not believe that autonomy was a proper goal for art, quite the contrary. His compositions and playing (first on the trombone and later on the piano) drew on a rhythmic complexity that he gleaned from everyday life, from the way people walked down the street and the rhythmic patterns of their work. "Every time I write something, it's about what I've been a part of or seen," he maintains. "If the community changes, then so goes the music."[71] *Songs of the Unsung* presents a story about jazz that contains no linear developmental narrative, no canon of great art or artists, and no embrace of modernist time or American space. It rejects the idea of the isolated and alienated artist and instead invests meaning in the power of art to transform social relations and people's senses of the self. "Our music is contributive, rather than competitive," Tapscott insists.

To fans of *Jazz*, Horace Tapscott's story probably seems eccentric, parochial, and insignificant, little more than a side man's engaging footnote to the real history of the art. The relentless delineation of particularities in Tapscott's tale, however, should not detract our attention from the more general claims it makes. Racism might be just one particular historical obstacle in the way of artistic genius to Wynton Marsalis, but it is a part and parcel of the music business to Horace Tapscott. From his perspective, the music industry does not just happen to reflect a legacy of racism that exists outside it in the broader society, but instead one of the core functions of the music industry and its categories is to produce and reproduce racism every day. Collective improvisation may be a wonderful artistic metaphor for social relations in Wynton Marsalis's universe, but it is a form of social organization and oppositional struggle in Horace Tapscott's world.

Modernist time, American space, and heroic artistry cannot be considered universal simply because they claim universal validity. Preston Love, Horace Tapscott's band mate in the West Coast Motown touring band of the 1960s, provides a perspective very similar to Tapscott's in his splendid autobiography, *A Thousand Honey Creeks Later: My Life in Music from Basie to Motown and Beyond*. Unlike the linear development of jazz from New Orleans to Chicago to New York, which Ken Burns and Wynton Marsalis use to connect jazz to the modernist city, Love tells the history of jazz from the vantage point of a working musician in Honey Creek, Iowa; Guthrie, Oklahoma; Big Spring, Texas; Alma, Nebraska; St. Cloud, Minnesota; and Roswell, New Mexico. He recognizes how Minneapolis and Albuquerque became key venues in the life of Lester Young. To be sure, Love pays proper tribute to the jazz greats he encountered in his life as an artist: Jo Jones, Freddie Green, Lester Young, Count Basie, and Dizzy Gillespie. Yet he also argues for the value of spontaneous moments when unheralded players reached extraordinary heights, like the chord changes that he heard George Salisbury play one night at the College Inn in Boulder, Colorado, the solo that Frank Sleet coaxed out of the alto saxophone during the first time he ever played the instrument, accompanying Jimmy Witherspoon's recording of "T'Ain't Nobody's Business," and the innovative playing on electric bass that Love heard Buster Coates perform repeatedly in small jazz clubs in Amarillo, Texas, and Clovis, New Mexico, in 1955.[72]

The life and career of Sun Ra also testify to the limits of thinking about jazz as coterminous with modernist time, American space, and artistic heroism. So alienated from historical time that he refused to acknowledge the day or even the year he was born, Sun Ra stubbornly insisted, "Me and time never got along so good—we just sort of ignore each other."[73] Although some observers noted his close resemblance to Herman "Sonny" Blount, born in Birmingham, Alabama, on May 22, 1914, Sun Ra did not acknowledge Alabama, America, or even the planet Earth as his space. "I had this touch of sadness in the midst of other people's parties," he explained. "Other people were having a good time, but I would have a moment of loneliness and sadness. It puzzled me, therefore I had to analyze that, and I decided I was different, that's all, I might have come from somewhere else."[74] He claimed that "somewhere else" was outer space, perhaps Saturn. Sun Ra encapsulated his strategic disidentification with modernist time, American space, and artistic individualism all in one sentence when he told an interviewer, "Liberty, too, is not all it's cracked up to be; even the liberty bell is cracked, for that matter, and it was liberty that led people to the use of crack."[75]

P-Funk impresario George Clinton recognized Sun Ra as a kindred spirit. "This boy was definitely out to lunch," he related mischievously, "the same place I eat at."[76] Yet there is more than eccentricity in Sun Ra's story. At stake here is not just an issue of a comprehensive mainstream history versus eccentric tales told by imaginative outsiders. Our entire understanding of music and society may hinge on what kinds of histories we valorize. Christopher Small rightly urges us to learn from the great African traditions that inform jazz music, to "learn to love the creative act more than the created object," and not to let our respect for the relics of the past inhibit our capacity to create culture relevant to our own experiences.[77] The history of jazz as creative act rather than created object can be represented in an infinitely diverse and plural number of equally true narratives.

The heroic narrative of *Jazz*, however, is designed as a genealogy of elitist blackness. It was consciously designed to counter a perceived excess of democratic thinking among Black intellectuals. Marsalis contends that Black professionals "are so gullible and worried about being accused of not identifying with the man in the street that they refuse to discern with the interest in quality that makes for a true elite."[78] This Black elite, like the white elite it hopes to join, derives its legitimacy precisely from its distance from the majority of the population. It offers roles as cultural brokers to elite and accomplished African Americans, but only if they will collaborate in the organized abandonment of Black communities. As James Kyung-Jin Lee argues, "Brokers are not simply middlemen, mediating and controlling access to societal power; brokers benefit from and, through their social being, affirm the asymmetrical relationships between the owners of capital and capital's owned, and manage that which is seen by the powerful and that which is left behind, all in the maintenance of this social order."[79]

Wynton Marsalis expresses his disdain of democracy openly. "The biggest problem with democracy, and with our education," he opines, "is that every opinion becomes law and fact, just because it exists. . . . Yet we mustn't forget that beneath all those opinions there is an underlying truth and reality."[80] Yet one might also say instead that all those opinions evidence multiple, conflicting, and contradictory realities and truths. Efforts to identify and honor a classical Black tradition in a country historically ruled by elite whites follow an understandable and ideologically overdetermined logic. Yet there is more to be learned from the history and enduring creativity of Black music than this. Los Angeles newspaper editor Charlotta Bass used to urge her constituents to look beyond the desire to see "dark faces in high places," to think about how the exclusion of Blacks from full citizenship and social membership in U.S. society was symptomatic of larger problems that could not be cured by integration alone, that it called instead for fundamentally new ways of knowing, thinking, and being. The true genius of Black music has not been confined to the production of individual "geniuses," but rather has been manifest in the plurality of new social relationships that the music has helped bring into being. The created objects and creative artists celebrated in *Jazz* do not tell us enough about the broader African American imagination and activism that gave their art its determinate shape. As Vincent Harding explains, "This people has not come through this pain in order to attain equal opportunity with the pain inflictors of this nation and this world. It has not been healed in order to join the inflictors of wounds. There must be some other reason for pain than equal opportunity employment with the pain deliverers."[81]

With its compression of modernist time, American space, and artistic struggle, the opening sequence of Ken Burns's *Jazz* captures a part of the truth about the history of jazz. But I suggest we turn to another compression of time, space, and struggle for an even truer and more useful understanding. It occurs in a story that trumpeter and arranger Clora Bryant tells in an oral history interview about jazz on Central Avenue. In my judgment, it encapsulates more of the experience of jazz in this country than all nine episodes of *Jazz*.

Bryant relates how hard it was for musicians to get paid by Curtis Mosby, manager of Central Avenue's Club Alabam. Mosby was an African American entrepreneur whose role as a cultural broker gave him power over the lives of aspiring Black musicians. He promised them good wages but was slow to keep his promises. Mosby's "deductions" for his purported expenses in providing food and drink to the artists sometimes canceled out all they had earned. Occasionally he would pay the right amount to keep in good standing with the musicians' union but then demand kickback from artists before he would let them play again. One night, blind singer Al Hibbler came to the club to demand money that Mosby owed him. As Bryant tells it, the blind singer shouted out, "You'd better give me my money or I'll shoot you" as he drew a pistol from his pocket. The blind man shouting and waving a pistol drew everyone's attention. Then, evidently remembering that his vision was impaired, Hibbler shouted to Mosby, "Say something so I'll know where you are."[82]

One joke about one artist and one club owner on one night in one city might not seem like an adequate substitute for the monumental reach and scope of *Jazz*. But Al Hibbler's anguish and anger help us see a side of the music business and the American dream that Ken Burns and his corporate sponsors will never show us. It may be true that jazz objectifies America, but it does so at least as powerfully through the promises that it breaks as through the ones that it keeps. Even Darby Hicks would have understood that.

5. Weeds in a Vacant Lot

The Hidden History of Urban Renewal

I wanted to be in a city where there were crossroads of transportation. Trains, buses, planes, where people are coming and going, conventions of all kinds, and migrations.
—C. L. Franklin

The dialogic processes that link music so powerfully to memory have made popular music an important register and record of the history of urban renewal. The performances and compositions created by Julius Hemphill before his untimely death in 1995 and the recording *Chávez Ravine,* by Ry Cooder, released in 2005, provide two examples of the role of music as an archive of urban history, as a repository of regret, resentment, and recrimination, and as a mechanism for making the memories of the past a useful and creative part of the present.

By the mid-1990s, the federal government and local municipalities had implemented more than 2,500 urban renewal projects in 992 U.S. cities. Federally assisted urban renewal during the decades of the 1950s and 1960s destroyed 20 percent of the central city housing units occupied by African Americans. Almost two-thirds of the people displaced by urban renewal have been Blacks, Mexicans, and Puerto Ricans. Ninety percent of the low-income housing units destroyed by urban renewal were never replaced. These programs constricted the housing market available to people of color, already artificially limited because of rampant discrimination in the real estate, home mortgage, and insurance industries. They forced people of color to pay higher prices for inferior dwellings in cities all across the country and led to the creation of new and overcrowded slums.[1]

Psychologist Mindy Thompson Fullilove estimates that urban renewal has destroyed more than sixteen hundred urban Black neighborhoods in the United States, leaving their residents displaced, dispossessed, disinherited, and (to quote David Roediger) "just plain dissed." Fullilove has coined the term *root shock* to describe the traumatic stress reaction that occurs when people lose all or most of their emotional ecosystems.[2] One of the hidden histories of racism in the United States lies in the loss of neighborhoods and the support structures they provided to communities of color.

For the majority of suburban whites, who derive direct benefits from the freeways, office buildings, and cultural centers constructed in downtown areas, the impact of urban renewal has been valuable but invisible. The homes and businesses it replaced have been long forgotten. For communities of color, however, urban renewal has been ruinous, its freeways and luxury urban enclaves a constant reminder of reckless destruction of valuable neighborhoods and social networks. History books and corporate journalism have not done a good job recording that history, but it permeates selected pieces of music written by artists affected by urban renewal's devastating consequences. One of those artists was Julius Hemphill.

Less than a year before he died, I conducted an interview with Hemphill in his apartment on Manhattan's Upper West Side.[3] Although I had closely followed the career of the composer and saxophone virtuoso over the years and had listened to nearly all of his recorded music, I had not seen him in person since the late 1960s, when he performed with the Black Artist Group in St. Louis. Mutual friends had warned me that Hemphill's physical condition was deteriorating rapidly, but I was nonetheless unprepared for the sight that awaited me when I entered his bedroom on that hot summer day in 1994. Hemphill lay on his back in bed, wearing only red running shorts on his slender frame. He looked emaciated and exhausted. One of his legs had been amputated up to midthigh, and the stump that remained jerked about spasmodically. Intravenous tubes carried fluids into his body from a bottle beside the bed. Hemphill's deep and rich voice still had the beautiful resonance that I remembered, but he spoke slowly, deliberately, and so softly that I had to place the tape recorder on the pillow right next to his head to pick up his words.

It pained me to see Julius Hemphill like this. I remembered what he had looked like as a young man, when his daring artistry, bold imagination, and imposing presence enabled him to command attention from everyone in the room. Yet, although it made me sad to speak with him under such circumstances, Hemphill's message was as instructive and inspirational as ever. He spoke passionately and eloquently about his efforts to envision and to enact an art that came from, and spoke to, the everyday life experiences of African American people. Affirming his faith in the energy and the imagination of his listeners, Hemphill articulated his intention to contribute to his community by transforming the aggravations and indignities they confronted into a critical consciousness capable of imagining and enacting their emancipation.

I asked Hemphill to tell me about the Black Artist Group (BAG) in St. Louis, a multimedia collective that he had helped to form in the mid-1960s. BAG brought together musicians, dancers, poets, actors, and visual artists for mixed-media performances in unlikely spaces. The group staged performances in multipurpose rooms of housing projects and school classrooms, in private lofts and public auditoriums. The organization and its activities provided a point of entry into the arts for many individuals who have subsequently secured great distinction in their fields: visual artists Oliver Jackson and Emilio Cruz; poets and spoken-word artists Arthur Brown, Ntozake Shange, Quincy Troupe, K. Curtis Lyle, Ajule Rutlin, and Malinke Elliott; actors Shirley Leflore and Vincent Terrell; and musicians Julius Hemphill, Hamiet Bluiett, Oliver Lake, Floyd LeFlore, and Charles "Bobo" Shaw.

BAG functioned as an alternative academy, to borrow the concept Robert Farris Thompson uses to describe sites where people with no recognized status in society as artists or performers hone their craft. While innovative and even revolutionary in its artistic vision, BAG drew productively on a long tradition of alternative academies in Black St. Louis, borrowing its forms, functions, ideas, inspiration, tools, and traditions from many sources, including from a WPA-sponsored "people's art center," from neighborhood jukeboxes and community drum and bugle marching bands, from grade school music, art, and drama classes, from gospel choirs, and from the speech, styles, sights, and sounds of the central city and its crowded, lively, and exuberant street life. BAG existed for only a short time before falling apart as a result of inadequate funding, internal dissension, and external opposition. For all of its achievements, it was a fragile and imperiled enterprise from the start. "We were like a weed in a vacant lot" Hemphill offered.[4]

A weed springs up in unexpected places. It pushes its way through seemingly impregnable asphalt and concrete. A weed grows in a vacant lot because no one bothers to uproot it, because everyone is looking the other way. A weed is hardy and hard to kill. A weed does not need to remain in its native soil to survive. It can be transplanted and survive and thrive elsewhere. The phrase "a weed in a vacant lot" provides an apt description of BAG and its importance. When Hemphill was asked about this earlier time in his life, it is significant that he described it with this spatial metaphor rather than in temporal terms.

The artists in BAG created innovative art in unusual spaces. They combined painting with music, and they mixed poetry with theatre. Most important, they sought to create an art that emanated *from* and intervened *in* the everyday life activities of the local African American community. They sought spaces for artistic expression independent of existing arts institutions and outside the confines of commercial culture. As Oliver Lake recalled years later, "We were voluntary specimens in an experiment to present culture as both an exclusive creation of the people and as a source of creation, as an instrument of socio-economic liberation."[5]

Julius Hemphill's memory of BAG as a weed in a vacant lot reveals a great deal about the group and perhaps about all of the Black Arts movement. Urban renewal in inner cities produced very little actual renewal but a lot of vacant lots. Like other 1960s Black Arts collectives emerging from similar circumstances, including the Association for the Advancement of Creative Musicians in Chicago (AACM), Strata and the Artists' Workshop in Detroit, and the Watts Writers Workshop and the Pan-Afrikan People's Arkestra in Los Angeles, BAG produced new artists, new audiences, and new art, primarily by developing new spaces for performance and participation.[6] The artists and activists responsible for BAG drew much of their inspiration from actual physical places that had been important in the lives of the group's members, including ghetto neighborhood businesses, public schools, concert halls, churches, and factories.

Yet these spaces and places were under attack at the precise moment that BAG and other collectives within the Black Arts movement emerged. Federally funded highways designed to speed commuters from white suburbs to downtown office buildings played a particularly pernicious role in destroying already scarce housing units available to African Americans. The roads themselves disrupted neighborhood life, imposed physical barriers to community cohesion, destroyed small businesses, and forced population flight from precincts, wards, and council districts that served as the basis for Black political power. The 1968 Housing and Urban Development Act created a lucrative and unregulated opportunity for bankers, brokers, developers, and speculators to reap windfall profits by selling substandard houses to minorities in inner-city areas. St. Louis was one of the cities that suffered most from the white-collar looting that this act and its implementation by the Nixon administration enabled. The program produced a 200 percent increase in inner-city housing costs between 1968 and 1972, but when bankers foreclosed on the mortgages of many of these uninspected and substandard dwellings, the Department of Housing and Urban Development then made inner-city areas ineligible for future loans, essentially destroying the value of Black neighborhoods for generations to come.[7]

Federal and city urban renewal projects bulldozed 780 acres of St. Louis in the 1950s and 1960s, destroying thirty-three thousand dwelling units.[8] The young artists who helped Julius Hemphill form BAG had been witnesses to urban renewal, highway construction, and the concomitant destruction of the community in which they lived. Their nostalgic memories of old spaces and their collective determination to build new ones originated, at least in part, from the impact of urban renewal on their lives. Their art sounded strident, militant, and even violent to outsiders, but its affective force came from the ruinous consequences of displacement and dispossession. As Richard Wright explained when asked in the 1940s about what critics described as the "violence" of his style, "The manner stems from the matter; the relationship of the American Negro to the American scene is essentially violent. He could not be kept in his present position unless there existed an apparatus of organized violence. Any attempt to deal with this situation must deal in terms of violence. I cannot deny the reality of my existence. It's what I've seen."[9]

Just as the violence of the lynch mob was the reality of existence for Wright, the systematic state-sponsored violence of urban renewal was the "organized violence" seen by creative artists within the Black Arts movement. BAG members Julius Hemphill, Oliver Lake, and Hamiet Bluiett became musicians because of their early experiences growing up in ghetto neighborhoods. Hemphill hailed from Fort Worth, Texas, from a district known as the Hot End, where musical models were not hard to find. "I didn't discover music one day," he explained to an interviewer. "I grew up with it all around me. I lived in the block where the nightlife would carry on. There were three juke boxes, and you could hear them about twenty-four hours a day."[10]

Oliver Lake was born in Marianna, Arkansas, but he moved to St. Louis as an infant. He learned to play cymbals and the bass drum because he wanted to join the American Woodman Marching Drum and Bugle Corps aggregation that he had seen in community parades through St. Louis's Ville neighborhood. Lake also received an early education in the blues from the jukebox at the Five Sisters Cafe, a family business that his mother co-owned and comanaged in the Ville. "The records were mostly gospel and blues—Muddy Waters, Lightnin' Hopkins, all those gutbucket guys," he later told an interviewer.[11] Lake remembers fondly the dynamism of the Black business district along Easton Avenue (later Martin Luther King Boulevard) near his house. "That whole block was alive," he recalls, "with tons of people walking back and forth."[12] Rhythm-and-blues singer Tina Turner lived ten houses away from Lake when she attended Sumner High School. "The blues have always been the basis of my music," he recalls, "even when I play chamber music, the blues are always there."[13]

Hamiet Bluiett grew up in Lovejoy, Illinois, near Scott Air Force Base in East St. Louis. Bluiett's house would shake and rattle every time air force jets flew above it. He became accustomed to the sound and even enjoyed it. He claims he took up the baritone saxophone because it was the first instrument he discovered that could replicate the sounds of windows rattling and walls shaking from sonic booms. Drawn into jazz and rhythm and blues by the success of Jimmy Forrest, a neighbor and family friend who scored a major hit record with "Night Train" (a cover of Duke Ellington's "Happy Go Lucky Local") in the early 1950s, Bluiett took his baritone saxophone into many musical settings that seemed not to be expecting the instrument. Because bands that Bluiett joined in college and in the navy were often unprepared for a baritone sax player, he learned to play parts written for alto on the baritone. "That's how I developed my high register," he remembers. Bluiett also played chamber music with the Gateway Symphony, but he found that group even more resistant to his sonic-boom style than jazz and rhythm-and-blues ensembles were. "I liked the sound [of the Gateway Symphony] when everyone was getting in tune," he recalls, but "not when we started playing."[14]

Although he played with extremely skilled classical and jazz musicians, Bluiett's admiration gravitated more toward eccentric innovators, such as the guitarist in rhythm-and-blues singer Marvin Gaye's band who played a fretless Fender bass and made chord changes that expanded Bluiett's "conception of what music might be."[15] He also admired Gaye's musicianship as a singer. "His concept of harmony was the most incredible thing I ever saw," Bluiett recalls. "He was right up there with Miles Davis, he blew me away."[16]

Davis, from East St. Louis, had gotten his first break as a professional musician in one of the St. Louis spaces later damaged by urban renewal. When Billy Eckstine's band (featuring Charlie Parker and Dizzy Gillespie) played at the Plantation Club in 1944, the establishment's white owners ordered Eckstine to enter the club through the back door only. They sought to prevent him from mingling with the club's white clientele. Eckstine defiantly entered through the front door and found himself fired from the job as a result. He scrambled to secure a new engagement for the band and found one when a local Black politician and club owner, Jordan Chambers, hired him to perform at the Riviera Club. At that venue, the group replaced an ailing trumpet player with eighteen-year-old Miles Davis, whose playing caught the attention of the very musicians who had long been his idols.[17]

Trumpeter Lester Bowie grew up in St. Louis, making music with many of the musicians who later became central to BAG. "St. Louis was really a great town for a young musician to grow up in," Bowie later recalled. "When I think back on it, it was really unbelievable."[18] Bowie received early training on his instrument from Enrico Carrion, who played with the St. Louis Symphony, but he also learned from watching local jazz trumpeters David Hines, Clark Terry, and Miles Davis. Bowie left for Chicago in 1965, before BAG became established, but his activities with the AACM (along with other St. Louis expatriates, Phil Cohran and Philip Wilson) helped inspire the founding of the St. Louis group.[19]

When many of the key members of BAG left St. Louis to tour Europe in the early 1970s, Bowie accompanied the group and performed with them along with his wife at the time, the great vocalist Fontella Bass, another St. Louis native. Bass's mother, Martha, sang gospel music with the Clara Ward Singers. Before joining with BAG, Fontella Bass had secured critical and commercial success as a rhythm-and-blues singer in the mid-1960s. She was best known for her hit song "Rescue Me," on Chess Records in 1966, but she felt drawn to the artistic and political daring of the improvisation favored in Hemphill's group. BAG musicians drew deftly on the classical, jazz, and gospel music of their community but also on rhythm and blues. Like so many other jazz musicians of their era, Hemphill and Bluiett had honed their craft as performers in touring rhythm-and-blues combos. Lake and Hemphill backed up Rufus Thomas, Solomon Burke, and Ike and Tina Turner on tours through small midwestern cities, including Iowa City (Iowa), Moline (Illinois), and Waynesville (Missouri).[20]

St. Louis might seem like an unlikely place for an avant-garde group like BAG. A staid midwestern metropolis suffering from a century of decline, the Gateway City has been the home of singularly uncelebrated cultural institutions: the International Bowling Hall of Fame, the Museum of Medical Quackery, the Dog Museum, and perhaps the only barbecue restaurant in the world named Take It 'N Git. In the 1960s, St. Louis lacked the arts infrastructure usually associated with an avant-garde. BAG member Vincent Terrell characterizes St. Louis's relationship to the arts in a simple couplet: "St. Louis, a very conservative laid-back town, goes to sleep when the sun goes down."[21] One time when BAG advertised a performance of Amiri Baraka's play *Police,* the local police actually showed up, evidently taking the advertising as a kind of a dare. Yet "the manner stems from the matter," as Richard Wright explained. The art activists in BAG produced radical forms of cultural expression, because their relationship to culture, community, and place was undergoing radical and dramatic transformations.

BAG emerged from the Mill Creek Valley, the St. Louis neighborhood most devastated by urban renewal. Decades of dislocation had left local African Americans embittered about the activities of the city's Land Clearance and Redevelopment Authority. Acres of empty and undeveloped blocks in the center of the city illustrated the failure of redevelopment to attract new investment or to replace the residential units destroyed by the process of "slum clearance." Local urban renewal authorities turned to Laclede Town, a low-rise federally funded housing project in the Mill Creek Valley, as their favored justification for urban renewal, as their prime example of the positive possibilities created by redevelopment.

Laclede Town could be seen from Highway 40 (the city's main commuting route between wealthy western suburbs and downtown) and from all sides of the otherwise empty urban renewal zone it occupied. The manager of the complex, Jerry Berger, sought to make Laclede Town a stable integrated community in a city increasingly polarized by residential racial segregation. Artists and activists in civil rights groups made up a natural constituency for integrated housing in St. Louis, so Berger attempted to make Laclede Town attractive to them. He granted them preferential treatment in rental applications and established the Circle Coffee House as a venue for live performances in a centrally located space in the complex.[22] Civil rights activists Percy Green and Ivory Perry took up residence in Laclede Town, using the nearby Berea Presbyterian Church, the bar Maurice's Gold Coast Lounge across the street, and the complex itself as a base for their community organizing. In the mid-1960s, Oliver Lake and Julius Hemphill moved into Laclede Town. Lake lived next door to Perry. Hemphill lived near Percy Green. Berger contracted with Oliver Lake to have the Lake Art Quartet play regularly at the Circle Coffee House, and Hemphill was one of the regular patrons of the establishment.

In an environment permeated by the exuberant self-activity of the civil rights movement and the self-affirmation central to the Black Arts movement, the Circle Coffee House quickly became a site for politically charged artistic expression as well as a locus for political consciousness raising. As anthropologist Victor Turner reminds us, "Pleasure becomes a serious matter in the context of innovative change."[23] The informal atmosphere and emphasis on experimentation at the Circle Coffee House encouraged an improvisational art that blurred the lines dividing music from poetry and audiences from performers. It enabled cultural workers to present their own readings and concerts in a place outside the control of commercial entrepreneurs and cultural institutions alike.

Members of the Circle Coffee House group developed ties with dancers trained at Katherine Dunham's art institute and community center in East St. Louis. They linked efforts with visual artists trained at the WPA-originated People's Art Center in North St. Louis. They allied themselves with musicians from local jazz and rhythm-and-blues ensembles, and they drew in artists engaged in preschool education and academic enrichment programs through the city school system as well as programs connected with the federal government's Office of Economic Opportunity's "war on poverty." One theatre group at Webster College (in suburban Webster Groves) put on a performance of Jean Genet's play *The Blacks,* recruiting African American actors, musicians, and dancers from the entire St. Louis area. The Black Arts community in the city at that time was so small that virtually every person who subsequently became central to BAG had a part in the play. Spoken-word artist and actor Vincent Terrell worked with visual artist Oliver Jackson teaching children at the Pruitt-Igoe Housing Project how to design sets that they could use in producing and performing their own plays.[24] Dancers, musicians, and poets staged weekly performances at the *Wall of Respect,* a mural emphasizing Black history located at the corner of Jefferson and Franklin, a few blocks from Laclede Town.

Prodded by activists in the antipoverty program and civil rights groups, the Arts and Education Council of St. Louis sought and received grants from the Rockefeller Foundation and the Danforth Foundation, each for one hundred thousand dollars, for "an experimental program of community cultural enrichment," providing classes in dance, theatre, and music for two thousand children and young adults in St. Louis and East St. Louis. The Arts and Education Council appointed Julius Hemphill as the director of the St. Louis program. He set up instructional programs in drama, dance, poetry, and music under the rubric of BAG, the Black Artist Group. Initially established in ground-floor rooms leased to Project Head Start and other antipoverty programs at the Pruitt-Igoe Housing Project, BAG eventually used the grant money from the Rockefeller and Danforth foundations to set up permanent studios and a performance space at the Sheldon Auditorium at 2665 Washington Avenue, about five blocks from Laclede Town.[25]

In fashioning their art, BAG drew on residual elements from the past and emergent aspects of the future. They took what they learned in neighborhoods that were disappearing in the face of urban renewal, such as the Mill Creek Valley, and attempted to create artistic and social spaces to anchor a new community in the process of formation. The headquarters of BAG in the Sheldon Auditorium comprised a new kind of urban space—a center for the arts intended less for individual uplift than for collective mobilization, a place where artistic and social barriers could be contested. Vincent Terrell remembers, "My specific intent was to provoke people, to bring their consciousness to the point of rebellion—that was my intent."[26]

Hemphill described the music made at BAG as "a sounding board for social issues," observing that "unsatisfactory conditions" affect everything in a person's life and therefore have to affect music.[27] But Hemphill also indicated that artists need to provide people with things the community needs in order to maintain credibility with their audiences. Artists had to earn audience respect by doing something for the soul *and* for the struggle. "We were just not trying to say that tooting this horn is going to solve all the problems in the world, particularly living under these wretched conditions over here," Hemphill explained. "That's a bigger issue than any kind of thing we might bring in there in terms of entertainment or whatever. Because first, it's got to be entertaining. If there's any deeper meaning or anything attributed to it, it's got to earn that. You can't just say this. It's got to earn that meaning. So we were more than happy to make the place available for some serious dialogue between the city's representatives and the people."[28]

Visual artists in BAG loaned their talents to community groups, making signs for a rent strike staged by tenants in public housing and for demonstrators protesting the lack of testing and treatment for lead poisoning among children in inner-city neighborhoods.[29] At the same time, those involved in BAG tried to create an artistic space appropriate to their political and social vision by transcending the limits of genre and form. Collaborations among musicians, writers, painters, and dancers encouraged individuals to reconceptualize the internal properties of their art by exploring the ways in which sight, sound, movement, and timing influence all artistic expression. Hemphill reconceptualized the saxophone as an extension of human vocal processes, as less of a musical instrument than a prosthetic for speaking and singing. He also spoke of music in terms that a sculptor might use, talking about it as a kind of "clay" that enables people to "just start making things."[30] In a 1970 interview, Oliver Lake explained how working with BAG made him reconceptualize the sounds he could make on the saxophone. "We try to make our music relevant to everyday life day-to-day existence," Lake asserted. "Often, we open our concerts with verbal phrases or lines of poetry. We use voices while we're playing, groans, moans, screams, but even these are aimed at relating to the lives of black people."[31]

Visual artist Oliver Jackson found that working with musicians taught him about the role of "time" in painting. "A musician knows when he is losing the attention of his audience right away," Jackson observes. "Working with musicians taught me about the whole matter of *time* in a painting, the need to eliminate the dead spots, the parts that don't move. From musicians, I learned how to get into a painting, to find an opening. And the most important thing you learn from the best musicians is: just *play the tune*. There are some tunes, certain thematic ideas, that call for lots of notes and speed and intricacy. Others simply have to be done with very few, and very simply. The same is true of a painting."[32]

In artistic terms, BAG succeeded in nurturing and promoting the talents of an extraordinary group of individuals who went on to secure subsequent fame and recognition as artists. These aesthetic achievements played a role in mass mobilizations and changes in individual consciousness in their community as well. They invited people to be artists who had few other invitations, and they encouraged people who had never been respected as citizens to exert influence on civic life. The BAG dance and drum ensemble offered dance classes on Wednesday nights and provided drum classes on Saturdays for a cost of only fifty cents per week.[33] Jazz saxophonist Greg Osby heard his first concerts as a youth because of BAG. "I always related to Julius Hemphill and Hamiet Bluiett," he later reminisced. "They used to play in these lofts around St. Louis. And while I was too young to get in, I'd sit outside where I could hear them just fine because they'd play real loud, with the windows open."[34]

The broader social movement of Black activism that was so central to BAG's genesis also enjoyed significant victories in the late 1960s and early 1970s. Percy Green's protests at construction sites called attention to discriminatory hiring practices in the building trades. They contributed significantly to the process that eventually produced federal affirmative action programs for the construction industry. Ivory Perry played a crucial role in the 1969 rent strike by tenants in public housing. Their struggle led Congress to pass legislation limiting the maximum rent for tenants in government housing projects all across the country. Perry led a similarly successful campaign to secure testing and treatment for children victimized by lead poisoning, ultimately resulting in a city ordinance banning the use of lead paint on the interior walls of residential buildings.[35]

These political and artistic victories jeopardized the main source of funding for BAG, however, when local elites protested to the Danforth and Rockefeller foundations about the group's actions. In the initial announcement of support for what was to become BAG, the Rockefeller Foundation defined the problems to be addressed by the group as primarily psychological and personal—the debilitating effects of racism and poverty on Black people themselves. "We believe that the arts, thought of in the broadest sense, do offer a direct remedy for some of the underlying ills—voicelessness, isolation, depersonalization—that affect the economically underprivileged members of our urban society," proclaimed George Harrar of the Rockefeller Foundation in announcing the original grant of two hundred thousand dollars in May 1968.[36] The foundation also argued that the arts themselves would profit by identifying, acknowledging, and refining the talents of inner-city residents. As the foundation asserted in a press release, "The American Negro has already shown, through his creative writing, his music composition, and his performance in music, theater, and dance, that he can make a valuable contribution to American society."[37]

Intending to speak to the psyches of deprived individuals and to augment the arts as they already existed, foundation officials were deeply disappointed by the practices that emerged from BAG. They complained that the group's "lessons and teachings have been mainly for blacks, not whites. Therefore the effect on black-white understanding has been very limited." They judged the group's theatre performances as having more "shock value" than "cultural value," complaining that "certain artists have been more interested in social reform than in art."[38] While conceding that "much that is good" came out of the program, the Danforth and Rockefeller foundations decided that BAG's accomplishments did not conform to the prescribed definitions of urban problems and the desired solutions as envisioned by the top officials of the foundations. Consequently, they terminated its funding. The foundation members' understanding of what constituted the "community" was clearly different from the definition used by members of BAG.

BAG lost its financial footing in the midst of a general attack on the institutions that generated and sustained the civil rights–Black Power movement in St. Louis. The war in Vietnam diverted money from the war on poverty during the Johnson administration. Revenue sharing and federal block grants initiated by President Nixon redirected funds away from direct aid to the poor, channeling them toward property tax relief for businesses, antiriot equipment for police and fire departments, and subsidies for constructing private office buildings and for civic amenities such as concert halls. The counterintelligence programs (COINTELPRO) of the Federal Bureau of Investigation secured the cooperation of the "red squad" of the St. Louis Police Department and of a young journalist named Pat Buchanan, then working for the conservative *St. Louis Globe-Democrat,* in vilifying, intimidating, and harassing a number of activists, including Percy Green and Ivory Perry. Vincent Terrell believes that BAG was infiltrated by the police. Given the documented cases of law enforcement officials placing undercover agent Darthard Perry in the Black Arts movement in Los Angeles and of carrying out covert attacks on Black Arts institutions in Detroit, he may well be correct.[39]

At the same time, seniority-based layoffs during the recessions of the early 1970s had an especially disastrous effect on Black workers, many of whom had secured access to skilled jobs only after the passage of civil rights legislation and direct action protests during the 1960s. As the last hired, they became the first fired. In addition, federal subsidies and incentives to move manufacturing to newly constructed plants in low-wage regions of the United States and overseas had an especially negative impact on Black workers in older industrial cities, such as St. Louis. Although some people connected with BAG obtained jobs at local educational institutions, most of the artists had to leave the city in order to find steady professional work as musicians, actors, artists, and writers. They enjoyed extraordinary success, artistically and commercially. Emilio Cruz moved to the Studio Museum of Harlem. Vincent Terrell became a successful actor and educator in Boston and New York. Robert Malinke Elliott gained recognition as a poet on the West Coast. Quincy Troupe joined the Watts Writers Workshop and earned distinction for his efforts as a poet, teacher, and biographer in New York and San Diego. Oliver Jackson attained great esteem and success as a painter in the San Francisco Bay Area. Julius Hemphill, Oliver Lake, and Hamiet Bluiett moved to New York, where they connected with David Murray (who was briefly married to Ntozake Shange, a St. Louisan, BAG alumna, and award-winning playwright) to form the World Saxophone Quartet.

Hemphill's vision helped shape the emergence of the World Saxophone Quartet, an ensemble that explored new sounds and sensations through its all-saxophone instrumentation. The group's success made it feasible for other musicians to explore similarly innovative lineups in groups such as Hornweb, Itchy Fingers, Manfred Schulze's Blaster Quintet, Kolner Saxophon Mafia, and De Zes Winden.[40] Hemphill substituted saxophones for human voices in his opera *Long Tongues,* a piece that deployed film footage, slides, and music by jazz saxophone players, a rhythm section, and members of the Washington Philharmonic Orchestra. With *Long Tongues,* Hemphill created a new kind of operatic space, paying tribute expressly to the kinds of spaces destroyed by highway building, suburbanization, and urban renewal. His setting for the opera was the legendary Washington, D.C., nightclub Crystal Caverns, which at different times in its history had been home to performances by swing bands, bebop ensembles, rhythm-and-blues acts, and jazz artists. Hemphill's libretto traced the history of the club from the early 1940s to its closing after the urban renewal that followed the destructive 1968 riots, instigated by the assassination of Martin Luther King Jr.[41]

The World Saxophone Quartet created a sensation in the jazz world during the 1980s. The group had no percussion or keyboard accompaniment. They made an art out of breaking the conventional rules of jazz performance. "We don't have drummers," Murray explained to a reporter. "We have heart beats."[42] Lake saw their art as a challenge to commercial culture, to "the almighty dollar which moves a lot of the stuff in America. You either fit or don't fit in this framework. It affects creativity and awareness because everyone pursues it. It comes before human life."[43]

Yet many of the very things that secured recognition and praise for the World Saxophone Quartet (WSQ) as innovators on the world jazz scene had grown organically and easily from local networks in St. Louis in the years when spaces existed that allowed them to flourish. Looking back at BAG from the perspective of his successful career with the WSQ, as a solo artist, and with other small ensembles, Lake emphasized, "The fact that we had poetry, dance, music, and so forth all together stayed with me. I've been doing that sort of thing pretty much throughout my career."[44] Similarly, on one of his last visits to St. Louis before his death, Julius Hemphill spoke fondly of his memories of a time when "there was a lot of interest in exploring unfamiliar territory, in putting on concerts instead of waiting for someone else to do it, in playing in places other than clubs."[45]

Although celebrated around the world as modernist innovators, the members of the World Saxophone Quartet shunned the label of the avant-garde, thinking of themselves as products of a musical and social environment that refused to recognize limits rather than one that honored limits all the more by self-consciously "transgressing" them. "I never really thought of myself as like that, avant-garde," Lake explained to a reporter in 1993. "At first it really used to make me mad because it was so limiting, but I've gotten used to it. I like to think of myself as a person who likes a lot of different styles."[46] Hemphill located his music similarly within community traditions rather than outside them, telling a reporter from *Down Beat,* "I think that the American people, particularly black people, have a kind of intimacy with the music that we play. There is a cultural dynamic that has to do with the reality of the music being all through the black communities. It results in a kind of awareness and exuberance that people bring from the whole history of listening to the guy next door."[47]

Deindustrialization destroyed the relatively high-wage jobs that enabled Black workers and their families to visit the nightclubs in Hemphill's hometown of Fort Worth, Texas, where he first heard professional musicians play, as well as in his adopted home, St. Louis, where he perfected his musical technique as a member of rhythm-and-blues bands. Tax cuts for the rich and property tax abatements for corporations demolished the financial base for the kinds of public school art and music classes that Hemphill and his fellow musicians took as students and later taught as practicing artists. Direct police repression against the civil rights and Black Power movements, as well as the gradual cooptation and incorporation of those movements' leaders into government positions, has blunted the sharp edge of radical activism that gave rise to cultural projects like the Black Artist Group.

All across the country, conservative attacks on public endowments for the arts and humanities have sharply curtailed projects designed to democratize the production and reception of art, like the ones that enabled Hemphill to secure commissions for his operatic, orchestral, and dance compositions. These assaults on the arts and on the government institutions and social movements that have sustained them in the past give more control over culture to a handful of corporations. They exercise oligopolistic control over commercial culture as well. These changes put even more power in the hands of private philanthropists and foundations, whose core concerns often compel them to isolate artistic products from the social matrices that give them determinate shape and meaning.

In his original and generative analysis of contemporary culture, Néstor García Canclini argues that commercial marketers and private foundations now serve as the primary patrons and generators of artistic activity, usurping a role formerly filled by social movements and the state.[48] Like so many of the revolutionary transformations of our time, this change has gone largely unanalyzed, even though it has enormous consequences. The imperatives of commercial culture, and of what Canclini calls tax evasion masquerading as philanthropy, are poor substitutes for the kinds of support previously given to artistic endeavors by social movements and the state. The new forms do not erase the oppositional potential of art by any means, but they do function to suppress systematically the kinds of self-expression and self-activity characteristic of the "community-based art making" and art-based community making that did so much to create new artistic and social spaces in the past by linking artistic practices to social conditions. The history of the Black Artist Group offers an important illustration of how the state and social movements during the 1960s combined to fashion a space for dynamic cultural activity. At the same time, this history shows how charitable foundations and commercial culture quickly reach their limits when they have to confront the kinds of creativity that emerged from the Blacks Arts movement in general and from BAG in particular. The destruction of antipoverty programs, cutbacks in state spending on the arts, and the defeats suffered by the social movements of the 1960s leave young people in St. Louis and other cities today with fewer options and opportunities for the kinds of self-expression that BAG nurtured and sustained.

No monument marks the spot where BAG once was, and no individuals have been able to pick up the torch that BAG members put down when they scattered to the far corners of the globe in the 1970s. In some ways the absence of a monument is appropriate, because it would contradict the spirit of a group based on improvisation, creativity, and the shake-up of categories to become an institution, immortalized yet fossilized. The conduits of commercial culture and foundation-supported expressions that now occupy the artistic spaces that once included egalitarian collectives like BAG also call our attention to the histories they have erased but ghost the present in the artistry of Oliver Lake, Fontella Bass, Julius Hemphill, Oliver Jackson, Hamiet Bluiett, Vincent Terrell, Robert Malinke Elliott, Ntozake Shange, Quincy Troupe, Lester Bowie, and many others in many different places. Through songs that recall their formative experiences in St. Louis, such as Julius Hemphill's "Messin' with the Kid," Hamiet Bluiett's "Night Train," and Oliver Lake's "Love Like Sisters," the members of the World Saxophone Quartet inserted into their art some of the energy, imagination, and inspiration they drew from their community and its social movements in the 1960s.

These performers and artists carried traces of their BAG experiences with them into their subsequent work. In addition, while historical appreciation and nostalgia alike feed a deep sense of loss about the disappearance of groups like BAG from cities like St. Louis, we have to acknowledge that these endeavors were fugitive and ephemeral even at their peak. Julius Hemphill came to St. Louis from Fort Worth and Jefferson City. Oliver Lake hailed from Marianna, Arkansas. Ntozake Shange lived in New York before she set foot in St. Louis. Vincent Terrell came to BAG after military service and several jobs in St. Louis factories. He began writing and performing poetry in the army with the help of two fellow soldiers, a Puerto Rican conga player and a Dominican bongo player.[49] Quincy Troupe also discovered poetry in the military, preferring "foreign" poets from Madagascar, Mexico, Martinique,

Nigeria, Cuba, and Chile to most of the U.S. poets that he read or heard.[50] Katherine Dunham's art center in East St. Louis drew on the great dancer's experiences in New York, Paris, and Haiti, as well as on local traditions and expressions. When Hemphill, Lake, Bluiett, Shange, Troupe, and Terrell moved to New York, they followed in the footsteps of previous exiles, including Josephine Baker and Miles Davis, who found St. Louis too harsh an environment for the survival of their art. Far removed from the physical places and cultural spaces that gave determinate shape to their art at one time, they continued to construct discursive spaces to keep alive the memory and the provocation of a different kind of culture. Their art was indeed ephemeral, fugitive, and elusive, but it retained the extraordinary moral power and sense of cultural connection characteristic of the art-based community making of the 1960s, evocative of the "weed in a vacant lot" that nurtured and shaped their talents.

Some people think weeds are ugly, that they fail to conform to the standards of beauty that earn plants designation as "flowers" rather than weeds. In Jack Conroy's Depression-era short story "The Weed King," a midwestern farmer tries to kill the Spanish nettle plants that threaten to take over his land. He pulls these weeds completely out of the ground, because that violent act is the only way to kill them completely. Yet the action of uprooting the Spanish nettle shakes its seeds and sends them off in a hundred different directions in the wind to appear as new weeds somewhere else. The same can be said for the members of BAG.

Ry Cooder's 2005 recording *Chávez Ravine* stages an excursion into another vacant lot, to the Chavez Ravine neighborhood in Los Angeles, razed by an urban renewal project for the purpose of building public housing but ultimately becoming the site of Dodger Stadium. Cooder grew up in suburban Santa Monica on the west side of Los Angeles. He never visited Chavez Ravine before the bulldozers leveled it to clear the ground for the ballpark. For this album, however, he selected the neighborhood as a symbol of all that has been lost in Los Angeles as fortunes were made and power acquired to make the city "paved over, malled up, high-rised, and urban renewed."[51]

By turning the lost Chavez Ravine into a site of discovery, Cooder continued the course that he has followed throughout his career as a romantic white interpreter of "lost" music created by people of color—by musicians from Hawai'i, the Bahamas, Cuba, and Afro-America. This lifelong project bears uncomfortable resemblance to colonial, anthropological, and folkloric efforts by whites to use the cultures of aggrieved groups for uplift, insight, and emotional renewal. According to this formula, people of color become what philosopher Elizabeth Spelman calls "spiritual bellhops, carriers of experience from which others can benefit."[52] Yet as he did with the *Buena Vista Social Club* from Cuba, Cooder shares this album with some hardy "weeds," people with direct links to the historical vacant lot his project explores and whose creative self-expression often transcends the limits of his particular artistic and social vision. *Chávez Ravine* is a cycle of fourteen songs telling the story of urban renewal from different perspectives. Cooder composed three of the songs and cowrote four others. He plays expertly on most of the tracks (on guitar, tres, and bajo sexto), and his characteristic nostalgia for little known "other worlds" permeates the production. Yet when he shares the microphone with Chicano musicians especially, the recording takes on an extraordinary energy, passion, and power.

Cooder's lineup includes a "who's who" of Chicano music. The great singer, songwriter, and parody artist Lalo Guerrero sings three of his own compositions. David Hidalgo of Los Lobos, Little Willie G of Thee Midnighters, East Los Angeles balladeer Ersi Arzivu, Don Tosti of the Pachuco Boogie Boys, Rudy Salas of Tierra, and sisters Juliet and Carla Commagere add important vocals. Original compositions by David Hidalgo and Little Willie G blend with old standards and new songs composed by Cooder, while Gil Bernal and Flaco Jiménez provide virtuosic accompaniment on the saxophone and accordion.

The "materials memory" of actual historical events permeates many of the songs on *Chávez Ravine*. In his liner notes, Cooder traces the intertextual genealogy of this project, from his discovery of Don Normark's book of photographs about the Chavez Ravine neighborhood to assistance he received in interpreting urban renewal from architectural and urban historian Dana Cuff. Cooder thanks Carolyn Kozo Cole, who supervised the photographic collection *Shades of LA* for the Los Angeles Public Library, "LA School" authors and urban historians Mike Davis and Phil Ethington, journalist and author Rubén Martínez, music experts Chris Strachwitz and Chuey Varela, and veteran Los Angeles activ-

ist and attorney Frank Wilkinson. Cooder uses these sources skillfully. Rarely have scholarly sources been mined so precisely and so
thoroughly in commercial culture. Indeed, the album may well be
American studies' greatest (and, so far, only) hit.

The songs on *Chávez Ravine* evoke the lively dynamism of the
barrio before urban renewal. "Poor Man's Shangri-la," "Three
Cool Cats," "Muy Fifi," "Los chucos suaves," and the remarkable "Chinito chinito" honor the vernacular culture of the streets,
the erotic energy of youth, and the aggressive festivity of working
people. These songs contain important evidence about the social
history of Los Angeles. They detail, for example, how the systematic segregation that Chicanos shared with other communities
of color produced mixed neighborhoods and lively sites for interracial contact. Lalo Guerrero's "Los chucos suaves" documents
the presence of Afro-Cuban rumba and African American boogie
woogie and jitterbug music in nightclubs patronized by Chicanos.
Cooder's cover of Don Tosti's "Chinito chinito" plays on the long
history of cultural coalescence and conflict between Latinos and
Asians in downtown and East Los Angeles through lyrics about
two Chicanas teasing a handsome Chinese man who works at a
local laundry. Although orientalist and even racist in its carica-
tured musical figures (deploying gongs and other devices symbolic
of the East to Western ears), the song displays unbridled affection
and admiration as well.

Little Willie G sings the beautiful "Onda callejera," a song he
cowrote with David Hidalgo. Their lyrics relate the story of the
zoot suit riots during World War II, the period in June 1943 when
packs of sailors, soldiers, and marines roamed Chicano neighborhoods in Los Angeles attacking young pachucos wearing zoot
suits.[53] Casual listeners might think that the leveling of the Chavez
Ravine neighborhood in 1959 had little to do with the hate crimes
perpetrated by military personnel sixteen years earlier, but as historian Eric Avila notes in his important book *Popular Culture in
the Age of White Flight,* the anti-Mexican racism that fueled the
riots (and afterward excused the rioters and blamed their victims)
helped make it possible for civic leaders to condemn neighborhoods
like Chavez Ravine (figuratively and literally) as "pachuco zones"
that had to be destroyed in order to revitalize the city.[54]

Perhaps most important, *Chávez Ravine* identifies urban renewal as one the main sources of enduring interracial enmity in

Los Angeles and as one of the main culprits in the destruction of interracial and intercultural cooperation. The city obtained land in Chavez Ravine and evicted its inhabitants through laws that allowed the confiscation of private property for the purpose of building public housing. After the land was procured, however, civic leaders in Los Angeles rejected public housing as socialistic and un-American. They changed the deed that gave the city title to the land and handed over the condemned property to Brooklyn Dodgers' owner Walter O'Malley. The City of Los Angeles purchased more than three hundred acres of land at Chavez Ravine from the Housing Authority for eight hundred thousand dollars after the 1952 referendum rejected building public housing on the site.[55] Mayor Norris Poulson offered the land to O'Malley as an inducement for him to move the team to Los Angeles and build a stadium on that site. O'Malley called the land "two hundred and ten taxable acres of hill ground that would be of interest only to goats"—a disingenuous description of a neighborhood that housed eighteen hundred families and occupied a choice location near downtown and at the intersection of three major freeways. Avila presents a former resident's very different view of the neighborhood before urban renewal:

> There were dances in the churchyard. Pageants held in the streets. Weddings in which the whole community joyously participated. . . . Flowers, gorgeous blooms, dahlias fit to grace any show display. Gardens, orchards, livestock. Cow's and goat's milk—cheese of every color, kind, and consistency. Cactus broiled, baked, preserved. At night, bonfires—music wafted over the air.[56]

The city gave O'Malley 315 acres of land worth anywhere from $2 million to $6 million, mineral rights under that land, a ninety-nine-year lease, complete control over revenues from parking, concessions, and tickets, $4.7 million worth of land preparation costs, and $5,000 of free surveying donated by Howard Hughes. In return, O'Malley built a $20 million stadium.[57]

Cooder's song "Don't Call Me Red" combines snippets of old radio programs, spoken-word testimony, and lyrics to delineate the story of how the neighborhood became the site of the baseball stadium hosting the Los Angeles Dodgers baseball team. The song relates the incident from the perspective of Frank Wilkinson, the head of the local housing agency who chose to go to prison rather than to testify about his associations and beliefs before the House Un-American Activities Committee.

Cooder connects the close-up story of Chavez Ravine in Los Angeles to broader processes and practices. He selects Hawai'ian slack key guitarist James Bla Pahanui to sing and play on the album's penultimate song, "3rd Base, Dodger Stadium." The lyrics portray the wistful memories of the neighborhood's former residents, who still identify their old homes by where they would be located inside Dodger Stadium. They remember the site as a place where neighborhood youths played baseball for free, not where suburban residents journeyed by freeway to watch professionals play. Pahanui has no direct relationship to Chavez Ravine, but he is well known in Hawai'i for his interpretation of songs such as "Waimanalo Blues," a piece detailing the destruction of local neighborhoods for high-rise ocean-view luxury apartments and tourist hotels.[58] His presence on "3rd Base, Dodger Stadium" locates the local story of Chavez Ravine in a broader context.

Yet there is a danger in Cooder's tribute to Chavez Ravine. Emphasizing the "little worlds emptied out" by urban renewal slights the efforts of displaced city dwellers to reconstitute the diversity and plurality of the city in their new suburban surroundings. The design aesthetic of the suburbs revolved around homogeneity and sameness, not only in the size and design of homes, but also in the racial makeup of the population. The growth of the suburbs, promoted by urban renewal, highway construction, and the channeling of federally guaranteed home loans to whites in the postwar period, created a new form of whiteness. This racially based cultural identity drew subsidies from key institutions, from direct discrimination and "steering" by realtors, from deed restrictions that prohibited the resale of suburban property to nonwhite buyers, from redlining by mortgage lenders and insurance companies, and even from hate crimes against families of color trying to move into prohibited neighborhoods.[59]

Yet the very homogeneity, uniformity, and blandness required by this combination of racial enmity and aesthetics made the intercultural creations of people of color even more appealing to the white children raised in these new suburbs. Rick and Barry Rillera, for example, formed the Rhythm Rockers band to entertain teenage audiences in the mostly white Los Angeles suburbs of Orange County in the 1950s. The Rillera brothers had a Filipino father and a Chicana mother. They took their first music lessons on the ukulele from the proprietor of a Hawaiian music store and learned how to play rancheras and boleros from their mother, who liked to listen to Chico Sesma's radio broadcasts of Mexican music. Their sister Nancy had Black friends who introduced her (and them) to the blues played by Lowell Fulson and B. B. King.[60] When Richard Berry, a Black vocalist from South Central Los Angeles, began singing with the Rhythm Rockers at Harmony Park in suburban Santa Ana, he noticed that the group had particular appeal to young Chicanos. The band often delighted listeners at Harmony Park with a version of Rene Touzet's "Loca cha cha." Berry took the beat of that song, added English-language lyrics, and composed "Louie Louie," the song that would be covered by the Kingsmen in 1964, much to the eventual (albeit completely unwarranted) consternation of the FBI (see chapter 7).[61]

The Rhythm Rockers did not become a successful recording act, but the musicians and singers they played with branched out into successful careers in different segments of the segregated music industry. Bill Medley and Bobby Hatfield became the Righteous Brothers, a group composed of two white males who sang songs in the "soulful" and Latin styles associated with Black and Mexican performers. Don (Bowman) Harris and Dewey Terry, both Black, became successful in rhythm and blues as Don and Dewey. Richard Berry had a small regional hit with "Louie Louie," although he never received the royalties owed him when the song became a hit for the Kingsmen. The Rillera brothers played with troubled "surf guitar" legend Dick Dale and eventually connected with Pat and Lolly Vasquez, two brothers from Fresno who recorded under the names Pat and Lolly Vegas, because their agent told them that the world was not yet ready to embrace a duo of Mexicans playing surfing music. Under the new name Vegas Brothers, adopted from the Nevada city synonymous with successful nightclub acts, the brothers hoped that they could go places that were denied to them as the Vasquez Brothers. In their early teens, with Pat on bass and Lolly on lead guitar, the Vegas Brothers had toured with Louisiana "swamp pop" star (and teen heartthrob) Jimmy Clanton. Drawing on the mixed Fresno neighborhood where they grew up and in which they interacted with Blacks who had moved west from Louisiana, they developed a bluesy sound. After their unsuccessful attempts to play surf music, they renamed themselves Redbone, the slang word employed in Fresno by displaced African Americans from Louisiana to describe a light-skinned black.

When Redbone performed at a Sunset Strip nightclub in the late 1960s, drummer Peter DePoe approached them and invited himself into the group. A Native American from a reservation in Washington, DePoe (also known as Lost Walking Bear) explained that the group needed him because they "sounded Indian," and he was an Indian. Taking inspiration from this comment, the Vasquez/ Vegas Brothers began performing in costumes resembling those worn by Plains Indians. They sang songs about Native American history, about the Paiute prophet Wovoka, the American Indian movement's takeover of Alcatraz Island, the nineteenth-century massacre at Wounded Knee, and its twentieth-century counterpart, which included a shootout between members of AIM and the FBI. When the brothers explained to their grandmother that DePoe's suggestion had led them to impersonate Indians onstage, she informed them that they *were* Indians. Their family had long known, but rarely mentioned, that the Vasquez lineage included Mexican Indians. When Peter DePoe left Redbone, Butch Rillera, the Filipino-Chicano from the Rhythm Rockers, replaced him.

Most listeners to Redbone's music knew nothing about the group's ethnic origins. It might have been difficult for them to comprehend that the band consisted of two Mexicans who pretended to be Indians because they had been unable to succeed as surf guitarists but who actually turned out to be Indian after all; that the band's drummer was Filipino and Mexican, a musician whose first instrument had been the Hawaiian ukulele, who had introduced Richard Berry to the beat of "Louie Louie," and who had performed with the Righteous Brothers and Don and Dewey before joining the Vasquez/Vegas Brothers in Redbone. Long after the physical spaces that gave rise to these interracial connections disappeared, they continued to influence the segregated popular music industry, even if only in extremely indirect form.

Like a weed in a vacant lot, the music of Redbone and that of Ry Cooder's *Chávez Ravine* keep alive memories of social sites that have been destroyed by urban renewal. They present testimony about the destruction of the emotional ecosystems of entire communities. They remind us of how society as a whole suffers from the absence of places that once existed. They do not undo the past, but their very existence testifies to the persistence and power of collective memory, the utility of music as a repository of social history, and the ways in which weeds pulled violently from the ground in one spot can throw out seeds that may blossom later in unexpected places.

6. Merengue

The Hidden History of Dominican Migration

> But the native intellectual who wishes to create an authentic work of
> art must realize that the truths of a nation are in the first place its re-
> alities. He must go on until he has found the seething pot out of which
> the learning of the future will emerge.
> —**Frantz Fanon,** *The Wretched of the Earth*

Anthony Santos's 1992 *bachata* **song** "Voy pa'lla" spoke to the
experiences of many of his fellow nationals from the Dominican
Republic. To the accompaniment of a lilting guitar and a steady
percussive beat, Santos's lyrics vowed that he was "going over
there" to find *la mujer qui me domina* (the woman who masters
me). At a time when nearly 10 percent of the population of the
Dominican Republic had immigrated to the United States, this
song about longing to be reunited with a loved one resonated with
the everyday concerns of many of its listeners.

Yet a deliberate ambiguity permeates the lyrics of "Voy pa'lla."
It is never clear whether *alla* (there) refers to the Dominican Republic or to New York City. Consequently the song could be interpreted both as an expression of diasporic longing for home *and*
as an expression of nationalist desire for reconnection with the
greater Dominican diaspora overseas.[1]

The popularity of "Voy pa'lla" exemplifies the crisis that con-
fronts traditional nationalisms in a transnational age. As Linda
Basch, Nina Glick Schiller, and Christina Szanton Blanc explain

in their influential and generative book *Nations Unbound,* transnationalism refers to "the processes by which immigrants forge
and sustain multi-stranded social relations that link together their
societies of origin and settlement."[2] Dominican history now takes
place in North America and Europe as well as in the Dominican
Republic, New York, San Juan, Madrid, and Rome in addition to
the nation's capital city, Santo Domingo de Guzmán.

Structural adjustment policies supported by the United States
have gradually shifted the Dominican economy toward offshore
manufacturing, tourism, and remittances from Dominican workers overseas. As many as one million Dominicans now live in the
United States and Puerto Rico, some four hundred thousand of
them in New York. In the early 1990s more immigrants arrived
in New York from the Dominican Republic than from any other
country.[3] So many Dominicans live in the Washington Heights
section of Manhattan that locals refer to the neighborhood as
"Quisqueya Heights," referencing the indigenous people of the
Dominican Republic.[4] The extensive migration that has taken
place from the city of Sabana Iglesias in the Dominican Republic
to Corona, Queens, leads many Dominicans to describe Corona
interlingually as "Sabana Church."[5] Hundreds of thousands of
Dominicans live in Spain, Venezuela, the Netherlands, Switzerland,
Greece, and Italy.[6] A Black Dominican immigrant, Denny Mendez,
even won the Miss Italy contest in 1996.[7] The two most favored
destinations for Dominican migration, however, remain the mainland of North America and Puerto Rico, locations that now play
an important role in the everyday lives of people in the Dominican
Republic as well.

Aspirants to elective offices in the Dominican Republic campaign on the streets of New York. All of the nation's political parties maintain offices and raise funds in the United States.[8] Leonel
Fernández Reyna, now filling his second stint as the president of the
Dominican Republic, spent his early years on Manhattan's Upper
West Side, held a U.S. "green card," and has vowed that once his
political service ends he intends to return to his family in New
York.[9] Newspapers from the Dominican Republic appear on news-
stands in the United States the day they are published. Dominican
journalists routinely report on the activities of Dominicans in
the United States, and television programs from the Dominican
Republic are broadcast simultaneously in the United States.[10]

These new social relations and cognitive mappings go beyond the traditional pattern of migration based on cycles of emigration, exile, and (perhaps) return. They entail the dynamism of circuits and networks through which people, products, culture, and capital move back and forth, maximizing individual and group opportunities by operating in more than one national or geographic context. The popularity of "Voy pa'lla" in the early 1990s emerged out of the crisis created for primarily "national" ways of knowing and being by the ever increasingly rapid mobility of products, people, ideas, images, capital, and culture in the transnational era.

It is fitting that a song (and a *bachata* song at that) emerged as one of the visible sites where Dominican nationalism would be troubled, problematized, and reconfigured. Few nations have grounded their nationalism in music more intensely and more specifically than the Dominican Republic. The *bachata* style performed by Santos had long been suppressed by Dominican elites, because it was identified with the dark-skinned poor and working-class majority of the nation. Merengue, on the other hand, has been the emblematic music of the island nation. Its champions associate it with the culture of the wealthy, light-skinned national bourgeoisie. The change from merengue to *bachata,* from light skin to dark skin, from lyrics about the island of Hispaniola to lyrics that might well be construed as referring to the island of Manhattan registers profound changes in Dominican national culture and subjectivity.

Few musical genres have been more fully infused with nationalist significance than the Dominican merengue. Characterized by lively 4/4 rhythms and an eighth note and four sixteenths at the end of every bar, the merengue originated with small combos orchestrated for the Hohner button accordion and a horizontally held double-headed *tambora,* a drum beaten by a gourd scraper *(guira)* on one side and by hand on the other.[11] The presence of the accordion reveals that transnationalism has a long history in the Dominican Republic (see chapter 10). In the nineteenth century, tobacco farmers in the Cibao region conducted extensive trade with Germany, receiving accordions in exchange for tobacco. Those accordions from Germany have played an important role in the national music of the Dominican Republic.

A rural music with a history that goes back to the 1840s, merengue first became associated with Dominican nationalism during the U.S. occupation of the country between 1916 and 1924. Bourgeois nationalists embraced the Cibao region's form of merengue as a distinctive marker of national identity in line with their program to mobilize Dominicans against the presence of U.S. Marines. Their efforts led to the conflation of merengue with Dominican nationalism during the dictatorship of Rafael Trujillo from 1930 to 1961.[12]

Trujillo came from a lower-middle-class family in San Cristóbal on the southern coast. He became familiar with the merengue music played by light-skinned residents of Cibao, near the north coast, during his military service. Trujillo put the power of the state behind merengue, because he viewed it as an emblematic icon of the nation's white, Spanish-speaking, and Catholic traditions, a source of national unity that provided a sharp contrast to the Dominican Republic's neighbors in Haiti, who were seen in this view as Black, French-speaking, and practitioners of vodou. Anxious about what he perceived as the threat to "white" Dominican identity from adjacent Haiti (even though people of African descent have lived in what is now the Dominican Republic since 1502) and eager to obscure the existence of his own Haitian grandmother, Trujillo used merengue at all official state functions and personal appearances. No one was allowed to leave a dance while the Orquesta Generalismo Trujillo played, not until the dictator himself departed, which, in at least one case, involved a stay of over twenty-four hours.[13]

Government promotion of merengue, however, went far beyond structuring ceremonial occasions of state. Trujillo used merengue music as direct propaganda. He commissioned musicians to compose some five hundred songs supporting his regime, making him one of the first dictators in history who literally, as well as figuratively, compelled his subjects to sing his praises. Songs with titles such as "Trujillo Is Great and Immortal," "Faith in Trujillo," and "We Venerate Trujillo" took center stage on the bandstands, in the jukeboxes, and in the record stores of the nation.[14] Trujillo's brother, José Arismendi (known as Petán), founded the Orquesta San José to play merengue songs during the 1940s and 1950s in a luxurious ballroom located inside the studio of his radio station, first called La Voz del Yuna (1942–45) and later called La Voz Dominicana (1945–61), the most powerful broadcast outlets in the country. At the dictator's insistence, the station played only merengue music during its nearly two-decade existence. Moreover, Arismendi banned any recorded music from the station, insisting on live performances exclusively during the station's twelve-hour broadcasting day. Consequently, the Dominican government kept a stable of merengue musicians from ten different ensembles on retainer around the clock to play on the station, further encouraging musicians in that impoverished country to master the genre.[15]

Merengue became an important tool for expressing Dominican national identity and for giving a local inflection to imports from abroad. Dominican bands created merengue arrangements of popular Brazilian sambas and Mexican rancheras. In the 1950s Felix del Rosario's arrangement of a South African song, "Skokiaan," for Antonio Morel y Su Orquesta, combined elements of merengue with U.S. big band jazz and South African *tsaba*.[16] Like many other aspects of official and popular culture in the Dominican Republic, the visual performance and lyrics of merengue during the Trujillo years valorized "whiteness," even though the dancing style associated with merengue stems from the dance steps invented by enslaved Africans, who had to confine themselves to dancing in small spaces because their owners kept their legs in chains. Despite their African origins, merengue songs exacerbated racial and class divisions within the country, marking as illegitimate those who did not conform to the idealized image.

Trujillo prohibited any direct acknowledgment of folk traditions with Haitian or African origins.[17] In 1937, these ideas took on deadly meaning when Trujillo ordered his troops to massacre Haitians. They murdered between ten thousand and thirty-five thousand people for the "crime" of being Haitian.[18] "Haitians are foreigners in our land," Trujillo explained. "They are dirty, rustlers of cattle and practitioners of Voodoo."[19] Many of the Haitians killed by Trujillo's troops resided on land that had traditionally been part of the nation of Haiti but was placed under the jurisdiction of the Dominican Republic by order of U.S. officials, who reconfigured the border between the two nations by giving disputed border land to Trujillo. In response to his slaughter, the United States negotiated a settlement that required Trujillo to pay an indemnity to Haiti of twenty-nine dollars for each officially "recognized" Haitian killed by his troops. The U.S. secretary of state Cordell Hull later referred to Trujillo as "one of the greatest men in Central America and in most of South America."[20]

Trujillo's racial politics expressed and exacerbated the core contradictions of the country itself. As Paul Austerlitz notes in his astute analysis, "While Trujillo massacred Haitians and propagated an anti-Haitian Dominican identity, he was of partial Haitian descent himself; while he proscribed blatantly African-influenced magic-religious customs, he practiced them himself; and while he chose a national music associated with what is arguably the country's most European region, *merengue ciabeno* itself has many African-derived characteristics. The music was an effective national symbol because it successfully articulated the contradictions of Dominican culture as well as of Trujillo's personality."[21]

People of African descent in the Dominican Republic learn to speak of themselves as *indio* rather than *negro*. Newspapers in the nation identify light- and dark-skinned Black people as either *indio claro* or *indio oscuro*.[22] Estimates of the number of Haitians in the Dominican Republic range from 150,000 to 500,000. Migration from the West Indies and Haiti has combined with intermarriage to gradually "blacken" the Dominican population, but as a result the official culture of the nation has become all that much more defensive and emphatic about its "whiteness."[23]

The aversive racism against Haiti cultivated within Dominican national culture has a political as well as a racial dimension. Dominicans celebrate February 27 as their national independence day, not because that is when they won their independence from Spain, but rather because on February 27, 1844, they secured their independence from Haiti by calling on Spain for assistance.[24] Although the light-skinned creole elite in Haiti has long held a near monopoly of power over that nation's political, economic, and military institutions, Haiti's national culture contains many elements that encourage the validation of Black identity as part of a larger program of egalitarian politics.[25]

The postrevolutionary Haitian republic outlawed slavery from the start, unlike the United States, the only other republic in the Western Hemisphere at the time. Antislavery sentiment also guided subsequent Haitian leaders, such as President Fabre-Nicholas Geffrard, who aided Dominicans struggling for independence from Spain by giving them supplies and refuge, largely because he preferred to share the island of Hispaniola with an independent Dominican Republic rather than with a Spanish colony, especially since Spain had not yet abolished slavery in Puerto Rico and Cuba.[26] Geffrard also ordered a special requiem mass in Haiti to mark the execution of the U.S. abolitionist John Brown in 1859.[27] The revolutionary ideals of Haiti's Black radical tradition threatened the racial basis for rule by the Dominican elite, and consequently they spared no expense in supporting reactionary forces on the Haitian side of the island. Trujillo secretly kept a retinue of Haitian politicians and public officials on his payroll throughout his years in power. Throughout his political career, President Elie Lescot of Haiti depended on covert funding from Trujillo.[28]

Within the Dominican Republic, the assassination of Trujillo in 1961, his succession by a brief period of popular reform, and the years of economic austerity and repressive rule by the dictator's former secretary Joaquín Balaguer (president for all but eight years between 1966 and 1996) have not diminished Dominicans' enthusiasm for merengue. In fact, because merengue received public support and secured market success during the Trujillo years, musicians from other genres, including the despised rural and lower class *bachata,* often adopted the tempos and instrumentation of merengue to make themselves sound more respectable.

Sometimes merengue artists deployed the genre against the politics of its patron. During the 1965 U.S. military occupation of the island (aimed at overthrowing the popularly elected president Juan Bosch and installing a regime that would support Trujilloism without Trujillo), merengue artist Johnny Ventura performed songs commenting on the crisis to raise the spirits and morale of the followers of Bosch's Partido Revolucionario Dominicano, noting, "Those of us who become artists and in some way are the voice of the people should use this voice to denounce wrongdoings, to show the way, to help us get along better."[29] Similarly, Cuco Valoy's "No me empuje" (Don't Push Me) was widely viewed as a rebuke to the U.S. troops.[30] Merengue has remained the most popular national music, even though it had been associated with a hated tyrant who demanded total control over the country's cultural life. As Dominican labor leader Fafa Taveras explains, merengue expresses national identity and national pride to a degree unmatched by any other cultural form.[31]

The permutations of Dominican merengue music over the past decades provide a particularly useful example of how commodity culture, transnational investments, remittances, and migrant labor paradoxically reinforce *and* subvert traditional understandings of the nation. When 10 percent of the population of the Dominican Republic migrated to the United States (and another 10 percent to Spain, Italy, and other destinations in Europe), merengue became even more important as a potentially unifying national symbol. Yet, experiences overseas transformed Dominican culture in significant ways that have changed merengue as well.

The influx of large numbers of immigrants into the United States since 1965 may seem like the cumulative consequence of millions of idiosyncratic individual decisions. Yet, as Saskia Sassen argues, it is the nations with the closest military, political, and financial ties with the United States that send the greatest numbers of migrants. "They" are over *here,* because "we" have been over *there.*[32] The geopolitical needs and interests of the United States as articulated by the national security establishment have played a central role in provoking immigration to the United States from Hispaniola, the island shared by the Dominican Republic and Haiti. Although the number of Haitian and Dominican immigrants to the United States has increased rapidly in recent years, the ties that bind those nations to the United States are neither recent nor idiosyncratic.

One important part of the traditional U.S. diplomatic strategy toward the Caribbean region has entailed expanding U.S. control over the Dominican Republic and propping it up as a white, Spanish, and Catholic alternative to Haiti's Black, French, and vodou-practicing society. In 1905 the United States took control of customs collections in all Dominican ports and installed George R. Colton, a retired army officer, as general receiver and collector for the Dominican Republic. Colton had previously served the empire as director of the customs service in the Philippines when U.S. troops began their occupation of that country.[33] The United States took control of all Dominican finances in 1907 through the Dominican–American Convention, a role it retained until 1940. A year after launching an invasion and commencing an occupation of Haiti, Woodrow Wilson authorized a formal "legal" military invasion of the Dominican Republic when it appeared as if a faction considered hostile to U.S. interests might attain power in the country. Captain Harry Knapp of the U.S. Navy's flagship U.S.S. *Olympia* issued a proclamation from the port in Santo Domingo dissolving the Dominican government and announcing a military occupation of the country by U.S. troops, which lasted until 1924.[34] Military rule enabled the United States to remove Dominican duties on products made in the United States, enabling manufacturers to flood Dominican markets with goods and destroy their local competitors.[35]

During this first occupation period, the American constabulary offered training to many Dominican military officers, including Rafael Leonidas Trujillo. He took power in a 1930 coup and presided over a brutal and corrupt dictatorship for the next thirty-one years, aided and abetted by a phalanx of U.S. allies from both the public and private sectors.[36] At the end of a chaotic period after Trujillo's assassination, right-wing military officials attempted to stop elections that seemed certain to bring to power liberal nationalist Juan Bosch. Loyal "constitutionalist" troops supported Bosch and distributed weapons to the Dominican people, but when they secured control of the capital, U.S. president Lyndon Johnson ordered yet another military invasion of the Dominican Republic, sending twenty-three thousand troops to the tiny country to prevent Bosch's return to power. Claiming that unidentified "communists" had taken over the leadership of the popular constitutionalist forces, the United States sanctioned covert and overt repression by right-wing military officers, orchestrating Joaquín Balaguer's election to the presidency in 1966. When Balaguer's policies exacerbated social and political tensions in the Dominican Republic, the United States followed a policy of encouraging migration to the United States as a safety valve designed to protect Balaguer's unjust, plutocratic, and ultimately dictatorial regime.[37]

Almost sixty thousand Dominicans immigrated to the United States between 1965 and 1969.[38] As early as 1968, the amount of money that entered the Dominican economy as remittances sent back home from workers in the United States exceeded what the Dominican Republic earned from the sale of its main export commodities, nickel and sugar.[39] Nearly one-third of the revenues brought into the Dominican Republic by "tourists" now comes from Dominicans living outside the country. Estimates of remittances from overseas workers now total between five hundred million and nine hundred million dollars.[40]

Within the Dominican Republic itself, consolidation of agricultural holdings by transnational corporations led to the displacement of rural residents to Dominican cities. The population of Santo Domingo de Guzmán doubled between 1961 and 1970. More than 50 percent of the Dominican population lived in urban areas by 1980.[41] Displaced from rural settings and unable to secure employment in cities, Dominican workers continued arriving in New York in large numbers during the 1970s and 1980s.

Austerity policies mandated by the International Monetary Fund and the World Bank made migration more attractive by making life in the Dominican Republic more difficult, continually undermining the earnings of Dominican workers. Patricia Pessar points out that the minimum wage for full-time work in the United States in 1980 was four times greater than in the Dominican Republic but climbed to six times greater by 1987 and to thirteen times by 1991.[42] Just as political terror (and U.S. bombing) in El Salvador fueled the growth of low-wage jobs in the garment industry in Los Angeles by producing refugees desperate for work, refugees whose availability enabled employers to violate minimum-wage laws and fair-labor practices, U.S. foreign policies favoring structural adjustment in the economy of the Dominican Republic instigated an influx of low-wage workers to New York, producing lasting consequences for the economy of that city.

The Dominican presence in New York helped drive down wages in the city while New York transitioned from a metropolis with an extensive number of high-wage jobs to one where janitors, domestics, child care workers, security guards, garment workers, low-wage factory operatives, and personal service workers became the fastest growing sectors of the labor force.[43] The "employer sanctions" provision of the 1986 Immigration Reform and Control Act did not lessen the demand for low-wage labor but instead encouraged manufacturers to "outsource" production processes (and transfer all risks) to undercapitalized immigrant entrepreneurs who routinely violated federal, state, and municipal labor regulations.[44] Dominicans rank with Puerto Ricans as the most impoverished ethnic groups in New York City. More than a third of "Dominicanyorks" live in poverty.[45] Almost 50 percent work as operatives, laborers, and personal service workers. Only 9 percent are self-employed, most of these as proprietors of extremely small businesses.[46] Hundreds of Dominican doctors in New York fill jobs far below those for which they trained, laboring for low wages as home care givers, paramedics, and research assistants.[47]

Dominicans carry their national consciousness with them to New York, but they encounter social relations significantly different from those they experienced back home. Interactions with dark-skinned Puerto Ricans, African Americans, and West Indians in the United States sometimes stir up old anxieties and antagonisms, but they also encourage escape from the constraints of Dominican racial categories. Some African Americans may initially view Dominicans as simply another group of foreigners with whom they have to compete for scarce resources, and some Dominicans might at first view inequality in the United States as a consequence of Black deficiencies rather than of white supremacy. But since members of both groups are viewed as equally "Black" by employers, police officers, teachers, landlords, and the media, they experience similar if not identical relations to the social distribution of suffering in the city.

The racial economy of New York City has enabled many Dominicans to reconsider their Afro-Dominican heritage. Musicologist Martha Ellen Davis notes the emphasis on African music and dance in the cultural work carried on by Luis Dias, Tony Vicioso, Bony Raposo, and Jose Duluc, among others. She notes, "In New York City where 'black is beautiful' has long been an integral part of the ideological configuration, their message is well received, celebrated, and subsidized."[48] Afro-Dominican dancer and choreographer Josefina Baez responds to the extensive intercultural dynamics of New York City in a piece titled *Dominicanish* (a play on Dominican, Spanish, and English). In this work, Baez incorporates Afro-Dominican elements into *kuchipudi*, a classical Indian dance form, and then blends that fusion with the movements enacted by the Isley Brothers in their performances of rhythm-and-blues music. Baez notes that she learned English as a young Dominican immigrant to New York City by watching performances on the *Soul Train* television show by the group she refers to as "los hermanos Isley" and "los Isley Brothers." Referring to the Isleys as her "professors," Baez raises her fist as she recalls the "poetry that they taught" her, proclaiming, "Fight the Power!"[49]

Dominican immigrant activists and ordinary citizens participated enthusiastically in the spring 2006 protests against House Resolution 4437, one of the most vicious anti-immigrant measures ever introduced in the House of Representatives. A few months later, Haitians and Afro-Dominicans in the Dominican Republic confronted yet another wave of assaults and deportations. A mob in the Hatillo Palma district of Monte Cristi attacked Haitians with machetes and burned down Haitian dwellings after learning that three Haitians had been charged with the killing of a

Dominican woman during a robbery. Mark Torres, a Dominican active in the binational immigrant Grupo de Acción Dominico-Haitiano, called for his fellow countrymen to protest against the attacks on Haitians and Afro-Dominicans. It would be hypocritical, he charged, to fight for immigrant rights for themselves in the United States without also speaking out on behalf of the Haitian immigrants who suffered from mistreatment and racism in the Dominican Republic. Living as migrants in the United States gave Torres and his group a new perspective on race in their country of origin as well as their country of arrival.[50]

Migration also upsets the gendered balance of power within families, requiring new roles and responsibilities of women while diminishing the historical privileges and power wielded by men. A 1981 survey found that more than 90 percent of Dominican women worked for wages outside the home in New York City, even though less than a third of them had been similarly employed when they lived in the Dominican Republic. Pessar's research reveals that wage work in the United States gives women leverage that enables them to secure their husbands' help with child care and house cleaning tasks. Dominican men in the United States need the incomes their partners earn, and, as a result, they can no longer make budget decisions unilaterally.[51]

On the terrain of culture, the Dominican community today experiences what Juan Flores calls "branching out," in reference to Puerto Ricans in New York. Flores argues that Puerto Ricans in New York move "toward those groups to whom they stand in closest proximity, not only spatially but also because of parallel cultural experience." Flores explains that this "growing together" is often misread as the "dissolution of national backgrounds and cultural histories" or as simple assimilation, but "the difference is obvious in that it is not directed toward incorporation into the dominant culture. For that reason, the 'pluralism' that results does not involve the dissolution of national backgrounds and histories but their continued affirmation and enforcement even as they are transformed."[52]

Dominican migrants to New York have often found themselves closer to Puerto Ricans there than they had been to those residing in their home country. Dominican Johnny Pacheco came to the United States in 1946 at the age of eleven. He participated in a broad range of jazz and salsa musical ensembles, eventually helping found Fania Records, the most important salsa label in the world during the 1970s.[53] Entry into Puerto Rican culture for him entailed contact with dark-skinned Afro-Cuban musicians, creative interaction with African American jazz players, and cultural and political alliances with the civil rights and Black Power movements of midcentury.

As early as the 1960s, racist treatment on the U.S. mainland propelled some Dominicans to embrace philosophies of Black Power and Black self-affirmation. Experiences in subsequent decades, both as immigrant low-wage laborers *and* as people racialized by North American categories in the United States, have further honed this racial consciousness.[54] During the 1980s, New York–based merengue artists brought these new experiences into their traditional music. In 1984, merengue trumpet virtuoso (and former postal carrier) Wilfrido Vargas released "El africano," an international merengue hit featuring lyrics with a decidedly stereotypical depiction of "primitive" Blackness. Yet Vargas also produced merengue versions of Haitian *konpa* music, including his 1985 hit "El jardinero," a song that blends *tamboras* and *guiras* with synthesizers, horns, and rap music.[55]

In the 1980s and 1990s, Juan Luis Guerra, a light-skinned musician who still lives in the Dominican Republic, recorded tremendously popular merengues that reject racist imagery relating to Haitians and dark-skinned Dominicans. Dark-skinned Cuco Valoy, who started his career during the Trujillo years and who has worked mainly in the Dominican Republic, arranged *bachata* songs as merengues, a gesture that elevated the status of *bachata*. In 1987, Blas Duran introduced the solid-body electric guitar to merengue with his song "Consejo a las mujeres," bringing touches of Anglo-American rock 'n' roll and Afro-American dance music to the genre. In the early 1990s, a series of female performers, including Millie Quezada and Alexandra Taveras, achieved star status in what had previously been an exclusively male genre. Lyrics of merengue songs often chronicle the experiences of workers and refugees. Certainly the desire to reach new audiences and secure greater exposure played a part in these changes, but the avenues open to merengue artists have depended on the new life circumstances of Dominicans in the United States.

The popularity of Juan Luis Guerra and his group 4:40 (named after the 440-hertz vibrations emitted at the A pitch on a tuning fork) provides a particularly significant illustration of the ways in which commercial culture can combine with ethnic life and labor to refashion a national culture. The son of a Spanish mother and a Dominican father, Guerra studied literature in the Dominican Republic. He drew inspiration from eclectic sources, from the poetry of Pablo Neruda and the music of the Beatles, the Rolling Stones, and Pink Floyd. Sometimes he detected familiar things in music from far away. He remembers hearing the version of "Till There Was You" recorded by the Beatles (featuring Paul McCartney) as "a kind of bolero, a *bachata* without bongos or maracas." Later on in life, Guerra adapted the sounds he remembered from his youth, deploying the cornets audible on the Beatles' "Penny Lane" and the violin arrangements on "Eleanor Rigby" in his production of "Ojala que llueva café" (I Hope It Rains Coffee) as performed by himself and his group 4:40.[56] After attending the Berklee School of Music in Boston, where he specialized in jazz but financed his studies by recording television commercials in the Dominican Republic, Guerra brought a new dimension to the merengue by slowing down the beat, adding jazz harmonies, and writing lyrics on social issues in the spirit of the great Cuban *neuva canción* singer–songwriter Silvio Rodriguez.[57]

Guerra's 1990 album, *Bachata Rosa,* sold 3.5 million units, an astounding total for any Spanish-language singer, much less one from a country as small as the Dominican Republic. By faithfully "covering" the *bachata* sound, Guerra derived remuneration and acclaim for mastering a working-class genre that he had previously ignored. Of course, his light skin and mastery of Anglo-American pop music forms enabled Guerra to receive rewards unavailable to most *bachata* performers. At the same time, however, Guerra also helped bring *bachata* and merengue closer together, securing augmented commercial viability for both.[58] His adventurous forays outside merengue traditions expressed the branching-out of Dominicans in New York City, and he used them to reexamine race relations within the Dominican Republic and beyond.

Guerra's song "Guavaberry" used calypso music and English-language lyrics to evoke the voices of Black *cocolos* (workers from Jamaica, the Virgin Islands, the Turks and Caicos, St. Kitts–Nevis, and Anguilla) in the Dominican city of San Pedro de Macorís (just as the Nicaraguan group Soul Vibrations had earlier accomplished for that nation's anglophone Black population along the Atlantic coast).[59] On his album *Areito,* Guerra called attention to the Taino Indians, the indigenous inhabitants of the Caribbean, especially on his salsa–merengue song "Si saliera petroleo" (If We Struck Oil), which refers to the Dominican Republic by its Taino name, Quisqueya.[60]

Guerra also employed Afro-Caribbean zouk rhythms from Martinique and Guadeloupe on "Rosalia." He recorded "A pedir su mano" (To Ask for Your Hand), a merengue version of the song "Dede Priscilla," by Lea Lignazi from the Central African Republic.[61] His song "El costo de la vida" (The Cost of Living) is based on a tune by Zairean guitarist Diblo, whom Guerra first heard playing at the New York night spot SOB's.[62] The appreciation that Guerra extended to African music with these songs may reflect a recognition of the huge influence merengue has had in Africa. Dominicans may routinely deny their African origins, but Africans can hear themselves when they listen to music from the Dominican Republic. Congolese musician Nico plays a Hawaiian steel guitar but refers to his music as merengue, because it sounds to him (and his listeners) like the "stuttering" accordions of Dominican merengue.[63]

Guerra and other contemporary merengue artists now acknowledge the rich cultural exchanges that have taken place between Dominicans and Haitians. Radio broadcasts and touring bands regularly brought Dominican merengue to Haiti, even when the two countries seemed on the verge of war. Angel Viloria enjoyed popularity as a merengue performer in Haiti (with the Haitian form of the genre), even though he was not popular in his native Dominican Republic. Despite official disapproval, Haitian music has often been popular in the Dominican Republic as well.[64] Catholic Haitians venerate the patroness of the Dominican Republic, the Virgen de la altagracia.[65] On *Mal de amor,* Guerra pays tribute to Haitian songwriter Nemours Jean-Baptiste, the founder of Haitian *konpa direk* music, who had been strongly influenced by Dominican merengue.[66]

Guerra's lyrics remind listeners that emigration has been a group experience as well as an individual decision, a product of global forces, not just local realities. Much of his band's initial popularity came from the Dominican community in New York.[67] The lyrics of Guerra's song "Visa para un sueño" (Visa for a Dream) express the anguish of people desperate to leave the Dominican Republic, both those who secure visas through legal channels and those who try desperately to cross the seas in makeshift rafts to immigrate illegally. The song's up-tempo rhythms and swirling orchestration suggest determination, but the sounds of helicopter rotors at the end remind listeners of the pain of those picked up in the sea off the coast of Puerto Rico and returned home by the INS, only to have to try to sneak out again the next day. Like Wilfrido Vargas's "La yola," which warns would-be refugees to Puerto Rico that they might be eaten by sharks, Guerra's "Visa para un sueño" documents the desperation of many of today's transnational migrants.[68]

In 1990 alone, U.S. Coast Guard patrols intercepted almost four thousand Dominicans in the waters near Puerto Rico, and authorities deported close to fifteen thousand Dominicans found to have entered Puerto Rico illegally. Perhaps as many as eighty thousand Dominicans have become permanent residents of Puerto Rico, finding employment as domestic workers and street vendors as well as in other low-wage occupations.[69] In Puerto Rico, rivalries and antagonisms divide Puerto Ricans from Dominicans to an even greater degree than they do in New York, yet at the same time merengue has become more popular than salsa in Puerto Rico, and members of a new generation of Dominican Puerto Ricans have been actively creating new cultural and political identities that differ from those available in either New York or the Dominican Republic.[70]

In "Ojalá que llueva café," Guerra takes his lyrics from an anonymously authored poem that he discovered in a small Dominican village, Santiago de los Caballeros. In it, he sings about the everyday experiences of campesinos, displaying powerful sympathy for their struggles to survive in the globalized economy.[71] Merengue's emphasis on dance, its history as the country's national music, and the lyrics of many songs make this genre one of the places where the immigrant community comes into existence as a distinctly new social entity formed out of both new and old common experiences, memories, and affective ties.

While merengue helps Dominicans in New York to draw selectively on their past to face the problems of the present, it also reflects the new opportunities available in the United States. Like Guerra, the New York Band brings an international flavor to Dominican national music, singing songs in Spanish, English, and French, as a means of seeking a broader market, to be sure, but in the process also enhancing pan-Caribbean and panhemispheric consciousness among Dominicans. The New York Band's merengue songs display strong traces of Trinidadian soca, a genre that is itself a blend of soul and calypso.[72] Cuco Valoy draws brilliantly on Cuban musical influences, and Wilfrido Vargas mixes zouk, reggae, *konpa,* and rap music with merengue and *bachata* into an eclectic new sound.[73] The band known as La Gran Manzana (The Big Apple) blended very new kinds of synthesizer music with some very old styles that clearly had Haitian origins.[74]

Differences between the United States and the Dominican Republic with respect to accepted gender roles have also influenced the course of merengue. The music of the migrant community reflects the changes in gender roles that have resulted from the new economic opportunities for Dominican women, who outnumber male migrants by at least a three-to-two ratio. Millie Quezada developed her career in multiracial, multicultural New York, leading a very popular family band, Los Vecinos. She claims that her group had no conscious intention of challenging gender roles within Dominican culture, but her sister and fellow band member, Jocelyn, argues that she thought of their efforts as a conscious assertion of gender equity. "We were making a statement," she explains, "because Dominican men are very male chauvinist; I mean, women stay home and cook. So, when we stood up in front of a band . . . women in the audience would identify with us. And the songs that we used to sing, we were attacking men: If you don't take care of your woman, you're going to lose her. So we had a lot of women fans, we still do."[75]

Similarly, the group Chantelle consists of three Puerto Rican women: Brenda Zoe Hernandez, Annette Ramos Sosa, and Doreen Ann Zayas. Fefita La Grande brings a woman's perspective to merengue through her performances as an accordionist and singer in working-class taverns in New York's heavily Dominican Washington Heights neighborhood.[76] Alexandra Taveras, who serves as lead singer for the New York Band, tries to incorporate a woman's point of view into her lyrics. "I tell the women we don't have to take everything that comes to us, and they love it," she explains. The members of Las Chicas del Can provide a decidedly less feminist image, structuring their stage show and attire largely for the scopophilic pleasure of men. Yet the mere presence of women like the group's trumpet player and leader, Maria Acosta, and vocalists Miriam Cruz and Eunice Betances onstage in merengue challenges the hierarchies of the past and has served as an inspiration to women throughout Latin America to take up instruments and join musical aggregations.[77] Merengue and *bachata* remain decidedly male-oriented musics celebrating the macho *tigerete* ideals of Dominican society, but the emergence in New York of female merengue and *bachata* artists signals at least the potential for change in the music's sex and gender coding.

Dominican migration has also changed the demographics of merengue listeners and performers. Deborah Pacini Hernandez reports that revenues secured from sales of Latin music and videos doubled between 1995 and 1998, with approximately a third of that total generated in the United States. The largest Dominican recording label, J&N, garners 75 percent of its sales in New York City, and Puerto Rico has become the second largest market for the company. The Dominican Republic now lags far behind in third place in the company's tallies of sales. Puerto Rican women singers now produce some of the most commercially successful merengue recordings.[78]

The reach of merengue and the scope of its influence on New York popular culture became clear in 2000, when Patrick Shannon, a blue-collar Irish American cable TV installer, emerged as an artistically respected and commercially viable merengue singer. Shannon first learned about merengue when he became friendly with Puerto Rican coworkers who invited him to join them at a local club. He taught himself Spanish by listening to Spanish-language radio broadcasts and watching Spanish-language television programs. "The only day I didn't listen to Spanish," he recalls, "was St. Paddy's Day." Shannon's song "Estase enamorada" climbed to number seventeen on Billboard's Latin Music charts, and he opened for Nuyorican singer Marc Anthony at the civic center in Hartford.[79] Just as some Puerto Ricans and Irish Americans become merengue stars, some Dominicans in the music industry in New York blend merengue with salsa, house, dancehall, and hip hop. Dark Latin Groove, Proyecto Uno, Fulanito, and Los Illegales bring together Dominicans, Puerto Ricans, and other Latinos to create hybrid music with no identifiable geographical home.

Dominican merengue artists have not tampered with their national music and launched an attack on Dominican national identity because they are postmodern theorists. Their new identities grow inexorably from the circumstances of their lives and labor. The music that once emblematized the ideal of a unified and racially homogeneous nation-state now reveals the multiracial character of the country and registers the inexorable interconnectedness of contemporary culture and commerce in a transnational frame. A music traditionally performed only by men and filled with lyrics from a male point of view now finds that many of its most important artists are women, who sing about the new realities that they, and their female fans, face in the transnational economy. Merengue still serves as a sensitive register of the social life of the Dominican nation, but the transnational nature of Dominican society reveals that nation to be more complex and more connected to other nations than the old nationalist merengues could ever admit.

The transformations that have occurred within merengue music are part of a larger pattern. After several centuries in which nationalism was the central modality through which people and nations entered modernity, transnational patterns and practices now seem on the ascendancy everywhere. Technological innovations such as containerization in shipping, computer-based "on time" manufacturing, Internet "e-commerce," and the simultaneous transmission and reception of information through satellite and fiber optic media all tend to make individual nations (as well as individual workers and consumers) seem like interchangeable components in a linked and fully integrated global system.

The eclipse of national projects by seemingly unaccountable transnational power comes as a crisis for millions of people around the world. The egalitarian and democratic reforms of the mid-twentieth century seemed to be just starting to address their hopes and aspirations for a better life. The new realities that we have come to subsume under the terms *globalization* and *transnationalism* come to us in the context of an orchestrated global counter-revolution against the very policies that emerged out of midcentury struggles for decolonization, national independence, civil rights, and social democratic reforms.

Every day more than thirty thousand children under the age of five in Asia, Africa, and Latin America perish from malnutrition or completely curable diseases.[80] One million orphaned and abandoned children in Africa now live homeless, fending for themselves on the streets. Nearly two-thirds of the 4.4 billion people dwelling in the poorest countries in Africa, Asia, and Latin America do not have access to basic sanitation facilities. One billion people in the world lack access to safe and uncontaminated water. Of the 828 million people that suffer from chronic hunger, nearly a third will die before their fortieth birthday.[81] Global income inequality enables entrepreneurs to profit from "sex tourism," which encourages wealthy European and American predators to purchase sex from desperately poor and virtually defenseless adults, teens, and children in the Caribbean and Asia.[82] Thousands of women in Latin America, Asia, and the Caribbean receive wages so low that they suffer from undernourishment, but they work in sweatshops that make sweatsuits and other exercise paraphernalia designed for affluent European and North American consumers seeking physical fitness while consuming diets loaded with sugar and fat.[83]

The nation-state does not disappear in our transnational age. Inequalities and differences among nations make transnational capitalism possible, putting each nation in competition with others in a race to the bottom—to provide the lowest taxes, the lowest wages, the poorest welfare benefits, and the weakest environmental and human rights laws. Nationalism and national rivalries increase in ferocity as the autonomy and independence of nations decline. Paradoxically, nationalism becomes one of the most important projects of transnational capital, because it is the very inequality produced by the existence of different nations that gives rapidly mobile capital both its profit-making potential and its apparent freedom from accountability and regulation.

Yet while the nation does not disappear, it does become transformed. When nationalism and national politics no longer serve as viable mechanisms for extracting concessions from capital, people increasingly augment their identities as national citizens with their diverse activities as transnational subjects, including their lives as consumers. Transnationalism produces new social relations that encourage the development of new social subjects. These subjects draw on unconventional archives and produce new cultural imaginaries, with new epistemologies, ontologies, and identities.

Transnational networks dramatically transform traditional gender roles and racial identifications; they bring to the surface many of the heterogeneous realities that the homogeneity of nationalism once obscured. The practices of the past that linked patriotism to patriarchy, permeated nationalism with pronatalist misogyny, and linked the destiny of the nation to the masculine privileges enjoyed by its men all become more visible and easier to confront once the nation no longer seems to deliver on its promises of a better future. At the same time, racism becomes revealed as both a national and a transnational project. The deadly links between race and nation become ever more evident, even in those nations that directly disavow any racial dimension to their national projects.

Perhaps most important, much of what seems radically new about transnationalism becomes exposed as part of a long history. The people of the Dominican Republic have never been as scattered around the globe as they are now. But they were never as unified at home or as uninfluenced by foreign culture and commerce as old-style nationalism encouraged them to believe. Emphasis on the seemingly separate, atomized, and discrete qualities of each national culture has occluded the always-international nature of the nation and its national symbols, even the merengue music that once signaled the autonomy of Dominicans from people from other nations but now registers their inescapably close interconnections.

7. The Hip Hop Hearings

The Hidden History of Deindustrialization

The playing field of contemporary culture may be new but it is still not level.

—Juan Flores, *From Bomba to Hip-Hop:*
Puerto Rican Culture and Latino Identity

In an early moment in Toni Morrison's 1977 novel *Song of Solomon,* teenager Guitar Baines voices a complaint to two men in a barber shop: he reports that the owner of the local pool hall will not sell him a beer. One of the barbers, Railroad Tommy, feels little sympathy for him. Summoning up the rancor he feels from a lifetime of disappointments, slights, refusals, and resentments, the barber points his finger at the youth and asks, "Is that all? He wouldn't let you have a beer?"

Drawing on his own bitter experiences, Railroad Tommy then offers the youth named Guitar a litany of all the other things he is *not* going to get in life, all the luxuries that the barber witnessed during his years working as a Pullman porter but never secured for himself: a private coach with red velvet chairs, a special private toilet, a custom-made eight-foot bed, a valet, a cook, a traveling secretary to attend to personal needs, enough money in the bank to get a loan without collateral, timber to sell, a ship to sail, a train to run, military honors, a breakfast tray with a red rose and warm croissants and hot chocolate delivered to your bed in the morning, pheasant baked in coconut leaves, vintage fine wine, and the dessert of ice cream inside a warm cake known as baked Alaska.

Intimidated by Railroad Tommy's torrent of bitterness unleashed by the complaint about not being able to buy a beer, Guitar Baines tries to lighten up the mood. "No baked Alaska?" he exclaims in mock horror. "You breaking my heart!" Seizing on the young man's choice of words, Railroad Tommy replies, "Well, now. That's something you will have—a broken heart." As the merriment dies in his eyes, Railroad Tommy adds, "And folly. A whole lot of folly. You can count on it."[1]

The exchange that Morrison stages between Guitar Baines and Railroad Tommy presupposes generational differences. Guitar Baines wants immediate gratification and pleasure today. His complaint does not get him any sympathy from Railroad Tommy, however, because the barber knows that many more disappointments and frustrations lie ahead. Yet the youth cannot possibly know why his elder is so upset. A shared sorrow produces conflict rather than connection between the two characters, because they see things from different generational frames.

This illustrative anecdote encapsulates many of Morrison's descriptions and plot devices in *Song of Solomon*. The novel revolves around intergenerational inheritance and antagonism, around the ways in which the pursuit of property and pleasure can cause suffering to others. Yet in a society based on property rights, not owning property can be hell. The long fetch of history in the novel shows that racism is an impediment to inheriting assets that appreciate in value and can be passed down to subsequent generations for Blacks. Only the injuries suffered by one generation become inherited by the next, not monetary wealth and property. The young condemn their elders constantly for the poverty and powerlessness that seem to be their lot without knowing the history of how things got that way, while the elders know so much about that history they can scarcely begin to communicate it to their children.

At a key moment in the novel, however, Morrison's narrator identifies the importance of work, achievement, and success. Money as an end in itself is corrupt, but discipline, dedication, work, and achievement in any endeavor are important. The narrator describes the farm that the protagonist's grandfather built after his emancipation from slavery. His hard work created a home and a business that encouraged other Blacks to think they could succeed too. His work "colored their lives like a paintbrush and spoke to them like a sermon," indicating that with discipline, determination, and work they could secure inclusion in a country whose history had been premised on their exclusion. "But they shot the top of his head off and ate his fine Georgia peaches," Morrison's narrator writes, explaining that jealous whites could not tolerate a success that would serve as a good example to other Blacks. "And even as boys these men began to die and were dying still," Morrison's narrator contends.[2] Cut off from their inheritance, denied the power of a good example, Blacks suffer the death of hope from the murder of Macon Dead Sr., and the injury continues across generations. They do not get a private coach with red velvet chairs, money in the bank, a ship to sail, or even baked Alaska. But they do inherit a whole lot of folly.

In 1994, Black youths across the United States encountered a whole lot of folly from an unexpected source, from some members of the Black Congressional Caucus. At a time of severe unemployment, systematic housing discrimination, educational inequality, and rampant police brutality, these representatives launched an inquiry into the lyrics of rap music. They responded to overwhelming structural problems in society with a moral panic—a publicity campaign designed to portray people *with* problems *as* problems. Moral panics about popular music have a long and dishonorable history. Adult anxiety about the behavior and values of young people has often led to attempts to blame the music young people like for disturbing cultural changes. In the United States at different moments during the twentieth century, efforts to suppress and censor Dixieland jazz, swing, bebop, and rock 'n' roll have all served as occasions where antiyouth and anti-Black discourses have blended together. It should not have been surprising, then, that hip hop would face the same fate. The moral panic over hip hop in the early 1990s took a novel turn, however, when these African American elected officials decided to take leading roles in attributing youth crime, drug use, and social disintegration in their communities to the popularity of "gangsta rap" music.

U.S. representative Cardiss Collins, of Illinois, a member of the Black Congressional Caucus, presided over hearings in 1994. Held in response to a request by C. Delores Tucker, of the National

Political Congress of Black Women, the hearings revealed deep divisions among Blacks, not only about the lyrics of gangsta rap songs, but also about the problems confronting African Americans in general. Although the sponsors of the hearings, key witnesses, and committee members all insisted that their efforts were directed solely against the music that young people liked rather than against the youths themselves, the hearings and the circumstances that brought them into being in the first place offered clear evidence of a deep chasm across generational lines.

Many witnesses at the hearings claimed that gangsta rap lyrics encouraged disrespect for women and that they glorified and promoted crime. The music's defenders claimed that the critics were blaming the messengers for news they did not wish to face, that gangster rap reported, recorded, and registered social changes that young people had seen with their own eyes, that gangsta rap was one of the few sites in U.S. society capable of telling the truth about the devastation caused by deindustrialization and disinvestment in inner-city communities, about the effects of economic restructuring, the failure to enforce civil rights laws, the pervasiveness of police brutality, and the evisceration of the social wage caused by tax cuts and shifts in government spending away from social services and toward military procurement. Largely absent from this debate was an appreciation of how arguments over song lyrics obscured the ways in which both neoconservative and neoliberal racial politics had driven a wedge between generations, not just among African Americans, but among young people and their elders in other groups as well.

Ostensibly a debate about culture and crime, about censorship and social behavior, the hearings about gangsta rap actually advanced the agenda of the enemies of the Black community by demonizing the victims of unjust social policies, by attacking the most public and visible manifestation of these problems in popular culture. Gangsta rap emerged in neoconservative and neoliberal cosmologies as the only plausible explanation for contemporary ruptures between genders and among generations and racial groups, because people in power refuse to take responsibility for their own actions, for the policies that have created the very problems they purport to decry. Their efforts to censor and suppress gangsta rap music have attempted to obscure the social causes and consequences of disturbing historical changes, rendering as individual and personal experiences that actually have broad-based collective origins and effects.

Invited to present her views as the first witness at the hearings, C. Delores Tucker invoked the moral authority of Martin Luther King Jr. on behalf of her cause. She alleged that if the martyred civil rights leader were alive today he "would be marching and demonstrating against the glamorization of violence and its corrupting influence, which has now become a part of our culture in the name of freedom. This freedom, freedom from responsibility and accountability, is not the kind of freedom that Dr. King, Medgar Evers, John Lewis, James Farmer, Rosa Parks and so many others risked their lives for."[3] Tucker claimed that for four hundred years African Americans had maintained a sense of humanity and morality that enabled them to survive the middle passage, slavery, and other horrors. But by the 1990s, "our morality, which has been the last vestige of our strength, [was] being threatened" by "lyrics out of the mouths of our own children," in her view.[4] Describing gangsta rap as "pornographic smut," Tucker alleged that this music provokes our youths to violence, drug use, and mistreatment of women. "This explains why so many of our children are out of control and why we have more black males in jail than we have in college," she charged.[5]

Syndicated radio talk show host Joseph Madison also invoked the legacy of the civil rights movement in his testimony at the hip hop hearings. "I was 23 years old when I became the executive director of the Detroit NAACP," Madison explained, establishing his credentials as an activist and an authority on the policies best suited to serve Black people. He told the committee, "When radio stations bombard the airwaves with these messages of hate, killing, and self-destruction, it will cause a conflict even within those families that may have taught other values." Citing the case of his own fourteen-year-old son, Madison told the committee that images of thugs and criminals projected by gangsta rap had turned his son from a young man who had been on the school honor roll and a star athlete into someone who began dressing like gangsta rappers, a youth who told his father in one conversation that he felt that time in jail would be preferable to the life he was leading in his middle-class home.[6]

Madison took pains to say that "this is not a confrontation with

young people," but then his subsequent testimony proved otherwise. After detailing how he had "educated" his son that "the pants
had to come off the hip and the shoe strings had to go back in, and
the language had to be cleaned up and the fascination with guns
had to end," he referred derisively to young rappers for saying that
"the older generation, the black leaders have done absolutely nothing. The black politicians have done nothing for this generation."
Madison answered that charge by taking it personally, asserting,
"Well, we obviously have more opportunities than we had 30, 40,
50 years ago and it was because many of us sitting here today sac-
rificed and gave our lives to see to it that this young generation has
at least the opportunity to do what they need to do. Have we com-
pleted it all? No. And there is a lot of work to do, but this is not
because we do not love our young people. It is just the opposite."[7]

Although often completely unaware of even the most elementary
facts about the lyrics, artists, and music they condemned, Tucker,
Madison, and other witnesses at the hearings were not incorrect
in their perception of a generation gap among African Americans.
Nor were they completely off base in detecting a certain contempt
and resentment among young Blacks about the civil rights movement and its record. Young people interviewed by a reporter for the
Pittsburgh Courier about holiday celebrations commemorating Dr.
King's birthday in 1996, for example, expressed this disdain clearly.
"Ours is not the same kind of struggle," one explained. "We really
don't know what it was like back then. All we know now is that the
only thing that counts in this world is money, power, and material
wealth." Another opined, "Dr. King believed in righteousness, but
that's not something you can take to the bank or to the grocery
store. To survive in this society today, you've got to be the firstest
with the mostest."[8]

These young people clearly did not know enough about the civil
rights movement, about Dr. King's Poor People's March, about his
support for striking sanitation workers in Memphis at the moment
when he was assassinated, or about the broad-based struggle for
jobs, education, and housing that accompanied efforts to secure
access to public accommodations. On the other hand, Tucker,
Madison, and other critics of African American youth did not
display enough knowledge about the circumstances facing young
people in their time, about the ways in which every significant institution in the society has made it clear to young people of color

that they do not count, that their parents are considered losers, and that their communities are largely places where no one would live unless they had no other choice. Gangsta rap has not caused this division, although it is an interesting and important symptom of it. The campaign to censor and suppress gangsta rap has, nonetheless, been enormously important, because it serves as a prototypical example of the ways in which conservative cultural and political mobilizations operate to obscure public understanding of who has power in our society and what they do with that power. It blames the victims and absolves the perpetrators.

During the 1980s, the number of children living in poverty in the United States increased by 2.2 million. Among European Americans, child poverty rose from 11.8 percent in 1979 to 14.8 percent in 1989. For Latinos, child poverty went from 28 percent to 32 percent. The portion of poor African American children increased from 41.2 percent to 43.7 percent during that decade. Neoconservative commentators blamed these increases in poverty on the mental and cultural deficiencies of minorities.[9] In fact, the fastest growing segments of the poverty population in this time period were young white families with children, families headed by married couples, and families headed by high school graduates.[10]

The effects of deindustrialization, however, exerted a particularly devastating impact on minorities, especially on entry-level workers beginning their careers. In 1979, 23 percent of male workers between the ages of eighteen and twenty-four received wages below the poverty line, but by 1990, that number rose to 43 percent. Only 6 percent of full-time workers between the ages of twenty-five and thirty-four received poverty-level wages in 1979, but 15 percent did so by 1990. The impact of these changes fell most harshly on communities of color. Between 1965 and 1990, Black family income fell by 50 percent, and Black youth unemployment quadrupled.[11] The share of low-income households headed by Blacks increased by one-third.[12] Fifty percent of Black males employed in durable-goods manufacturing in five Great Lakes states lost their jobs as a result of computer-based automation or capital flight between 1979 and 1984.[13] For many young people who came of age as witnesses to the era of deindustrialization, the "victories" of the civil rights generation seem insubstantial. They came to know the meaning of race through their experiences, from long periods of unemployment, sporadic work at entry-level low-

wage jobs, pervasive housing discrimination, stark educational inequality, oppressive police brutality, and toxic levels of environmental pollution in their neighborhoods.

The economic conditions that inner-city youths faced in the
1980s and 1990s were inflected by both their generational and
their racial identities. Adults of the civil rights generation witnessed enormous changes in the racial rulebook of U.S. society in
their lives, but continuing and cumulative discrimination in housing, employment, and education has worked to prevent them from
acquiring assets that appreciate in value to a sufficient degree that
they can be passed on to the next generation. As Melvin Oliver
and Thomas Shapiro demonstrate clearly and definitively in *Black
Wealth, White Wealth,* past and present discrimination in real estate and other forms of asset accumulation leaves Black parents far
less able than white parents to pass on their class status to their
children. Only slightly more than one-third of Black adults with
upper-level white-collar jobs successfully transmit their class status
to their children, while it is extremely rare for white children from
that background to fall in class status. In addition, twice as many
Black children as white children fall from upper-level white-collar
backgrounds to lower-level blue-collar positions. For blue-collar
families, the statistics are even starker. Almost 60 percent of whites
from blue-collar backgrounds rise in class status, but only slightly
more than one-third of Black children experience similar upward
mobility. One half of Blacks from upper-blue-collar families wind
up at the bottom of the occupational hierarchy. Fewer than 30 percent of Blacks from lower-white-collar families move into professional jobs, but more than 50 percent of whites from lower-white-
collar families move up into the professions.[14]

Under these circumstances, one could well understand citizens,
congressional committees, and mass media outlets engaging in
anxious debate about infant mortality, child nutrition, and health
care, about youth education and employment, about the routine
and pervasive violations of fair housing and fair lending laws that
leave people from different races with starkly different opportunities and life chances. These discussions did indeed take place, but
they attracted far less attention and played much smaller roles in
the popular political imagination than cultural controversies about
mass media images and their purported influences and effects. The
reasons for this imbalance are multiple and complex, but one aspect

of the problem stems from the strategic utility of questions about the evils of commercial culture for people interested in suppressing social memory and silencing social theory at the grass roots. The controversy over gangsta rap is only the latest in a long line of historical moral panics about mass media and social relations, panics that have almost always stemmed from the same sources and produced the same results.

During the Great Depression of the 1930s, for example, motion picture censors took aim at gangster films because they made crime seem like a logical response to social conditions rather than a grievous violation of personal and public moral codes. As Jonathan Munby has shown, sound films enabled Edward G. Robinson and James Cagney to bring the actual speech of an ethnic urban underclass to a broad audience, and their tremendous popularity (many theaters had Robinson and Cagney "imitation" shows before screenings) disclosed a broad desire to register the suffering and express the resentments of those who suffered most from the Depression.[15]

Gangster films, however, defamed Italian, Irish, Greek, and other ethnic Americans by reinforcing the association between ethnic identity and urban crime, echoing the vicious hatreds that had been widely disseminated by nativists and eugenicists during the 1920s as reasons to curtail immigration. These views were implicitly conservative, because by grounding the plight of the lower classes in their biological makeup, they portrayed efforts at social reform as futile. Yet many viewers of gangster films drew directly opposite conclusions, identifying with the "gangsters" as symbols of their own desire for upward mobility, as emblems of suppressed ethnic and class anger, and as icons who escaped the humiliating stigma of ethnic and class subordination through daring action and stylish consumption.[16]

Aware of the oppositional potential of such narratives, some representatives of conservative Catholic groups participated in censorship efforts enthusiastically during the Great Depression. Because Anglo-Protestants drew on vicious and pervasive anti-Catholicism in pressing for an end to immigration, for the deportation of alleged subversives and criminals, for the prohibition of alcohol consumption, and for the censorship of popular music and film, some respectable Catholics felt defensive. It is not unusual for members of aggrieved communities who have been defamed as not only alien but also nonnormative to embrace rigorous restraints on themselves, performing normativity in the face of their enemies in hopes of disproving the stereotypes.[17] During the Great Depression, conservative Catholics supported censorship in the hope of proving themselves and their entire religious group to be normative, moral, clean, and decent. They viewed the "glorification" of the Irish, Italian, or Greek gangster as ammunition for their enemies. Consequently, they sought to disrupt the link that connected ethnic identity to criminal behavior. In the process, however, they helped Anglo-Protestants to mute collective memories and to suppress social analyses of the conditions that immigrant and ethnic communities confronted. Disconnected from social causality, the gangster became an individual aberration whose "deviance" could be addressed only by repressive state power or by individual psychological treatment rather than meliorative social reform.

Similarly, during the post–World War II period, the House Un-American Activities Committee held repeated hearings into alleged Communist subversion in Hollywood. Committee counsel repeatedly asked actors of Jewish ancestry to disclose their original names, as if Emmanuel Goldenberg became Edward G. Robinson or Morris Carnovsky became Chester Morris because of a secret Communist plot rather than in response to American anti-Semitism. Witnesses were asked to spell out their non–Anglo Saxon names, even though the committee (having sent them subpoenas) knew perfectly well how they were spelled. The spelling exercise was designed to emphasize the foreign (and often Jewish) ancestries of the witnesses. This enabled the committee to create the impression that challenges to capitalism did not, and could not, originate in America. As part of a larger conservative ideological assault, HUAC wanted to brand the New Deal itself as subversive, to portray its thought and culture as foreign to America, to misrepresent antifascism as procommunism. The premise that only something outside the United States could account for anticapitalist attitudes led an otherwise largely cooperative and compliant Clifford Odets to protest to the committee that he had not been radicalized by anything said to him by members of the Communist Party. Odets insisted on telling the committee about the domestic origins of his alienation, recalling how his mother "worked in a stocking factory in Philadelphia at the age of eleven and died a broken woman . . . at the age of forty-eight."[18] Odets's efforts to bring historical memory and social analysis back into the discussion proved futile. The success of HUAC came not through any exposure of actual Communist influence in Hollywood but rather from the articulation and dissemination of the idea that analyses of unequal and unjust social relations in the United States stemmed from the malicious actions of nonnormative individuals rather than from honest observation of social conditions.

Attempts to silence, regulate, and even criminalize rap music in the United States during the 1990s followed this same trajectory. These attempts emerged most clearly through what Leola Johnson calls "one of the most sustained censorship drives in United States history."[19] By examining the origins and evolution of these censorship efforts, we can see how the hip hop hearings blamed the messenger in order to occlude the clear connections between the fantasies circulated in gangsta rap and the harsh realities of societal conditions.

Assistant Director Milt Ahlerich of the Federal Bureau of Investigation sent a letter in 1989 to Priority Records in Los Angeles complaining about a song that he did not name but was obviously "F—— the Police," on the label's album *Straight Outta Compton,* by the group N.W.A.[20] Hiding behind the passive voice to disguise the agency of the bureau, the FBI official described the song as something that had been brought to his attention, although he did not say by whom, how, or why. Protecting himself against charges of censorship, Ahlerich explained that he was writing the letter merely to share his thoughts and concerns with company executives. He did not indicate how frequently the assistant director of the FBI took time out from fighting crime to share his personal thoughts and concerns with music producers. Later in the letter, however, Ahlerich claimed directly that he was expressing "the FBI's position relative to this song and its message." Complaining that the song "encouraged violence and disrespect for the law enforcement officer," the letter went on to state, "We in the law enforcement community take exception to such action."[21] Ahlerich later admitted to reporters that the FBI had never before taken an official position on any piece of music, literature, or art, apparently forgetting the bureau's zealous but futile efforts to decipher the lyrics of "Louie Louie" by the Kingsmen, an episode probably known in crime-fighting annals as "the Great Louie Louie Scare of 1964."[22] Nor could the bureau admit that it was, at that very moment, engaged in a twelve-year struggle to keep "confidential" a sheet of paper containing the lyrics of John Lennon's 1971 song "John Sinclair," even though the lyrics had been publicly available for years, printed on the back of the jacket of Lennon's album *Some Time in New York City.*[23]

Ahlerich conceded in his letter that nobody in the bureau had actually purchased *Straight Outta Compton* or at least would admit to having purchased it. Thus, he could not explain exactly how the song came to his attention, except by citing unstipulated actions by "responsible fellow officers" whom he did not name.[24] Directly or indirectly, however, the bureau's letter about "F—— the Police" encouraged officers around the country to take action, and they did. Taking time out from the efforts to enforce the law, officers around the country set up an informal "fax" network designed to prevent public appearances by N.W.A. Off-duty officers withheld concert security services from the group, making it impossible for promoters to secure insurance for N.W.A. appearances.[25] Police harassment jeopardized or canceled the group's shows in Washington, D.C., Chattanooga, Milwaukee, and Tyler (Texas). N.W.A. performed in Cincinnati only because members of the Cincinnati Bengals professional football team (including city council member Reggie Williams) spoke up on their behalf. When members of the group sang the first few lines of "F—— the Police" in Detroit, officers rushed the stage, fought with arena security staff, and followed N.W.A. to their hotel, where they detained the group for fifteen minutes. "We just wanted to show the kids," one officer explained to a reporter, "that you can't say 'f—— the police' in Detroit."[26] Of course, by saying that, he violated his own rule. Then again, what he probably meant to say was that *they* can't say those words in Detroit.

The crusade against hip hop emerged within local politics in Florida one year later. A federal district court judge in Fort Lauderdale agreed with a complaint by conservative activist Jack Thompson, ruling the rap album *As Nasty as They Wanna Be,* by 2 Live Crew, to be obscene. Two years earlier, Thompson had been a candidate for the position of prosecuting attorney in Dade County, Florida, on the Republican ticket against the incumbent (and later U.S. attorney general) Janet Reno. At one campaign appearance, Thompson handed Reno a prepared statement and asked her to check the appropriate box. The statement read, "I, Janet

Reno, am a ___ homosexual, ___ bisexual, ___ heterosexual." It continued, "If you do not respond . . . then you will be deemed to have checked one of the first two boxes." Luther Campbell, known as Luke Skywalker, the leader of 2 Live Crew, had supported Reno, conducting voter registration drives on her behalf during that race.[27] Six weeks after losing the election, Thompson wrote letters to Janet Reno and to Florida governor Bob Martinez demanding an investigation of 2 Live Crew for possible violation of state obscenity statutes and racketeering codes in conjunction with *As Nasty as They Wanna Be*.[28]

Two days after the federal court ruling declared *As Nasty as They Wanna Be* obscene, a Broward County sheriff arrested Charles Freeman, a twenty-eight-year-old Black man and the owner of a music store, for the crime of selling a record and tape version of *As Nasty as They Wanna Be* to an adult undercover deputy. Officers put Freeman in handcuffs and took him to the police station. He was subsequently convicted of a first-degree misdemeanor. Sheriff's deputies also arrested two members of 2 Live Crew later that week for singing lyrics from the album at an adults-only concert.[29] An appeals court later overturned the district court's ruling, declaring *As Nasty as They Wanna Be* not to be obscene. Thompson's efforts, however, did persuade the Musicland stores with 752 outlets and the Trans World Stores with 450 branches to drop 2 Live Crew's album from their inventories.[30] At the same time, U.S. Marine Corps officials, with a zeal never previously detected in regard to the presence of "pornography" on military bases, announced that base stores in Yuma, Arizona; Beaufort, South Carolina; Jacksonville, North Carolina; and Oceanside, California, had removed the group's album from their shelves.[31]

The videotaped beating of Rodney King by members of the Los Angeles Police Department in March 1991 and the mass violence directed against persons and property when a Simi Valley jury found the accused officers not guilty on April 29, 1992, set the stage for the next wave of attacks against rap music. For many hip hop artists, fans, and critics, the Los Angeles rebellion demonstrated the broad community consensus behind hip hop's claims of police misconduct. They believed that rap songs like N.W.A.'s "F—— the Police" had been prophetic but ignored. For these observers, there was truth in the claim made by Ice Cube when he was still with N.W.A.: that rappers are "underground street reporters."[32]

The Isley Brothers. Photograph copyright Waring Abott / MichaelOchsArchives.com.

'N Sync. Photograph copyright Sue Schneider / MichaelOchsArchives.com.

The Fugees. Photograph copyright B+ for www.MOCHILLA.COM.

El Peladillo (Jesus Garcia). Photograph by Helena
Simonett, 1994. Courtesy of the photographer.

Banda dancers in Mexico City. Photograph by Helena
Simonett, 1998. Courtesy of the photographer.

Willie Colón. Courtesy MichaelOchsArchives.com.

James Gadson, Earl Palmer, Paul Humphrey, and Derf Reklaw. Photograph copyright B+ for .

Paul Humphrey, Babu, Jrocc, Numark, Cut Chemist, and Shortkut.
Photograph copyright Natasha Calzatti for www.MOCHILLA.COM.

Derf Reklaw in the foreground and Keepintime DJs in the background. Photograph copyright Natasha Calzatti for WWW.MOCHILLA.COM.

Shortkut, James Gadson in the foreground. Photograph copyright B+ for WWW.MOCHILLA.COM.

Invisible Skratch Piklz: Mixmaster Mike, Shortkut, Q-Bert, D-Styles, and Yoga Frog. Photograph copyright B+ for www.MOCHILLA.COM.

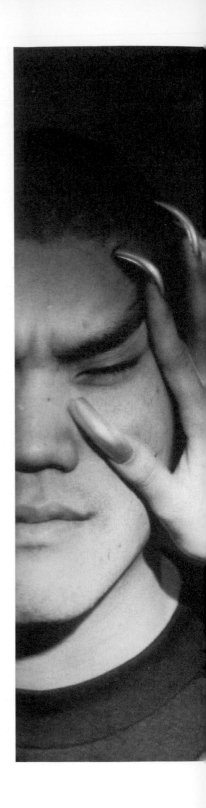

Keykool and Rhettmatic. Photograph copyright
B+ for www.MOCHILLA.COM.

The Dixie Chicks, from left to right, Emily Robison, Natalie Maines, and Martie Maguire. Photograph copyright Sherry Rayn Barnett / MichaelOchsArchives.com.

In contrast, others saw the riots as a consequence of the views and attitudes popularized by rap music. In May 1992, then Democratic presidential candidate Bill Clinton scolded rap artist Sister Souljah for commenting that she understood the "logic" behind attacks on white people during the rebellion. Souljah noted that if Blacks could attack one another violently every day in the ghetto, it should not be surprising that they would lash out at whites during the riots. Clinton distorted her remarks, however, condemning her as if she were calling for attacks on white people. Less than a month later, a group calling itself the Combined Law Enforcement Association of Texas (CLEAT) denounced the song "Cop Killer," which had been released several weeks before the riots on Ice-T's successful album *Body Count*, recorded with his speed metal band. Even though "Cop Killer" is not a rap song, Ice-T's long history as a rap artist and his visibility in films as an actor playing roles about inner-city life led many critics of the song to refer to it as gangsta rap. CLEAT called for a boycott of all products by Time Warner, the conglomerate distributing *Body Count*. It demanded the removal of the song and album from stores.

Two days after CLEAT announced its campaign against "Cop Killer," Los Angeles City Council member Joan Milke Flores, a Republican, joined the Los Angeles Police Protective League and the Fraternal Order of Police in asking the city council to demand that Time Warner stop selling the song. Vice President Dan Quayle attacked Ice-T at a national convention of radio talk show hosts, and President George H. W. Bush denounced the rap artist at a national police association conclave. Sixty members of Congress declared "Cop Killer" to be "vile and despicable." Oliver North's "Freedom Alliance" urged the governors of all fifty states to bring criminal charges against Time Warner for distributing the song, and North hired Jack Thompson to represent these concerns at Time Warner's annual stockholders meeting.[33] The National Association of Black Police officers, however, opposed the boycott of Time Warner and the attacks on "Cop Killer." They identified police brutality as the cause of much antipolice sentiment, and they proposed the creation of independent civilian review boards "to scrutinize the actions of our law enforcement officers" as a way of ending the provocations that cause artists such as Ice-T "to respond to actions of police brutality and abuse through their music." Their statement noted wryly that "many individuals of the law enforcement profession do not want anyone to scrutinize their actions, but want to scrutinize the actions of others."[34]

Time Warner initially stood behind the song on free speech grounds. Ice-T announced his resolve to defy the pressure against him and his song. As the complaints mounted, however, both the artist and his label caved in. In Greensboro, North Carolina, police officers delivered an ultimatum to the management of one retail store that, if it kept selling *Body Count,* the police would not respond to any emergency calls at the establishment. Managers removed the album from the store's inventory.[35] Time Warner severed relations with Paris, a Bay Area rapper best known for his political lyrics attacking capitalism and celebrating the history of Black activist groups like the Black Panther Party.[36] Police departments around the country began requesting the managers of their pension funds to divest themselves of Time Warner stock. Ice-T had difficulty securing performing and speaking engagements because of police harassment. By August, Ice-T announced his decision to remove "Cop Killer" from the *Body Count* album. Early in 1993, when Time Warner executives asked Ice-T to make changes on the cover of his new album, *Home Invasion,* the artist severed his ties with the company completely.[37]

Starting in 1993, African American individuals and groups joined the campaign against rap music. Calvin Butts, pastor of the Abyssynian Baptist Church in Harlem, (and later appointed president of the State University of New York College at Old Westbury by Republican governor George Pataki) condemned rap music from the pulpit before attempting to drive a steamroller over a pile of compact discs and cassette tapes.[38] Los Angeles attorney Eric Taylor charged that African Americans like himself had just begun to realize the dreams of Frederick Douglass, Malcolm X, and Martin Luther King Jr. when "another movement was emerging within the same community that quickly began tearing away at epic civil rights advancements. It labeled many blacks who have endured systemic obstacles to take part in the American Dream as 'sell-outs.' Ironically this movement has found a voice, and to some, legitimacy in gangsta rap music."[39] Detroit ministers James Holley and Wendell Anthony called for a boycott of rap music, decrying it as "immoral, racist, and decadent."[40] In October 1993, the National Urban League and the National Association for the Advancement of Colored People started to host youth forums attacking gangsta rap, and the National Political Congress of Black Women launched demonstrations at retail record outlets against the sale of "obscene" rap songs.[41]

Early in 1994, Senator Carol Mosley Braun and Representative Cardiss Collins, both Democrats from Illinois, responded to entreaties by C. Delores Tucker, of the National Political Congress of Black Women, to hold legislative hearings about rap music. As Leola Johnson astutely notes, Mosley Braun and Collins shifted the focus of attacks on rap music away from its supposedly seditious stance toward the police and instead critiqued the music as obscene, misogynist, and threatening to decency within Black communities. Although the legislators denied any intention to promote censorship, they did remind record industry executives, not so subtly, of the power of Congress to pass laws affecting the industry's financial position, such as the Audio Home Recording Act, implying that some form of self-censorship would secure future cooperation from legislators.[42]

In her opening remarks to the hip hop hearings, C. Delores Tucker testified on behalf of the National Political Congress of Black Women that rap music glamorizes violence, degrades women, exposes children to smut, incites violence, and seduces young people into lives of crime. She argued that freedom of speech was not an issue, because rap lyrics are obscene, and "it was never intended by the Founding Fathers of this Nation that First Amendment rights be for the protection of obscenities."[43] Unlike Representative Collins, who seemed to favor an improved parental advisory rating system for popular music, Tucker argued that rap music should be banned because of the harm that it does to Black communities.

Committee member Clifford Stearns, a Republican from Florida, cited Joe Madison's testimony at a later hearing but gave it a slightly different spin. Attempting to reconcile Tucker's and Madison's views on misogyny, pornography, and intergenerational tensions among Blacks with the broader conservative agenda embodied in the attacks on "F—— the Police," *As Nasty as They Wanna Be,* and "Cop Killer," Stearns noted Madison's remarks about his son's expressed preference for jail over his middle-class home and existence. Stearns opined, "For this reason, I am greatly disturbed by the proliferation of a music, a style, and class, and type that advocates the killing of police officers, the denigration of women, and the need for violent revolution."[44] Madison's actual testimony merely claimed that rap music made his son wear the wrong clothes and wish to leave his middle-class home, not that it advocates the killing of police officers, the denigration of women, or the need for violent revolution, but evidently Stearns felt the need to freestyle his own "rap" on the material given him by Madison.

Conservative spokesperson and former "drug czar" and secretary of education William Bennett followed Stearns's logic in 1995 when he teamed up with C. Delores Tucker in a joint public attack on "hate and sexism in rock and rap music and its corporate sponsors."[45] At the same time, Kansas senator Bob Dole launched his campaign for the Republican presidential nomination with a spirited condemnation of motion picture violence and gangsta rap music.[46] The systematic and sustained attack on rap music by white conservatives and Black liberals, by the FBI and police officers' associations, by local prosecutors and state governors, by members of the House of Representatives and the Senate, by presidential candidates and presidents might indicate that rap music genuinely poses a threat to public decency and safety. Yet the bad faith, cynicism, and opportunism of rap's opponents reveal something less than sincere concern for public morality.

The FBI might have had more credibility in its complaints about N.W.A.'s "F—— the Police" if it had had a better record in responding to the 47,000 cases of police brutality reported to the Department of Justice between 1986 and 1992, of which only 15,000 were investigated and only 128 were designated for prosecution.[47] Alabama governor Guy Hunt, one of the first public figures to attack Ice-T's "Cop Killer" in 1992, would have been a better spokesperson for law and order had he not looted his inaugural fund to pay his personal expenses, a felony offense for which he was convicted and sentenced to a $211,000 fine and ordered to perform a thousand hours of community service in 1993.[48]

Oliver North would have been a more convincing spokesperson for law and order in the campaign to punish Time Warner for "Cop Killer" had he not himself defied the law against covert aid to the Contras in Nicaragua as a White House aide in the Reagan administration, a crime for which he was convicted, before an appeals court overturned the verdict as a result of one of those legal technicalities that conservatives always complain about until they are the direct beneficiaries of them. Jack Thompson would have been a more convincing opponent of *As Nasty as They Wanna Be* had he not targeted an entertainer who supported his opponent in the previous election. Bob Dole would have been a more convincing crusader against motion picture and music violence had he not singled out only the products of firms whose executive officers donated money to Democrats while expressly exempting from his critique films by Arnold Schwarzenegger, a Republican whose *Terminator* films portrayed every bit as much fantasy violence against the police as any song by N.W.A. or Ice Cube.

Singer Dionne Warwick, a cochair of the National Political Congress of Black Women and a witness against gangsta rap at the hip hop hearings, would have been a more credible defender of "our children" from the alleged damages done to them by commercial popular music if she were not also the official on-camera spokesperson for a "psychic friends hot line" that encouraged children and adults to spend three dollars a minute on a telephone service that connects callers to "psychics" who purport to have special insights into the future. Warwick's concern for the corrupting evils of gangsta rap might have been more persuasive had she not agreed to a plea bargain in a Florida courtroom on June 5, 2002, to enter a drug treatment program in return for having charges dropped against her for possession of eleven marijuana cigarettes in a lipstick container at the Miami International Airport a month earlier.[49] William Bennett, the author of the *Book of Virtues*, might have been a more convincing critic of the morality of other people had the *Washington Monthly* not reported that he had lost an estimated eight million dollars gambling at casinos and if he had not opined on his syndicated radio program that aborting Black babies would eliminate most of the crime committed in the United States. Bennett noted that that he opposes such a solution, not because it is genocidal and racist, but because he opposes abortion. He never revealed any evidence for his assumption that Blacks commit most of the crime in the United States.[50]

Perhaps the chair of the National Political Congress of Black Women, C. Delores Tucker, would have had more credibility in her campaign against the immorality of rap music had she not been fired as Pennsylvania's commonwealth secretary in 1977 for running a private for-profit business at state expense, had she not used state employees to write speeches for which she received $66,931, had she and her husband not been found to owe close to $25,000 in real estate taxes in 1973 on twelve properties that they owned in the North Philadelphia ghetto, and had she not set up a meeting in August 1995 in which she proposed that Time Warner create a record distribution company for her and give her control over the highly profitable Death Row Records label. When executives from Death Row Records filed suit against her for trying to interfere with their contracts with Time Warner, Tucker explained to a reporter that "whatever they accuse me of doing, it would be worth it to protect children," a comment that Dave Marsh notes "is markedly different than 'not guilty.'"[51]

Bad faith, personal hypocrisy, and political opportunism have been important features of the campaign against rap music, but they do not explain why the campaign exists or why it has largely succeeded. Like most conservative mobilizations over the past three decades, the crusade against rap music identifies real problems in people's lives: hostility between men and women, disintegration of family and community networks, urban violence, intergenerational tensions, and the materialism, vulgarity, and scopophilia of much popular culture and advertising. But like most other "moral panic" crusades, the campaign against rap music takes these social realities out of historical context, hiding their causes and consequences by making them matters of personal and private morality. The crusade against rap music suppresses social memory by claiming that only culture counts, that history—in this case deindustrialization, economic restructuring, white backlash against the civil rights agenda, and neoconservative politics—has nothing to do with the social disintegration in our society. Criticizing rap music enables conservatives and their allies to run away from their own responsibility for today's social problems, to blame cultural responses to intolerable conditions *for* those conditions.

The attack on rap not only suppresses social memory; it also silences social theory. Because conservatives have a theological faith in the infallibility of "the market" to convert private greed into public good, they can explain systemic social breakdown only in terms of the deviant actions of individuals. As a result, Vice President Dan Quayle attributed the Los Angeles rebellion to "a poverty of values in the inner city," and Pat Buchanan and Bruce Hershensohn argued that a return to prayer in the schools would address the root causes of the riots. The attack on rap music grows logically from that denial of history and of social theory. If we have bad conditions, it must be because of bad people and their private decisions, not because of the systematic structuring of privilege and advantage for a few as a result of the systematic exploitation of and disadvantage for the many, not because of economic restructuring, the role of low-wage labor and unemployment in the new transnational economy, disinvestment in social institutions and the social wage, and the abandoned enforcement of civil rights laws and principles.

Not only does rap music make a convenient target for this crusade, but it is also a practice and an institution offering an alternative to the suppression of social memory and social theory. Early in the Reagan years, a White House aide announced the administration's goal as "defunding the left," a phrase used routinely by Pat Robertson and others to explain the philosophical agenda uniting diverse activities from attacks on the NEA to campaigns for school vouchers. As much as any institution in our society, hip hop culture and rap music have been repositories of social memory, from the basic musical techniques of sampling songs from the past to their lyrical concern for Black history, from their specificity in detailing the devastation of inner cities to their eloquence in expressing the feelings and experiences of people that mainstream media and institutions ignore.

Throughout the sustained censorship campaign against hip hop, rap artists and their defenders have conceded that the music's lyrics are sometimes obscene, sometimes celebratory about violence, and sometimes sexist and misogynist. They have also pointed out, however, that critics often forget that rap lyrics use metaphors—that Ice-T's "Grand Larceny" is actually about "stealing" a show and that his "I'm Your Pusher" is actually an antidrug song celebrating "dope beats and lyrics" with "no beepers needed."[52] While acknowledging and often condemning obscene, violent, and misogynist lyrics, they contend that these features were incidental to the music's main purpose: telling the truth about the conditions experienced by young people, especially those in inner-city ghettos and barrios. "This is our voice," argued Vinnie Brown, of the group Naughty by Nature. "If it wasn't for rap, you would never know that these horrors are going on in the community."[53] Chuck D, of Public Enemy, explained, "Hip-hop is not exactly a music. It's damn near real life."[54]

Rap music has created a discursive space open to young people who have little access to any actual physical space. They have found themselves largely not wanted as workers, as students, as citizens, or even as consumers. Police officers, private security guards, and gang violence have constrained their access to public spaces, and politicians and the mass media have demonized them as criminals responsible for the poverty of their own neighborhoods. Through rap music, they tell the story as it appears to them. Bushwick Bill, of the rap group the Geto Boys, stressed the material dimensions of hip hop as a response to ghetto conditions in his answer to Senator Dole's attack on violence in rap music. "Dole, who opposes affirmative action, has now bashed rap, which is the number one form of jobs to be had for a lot of inner city youths, as even if you don't rap, engineer, or produce, you can get paid to put up posters, pass out fliers, distribute promotional tapes, work on music video sets, do security, promote a club, just all kinds of things you can get paid to do. Not only is Dole's attack another attempt to censor us because this is our creative art form talking about what's going on, but also rap has been a way to get out of the ghetto without violence or selling drugs."[55]

Television personality and *Soul Train* host Don Cornelius astutely described rap music fans as young people who realize that they have been given the worst of everything this society has to offer. "They are people who nobody really has spent much money on or spent much concern on. They are part of a more or less forgotten community. Along come these young rappers with all of this negative commentary who are saying, 'we know that you are there, we know what your problems are, we not only know what they are, we are willing to dramatize and comment on these problems in our records.'"[56]

A study by the California legislature in 1982 revealed that deindustrialization, capital flight, and neoconservative economic restructuring in the late 1970s had produced a 50 percent rise in unemployment in South Central Los Angeles, while purchasing power there had dropped by one-third.[57] In Los Angeles at the time of the 1992 rebellion, the African American poverty rate reached 32.9 percent, Black unemployment hovered between 40 and 50 percent, and forty thousand teenagers (20 percent of the sixteen- to nineteen-year-olds) were both unemployed and out of school.[58] In one study, nearly 5 percent of all Blacks reported being unjustly beaten by the police. Civilian deaths resulting from police brutality have long been at least nine times more likely to happen to Blacks than to whites.[59] Contrary to C. Delores Tucker's claim that violence promoted by rap music is the source of "the greatest fear" in Black communities, rampant discrimination, environmental hazards, on-the-job injuries, inadequate access to medical care, police brutality, and hate crimes remain the sources of the greatest threats to Black people and to other exploited and aggrieved populations. Even in respect to violence, the definitive sociological study in the field shows that "socioeconomic inequality between races, as well as economic inequality generally, increases rates of criminal violence" and that "aggressive acts of violence seem to result not so much from lack of advantages as from being taken advantage of."[60] Thus, Black-on-Black crime would be lessened by policies producing greater equality and opportunity.

Rap music has chronicled the devastation of inner cities and the demise of jobs, services, and opportunities during twenty-five years of neoconservative contraction of the industrial economy and the welfare state. Moreover, rap artists and their defenders have understood that many of the attacks on rap have been aimed at obscuring these realities. Rap artist Michael Franti, formerly a member of Disposable Heroes of Hiphoprisy and later the leader of Spearhead, argued, "Rap didn't start the phenomena of people killing each other or mistreating women in our community. Education and welfare cuts and a buildup of jails has more to do with it. . . . Nobody got mad when Eric Clapton sang 'I Shot the Sheriff.' You've got *The Terminator,* a whole movie about blowing cops to bits, and there's Arnold Schwarzenegger posing with George Bush. It's hypocrisy."[61]

Representative Maxine Waters, a Democrat from California, spoke bluntly about the attack on rap. "Let's not kid ourselves. There are those who have a political agenda in seeking to distract people from other issues. Sometimes our friends, the conservatives, are having a field day. They have always believed blacks cause most of the crime in America. After all, they say, look at the inordinately high number of blacks in prisons and on death row. Now their evil propaganda stands virtually unopposed in today's public debate over rap music."[62] In a similar vein, David Harleston, a music industry executive associated with a popular hip hop label, Def Jam Recordings, claimed, "It is increasingly apparent that certain opponents of hip hop music are of the misguided view that if we do not hear about the issues raised and addressed in the music, then those issues will not exist. In fact, one could argue that efforts to suppress hip hop artists are efforts to ignore unpleasant realities that exist in America's back yard. Such a view simply denies reality. Silencing the messenger will not extinguish the problem."[63] Tricia Rose, author of *Black Noise,* the best book on hip hop, described the 1994 hearings chaired by Senator Mosley Braun and Representative Collins as "a form of empty moral grandstanding, a shameful attempt by politicians to earn political favors and ride the wave of public frenzy about crime while at the same time remaining unable and often unwilling to tackle the real problems that plague America's cities and their poorest black children."[64]

Members of the civil rights generation are not wrong to detect resentment of them within gangsta rap, but their interpretation of the causes of the chasm between them and inner-city youths is misdirected. In a brilliant chapter on gangsta rap in his indispensable book *Race Rebels,* Robin D. G. Kelley argues that the use of the word *Nigga* by gangsta rappers, a word choice deeply offensive to many in the civil rights generation, is an attempt to speak to "a collective identity shaped by class consciousness, the character of inner-city space, police repression, poverty, and the constant threat of intraracial violence."[65] In short, this word choice is a form of what Kelley calls "ghettocentricity," a moral choice to identify with the poorest and most aggrieved part of the collective community while rejecting individual solutions predicated on a personal upward mobility premised on forgetting the suffering one leaves behind for others to face. Most important, it represents an unwillingness to disidentify with the poorest, most despised, and most aggrieved members of the Black community.

As Michael Eric Dyson explains, "Gangsta rap is largely an indictment of mainstream and bourgeois black institutions by young people who do not find conventional methods of addressing personal and social calamity useful. The leaders of those institutions often castigate the excessive and romanticized violence of this music without trying to understand what precipitated its rise in the first place. In so doing, they drive a greater wedge between themselves and the youth they so desperately want to help."[66]

These intergenerational tensions are not new; they are part of the price Black people have always paid for white supremacy in America. White parents may imagine that they command the loyalty of their children purely through moral suasion, but like other forms of whiteness, white parental authority is heavily subsidized by the state. Peggy Pascoe points out that antimiscegenation laws were aimed not so much at banning interracial relationships or even interracial sex as at preventing the passing of property across racial lines. Black parents, conversely, find their authority routinely undermined by public and private policies designed to impede the accumulation of assets and intergenerational transfers of wealth within Black families. A character in James Baldwin's 1968 novel, *Tell Me How Long This Train's Been Gone,* articulates the implications of these policies for many Black youths in an eloquent soliloquy: "I was very nearly lost because my elders, through no fault of their own, had betrayed me. Perhaps I loved my father, but I did not want to live his life. I did not want to become like him, he was the living example of defeat. He could not correct me. None of my elders could correct me because I was appalled by their lives. I was old enough to understand how their lives had happened, but rage and pity are not love, and the determination to outwit one's situation means that one has no models, only object lessons."[67]

In their desire to be seen, to wield the symbolic and material currency of American society, some rappers *do* rely on misogyny, abusive language, and eroticized brutality. How could it be otherwise, given the values, social relations, and reward structures of our society? But in a subculture that has made an art form out of talking back, the best rebukes of these rappers have come from within, from women rappers like Queen Latifah, M. C. Lyte, and Lauryn Hill, from politicized male rappers like Public Enemy and KRS-1. In addition, artists and intellectuals have utilized other media to provide important metacommentaries on hip hop that evade the facile condemnations that dominated the hip hop hearings. For example, rap artist Sister Souljah's book *No Disrespect* combines a moving memoir and a searing indictment of sexism, while Michael Eric Dyson's *Between God and Gangsta Rap* eloquently explores the ambivalence toward the genre felt by a man who is a father of a teenage son, an ordained Baptist minister, a university professor, and a knowledgeable and discerning fan of hip hop.[68]

Government censorship and regulation or private mobilizations and moral panics cannot cure the ills that they misidentify and misattribute to rap music. But nurturing the social memory and social theory found in some rap music might lead us to a more mature and more responsible understanding of our problems and their solutions. Representative Maxine Waters, of California, whose district encompasses many of the neighborhoods from which gangsta rap emerged, offered an example of precisely that kind of analysis in her testimony before the hip hop hearings. Pointing out that hip hop emerged from the bottom up, from children who created an art form in their garages and basements, Waters praised the success of rap artists in communicating their experiences to a wider world. "For decades, you and I and so many others have talked about the lives and the hopes of our people," she told the committee, "pain and the hopelessness, the deprivation and abuse. Rap music is communicating that message like we never have. It is, indeed, as was described, the CNN of the community causing people from every sector, including black leadership, to listen and pay heed."[69]

Conceding that gangsta rap often contains lyrics that offend her, Waters related that she had grown up in a Black community in St. Louis, where she heard obscene words many times before she ever heard them used by gangsta rappers, that she remembered them uttered by the most highly esteemed adults in church on Sunday morning. "I don't say to people, you should use them. I don't encourage them, but we had better stop pretending like we are hearing them for the first time."[70] Most important, Waters detailed her efforts to work with, rather than against, young rap artists, bringing them to Washington to meet with the Black Congressional Caucus and the Black Women's Forum and sponsoring a program, L.A. 17 to 30, designed to attract ghetto youths into vocational training as well as high school and community college courses and to place them in gainful employment.

The silencing of social memory and the suppression of grass roots social theory within hip hop are not a matter of concern for African Americans exclusively. They are a process that harms our whole society. For in erasing history from public debate, we unduly constrain our understanding of the present. The demonization of Black people in general and of inner-city youth in particular often proceeds through an argument that claims that poverty does not cause crime, that Depression-era Americans endured hardships nobly, and that the problems facing aggrieved racial minorities today stem solely from the internal moral and cultural failings of those groups. But in the 1930s, when white people were among the poorest parts of the population, many of today's dynamics prevailed. The humiliating subordinations and indignities of poverty ripped families apart then as they do now. Despair and rage over inequality provoked criminal behavior then as they do now, and they gave rise to popular preferences for sadistic and vengeful representations of social life then, the same as now. C. L. R. James shows in *American Civilization* that during the 1930s the gangster film, violent comic strips like Dick Tracy, and detective stories and motion pictures gave voice to popular desires for representation of what the Depression had done to them, for expression of the anger they felt—and feared. Writing about the plays of Clifford Odets during that decade, Robert Warshow later zeroed in on the intergenerational tensions between parents disappointed in their children and children who thought that their parents evaded the central fact of American life: "without a dollar you don't look the world in the eye." Warshow sees the young people in Odets's plays and the entire generation they depicted as internalizing cynicism but nonetheless engaging in the strongest subversion: "taking capitalism without sugar."[71] Young rap artists and their listeners tried taking capitalism without the sugar in the late 1980s and early 1990s. More than anything, they sought an art that refused to lie, that refused to run from the hard facts and harsh realities of their time.

William Drayton, who played Flavor Flav, the mischievous trickster in the rap group Public Enemy, used to wear a facsimile of a stopped alarm clock on his jacket, telling audiences, "We know what time it is." Part of the purpose of gangsta rap and all hip hop has been to tell people what time it is. When Japanese troops occupied Singapore during World War II, they translated the names of all the streets into Japanese, imposed the Japanese calendar and year on the locals, and even mandated that standard time in Tokyo would prevail in the Singapore time zone. The Japanese military and colonial administrators understood the importance of imposing their own sense of what time it was on their victims and of eliminating potentially alternative memories and histories. The attack on hip hop in the 1990s sought to solidify the power of dominant groups by suppressing social memory in similar fashion.

The collective memory at the heart of hip hop contains a material memory of the racial and generational dimensions of deindustrialization that would otherwise have remained hidden from history. It is not surprising that this kind of cultural expression attracts the wrath of powerful critics, but it is tragic that so many of them have been gullible enough to believe that battles over music censorship actually concern conflicts over music and morality rather than over power, privilege, and persecution. More than a decade after the hip hop hearings, rap music remains a source of enormous profits for the music industry. The censorship campaigns of the 1980s and 1990s embodied in the hip hop hearings did nothing to diminish the amount of misogyny and obscenity in the music's lyrics. These efforts did succeed, however, in frightening recording companies and radio stations away from politicized rap, away from songs with lyrics that critique dominant institutions in U.S. society. With the notable exceptions of Lauryn Hill, Dead Prez, Mos Def, Talib Kweli, and a few others, most rap lyricists today place sexual pleasure and consumer purchases at the center of the social world. Censorship made sexism, misogyny, and materialism *more* prevalent in hip hop rather than less. Only politicized answers to public problems have disappeared.

The sexism, misogyny, and materialism that govern hip hop today help fuel corporate synergy and high profits for investors. Sean Combs, the performer known sequentially as Puff Daddy, P. Diddy, and then Diddy, has made singularly unimpressive contributions to hip hop, but his celebrity status has enabled him to become chief executive officer and chairman of the board of directors of the Sean John clothing company. His firm outsources production to low-wage workers in impoverished parts of the world, such as Choloma, Honduras, where women and children who make Sean John sweatshirts that retail for more than fifty dollars receive less than twenty-five cents per shirt. The National Labor Committee, an antisweatshop activist group, reported that the managers of Southeast Textiles in Choloma refused to make contributions to an employee health plan, fired workers if they became pregnant, denied them water and bathroom breaks, and dismissed them if they complained. They also discovered that the 20 percent of the workshop not devoted to making clothes for Sean John produced clothing for Rocawear, a firm founded by hip hop artist Jay-Z and producer Damon Dash.[72]

When former Run–DMC member Russell Simmons sold his Phat Fashions clothing line to the Kellwood Corporation in 2004 for $140 million, he proudly lauded hip hop as "the best and most important brand-building force in America."[73] Unlike many contemporary entrepreneurs, Simmons has used his resources to promote many of the interests of the consumers who buy his products. He has sponsored voter registration drives, worked with hip hop artist Wyclef Jean to organize rallies against budget cuts in education, and lobbied the state legislature against the harsh and repressive "Rockefeller Drug Laws" in New York State.[74] Yet Phat Farm subcontracts work to shops charged with violations of fair labor practices by the Garment Workers Center in Los Angeles and refuses to deal with SweatX, a unionized clothing company that pays fair wages and provides decent working conditions.[75]

Does Simmons's success show how powerful hip hop is? Does it demonstrate that inner-city youths have built a multibillion dollar industry that helps shape important areas of American life? Does it offer hope that entrepreneurs dependent on the prestige from below, emanating from the style of inner-city youths, may actually help those youths as well? Or does it prove how weak hip hop is? Does it show that it has been easily and fully co-opted into just another novel style, just another marketing opportunity? Does Russell Simmons's activism demonstrate how open the U.S. political system is or how closed it has become? Does his political work express the unvoiced and unmet demands for justice of an ignored generation, or does it merely add marketing cachet to his product line and prove that no voices are heard in this society unless they represent the interests of capital?

The exploitation of workers in sweatshops does real harm to real people. It provides unfair gains and unjust enrichments for investors and is dependent on the perpetuation of inequality, intimidation, and injustice. Yet the guardians of morality who found themselves sufficiently motivated to conduct congressional hearings and issue widespread condemnations of the words spoken on rap recordings in the early 1990s have not yet managed to utter a word of protest against hip hop's ties to sweatshop labor. They are interested in Russell Simmons's business and his celebrity status but have done next to nothing to provide the young people whose tastes have made Russell Simmons rich with jobs that pay decently, much less with meaningful participation in the key decisions that affect their lives.

Today's hip hop artists and entrepreneurs can be as materialistic "as they wanna be" and even "as nasty as they wanna be" as long as it's all about a salary and not about reality. By the middle of the first decade of the twenty-first century, it has become clear that hip hop plays a very different role in society from the one it played in the late 1980s. Despite all the good efforts by committed artists and activists at the local level, hip hop is much more significant as a marketing category than as a cultural or political force. As twenty-five-year-old Allan Mashia argued at the National Urban League Influence Summit plenary session on hip hop and social conscience in 2005, "What hip hop is now is not what it was . . . hip hop made you proud to be Black and inspired you to be positive and make something of yourself."[76] Of course, P. Diddy and Russell Simmons *have* made something of themselves but, like Macon Dead Jr. in *Song of Solomon*, only by exploiting others. The theft of inheritance perpetrated on Black people by discrimination and the dynamics of a system that allows inclusion only to those willing to police the boundaries of exclusion zealously against others stand behind the intergenerational bickering manifest during the hip hop hearings—and behind many other kinds of folly as well.

Yet we need to remember that Railroad Tommy's pessimistic prediction is not the dominant message of *Song of Solomon*. At the end of the novel, Milkman Dead learns how to do the impossible, how to ride the air by surrendering to it. Like his grandfather who built a farm in the face of vigilante violence in the era of Reconstruction and like the hip hop artists, activists, and intellectuals who have made an art form and a political praxis out of talking back, he learns that conscious action in the world makes all the difference, that for all our disappointments, resentments, and regrets, there is still important work to be done. The legendary hip hop act Erik B and Rakim claim, "It's not where you're from, it where you're at," as a way of inviting people from different backgrounds, neighborhoods, races, and countries to unite, to prove their worth through their artistry, initiative, and imagination. Toni Morrison's narrator in *Song of Solomon* makes the same appeal in a different way, describing how the work of Macon Dead Sr. led by example. In words that apply to the best works of hip hop and the best activism of social movements, she writes:

> "You see?" the farm said to them. "See? See what you can do? Never mind you can't tell one letter from another, never mind you born a slave, never mind you lose your name, never mind your daddy dead, never mind nothing. Here, this here, is what a man can do if he puts his mind to it and his back in it. Stop sniveling," it

said. "Stop picking around the edges of the world. Take advantage, and if you can't take advantage, take disadvantage. We live here. On this planet, in this nation, in this country right here. Nowhere else! We got a home in this rock, don't you see! Nobody starving in my home; nobody crying in my home, and I got a home, you got one too! Grab it. Grab this land! Take it, hold it, my brothers, make it, my brothers, shake it, squeeze it, turn it, twist it, beat it, kick it, kiss it, whip it, stomp it, dig it, plow it, seed it, reap it, rent it, buy it, sell it, own it, build it, multiply it, and pass it on—can you hear me? Pass it on!"[77]

8. Masquerades and Mixtures

The Hidden History of Passing

The terms by which we are hailed are rarely the ones we choose (and even when we try to impose protocols on how we are to be named, they usually fail); but these terms we never really choose are the occasion for something we might still call agency, the repetition of an imaginary subordination for another purpose, one whose future is partly open.

—Judith Butler, *Excitable Speech: A Politics of the Performative*

The 1980s and early 1990s witnessed an upsurge in the popularity of Vietnamese music in the United States. The concentration of Vietnamese Americans in Westminster, California (known as Little Saigon), coupled with the entrepreneurial skills of astute producers aware of the community's hunger for its familiar music, led to the creation of a highly lucrative market.[1] It is not unusual for immigrants, exiles, and refugees to treasure the music that reminds them of home, but music making for diasporic Vietnamese in the United States presented singularly unusual challenges. Because the intensity of anticommunist politics among many Vietnamese in the United States precluded the importation of music from contemporary Vietnam, community musicians in California in the 1990s attempted to re-create the Vietnamese music they remembered from the years before the Communist victory in their country, music from the years 1954–73. Aided by the existence of a thriving Mexican music industry in the area, which gave them access to studios and session musicians (many of them Mexican), Vietnamese entrepreneurs and producers created a contemporary popular music based on the revival of old songs and the composition of new ones with the feel of a previous era. Almost all of the singers in the genre were Vietnamese Americans, but two notable exceptions illustrate the complex relationships that link music and identity.

Patrons at one particular Vietnamese-themed nightclub in Orange County enjoyed the comedy and song stylings of a master of ceremonies and performer who spoke fluent Vietnamese and stood on stage wearing a traditional *ao dai* outfit with long scarf and hat. Yet this entertainer was neither Vietnamese nor Vietnamese American, but rather an Anglo American named Rick Murphy. He told his receptive audiences that he wanted to simulate the atmosphere in a real Vietnamese teahouse as closely as possible and rapidly became a local favorite.[2] A singer calling herself Dalena proved even more successful, securing international success among Vietnamese expatriates for her perfectly rendered sentimental ballads. Yet Dalena did not understand the words she was singing and spoke no Vietnamese. A Scandinavian and Scotch Irish woman born in Muncie, Indiana, Dalena picked up Vietnamese music while working in a restaurant in Orlando, Florida. She learned her songs from the jukebox but sang them so well that she became a favorite of audiences eager to be reminded of the home they imagined for themselves in retrospect while in exile.[3]

Rick Murphy and Dalena are exceptions, but they are not alone. Patrick Shannon, an Irish American cable television company worker, learned Dominican merengue from his Puerto Rican co-workers and went on to star in the genre, as we saw in chapter 6. Judy Cheeks, an African American and Native American who was the daughter of gospel singer Julius Cheeks, found success both as a singer of the globally popular dancehall hit recording "Mellow Loving" and as the host of a television show in Germany, where she sang duets in German with a puppet purporting to be a singing hamster.

Rick Murphy and Dalena found themselves successful in a genre that seemed inconsistent with their embodied identities. The novelty of their presence in Vietnamese music raises important questions about who belongs where and who can sing what. The vexed relationships that make music a significant marker of racial identity are something we inherit from history, but both the past and the present are rarely as finite and fixed as they appear.

Long waves of experience enable us to speak about jazz, hip hop, and Detroit techno as significant sites for understanding elements of Black history. They also guide our explorations of merengue, banda, and salsa as key components of Latinidad. Long waves of history stand behind the marketing of popular music as a key component in the social construction of whiteness. History does not, however, leave any of us with any simple, discrete, atomized, or isolated identities. Racial identities are fictive identities, even when they have factual social consequences. Racial groups have relations with one another that shape the identity of each group. Individuals learn their racial identities through complex encounters with others. Many individuals belong to more than one racial group. Ruth Wilson Gilmore talks about race as a fatal coupling of difference with power. Racial difference helps determine who has power. Consequently, racial identities are contested and conflicted rather than firm and fixed. Yet the fluidity of racial identities is often hidden from view by the seemingly natural character that race assumes in racialized societies. For that reason, racial identities that appear atypical, accidental, or artificial can teach us a great deal about race as a socially constructed category.

African American musicians have often passed as members of other races in order to escape anti-Black racism. Jelly Roll Morton had to pass as a "Cuban" in order to secure lodging in Richmond, Indiana, when he went there to record with the all-white New Orleans Rhythm Kings in 1923.[4] Morton's "Mexican" friend Anita Gonzalez often hired black musicians to play at the saloon she owned in Nevada. Only Morton and a few other close associates knew that the person posing as Anita Gonzalez was really Bessie Johnson, a light-skinned creole from Mississippi who had to pass as Mexican (and therefore white) in order to own property and maintain a business in Nevada in that era.[5]

The complexities of race sometimes outpaced the ability of racists to police its boundaries. The touring band led by Lee Collins especially vexed local authorities in Hattiesburg, Mississippi, in 1920. The band's personnel included a light-skinned Black creole drummer, a Japanese American clarinetist, and a Mexican playing bass. The police received complaints about the race mixing the group was carrying on, but the officers were unsure whether this was an integrated band (and hence illegal) or not, because they did not know for sure if the Mexican or Japanese American could be considered white. They decided to prevent the Japanese American from performing but left the rest of the band intact. At one dance in San Antonio in the 1920s, police officers ran a rope across the dance floor to keep whites and Blacks apart but then had to deal with complaints from a group of dark-skinned Mexicans who insisted they were white.[6]

These ambiguities sometimes encouraged members of one aggrieved group to masquerade as members of another. In the early 1950s, the popularity of the television program *Adventures in Music with Korla Pandit* helped establish the commercial viability of the newly established medium in Los Angeles. Pandit played romantic mood music on a Hammond organ, exuding an air of mysterious spirituality. He told interviewers that he had been born in India, the son of a high-caste Brahman government official and a French opera singer. Pandit never said a word on the air, but his delicate features and soulful stares into the camera caused a sensation among female viewers. Sporting turquoise, maroon, and burgundy turbans, crowned by a single topaz jewel in the center of his forehead, and dressed in white shirts with elaborate French cuffs set off by ornate cuff links under dark, double-breasted, pinstriped suits, Pandit's exoticism and elegance made him a powerful object of romantic desire and a welcomed "guest" into millions of Southern California homes during his daily telecasts.[7]

Not many of Pandit's viewers knew, however, that the people from India who wear turbans are Sikhs and that Sikhs do not adorn their turbans with jewels. Fewer still knew that the man they recognized as Korla Pandit had previously played piano and organ in nightclubs, on records, and on the radio in Southern California as "Juan Rolando," an entertainer who told his employers he was Mexican. Yet this, too, was misleading. Only after his death in 1998 did it become generally known through the research of journalist R. J. Smith that the man known as Korla Pandit and Juan Rolando was actually John Roland Redd, an African American born in 1921 in Columbia, Missouri.[8] In Missouri, Redd's father, Ernest S. Redd, served as pastor at Columbia's Second Baptist Church, an African American landmark in that university town. John Redd played jazz and blues music in local bands in which he often encountered Sir Charles Thompson, an artist who later went on to establish an international reputation as a bop pianist. John's brother, Speck Redd, went on to play piano at Howard and Seymour Gray's Sepia Club in Des Moines, Iowa. Speck Redd gave music lessons to many of that city's aspiring musicians, including piano virtuoso Roger Williams and Louie Bellson (who later switched to playing drums). Speck Redd even had his own local television program in Des Moines, *Speck Redd Plays*.[9] Yet John Roland Redd followed another path.

Redd left Missouri and moved to California in the 1940s, hoping to escape the pervasive white supremacy in Boone and Callaway counties, a part of the state of Missouri that locals sometimes referred to as Little Dixie. Los Angeles, however, did not turn out to be the paradise that Redd imagined it would be. Anti-Black discrimination kept him from joining the white local of the musicians' union, depriving him of access to most of the high-paying studio, radio, and nightclub jobs. Moreover, the city's rampant and pervasive residential segregation and racialized policing exposed him to repeated humiliations. While boarding in the home of a Mexican American family in Orange County, Redd came to feel that he could improve his employment opportunities by taking advantage of his comparatively light complexion. He adopted the Spanish-language versions of his first and middle names, turning John Roland Redd into Juan Rolando.[10] As Juan Rolando, he found employment as a recording artist and studio musician. But he discovered that anti-Mexican sentiment in Los Angeles often turned out to be almost as intense as anti-Black racism. While playing the organ for the radio program *Chandu the Magician* (about a mystic who traveled to distant lands and solved crimes), Juan Rolando decided to play a new role, to become Korla Pandit, a visitor from the mysterious East!

As Korla Pandit, Redd/Rolando soon secured work as the organ player for *Hollywood Holiday,* a daily program broadcast from a restaurant at Sunset and Vine. That job led the keyboardist to steady work on a television puppet show called *Time for Beany* and eventually to *Adventures in Music with Korla Pandit.* The instrumentalist found that Korla Pandit could go places that Juan Rolando and John Roland Redd were not welcome. In 1948, he married a white woman, Beryl DeBeeson, a blonde who worked at Disney Studios as an airbrush artist. On the television screen, the racial mores of Los Angeles at midcentury allowed white women in all-white suburbs to swoon over the televised image of a mysterious and exotic visitor from India, but they would never have allowed similar attention to be directed toward a Black man.

By declining to speak on the air, Redd hid his identity, but this also proved to be a profitable career move for him. It cultivated an air of mystery about Korla Pandit. Friends sometimes joked, however, that the man who never spoke during his television broadcasts would never shut up in real life, except for carefully avoiding conversations with strangers, especially with actual South Asians. Oddly enough, he developed a close friendship with and was often seen in Hollywood in the company of Sabu, an Indian actor who appeared regularly in motion pictures as the "boy" known for tending elephants in his native land. Relatives and friends confided that Redd affected an Indian accent in public for so many years that he actually became very difficult to understand in unaccented "standard" English. "It was strange," recalled Pandit's nephew, Ernest Redd. "It got to a point he didn't even speak very good English because he had talked that Hinduism or whatchacallit for so long."[11]

Like Korla Pandit but for different reasons, Harry Kitano also "passed" as someone from South Asia in order to escape the stigma attached to his historical identity. When World War II began, the U.S. government incarcerated Kitano and his family at the Santa Anita Detention Center, in California, along with thousands of other Japanese Americans. Later, they were sent to the Topaz Detention Camp, in Utah. The Kitano family found itself part of the U.S. government's roundup and imprisonment of more than one hundred thousand West Coast Japanese Americans, many of them citizens, none of whom had committed any documented acts of espionage.

In high school, Kitano had played jazz trombone. He especially admired Tommy Dorsey's solo on that instrument in the Dorsey band's version of Rimsky-Korsakov's "Song of India." After being released from the camps and relocated by the government, Kitano found work as a trombonist in dance bands traveling throughout the Midwest. He changed his name to Harry Lee, passing as Chinese in order to evade the anti-Japanese hysteria generated by demagogic responses at home to the war in the Pacific. In 1945, his band's performances featured a solo by "Harry Lee" on the trombone, playing "Song of India." Kitano would wrap a hotel towel around his head as if it were a turban, playing Dorsey's famous solo one octave lower to give it a more "exotic" feel. The band leader introduced Lee as a "gen-u-wine" Indian, a humorous claim, since the trombonist clearly appeared to be a Chinese man pretending to be Indian. In truth, however, he was a Japanese American pretending to be a Chinese American impersonating a South Asian Indian by replicating a white trombonist's solo in a "Black" version of a song evoking India written by a Russian![12]

Korla Pandit's racial masquerade entailed passing, first as Mexican and later as Indian, in order to surmount the barriers put in his path by anti-Black racism. Harry Kitano passed as Chinese American in order to keep a job that required him to appear in public without "giving away" his Japanese American identity in order to escape the hateful acts and stigma directed at that identity. The ability of Pandit and Kitano to fool the public so successfully underscores the constructed and artificial nature of racial categories in a way that might lead us to new and productive ways of thinking.

The pernicious pathologies of racism make it impossible for people either to evade completely or to embrace totally the racial categories by which they are defined. People have to be realistic and recognize racism's power and at the same time reject the idea that knowing a person's race tells anything definitive about the person. The performative dimensions of John Roland Redd's racial masquerade as Juan Rolando and Korla Pandit can offer us important understandings of where antiracist thought and action might emerge within already existing social relations and social identities.

In U.S. society, where opportunities and life chances are systematically skewed along racial lines, where housing segregation and racial profiling routinely relegate people of different races to different physical and social spaces, the rule of race often remains unchallenged and unquestioned. Racial segregation is so pervasive that it comes to seem natural, necessary, and inevitable. Under these circumstances, race provides protective cover for widespread injustice and inequality. As W. E. B. Du Bois demonstrated in *Black Reconstruction in America*, racism makes it easy for people with privilege "to discount and misunderstand the suffering or harm done to others." Du Bois noted that "all consciousness of inflicting ill disappears" once degradation and exploitation are "hidden beneath a different color of skin."[13] Desperate poverty, onerous labor, poor health, and inadequate shelter come to be seen as the personal qualities of members of particular aggrieved groups rather than the results of exploitation and exclusion.

For those people who identify themselves (or who are identified by others) as mixed race, however, the artifice of race is often visible, self-evident, and even inescapable. People whose families include members of different races, for example, can rarely take race for granted. If for no other reason than self-defense, they need to learn the nature of the racial regimes that they and their relatives are certain to encounter, even in the most casual social interactions. Under the best of circumstances, mixed-race identity requires a performative dimension similar to the racial masquerading of Korla Pandit. Under some circumstances, it can provide a useful optic on power, a privileged standpoint from which important aspects of social relations can be absorbed, analyzed, and understood.

Yet mixed-race identity can also be a source of great personal pain and considerable political disempowerment. Of course, *all* people are mixed race, because pure races do not exist. The history of humans has been a history of intermixing.[14] Even among those who recognize that *all* identities are socially constructed, that *all* ethnic groups are coalitions, and that *all* racial identities are political, provisional, and strategic constructions rather than biological or anthropological facts, mixed-race people can sometimes find themselves unwanted in any group, ridiculed as disloyal, despised as the "other's other," because they carry within their embodied selves an identity that seems to threaten the unity and uniformity of aggrieved collectivities.

This identity can be something of a mystery to those identified by it. "I think I must be a mixed blood," confides Cherokee artist Jimmie Durham, seemingly referring to the vexed question of how much Indian ancestry is required to designate an individual as a true Native American. But then, with a joke that calls into question the very categories that cause controversy, Durham notes, "I claim to be male, although only one of my parents was male."[15]

One difficulty that mixed-race people confront comes from the strong solidarity that has been built within and among aggrieved racial groups through metaphorical and metonymic references to biology, to common bloodlines and bones. In her brilliant analysis of gender, orality, and vulgarity in Jamaican culture, Carolyn Cooper points to "the metonymy of blood and bone" embedded in novelist Vic Reid's definition of a true griot. Ordinary storytellers can get their wisdom from anywhere, Reid's narrator tells us in *Nanny Town,* but the knowledge of a griot comes from deep inside, "like an echo in the bone or a noise in the blood."[16]

Artists, intellectuals, and activists working within antiracist contexts have often made much of these noises and echoes. A strong and evocative tradition appealing to embodiment and ancestry has been an important form of self-defense for members of aggrieved communities. Black nationalism, Chicanismo, the American Indian movement, separatist feminism, and many other forms of identity-based mobilization have made permanent and enduring contributions to the struggle for social justice. Because social inequality is so often inscribed on the body, solidarity based on skin color, phenotype, and sex, on shared experiences or shared ancestry, has functioned frequently as a means of turning hegemony on its head, a way of transforming negative ascription into positive affirmation, and a vehicle for building identification with a common "us" instead of an isolated "me."

Yet appeals to blood and bone have ultimately proved themselves unreliable and unsuccessful. They privilege biology over belief and promise more sameness than any group's experiences can actually sustain. By emphasizing the identity of the victim rather than the innate injustices of victimization, movements based solely on identity can encourage each group to seek gains at the expense of others, to settle for placing different faces in high places, rather than using the knowledge that all oppressed groups have about the necessity to challenge *all* exploitation, dehumanization, and injustice.[17]

Because of the history of identity-based solidarity within aggrieved racial groups, mixed-race people understandably might feel tempted to fashion a firm and fixed identity category out of their diverse experiences. Embodiment and ancestry seem to determine the social status of mixed-race people, and consequently they might serve as important symbols of struggle. Yet symbolism is not substance. A closer look at the experiences of "raced" people in struggles for social justice reveals that reliance on firm and fixed identities has been more apparent than real.

Even the most militant forms of nationalism have never assumed that all members of an aggrieved group are alike. On the contrary, nationalist movements have characteristically struggled to impose clear political meanings on diffuse group identities, often devoting much more time to changing ideas and attitudes within their own groups than on battling those outside. By promoting the term *Chicano,* for example, Mexican American activists of the 1960s and 1970s sought a political rather than a biological source of self-definition. The term *Chicano* inspired them to build egalitarian solidarity around the needs of the most despised and oppressed part of their community, to disrupt the U.S. "ethnic" model of assimilation through deracination by evoking the mythical Aztlán, a nation that could not be easily absorbed into the national projects of either the United States or Mexico. Chicano militants attempted to build a common political project for a community that they recognized as deeply divided by region and religion, by language and legal status, by gender and generation. Similarly, the Asian American movement built a new collective U.S. panethnic identity among people with a wide range of class positions, people whose ancestors came from many different national backgrounds, spoke different languages, and practiced distinctly different religions.

The history that we now remember as made by nationalist identity-based struggles often, in fact, proceeded through recognition of intercultural and interethnic connections. In a revealing reflection, Chicano scholar–activist Carlos Muñoz recalls, "When we started the movement in the '60s, we tried to redefine ourselves as a mixed-race people of color both Spanish and Indian. Then, as we developed Chicano Studies, we discovered that African slaves were also taken throughout Mexico and elsewhere in the Americas, in the Vera Cruz and Acapulco areas in particular. We discovered that Asians were also taken to Mexico and Latin America. For example, the Spanish at one time brought Filipino slaves to Mexico."[18] The search for an authentic original Mexican identity foregrounded differences within the group and pointed the way toward alliances with other aggrieved communities.

Similarly, recently deceased (and greatly missed) attorney, activist, and cultural worker Chris Iijima remembered the construction of Asian American identity as a means to an end, not an end in itself. "It was created as an organizing tool to mobilize Asians to participate in the progressive movements of the times," Iijima asserted. "It was as much a mechanism to identify with one another as to identify with the struggles of others whether it is African Americans or Asians overseas, and it was less a marker of what one was and more a marker of what one believed," he concluded.[19]

Decisions about the present and future of mixed-race consciousness and political affiliation need to be made with a full understanding of the figurative meaning of embodiment and ancestry within the "race-based" tradition of social justice struggles. What seem on the surface to be essentialist appeals to embodiment and ancestry often turn out, on closer inspection, to be figurative ways of locating people in the present as the inheritors of historical traditions of struggle, suffering, sacrifice, and success, not as people with unmediated and unproblematic access to noises in the blood and echoes in the bone. These identities are, to echo the characteristically brilliant insight of historian Robin Kelley, not so much about blood lines as about bloodshed.

Oneida poet Roberta Hill tells us about some of the echoes she feels in her bones in "Preguntas." In the poem she describes her literature professor, Hernan Vidal, a political refugee from Chile. He tells Hill, "Your bones contain your people's history." She discovers a seemingly literal (rather than figurative) dimension to his statement when she visits her home state and learns "there is a bounty for brown women like me." Instead of the usual announcements for "turkey shoots," competitions in which sharpshooters vie for prize Thanksgiving turkeys as rewards for marksmanship, Hill finds a sign at a local pizzeria in Medford, Wisconsin, that vents anti-Indian hatred by proclaiming "The First Annual Indian Shoot." Hill writes, "I felt the bones in my fingers / and I scruffed them across the sign. / 'It is not the first,' the right fingerbones sang. / 'It has never been annual,' the left ones added."[20]

Hill's bones speak directly to her in this poem. They testify to the horrors of history and their continuing legacy in the present. But the "wisdom" in Hill's bones is activated, informed, and augmented by the experiences that her Chilean teacher had with political repression in South America. Hill connects the lessons she learned early in life from her father's "singing" and "sobbing," from "his struggle against the daily snare of being declared worthless," to the "cloud of loneliness and loss, of solidarity with those who suffer" that she sees on her professor's face. She expresses gratitude to her teacher, because the resemblance between her suffering and his teaches a larger lesson. Her suffering is not her peculiar and particular burden, not just a personal inheritance, but rather part of a broader context of injustice. It has more to do with the sickness of her enemies than with any deficiencies in her. "You have helped me understand," she tells both her father and Professor Vidal, "their fear of the dark is not my identity."[21]

Within aggrieved racialized communities, dancing has often been figured as a means of summoning up the ancestral presence. Through collective ritual, dancers' bodies seem to remember what the mind may have forgotten. Haitian vodou and rara ceremonies directly seek communication with the ancestors. The ring shout serves as a constantly renewable source of moral instruction and solidarity for African Americans.[22] Participants in Danza Azteca collectives burn sage and reenact ancient dances to locate themselves within a long tradition of indigenous and Mexican artistry and religious belief.[23] Pilipino Cultural Nights on college campuses salute ancestors by presenting elaborate production numbers organized around *kalapati, binasuan, tinikling,* and other folk dances of the Philippines. From the ghost dance to the grass dance, many instances of American Indian cultural revival and ethnic renewal have revolved around embodied activities that make ethnic identification a physical as well as an ideological process.[24] Dancing like this creates the very solidarity it invokes. Although seemingly speaking to the past and to the ancestors, these ritual performances also call a community into being through performance, staging solidarity in the present to point the way toward the future. The active process of coordinated and collective movement inscribes in the body the very messages it purports to find there; it creates a past capable of serving the present, using the imagined unity of the past as a guideline for the present and the future.

It is not that noises in the blood and echoes in the bone do not exist. The true griots in Jamaica that Vic Reid celebrates hear the same sounds that W. E. B. Du Bois detected in the spiritual "sorrow songs" that, he said, "stirred me strangely," even though he did not know the meaning of the words they contained. The words of these songs simply served as place markers for a deeper shared historical experience. Du Bois explains that these inchoate words and ancient melodies came from his grandmother's grandmother, "who was seized by an evil Dutch trader two centuries ago." She sang her song to her child, and "the child sang it to his children and they to their children's children, and so two hundred years it has traveled down to us and we sing it to our children, knowing as little as our fathers what its words may mean, but knowing well the meaning of its music."[25]

Frederick Douglass heard those same noises in the blood in songs that seemed to him made up of "unmeaning jargon, but which, nevertheless, were full of meaning to themselves."[26] For Tongva artist L. Frank and Chinese American writer Nellie Wong, noises in the blood are also heard literally as well as figuratively. "Sometimes when I'm working with soapstone, I can hear the voices of the ancestors," says Frank.[27] Wong contends that in order to begin writing her story she had to hear the voices of her ancestors, both the women heroes of Chinese lore and history and the unheralded courageous women of her parents' ancestral village in Guangzhou.[28]

Contact with ancestors can inform, authorize, and empower artists, intellectuals, and activists in the present. "I come from a long line of eloquent illiterates whose history reveals what words don't say," explains Chicana poet Lorna Dee Cervantes.[29] Farah Jasmine Griffin shows that the ancestor figure in Black fiction functions to remind readers of the strength and sustenance they can draw from the past. In the writings of Toni Morrison, Griffin notes, fiction itself can serve as a surrogate for actual ancestors.[30] Bahamian poet Marion Bethel's tribute to the feminist activist group DAWN positions politics in the present as a partial means of paying debts to the past. Her poem "And the Trees Still Stand" addresses ancestors directly, proclaiming that "we" are here because "you" made a road for us, beat back the bush, raked rocks and stones, pitched scalded tar, and uprooted trees "to turn that unchartered road into a journey with landmarks."[31] However much we recognize that these metaphors and metonyms are constructed, fabricated, and strategically deployed, we must also recognize that their power to mobilize a solidarity based on sameness has been an important vehicle for the antiracist struggle. And it is precisely this solidarity through sameness that seems denied to people identified or identifying themselves as mixed race.

What do echoes in the bones and noises in the blood mean to mixed-race people? What can they mean to former Black Panther Johnny Spain, who felt that he had to keep secret his mother's white identity in order to be part of the Black struggle?[32] What can they mean to scholar Tiya Miles, some of whose Cherokee ancestors likely owned some of her Black slave ancestors? What can they mean to Marie and Anita Daulne of the music group Zap Mama, two sisters whose Belgian father was killed by Congolese revolutionaries in that nation's war for independence and whose politically suspect status forced their Congolese mother to flee the country with them and migrate to Belgium? What can echoes in the bone and noises in the blood mean to the 600,000 Asian Americans who are also Latino, to the 1.7 million Latinos who are also Black, to the 93.6 percent of the people who claim Native American ancestry yet report their race to be white?[33] Exactly which noises and which echoes resonate for Cape Verde Islanders, whose ancestors are both Portuguese and African; for Lumbees, whose ancestors are white, Black, and Native American; or for Garifunas, whose ancestors are Blacks but not slaves, Indians but not North American, citizens of Belize, but also of Honduras, Guatemala, and the United States, and "native" speakers of English, Spanish, and Garifuna?

Musicians from intercultural backgrounds have often been seen as members of only one group. Blues guitarist Lowell Fulson was born on an Indian reservation in Oklahoma in 1921 and had Black and Indian ancestors. Yet he seemed "only" Black to audiences impressed by his mastery of the southwestern style of blues singing and guitar playing pioneered by Blind Lemon Jefferson and T-Bone Walker (who also claimed Indian ancestry).[34] Blues musician Hammie Nixon claimed Native American and Black ancestry, as did jazz singer Helen Humes.

Eddie Durham played electric guitar and trombone brilliantly for African American Texas and "Territory" swing bands in the 1930s and 1940s. Few people knew that Durham's father had one Irish and one Mexican parent, and his mother's parents were Black and American Indian.[35] Blues singer Tommy McCracken identifies himself as Black, Irish, and Native American. During the 1950s, New Orleans guitarist Earl Stanley seemed black to audiences as well as to members of the Night Trains and other ensembles with which he performed. Stanley's mother was Black, but his father was a Yaqui Indian who instructed his entire family to play Mexican music at home. Yet commercial opportunities in rhythm and blues led Stanley to emphasize the Black side of his heritage.[36] Ragtime piano virtuoso Louis Chauvin was Black and Mexican, as was the New Orleans clarinetist Lorenzo Tio. Charles Mingus's grandmother was Chinese and perhaps also Mexican. James Brown claimed Afro-Asian ancestry from his mother's Caribbean side of the family as well as Native American heritage.[37]

The unease that mixed-race people can face holds enormous import at the present moment, because neoliberal and neoconservative opportunists seeking to undermine enforcement of U.S. civil rights laws have seen the existence of mixed-race people as a strategic wedge that might be used to reject claims for social justice from aggrieved racial groups. In order to evade their responsibilities to communities of color for the continuing effects of the unfair gains and unjust enrichments generated by past and present discrimination, neoliberals and neoconservatives alike seize on the existence of mixed-race people as a means of representing race in the United States as personal, private, individual, and idiosyncratic rather than institutional, ideological, collective, and cumulative. They hope that a proliferation of new identities will fragment the solidarity of aggrieved groups and frustrate race-based remedies for discrimination, such as affirmative action. If racial identities are uncertain and racial boundaries unclear, then the privileges of white supremacy can be secured, and the manifestly racist injuries suffered by the victims of discrimination in housing and employment—from mortgage and insurance redlining, from racial profiling, and from environmental racism—will not be remedied. Although these provocateurs generally demonstrate no sincere interest in and no actual knowledge about the experiences, problems, or perspectives of mixed-race people, they nonetheless see great tactical utility in the mixed-race category. As David Parker and Miri Song warn us, "The topic of 'mixed race' can bring out the worst in people."[38]

Deliberately confusing a desire for recognition with a renunciation of rights, conservative University of California regent Ward Connerly argued that the successful effort to allow individuals to check more than one racial category on the 2000 census form represented "a protracted outcry over the census's focus on race."[39] Liberal historian David Hollinger argues that mixed-race people are now performing a valuable service to American society by making ethnoracial affiliation a matter of individual choice and preference rather than a matter of external or institutional ascription. "It is the willingness to form new communities rather than merely remaining loyal to old ones," Hollinger argues, that distinguishes mixed-race people as "worthy" in comparison with the disreputable raced subjects who are rejected by Hollinger because they remain loyal to old racial categories that no longer have determinate meaning in his eyes.[40]

Yet Hollinger makes it clear that the voluntary choice made by mixed-race people must agree with the one that *he* has chosen for them. As George Sanchez points out in his devastating critique of the fantasy of "mixed-race" identity as the cost-free solution to the racial ills of the United States, Hollinger's argument is racist, because it is based on biology, alleging that it is the mixed gene pools of mixed-race people that force them to choose a mixed-race identity. Hollinger's argument is also totalitarian, because his formulation allows mixed-race people to identify *only* as mixed race. For Hollinger, if they choose a white identity, they reinforce white supremacy, but if they identify completely with an aggrieved community of color, they reinscribe the "ethnic nationalism" that Hollinger despises. To satisfy him, mixed-race people must choose a dual existence, must serve as bridges between cultures and colors. As Sanchez astutely notes, "What a burden for these super-Americans to shoulder! What an abandonment of responsibility by those of us who appear to be bound by one racial identity!"[41]

Connerly and Hollinger are so eager to make race, and especially blackness, disappear that they do not even bother to investigate the history of societies like Brazil, where the elimination of overt racial categories in law makes race even more powerful in shaping actual opportunities and life chances.[42] They do not notice that allowing people to check more than one racial classification on the census entails *more* emphasis on race rather than less. As Liz Guillen of the Mexican American Legal Defense and Education Fund argues, "The fact that so many people checked the mixed race box signifies a cry for the census to capture who I really am, not to ignore race completely."[43] Connerly and Hollinger know so little about the history of ethnogenesis in the United States that they fail to discern that social movements for justice along racial lines have never been based solely in biology but rather in collective and deliberate efforts to build new communities by giving an internal political meaning to external ascription. Hollinger, in particular, is so eager to evade the overwhelming evidence that shows the salience of race in determining opportunities and life chances that he portrays the radical solidarity of Blacks in fighting against contemporary discrimination and exclusion as merely an outdated loyalty to a "past" community.

What were the architects of Asian American and Native American panethnicity doing in the 1960s and 1970s if not creating new voluntary communities based on shared intellectual and cultural understandings? What were the advocates of Chicanismo and Black Power doing if not giving a political definition to a presumed biological identity and then striving to persuade others in their groups to adopt those politics? As Alexandra Harmon emphasizes in discussing Native American ethnogenesis, "Virtually every characteristic or practice that has marked Indians in the past—name, physical appearance, language, location, method of governance, religion, kinship system, and even group life itself—can lapse without necessarily dimming people's determination to be counted as Indians."[44]

Moreover, we are connected to one another even when we do not share bloodlines. As Luis Alberto Urrea writes, "People daily speak a quilt of words, and continents and nations and tribes and even enemies dance all over your mouth when you speak. The tongue seems to know no race, affiliation, no breed, no caste, no order, no genus, no lineage. The most dedicated Klansman spews the language of his adversaries while reviling them."[45]

It should not be surprising that the enemies of antiracist activism deliberately misrepresent antiracist strategic political, cultural, and intellectual formulations as biological essentialism. In so doing, they shift attention away from critiques of normativity and whiteness, putting antiracists on the defensive, as if they were the authors of the racist categories they find themselves forced to confront. Yet some of the underlying assumptions within antiracist politics sometimes actually encourage these distortions. Too often, they take their own group's history for granted and fail to foreground the lessons they have learned over the years through long and difficult struggle.

Like most social movements of the industrial era, the antiracist activism of the civil rights era relied on the solidarity of sameness. It built organic solidarity around common experiences and common identities, deciding that identities like race produce commonalities that are more important than the differences that divide the identity group. They knew that all ethnic groups are coalitions, that all identities are socially constructed, that there has never been one way to be Black, or one way to be a worker, or one way to be a citizen, or one way to be gay or lesbian. But especially given the pressures on them to disidentify with low-status groups, it was often extremely satisfying to be with people who seemed similar to themselves, who shared a common language, religion, skin color, cuisine, or culture. Radical solidarity based on a common racial identity not only turned negative ascription into positive affirmation; it also functioned as an alternative to the radical divisiveness and disidentification that often plague aggrieved groups, because their members constantly compete with one another for scarce resources and limited prestige, see a mirror of their own humiliation and debasement in the faces of people who look just like them. Yet this organic solidarity often exacted a high price by making antiracists expect to find (or feign) more uniformity within groups than actually existed. It encouraged them to seek uniformity rather than unity, to confuse identicality with identity. By denying the divisions that existed within their own ranks, they deprived themselves of the dynamism of difference—the consciousness and knowledge that can come only from seeing a problem from more than one perspective, the processes that fashion group identity from the full range, complexity, and contradictions of collective experience.

Moreover, the desire for sameness always leads to disappointment, to divisive fights about who is Chicano enough or Black enough or Indian enough. As Maryse Conde argues in respect to the legacy of negritude in the francophone Caribbean, the exhilarating promises of "likeness" and "similarity" that nationalist mobilizations promoted only set the stage for deep disillusionment and sectarian divisiveness when Afro-Caribbeans like herself started to realize that they could not solve their own problems through references to an idealized and undifferentiated pan-Africanism. "Without Negritude," Conde contends, "we would not have experienced the degree of disillusionment that we did."[46] She notes that emphasis on a shared pan-African identity during anticolonial struggles often occluded gender differences, reminding us that unveiled Algerian women carried and detonated bombs in the war of independence from France, only to find themselves veiled and disenfranchised in the nation their sacrifices helped to create.

When mixed-race people see themselves as lacking secure and fixed points of reference, as vexed by choices about what their identities mean, they are not different from "raced" people, from people who have learned that solidarity based on identity is limited but that solidarities based on identities are unlimited, that we cannot draw our politics from our identities but instead must construct our identities through our politics. Racial identifications and identities are historical, socially constructed, and strategic. They are not good sources of safety, security, or certainty. They are based on legacies of belief as well as those of blood and bone. Their noises and echoes come to us by choice as well as by chance; they are inherited *and* invented, found *and* fabricated, determined *and* dynamic.

Ethnic studies activists, intellectuals, and artists have often made their greatest contributions in spaces that might not seem to belong to them by birth. Chinese American ancestry does not diminish Grace Lee Boggs's heroic contributions to the African American freedom struggle.[47] Yemeni farmworker Nagi Daifallah became a martyr to the Chicano movement when he was shot and killed by a county sheriff in California in 1973 because of his activism in the United Farm Workers (UFW) union.[48] Led by Chicanos, including César Chávez and Delores Huerta, the UFW itself emerged out of the Filipino Agricultural Workers Organizing Committee, led by Larry Itliong and Philip Vera Cruz.[49] Chicano Ralph Lazo presented himself as a Japanese American during World War II and endured internment at the Manzanar Relocation Center so that he could stay with his Japanese American friends from Los Angeles's Belmont High School. "Who can say I haven't got Japanese blood in me?" Lazo asked incredulous relocation officials when they discovered his identity and ordered him released from the camp.[50] Yuri Kochiyama's internment camp experiences motivated her later participation in Malcolm X's Organization of Afro-American Unity as well as in the Puerto Rican independence movement.[51] The flag flown by activists in the American Indian movement at Wounded Knee, South Dakota, in 1973 featured four colors—red, yellow, black, and white—to represent four races and four directions.

Although rarely acknowledged by their identities, mixed-race people have routinely played important roles in progressive politics and interethnic antiracist activism. In many cases their mixed-race heritage has proved to be an advantage, not because of biology, but because it armed them with the situated knowledge of more than one group. William Apess wrote *A Eulogy on King Phillip,* one of the most powerful condemnations of North American anti-Indian racism. Its author, a participant in the Mashpee revolt, was a Christian convert who claimed a Euro-Indian father and a Pequot mother (although some scholars believe she might have been an African American slave).[52] Lucy Parsons is often celebrated for her work as a labor activist, anarchist, and communist but is rarely recognized as an individual with Mexican, Black, and Native American ancestry.[53] Bob Marley has become a global symbol of Black nationalism, even though his father was white. The reggae music that he is famous for emerged from the combined efforts of Black, Chinese, and East Indian artists and producers. As previously mentioned in chapter 2, even *ganja,* the word Marley and other Rastafarians used for their sacramental herb, is of East Indian origin.[54]

An Anishinaabeg (Ojibwe) activist and two-time candidate for vice president of the United States, Winona LaDuke draws on the activist example of her father, Vincent LaDuke, from the White Earth Reservation, in Minnesota, but also from the experiences of her mother, Betty Bernstein, a Polish-Ukrainian Jewish American from the Bronx, as well as from the work of her grandmother Helen Bernstein, who was a trade union organizer and antifascist activist in the 1930s and 1940s. Poet, author, and teacher June Jordan has been rightly recognized for her incomparable contributions to Black culture and the Black freedom movement, but Jordan herself felt it was very important to acknowledge that her father was Black and Chinese and that her mother was Black and East Indian.[55]

The ability of raced and mixed-race activists, artists, and intellectuals to draw lines of belief and to act in arenas not determined by their skin color or phenotype may hold one key to formulating a politics of mixed-race identity in the present. In California at the end of the twentieth century, the number of babies designated by their parents as "interracial" exceeded the number of babies designated as Black, Asian American, or Native American.[56] What are the noises and the echoes that will resonate for them? What role will they play in identifying the things that divide us and the things that might unite us in the future? Will they campaign to build a panethnic collectivity out of "mixed-race" identity? Will they seek to maximize their own self-interest by strategically disidentifying with aggrieved communities of color, by seeking inclusion for themselves by policing the exclusion of others? Or will they use the particular and specific situated knowledges they possess to serve as weapons against racist exploitation and hierarchy? These choices are not so different from those confronting people who identify themselves as white, Black, Asian American, Native American, or Latino. None of us has had the luxury of picking our parents or our pigment, but all of us have the obligation to pick our politics and our principles.

Social movements by aggrieved racialized groups often deploy a common identity as a strategic source of organic solidarity. Yet, no single social group is ever so powerful or so united that it can secure meaningful victories on its own without any outside help. Activists in antiracist struggles always need to change others and themselves in order to change society, to bring into being new identities, identifications, and affiliations. Cultural and political activism must enact what it envisions, must produce new social relations in the course of struggle in order to bring about what Karl Marx called the alteration of people on a mass scale, ridding themselves of "the muck of ages"—the inherited and largely uninterrogated categories, classifications, characteristics, and qualities that constrain our actions and our imaginations.[57]

Strategic anti-essentialism has been a particularly effective way for antiracist activists to effect affiliations and alliances grounded in interethnic ideologies, epistemologies, and ontologies. Gayatri Spivak defines strategic essentialism as the tactical embrace of a single social identity in order to advance collective claims for social justice. Under conditions when the things that unite members of a particular group are more compelling than the things that divide them, strategic essentialism makes sense. When racial profiling causes police officers to stop African Americans for "driving while Black," a unified response from the Black community is warranted, regardless of that community's heterogeneity and diversity. When pervasive domestic violence threatens the safety, security, and dignity of all women, however, Black women may well want to speak out as "women," a strategic essentialism that for the moment emphasizes gender commonalities, even across racial lines.[58]

Strategic anti-essentialism, on the other hand, entails identifying with a group to which you do *not* belong, presenting yourself as someone else in order to express more effectively who you actually are. Though Willa Cather's studies of the "Orient" were ethnocentric and even racist, they nonetheless opened up to her a world of sensuality that she projected onto frontier life in Nebraska and New Mexico in her historical novels. Her decision to tell the story of *My Ántonia* in the voice of a male narrator enabled her to express lesbian desire at a time when it would not have been possible to voice that desire directly in print.[59] Working-class Blacks in New Orleans parade in the streets masquerading as Plains Indians every Mardi Gras day and every St. Joseph's day, because playing "Indian" enables them to take on the identity of heroic warriors resisting white oppression without bringing on direct repression from the local white power structure. Yet the message comes through clearly to other Blacks. Community activist Jerome Smith remembers thinking of Mardi Gras Indians as part of a culture that "unconsciously made statements about black power . . . the whole thing about excellence, about uniqueness, about creativity, about protecting your creativity."[60]

Strategic anti-essentialism can enable open expression of suppressed parts of one's own identity. Yet in depending on racial disguise, it can do more to harm than to help antiracist efforts. Inhabitants of the actual Orient were not aided by Willa Cather's appropriation of orientalist stereotypes, and the cause of American Indians could hardly be helped by the Mardi Gras Indians' reiteration of Indian stereotypes from Wild West shows, dime novels, and John Ford films, even though some New Orleans tribes made sincere and laudable efforts to understand and assist Native American activists. When coupled with "branching out," however, strategic anti-essentialism can serve broader purposes.

Juan Flores identifies "branching out" as a characteristic cultural and political strategy of Puerto Ricans in New York. Defamed and discriminated against as foreigners even though they are U.S. citizens, relegated to low-wage jobs, and restricted to crowded barrios while enduring ridicule for failing to "assimilate," Puerto Ricans find themselves portrayed as a racial menace to North American whiteness, even though they did not think of themselves as "nonwhite" in Puerto Rico. In response, Nuyoricans fashion a selective connection to and interaction with North American cultures, branching out to Black Americans, other migrants from Latin America and the Caribbean, other "unwanted" groups such as Chinese Americans and Arab Americans, and "more cautiously" to Irish, Italian, and Jewish Americans, without ever seeking absorption (and deracination) in a "white" center. The polylateral points of connection afforded by branching out enable Puerto Rican New Yorkers opportunities to remain "ethnic" without being either "always ethnic" or "only ethnic," to create new identities without having to surrender the historical consciousness and situated knowledges specific to their group.[61]

The odyssey of musician Lee Brown offers an illustrative demonstration of the utility of branching out, but it also evidences the perils of racial masquerade. Like John Roland Redd, Brown passed through multiple identities in fashioning a career in popular music. Born into an African American family in Newark, New Jersey, in 1919, Brown remembers his youth as a constant battle against segregation and discrimination. In an autobiography published in 1967, he presents himself as someone who lived by the precepts of the Black Power movement all of his life. He claims that when he was twenty, he was so upset by the practices of motion picture theater managers in Newark, who restricted African Americans to seats only in the balcony, that he joined a delegation attempting to negotiate a change in policy. When their overtures were rejected, they resorted to direct action. "One Sunday when the theatre was filled to capacity," he recalls, "we all got up in different parts of the balcony and shouted FIRE!! We repeated this procedure every week for a month and colored people began to sit in orchestra seats."[62] Brown presents incident after incident in which he and his friends broke the color line through some form of militant direct action like this.

Yet the "essentialist" Black Power strategies popular in the 1960s, when Brown wrote his book, do not always conform to the strategies he reports himself pursuing in actual contests against racialized power. Brown's approach draws more on strategic anti-essentialism and on branching out than on Black nationalism. Brown learned early that racial ambiguity could work in his favor. When the musicians' union refused to admit him and the other musicians in his band into the all-white local, light-skinned Pancho Diggs joined on his own, because he was able to pass for white. Union officials were furious when they discovered they had admitted a Black member, but because Diggs had a valid union card, they could not prevent the whole band from receiving union scale. Once the dual-wage system was broken, the union relented and allowed Brown and the other musicians to join.[63]

Brown chafed at many of the restrictions imposed on him as a young Black man in Newark. He found himself barred from employment by the city's largest and best-paying companies. He had to watch high school classmates with grades far worse than his secure jobs for which he was turned down. Brown wanted a better job than the ones that seemed available to him, so he hit on a novel strategy. Noting the popularity of "Sabu, the Elephant Boy" (the very South Asian character played by the close friend of Korla Pandit, mentioned earlier in this chapter), Brown noticed that Sabu's skin color was similar to his own.[64] He approached a seamstress and commissioned her to make him some turbans. His friends just laughed when they saw him dressed as Sabu, but Brown discovered that white people who did not know him showed him much more respect in a turban than they had when they believed him to be an American Black.

Brown began calling himself "Ram Singh." He moved to Los Angeles and secured a job as chauffeur to Hollywood film star Errol Flynn. He found that Ram Singh could do things that Lee Brown could not: stay in luxury hotels, date white women, and draw respectful bows "from the southern ofays" in his neighborhood.[65] Brown carried his disguise to a new level after working for Flynn for eight months. The actor was accused of having sex with underage girls and did not want his chauffeur available for questioning by the police, so he paid Ram Singh five hundred dollars to leave town. But before he could depart, Brown experienced a sudden appendicitis attack and had to be taken to a hospital emergency room. The cab driver who drove him there, noticing that he had passed out, stole his wallet before dumping him at the hospital. None of the physicians knew who he was, and Brown had no proof of his identity. Not wishing to be Lee Brown again but unable to continue as Ram Singh in order to protect Errol Flynn, Brown told his doctors that his name was Babs Gonzales.

Brown claims that as a child, he and each of his three brothers were nicknamed Babs (which, if true, must have presented some difficulties for people trying to reach them by phone). The "Gonzales" was a generic Spanish surname that Brown chose because he believed, as "Juan Rolando" did, that he would encounter less discrimination as a Mexican American than he would as an African American. Brown bought a Spanish-language dictionary and started associating with Mexican street hustlers on Sixth Street in downtown Los Angeles. His local draft board in Newark was looking for Lee Brown, but since he had secured legal papers identifying himself as Babs Gonzales, Brown thought he would be safe. Unfortunately, his mother told federal officers where he was.

They traveled to Los Angeles and sent him back east by bus. On the journey, he spoke only Spanish so that he could be served at bus station lunch counters. One time he even brought back food for two Black women on the bus, whose patronage was unwelcome at the lunch counters that were nonetheless willing to provide service to a "Mexican" like Babs Gonzales.

One additional disguise was necessary before he could escape the draft. The man known as Lee Brown, Ram Singh, and Babs Gonzales reported to his preinduction physical in Newark wearing women's clothes, with his toenails and fingernails painted bright red. When the army rejected him, he was free to become Babs Gonzales again and resume his career as a jazz pianist and singer. As the leader of the jazz group Three Bips and a Bop, Gonzalez enjoyed international recognition and acclaim putting lyrics to bebop instrumentals. A stint in Paris even enabled him to learn enough French to cross the color line in a restaurant in Atlanta, Georgia. When no one offered him service, Gonzales began speaking loudly in French. Fearing an international incident, the manager not only served him but picked up the tab for his drinks.[66]

It is not completely clear whether the autobiography of Lee Brown/Ram Singh/Babs Gonzales is an accurate account of events or simply another exercise in creative masquerade. His peculiar punctuation system puts everyone's name in quotation marks, as if "Ben Webster," "James Moody," and "Harry Edison" might be pseudonyms. He even puts the names of cities in quotation marks, as if "Newark," "Paterson," and "Trenton" might really be named Lee Brown, Ram Singh, or Babs Gonzales. But even if it is only performance, the book is a powerful example of how strategic anti-essentialism and branching out can augment opportunities and allow for the elasticity of identities.

Brown's story is similar to that of Johnny Otis, an ethnic Greek who became "Black by persuasion"; to the story of Little Julian Herrera, the first Chicano doo-wop rock 'n' roll heartthrob, who actually turned out to be a Hungarian Jew; to the story of Narcisso Martinez, who sold recordings of polkas under his own name to Mexicans but marketed the same recordings as "Louisiana Pete" when selling to Cajuns and as "the Polski Kwartet" when selling to Polish Americans; and to the story of Korla Pandit. Lee Brown combatted the everyday indignities of racial discrimination by carrying social construction to an extreme. By proving that identities can be learned and performed, he was able through strategic anti-essentialism and branching out to prove that belief and belonging are not always matters of blood or bone.

Activist organizations today constantly grapple with the complexities of identity categories. Asian Immigrant Women Advocates originated as an Asian American feminist organization committed to advancing the interests of new immigrant women from that continent. But they found that job segmentation and environmental racism mandated that any efforts to help Asian immigrant women had to assist Latinas as well. Korean Immigrant Worker Advocates in Los Angeles started out trying to organize Korean low-wage workers in Los Angeles sweatshops and restaurants. They discovered that in order to help Korean low-wage workers, they had to ally with Latino and Latina workers against Korean immigrant capitalists. The Bus Riders Union in Los Angeles was formed to challenge the neighborhood race effects that leave inner-city bus riders with expensive but inefficient transportation as a way of subsidizing luxury trains for suburban commuters. Their multiracial organizing team realized that transit racism meant that the 15 percent of inner-city bus riders who are white suffer from neighborhood race effects aimed at people of color and that the small percentage of suburban train riders who are people of color benefit from the possessive investment in whiteness. Consequently, they filed a civil rights suit to challenge transit racism. The suit stipulated that, for purposes of this case, the inner-city bus riders who are white should be treated as people of color and the suburban trade riders who are African American, Asian American, and Native American should be treated as if they were white. The Bus Riders Union won a settlement because of that suit, a settlement that has brought lower fares and better service to inner-city bus riders on new nonpolluting buses, purchased solely because of the union's activism.

The pain and political frustrations of mixed-race people are real. They cannot be wished away by glib formulations or erased by the example of a few inspired eccentrics. Like all racial identities, the "mixed-race" category can be neither entirely embraced nor entirely evaded. But it can be analyzed, and understood, and utilized as a standpoint from which to fight against all forms of dehumanization, exploitation, oppression, and suppression, following the example of the race-specific activism by Asian Immigrant Women

Advocates and Korean Immigrant Worker Advocates as well as by the consciously multiethnic organizing of the Bus Riders Union. As an embodied identity, "mixed race" is an accident of history. As an epistemology and a situated knowledge, as a standpoint from which to create strategic anti-essentialism and branching out, it is a powerful weapon of the struggle available to everyone.

In her poem "Child of the Americas," Jewish Puerto Rican writer and poet Aurora Levins Morales proclaims the virtues of her mixed identity. Like the Yoruba elders of West Africa and the vodou believers in Haiti, she focuses on the trope of the "crossroads," the place where different paths converge, where painful collisions happen, but also the place where moral and political choices can make things better. Speaking literally for herself but figuratively for all of us, she ruminates on an identity that has Africa in it but is not African; that has indigenous elements but no direct access to them; that is European but no longer has a home in Europe. She proclaims herself a new creation, made by history. "I was born at the crossroads," she confides, "and I am whole."[67]

9. Salsa

The Hidden History of Colonialism

Not coincidentally, the richness of *boricua* cultural production and discourse is, to a great extent, a result of the constraints placed upon Puerto Rican economic and political agency.

—Frances Negrón-Muntaner, *Boricua Pop: Puerto Ricans and the Latinization of American Culture*

Puerto Rican salsa singer Héctor Lavoe, famous for his distinctive vocals with Willie Colón's band, died and was buried in New York City in 1993.[1] Lavoe succumbed to a heart attack, aggravated by a long battle with AIDS. Mourners throughout the hemisphere (including the estimated 35 percent of the population of Puerto Rico that resides on the North American mainland) staged prayer vigils and memorials to honor him. Yet many of Lavoe's fans in Puerto Rico viewed their great cultural hero's interment in the Bronx—in the earth of the island's primary colonizer—to be a national disgrace. Some of them launched a campaign to have the singer's body exhumed from St. Raymond's Cemetery so that he could be reburied in Puerto Rico. Although Lavoe's family stated emphatically that they simply followed the singer's own clear request to be buried in the Bronx, nationalists in Puerto Rico were not placated.[2]

The battle over where Héctor Lavoe's grave belongs serves as a surrogate for a broader question about where Puerto Rico and its people "belong," especially at the turn of the twenty-first century, when transnational migration, communication, and commerce complicate the nature of national identities for all people. As members of the world's oldest continuous colony, Puerto Ricans have never fully controlled their own destiny. Conquest, occupation, and exploitation have long shaped the contours of life on the island. "Puerto Rico is like a stray dog," comments visual artist Jaime Carrero. "We've been pushed around for 500 years."[3] Yet colonialism has never been simply a local matter; the history of Puerto Rico has been played out on a global scale.

Immigrants to the U.S. mainland from Puerto Rico have sailed or flown over the waves of the Atlantic Ocean, but their journeys have also been propelled by long waves of history connecting the mainland to its colonial possession. The United States seized Puerto Rico by force. It imposed citizenship on Puerto Ricans as part of a broader strategy to secure control over the island's natural resources and to take advantage of Puerto Rico's strategic military position as the gateway to the Caribbean. The Jones Act of 1917, which granted U.S. citizenship to Puerto Ricans, also codified and confirmed their colonial status. Puerto Ricans could not vote in presidential elections, yet U.S. presidents could veto laws passed by the Puerto Rican legislature. An auditor from the U.S. Treasury Department claimed final jurisdiction over the finances of Puerto Rico, and the U.S.-appointed commissioner of education supervised the selection of teachers in local schools and retained complete control over their curricula.[4] Coastwise shipping laws mandated that only ships built in the United States and manned by U.S. crews could conduct seaborne trade in Puerto Rico, adding an estimated 15 percent to the cost of the island's exports and imports.[5]

The restrictive immigration policies aimed at excluding southern and eastern Europeans from the United States between 1924 and 1965 unwittingly increased Puerto Rican migration to the U.S. mainland, because displaced urban and rural dwellers from the island filled the low-wage labor jobs that had previously gone to European immigrants. Puerto Ricans and southern Blacks swelled the ranks of migrant workers in agriculture and low-wage workers in industry during this time. Nearly one million Puerto Ricans moved to the North American mainland between 1940 and 1960.[6] The frequency of movement back and forth between the island and the mainland, the creation of mutual support circuits and networks linking dispersed sites, and the emergence of new cultural practices that conformed completely to neither the culture of their place of origin nor the culture of their place of arrival, all display the properties that contemporary scholars identify as transnational: "'multi-stranded social relations' that place immigrants simultaneously within their places of origin and settlement."[7]

Although European immigration during the industrial era actually contained more of these processes than contemporary scholars generally acknowledge, it is clear that today's immigrants to the United States from Latin America, Asia, and Africa display transnational practices that have a long and well-established history among Puerto Ricans. As Juan Flores argues, "Far from being unique or exceptional, the cultural disjunctures, ambiguities, and reconnections undergone by Puerto Ricans in both localities [Puerto Rico and the U.S. mainland] are paradigmatic of experiences familiar to more and more people, and nations, of the world."[8]

Like Héctor Lavoe, millions of Puerto Ricans have been forced to make a "home" for themselves far from home. Puerto Rican history happens in Newark and New York, in Miami and Milwaukee, in Hartford and Honolulu. Puerto Ricans speak Spanish and English. The politics of Puerto Rican identity entails complex antagonisms and affinities between Puerto Rico and other places, especially Spain, the United States, Cuba, Mexico, and the Dominican Republic. Puerto Ricans come to the U.S. mainland as Spanish-speaking immigrants from a colonized nation but also as U.S. citizens. Every facet of their lives in Puerto Rico has already been influenced by the U.S. government before they emigrate. They migrate to the very country whose policies compel them to seek escape.

The controversy over the interment of Héctor Lavoe emerged out of a long history of strife, suffering, struggle, and symbolic contestation. For Puerto Rican nationalists, the New York City burial of a beloved icon of the music most closely identified with the national aspirations of their people constituted a deep insult and injury. Yet the transnational history of salsa music and the significance of the parts of Puerto Rican history that have occurred off the island make the issue more complex than the nationalist formulation acknowledged.

Puerto Rico's most famous nationalist song, "Lamento borincano," was not composed in Puerto Rico. It was written in New York City by Rafael Hernández, a Puerto Rican national treasure who spent long stretches in his life in Mexico and the United States.[9] Hernández's Afro–Puerto Rican parents worked in the tobacco industry near Aguadilla, on the island's northwest coast. Like many other Puerto Rican workers, he came to New York after World War I in search of employment. During the days, Hernández worked a series of menial jobs in factories and restaurants. In the evenings, he played and sang his music, working for tips on street corners and in the bars and restaurants of East Harlem. In an urban setting far from home, Hernández composed "Lamento borincano," a song saluting the industrious—and mostly white—peasants from a rural part of the island, despite his own African ancestry. Hernández's song went on to have an enormous impact on island politics. In the 1940s, Luis Muñoz Marín (also an émigré *bohemio* in New York during the 1930s) used the song as the anthem for his political party, the Partido Popular Democratico.

Although iconic in the history of Puerto Rico, "Lamento borincano" attracted admirers throughout the Americas. José Luis González attributes its enduring popularity in Central and South America to its eloquence in expressing "a social reality that far from having become 'past history' is still fully alive" in the problems confronting peasants in El Salvador, Bolivia, Guatemala, Paraguay, Ecuador, and many other nations in the hemisphere.[10] Yet the song holds special meaning for Puerto Ricans as a symbol of their specific national aspirations and experiences. The lyrics of "Lamento borincano" present an allegorical interpretation of the history of Puerto Rico, but the song also registers the impact of emigration on Puerto Rican life and culture, expressing a perspective that has resonated powerfully with the many Puerto Ricans who have been forced to view their homeland from afar. Away from home, they often feel most attached to the parts of Puerto Rico that seem least like the North American urban neighborhoods to which they have migrated.[11]

Yet the glorification of the *jibaro* as the quintessential sign of Puerto Rican identity also responded to complicated racial politics on the island and the U.S. mainland. Frances Negrón-Muntaner notes astutely that nationalist pride often bears a direct relationship to the forms of negative ascription used to shame the nation. In the case of Puerto Rico, Spanish and U.S. colonizers viewed the island's mixed-race (Taino–Black–European) people with disdain, decried the poverty of the population, and ridiculed the reluctance of Puerto Ricans to take up arms either to defend Spanish rule or to oppose it (as the Cubans had). Negrón-Muntaner notes how the image of the mountain-dwelling, Spanish-speaking, creolized, light-skinned European *jíbaro* warded off the shame of a nationality derided as poor, devoid of culture, Black, and queer (both in the sense of being nonnormative among nations and in the sense of being putatively unmasculine, because its men had not taken up arms in the war of 1898).

"Lamento borincano" became a widely acknowledged symbol of Puerto Rican nationality, extolling *jíbaro* life in Puerto Rico almost as soon as the bolero was first recorded on July 14, 1930. Yet this recording did not take place in Puerto Rico either. A small combo led by Manuel "Canario" Jiménez first put the song on record in New York. Canario had left Puerto Rico as a teenage stowaway, spending his early adult years working as a merchant seaman. Although his trade took him away from music making for months at a time, he returned to New York after each voyage and attempted to maintain a career as a musician. He knew Rafael Hernández well by the time he recorded "Lamento borincano," having joined the composer's ensemble, the Trio Borinquen, in 1925.[12]

Throughout the twentieth century, working-class migration from the Caribbean and South America to New York City offered Puerto Rican musicians an opportunity to expose new audiences to the rich musical traditions of their homeland. Yet migration also changed the music they played. In New York, they produced fusions of different regional forms that most often remained isolated from one another on the island. At the same time, they brought the music of Puerto Rico into more direct dialogue with African American and other Afro-Caribbean musical forms, figures, styles, and genres. Canario distinguished himself in New York as the master of the *plena*, a music that originated in Puerto Rico's coastal cities. Yet, he grew up in the mountains, not on the coast. In fact, Canario had never heard *plena* music in Puerto Rico. He learned it only after meeting émigrés from coastal regions after he moved to New York.[13]

Not only did the popularity of *plena* in New York allow émigré Puerto Ricans to overcome regional divisions away from the island, but it also entailed a racial reconciliation. The *plena* and *bomba* genres had low prestige in Puerto Rico, principally because they were the musical genres most directly identified with Afro–Puerto Ricans. Cultural brokers and the institutions they controlled on the island anxiously emphasized the European heritage of Puerto Rico, insisting that the island's emblematic cultural products came from those areas with the least African presence. In New York, however, Afro–Puerto Rican styles like *plena* and *bomba* became the very forms that embodied Puerto Rican identity and consciousness. The long careers and extraordinary commercial success of New York–based Puerto Rican *plena* and *bomba* musicians Mon Rivera and Canario testify to the centrality of these forms to the Puerto Rican identity that emerged in New York.[14] Bands based in Puerto Rico led by Rafael Cortijo and César Concepción played regularly in New York for weeks on end. During the 1940s, Concepción's orchestra made frequent trips to perform in carnival celebrations in Caracas, Venezuela.

The success of Puerto Rican music in New York and Caracas changed the island in turn, when these musicians exerted enormous subsequent influence on the contours of cultural production and reception back home. Juan Flores identifies diasporic cultural productions exported back to the nation of origin as "cultural remittances," a concept that grows directly out of the dialogic relationship between New York and Puerto Rico but has enormous relevance for many other diasporic populations and their countries of origin around the globe.[15]

The transformations of *plena* and *bomba* in New York stemmed, in part, from their political utility. *Plena* songs have a long history of topical lyrics, similar to calypso in the Anglo-Caribbean West Indies. Like Jamaican *mento, plena* is often described as a "singing newspaper."[16] *Bomba* signifies plantation slave culture through its distinctly African dance forms but also because it is played on barrel-shaped drums, a tradition that started when African slaves pounded out rhythms on the barrels used for manufacturing and storing rum, the very commodity for which their labor was expropriated.[17]

The life histories of Rafael Hernández, Rafael Cortijo, Canario, and so many other Puerto Rican musicians demonstrate that New York City has been a central site for the creation, distribution, and reception of Puerto Rican culture. U.S. colonial policies promoted emigration from the island, ostensibly to reduce the density of Puerto Rico's population but really to enable the consolidation of large landholdings by agribusiness firms.[18] Absentee U.S. land-owners eventually came to control three-fifths of the island's sugar industry while an ever-increasing number of Puerto Rican farm-ers lost their small landholdings and became wage workers in the postwar period.[19] The political and economic strategies available to generations of low-wage workers from the island have included migration to the U.S. mainland and other sites as one of the few measures open to them to combat the limited economic oppor-tunities available at home as a direct result of U.S. control over Puerto Rico.

Puerto Ricans do not cross a national border in coming to the North American mainland (or to Hawai'i), but the cognitive map-ping of their community requires the ability to see events on the mainland and on the island as relational and mutually constitutive, as linked parts of a dialogic history that continuously takes place both *aquí* (here) and *allá* (there). The tale of how Rafael Hernández came to New York in the first place offers an illustrative anecdote emblematic of the complex cultural patterns that diasporic Puerto Ricans have historically confronted and created.

In the early months of U.S. participation in World War I in 1917, African American composer and band leader James Reese Europe traveled to Puerto Rico. He went to recruit musicians to play in a band attached to the 369th Infantry "Hellfighters" Band of the New York National Guard, an all-Black unit. The regiment's white commanding officer, Colonel William Hayward, wanted to orga-nize "the best damn brass band in the United States Army" in order to raise the reputation of African American soldiers, to convince the army to deploy them in combat, and perhaps to end segregation in the military altogether. Hayward hired Europe to organize his "dream" band because of the musician's many previous successes as an artist and entrepreneur. Europe had staged the first concert ever by a Black orchestra in Carnegie Hall, and he secured the first recording contract given to an African American ensemble.[20] He organized other musicians to form mutual benefit societies, and his "society orchestra" introduced the fox-trot to U.S. audiences by providing accompaniment and choreography for the popular white British dance team of Vernon and Irene Castle.

James Reese Europe could not persuade enough New York musi-cians to give up their lucrative careers to join the army, so he con-vinced Hayward to let him recruit Black musicians elsewhere.

He found the brass players that he needed in New York but was frustrated in his efforts to hire enough reed players, specialists Europe particularly desired to give his band the ability to simulate the powerful effects that string instruments give to an orchestra. Europe convinced Hayward to send him to Puerto Rico, where he recruited nearly half of Manuel Tizol's San Juan Municipal Band into his ensemble—thirteen musicians in all, one of whom was Rafael Hernández.[21]

Accustomed to playing classical music from scores, Hernández and the other Puerto Ricans who joined the band had to learn to improvise and to play without sheet music in order to perform in the manner commonly expected of Black musicians.[22] Yet they already enjoyed considerable experience as improvisers playing *contradanzas* and *danzones* in the Caribbean. Moreover, the kinds of jazz playing performed by members of Europe's orchestra in New York reflected Latin influences in early New Orleans jazz, especially improvisations by lead clarinetist and cornet players, as well as the syncopated rhythms that shaped early ragtime.[23]

The Puerto Ricans in Europe's band were not "Black" in any meaningful sense in Puerto Rico, but once they joined the 369th Infantry "Hellfighters" Band, they took on the identity, and status, of African Americans. Almost as soon as they arrived in the United States, they marched triumphantly in a parade in Harlem, hailed by admiring crowds as heroes of "the race." The echoes of that reception were still in their ears when Europe and his band members were exposed to the harsh and punitive prejudices of white supremacy. The U.S. Army's top brass refused to give them weapons or to let them train with other guard units. They assigned them to receive basic training in the Jim Crow segregated South, in Spartanburg, South Carolina. Although the band played popular (and free) concerts for townspeople, the presence of a military unit composed of Blacks frightened and offended many local residents. Spartanburg whites harassed members of the unit repeatedly. Army officials refused to defend the Black troops from white vigilante violence and, in fact, gave in to the harassment. They decided that the unit would be safer on the front lines of combat in France than back "home" in South Carolina, so they sent the regiment overseas after only three weeks of basic training.

The Puerto Rican and Black soldiers in the 369th Infantry regiment received better treatment from the French people than they received from the citizens of Spartanburg or from their own fellow soldiers. Instead of welcoming the contributions that the regiment might make to the war effort, the U.S. military command in France refused to let the 369th Infantry into combat. The officers feared setting a precedent that might lead to integration of the army in the future. The French army, however, needed reinforcements and did not mind if the soldiers fighting on their side were Black. Thus, Europe and his Black and Puerto Rican musicians entered combat, not as U.S. soldiers, but as members of the Sixteenth Division of the Fourth French Army.

By moving from San Juan to Harlem, Rafael Hernández and his fellow Spanish-speaking Puerto Rican musicians had become "Black" in a new way. Their journey to South Carolina and to the front lines in Europe changed them in other ways. Because of North American exclusionary racism, they found themselves unwelcome in South Carolina but entitled to a remarkably strange and composite identity in the war—as *Spanish*-speaking light-skinned *Black* soldiers fighting against *Germans* for the *French* army under the command of an *African American* man from the *United States* whose last name was *Europe*!

The Puerto Rican and North American Black soldiers in Europe's regiment served with distinction, both as soldiers and as musicians. They earned adulation from their allies in France. Musicians attached to the French army were so impressed by Europe's band that they asked him for sheet music so they could play the same arrangements. When they failed to reproduce the sounds that Europe's band made, they became suspicious and demanded the opportunity to inspect the Black musicians' instruments, because they were convinced that only "trick" horns and reeds could make those inspiring and unusual sounds. Europe and his men received recognition and respect in France that were denied them by officers and enlisted men from their own country. In a characteristically mean-spirited measure, high-ranking officers ordered military police to harass the unit while it waited for passage home at the war's end. The white officers wanted to "prepare" the Black soldiers for their return to the United States by making sure that they would not go back to North America with too much pride or with the expectation of continuing to receive the dignity, respect, and freedom that they had enjoyed in Europe.[24]

When the war ended, many of the Puerto Rican musicians in

the unit moved to New York. Rafael Hernández joined his sister, Victoria, who had arrived in the city in 1919. She operated a store near 115th Street on Madison Avenue, supplementing her income from selling groceries by selling phonograph records and giving piano lessons. Musicians and fans flocked to her establishment throughout the 1920s. In 1930, Victoria Hernández started her own record label.[25]

Puerto Rican musicians in New York after World War I found themselves forced once again to confront the North American racial order. Light- and dark-skinned Puerto Rican musicians had played together in San Juan and in the 369th Infantry "Hellfighters" Band in France, but they had to perform with separate orchestras in New York. Dark-skinned musicians such as trombonist Fernando Arbello and tuba player Ralph Escudero secured positions with an African American band led by Fletcher Henderson. Light-skinned Louis "King" Garcia appeared in white bands led by Benny Goodman and Tommy Dorsey. Miguel Ángel Duchesne played "hot" Spanish trumpet in the band of a notoriously "cold" Anglo, Paul Whiteman.[26] Trombonist Juan Tizol's racial ambiguity in North America, on the other hand, enabled him to play for both the orchestras of Duke Ellington, who was Black, and Harry James, who was white. Noble Sissle, who served as James Reese Europe's African American assistant director of the 369th Infantry "Hellfighters" Band, hired Francisco Tizol, from the prominent San Juan musical family, to play in the orchestra for the musical *Shuffle Along,* which Sissle cowrote with Eubie Blake. Sissle also employed dark-skinned Puerto Rican trumpeter August Coen, who later played with bands fronted by Duke Ellington and Fletcher Henderson.[27]

New York was not the only destination for Puerto Rican musicians and not the only place where transnational practices emerged and thrived. Manuel Peña, whose father conducted the municipal band in Humacao, Puerto Rico, migrated to New York in 1929, hoping to earn a living as a prizefighter. He found more success, however, as a musician, but not with a mainland U.S. ensemble. He joined a Filipino orchestra, feeling at home because of the similarities between Puerto Ricans and Filipinos: both immigrants from island nations colonized by Spain and acquired by the United States in 1898, both accustomed to learning English as a second language because of colonial education, and both motivated to seek employment as entertainers in order to escape the low-wage work awaiting them in the fields and factories of their homelands and the United States. Pepito Arvelo applied the music lessons he had learned in Puerto Rico to his career as a guitarist in a Hawaiian group during the mid-1930s.[28] The transition was an easy one, in part because of the migration by Puerto Rican sugarcane cutters to Hawaii at the turn of the century and their consequent influence on Hawai'ian culture. For many years, one of the most popular radio shows in the islands was *Alma Latina,* hosted by Nancy Ortiz, who programmed a steady rotation of salsa and *cachi cachi* music. The foods that Hawaiians refer to as "pateles" and "ganduli rice" originated in Puerto Rico as *pasteles* and *arroz con gandules,* although Puerto Ricans in Hawai'i often prefer to add Korean kimchi to their *pasteles.*[29]

Parallel relations with U.S. colonialism and shared subservience to transnational sugar companies crafted connections between Hawai'i and Puerto Rico, but the uncertain and unpredictable aspects of migrants' lives also left diasporic Puerto Ricans with uneven and irregular relations with the culture of their homeland. During the first decades of the twentieth century, Puerto Rican culture in Hawai'i remained so isolated from home that musicians in Hawai'i did not notice the growing consciousness of Afro–Puerto Rican roots that flourished because of migration to North America. As a result, Hawai'ian musicians of Puerto Rican descent did not generally play bongos or conga drums until World War II, when they learned about them from Puerto Rican soldiers in the U.S. Army stationed in Hawai'i.

Destinations outside the United States and its holdings also beckoned diasporic Puerto Rican musicians. Rafael Hernández lived in Cuba during the early 1920s, a time when *son* music began to be recorded commercially, and he made singular contributions to Cuban dance music in those years. He worked in Mexico during the 1920s before starting the Trio Borinquen in New York in 1926, as mentioned earlier in chapter 4. Taking their name from the indigenous people of Puerto Rico, this trio, made up of two Puerto Ricans and one Dominican, played both Puerto Rican and Dominican music. When they performed in the Dominican Republic, they transposed their name to the Trio Quisqueya, in honor of that nation's indigenous people.[30] Labor as a merchant seaman, however, led one of the members of Trio Borinquen to go repeatedly to sea, so Hernández dissolved the group and formed his Victoria Quartet. Hernández lived in Mexico for many years, marrying a Mexican citizen before returning to Puerto Rico in 1947, at the request of then governor Luis Muñoz Marín.[31]

Puerto Rican musicians in New York most often found work in Cuban bands, especially Black and mulatto musicians capable of drawing on Afro-Latin elements that were muted sometimes in Puerto Rican music but prominent in Cuban songs. When Puerto Ricans played with Frank Grillo's outfit they belonged to a group called Machito and His Afro-Cubans, even though they were not Cuban. Cuba's reputation as the birthplace of so much Afro-Caribbean music gave all things Cuban an inflection of "authenticity," leading Puerto Rican Gilberto Calderón to give himself the stage name "Joe Cuba" during the 1950s. Restaurants with customers and cuisines from all over the Caribbean sometimes advertised themselves as "Cuban" for commercial purposes.[32]

Musicians from other communities participated in making Puerto Rican music as well. Before World War II, bandleader Alfredo Mendez hosted a popular New York radio program *La hora hispana,* using Rafael Hernández's "Lamento borincano" as his theme. Few of his listeners knew that the musician they recognized as Alfredo Mendez was really Alfred Mendelsohn, a Jewish pianist from New York who took on a Puerto Rican identity to make his music more commercially appealing to Latin audiences. Years later, in the 1970s, Lawrence Ira Kahn, another Jewish musician, would gain fame as the leader of Orchestra Harlow, an aggregation playing Puerto Rican music under the direction of Kahn, who now called himself Larry Harlow. He even recorded a song titled "Yo soy latino" (I Am Latino). His artistry confirmed that affirmation, even if his embodied identity did not. Unlike Alfredo Mendez, however, Harlow acknowledged his origins openly, billing himself among Puerto Ricans as "El Judio Maravilloso"—the Marvelous Jew. During the 1940s and 1950s, Afro-Cuban and Puerto Rican music at New York City's Palladium, on Fifty-second Street, drew diverse crowds of "blacks, Anglos, Latinos, Jews, Italians, and even Chinese."[33] Nuyorican musicians Charlie and Eddie Palmieri grew up in a Jewish neighborhood in the Bronx, where they learned to play piano from a great African American classical composer and pianist, Margaret Bonds. Yet they also nurtured their musical artistry at summer camps outside the city run by Puerto Rican labor groups and social clubs.[34]

Just as Mendelsohn and Kahn passed for Puerto Rican, Herman Santiago and Joe Negroni passed for Black as members of Frankie Lymon's backup group, the Teenagers, during the 1950s. In the 1960s Joe Cuba, Johnny Colón, and Pete Rodríguez, among others, played and recorded rhythm-and-blues-oriented Latin bugalu hit songs, in part because of the close interactions among Blacks and Puerto Ricans in New York City, but also because much of 1950s and 1960s rhythm-and-blues music by Blacks reflected so many "Latin" elements in songs, for example, Lavern Baker's "Tweedle Dee," Bo Diddley's "Say Man," and the Drifters' "Sweets for My Sweet" and "Save the Last Dance for Me." During the 1970s, Afro-Filipino Joe Bataan had a major hit record, "The Bottle," among Puerto Ricans. He explained, "My father was Filipino and my mother was African American, and my culture is Puerto Rican."[35] In the same era, the African American disco group Chic scored a hit with "Le Freak," a song based on Latin bugalu and a variety of other Puerto Rican dance forms.

In the early years of hip hop, Puerto Rican disc jockey Carlos Mandes emerged as a prominent figure in the African American community, using the stage name "Charlie Chase."[36] Many of Chase's radio listeners assumed he was Black, even doubting that he could be the "real" Charlie Chase when they encountered him in person. He recalls, "A lot of Blacks would not accept that I was Spanish. You know, a lot of times because of the way I played they thought I was Black, because I rocked it so well. When they saw me, they still wouldn't believe it. They are like, 'No, that's not him!' But I was the type of kid that, you know, I always grew up with Black people; my best friends were always Black people. You know, I don't know why. My daughter's godfather is Black. He's like my brother, that guy."[37] Chase came to his work as a hip hop disc jockey, mixer, sampler, and scratcher from a career of playing bass in salsa bands, a history that gave him an enormous inventory of riffs that worked perfectly as samples for hip hop.[38]

In the wake of Fidel Castro's revolutionary insurgency in Cuba, many of that nation's musicians fled to New York, where they could make a living playing familiar music, their quest aided in no small measure by the large Puerto Rican presence in the city.

Puerto Ricans exposed the Cubans to elements of *plena, bomba,* and *jibaro* music, injecting new vigor into salsa through the early work of Conjunto Clásico, Willie Colón, and El Gran Combo, all of whom featured reprises of traditional *bombas* and *plenas*.[39] When salsa reached the zenith of its commercial popularity in the 1970s, it was widely regarded as Cuban music played by Puerto Ricans, but it secured its largest single market in Venezuela, with a huge following also in Colombia, and numbered among its leading entrepreneurs and performers Johnny Pacheco, a Dominican who moved to New York when he was eleven, Afro-Filipino Joe Bataan, and Ruben Blades, the son of a Panamanian detective who played bongos and a Cuban woman who sang boleros and was herself the daughter of a Colombian college graduate, Emma Bosques, who took her young grandson Ruben to premieres of U.S. musical comedies.[40]

These innovators of the 1970s followed a well-worn path of trans-Caribbean collaboration and creativity in their music. During the 1950s, Colombian expatriate Nelson Pinedo sang with the Cuban band Sonora Matancera. Puerto Rican Daniel Santos preceded Celia Cruz as the main vocalist in Sonora Matancera. Santos later married a Colombian and continued his career in that country after setting up residence near Cali.[41] His memorable renditions of the songs of Rafael Hernández and Pedro Flores in New York in the 1940s have had enormous impact throughout the hemisphere, making Santos a revered icon in different ways in New York, Colombia, Cuba, Venezuela, the Dominican Republic, and Peru.

The complex transnational relationships that structure Puerto Rican music can confound commentators and critics attempting to craft linear chronological narratives about the music's history. Compared with writers located on the mainland of North America, those based in the Caribbean tend to pay more attention to innovative artists working in Black musical forms, such as Ismael Rivera and Rafael Cortijo, who blended the Cuban *conjunto* format with Puerto Rican *plena* and *bomba,* taking them from the streets into nightclubs. Afro-Caribbean musicians throughout the hemisphere, but especially in New York, began to develop greater contacts with musicians from Africa during the 1970s. Puerto Ricans Tito Puente and El Gran Combo both recorded versions of "Pata pata," a composition by South African singer Miriam Makeba in the 1960s.

Manu Dibango, an African from Cameroon, had a Latin-flavored international hit with "Soul Makossa" in 1973. He played the closing set at the second annual "Our Latin Thing" concert at Yankee Stadium in 1973 and subsequently toured the Caribbean with salsa's hottest ensemble, the Fania All-Stars. Dibango gave a triumphant performance in San Juan on that tour, introducing himself to the audience in Spanish and dazzling listeners and dancers with his mastery of salsa rhythms.[42]

Lise Waxer's brilliant study of music in Cali, Colombia, documents the influence of Puerto Rican music and musicians in that metropolis, as well as their subsequent significance in shaping music made back home in Puerto Rico.[43] Popular culture in Cali in the 1980s revolved around the localization of salsa, which went by the name *musica antillana*. Migrants to Cali came from different regions of Colombia with antagonistic and divergent cultural traditions. Since *musica antillana* belonged to none of them but was familiar to all, it became the musical lingua franca in the city. Furthermore, the Colombians inflected the music with their own accents and augmentations as well as with elaborations taken from other forms of popular culture. They showed old Mexican films from that nation's golden age of cinema in the discotheques of Cali, blending the local salsa culture with the music, dancing, outfits, and attitudes displayed in motion pictures by Tin Tan, Antoinetta Pons, Resortes, and La Tongolele. Jukeboxes, known as *rockolas,* provided music for working-class audiences too poor to pay the cover charges demanded by venues featuring live musicians. In a move that anticipated the drum machines of disco and hip hop, Cali entrepreneurs mounted drum sets on small platforms over the *rockolas* and hired drummers to play along with the records, adding rhythmic emphasis to songs already orchestrated for extensive percussion sections.[44]

The significance of salsa in Colombia became so great that opposing armies even claimed the music as their own. The Colombian Third Army Brigade stationed in Cali included a permanent salsa band, probably the only such military orchestra in the world. In the 1970s and 1980s, however, the Colombian Maoist guerrilla force M-19 also embraced salsa. Clandestine meetings of the revolutionary group featured discussions with musicians and musicologists about the potential of salsa as an instrument of revolutionary struggle in pursuit of what the rebel leader Jaime Bateman termed *la social vacancería* (societal grooviness), an agenda promising joy and happiness to all.[45]

Puerto Rican music has influenced and been influenced by music from Europe, Africa, and Asia. It has played a role in Black and white jazz traditions, rhythm and blues, disco, and hip hop as well as in Hawaiian music. The politics of identity that emerge within Puerto Rican music are matters of culture and color as much as country of origin. They express the nationalism of a people that have long been international and transnational. Although we must not lose sight of the terrible price Puerto Rico has paid for its colonial status, it is also true that the complicated dialogue Puerto Ricans have been forced to have with other cultures renders their experience particularly relevant to today's transnational global culture. Puerto Rican identity contains no single immutable essence but rather a historically grounded set of circumstances that expand and contract, branch out and withdraw, change through contact with others but also remain the same.[46]

Puerto Rican cultural practices have been extraordinarily adaptable and contested, but they have not been infinitely open. Frances Negrón-Muntaner demonstrates that culture plays an unusually important role in Puerto Rican politics, because the maintenance and preservation of a distinct culture has been a great political victory for a people unable to win national or economic independence from the United States.[47] Yet this has also made Puerto Rican culture vulnerable to political appropriation and distortion. In an emblematic episode, Luis Muñoz Marín (who rose to power to the strains of "Lamento borincano" as his theme song) tried once again to recruit the music of Rafael Hernández for his own ends in the early 1950s. As part of the strategy of establishing Puerto Rico as a commonwealth under the domain of the United States, the governor asked the composer to change the words of "Preciosa" so that the line describing "the tyrant's black wickedness" would be rendered "destiny's black wickedness." If the change was intended to obscure the reputation of the United States as tyrannical in Puerto Rico, the attempt failed. Popular protest marked by intense anti-U.S. sentiment prevented the revision, compelling Hernández to restore the original lyrics.[48] Hernández's inability to change the lyrics of his own song because of popular protest reveals a part of how Puerto Rico's dispersed population returns again and again to

the hurts of history that created Puerto Rican national consciousness in the first place.

Like many new immigrants, Puerto Ricans come to the mainland of North America from a colonized homeland where English
is not the native tongue. Yet like African Americans, they are citizens of the United States who endure discrimination and exploitative working conditions largely because of their color. Puerto
Rican migration stems from the misery of a rural proletariat, but
the island's people have become the most urbanized ethnic group
in North America, more likely to live in inner-city areas of large
cities than any other group, including African Americans. Thus,
Puerto Ricans can play a crucial role in coalitions that unite communities of color on the basis of common confrontations with white
racism, but they are also an integral part of the pan-Latino identity
that unites Spanish speakers from Latin American countries in a
common history and culture.[49]

Puerto Rican music has been made in many places by people of
many different nationalities, but in each case it has inflected and become inflected by the music of the country in which it is produced.
Even in Hawai'i, a group of Puerto Ricans calling themselves the
Hawaiian Gentlemen played an indigenous song, "Pua 'Olena," as
a bolero. Juan Flores explains the rich dialogue with Black culture,
evident in genres such as Latin bugalu, as a manifestation of the
ways in which Puerto Ricans become more aware of the African
elements in their culture when they move to New York and notice
the full dimensions of anti-Black racism at work.[50] Piri Thomas
describes this process eloquently in *Down These Mean Streets,* in
which he identifies strongly with African Americans, even though
his father constantly lectures the family about the value of their
light skin.[51]

At the same time, shared class positions and affinities of language and culture give a strong Puerto Rican quality to the pan-
Latino culture created by migrants from many different national
groups in New York. Flores speaks of Puerto Rican culture as
"branching out," as changing through contact but moving in all
directions toward other people of color, not trying to move toward
a presumably white Anglo center.[52] Situated in more than one
identity, susceptible to dynamic change when experiences in exile
awaken repressed consciousness of the indigenous and African

roots of their culture, Puerto Ricans have fashioned a dynamic culture that refutes simple binary divisions of separatism versus assimilation or tradition versus transculturation.

Thus, the controversy over where Héctor Lavoe would be buried allowed for no simple solution. The nationalists correctly called attention to the colonial relationship between the island and the mainland. Yet long histories of colonialism, migration, and exile leave Puerto Rico with a vexed relationship to nationalism. Puerto Ricans living off the island have often played important roles in the island's struggles for self-determination, statehood, and independence. In the nineteenth century, Ramón Emeterio Betances campaigned against Spanish rule over the island from exile in France.[53] Between 1936 and 1947, the U.S. government incarcerated Pedro Albizu Campos in the federal penitentiary in Atlanta, Georgia, because of his pro-independence agitation and organization.[54]

No less than its politics, Puerto Rican culture has also survived and thrived off the island. The great poet Julia de Burgos studied in Cuba, wrote poetry while employed as a factory worker and a lab technician in New York, and died in a Harlem hospital.[55] Five thousand Puerto Ricans migrated to Hawai'i at the turn of the twentieth century to work on sugarcane plantations. Their influence on Hawai'i endures to this day in the musical form known as *cachi cachi,* played on the quarto and derivative of the Puerto Rican *jibaro* style.[56] Puerto Rico's most successful politician, Luis Muñoz Marín, grew up in New York's Greenwich Village as the son of an exiled nationalist. He attended Georgetown University in Washington, D.C.[57]

Contemporary Nuyorican visual artist Papo Colo prefers his "exile" condition in New York to living in Puerto Rico, precisely because it offers him critical distance from the island. "I can't return to my country. It is a victim of maracas and cement," he explains in reference to Puerto Rico's function as an exotic vacation site for North Americans.[58] Nuyorican poet Pedro Pietri dramatized the ambiguous identity of Puerto Rico by collaborating with photographer Adal Maldonado to produce mock passports purporting to give the bearer permission to travel "overseas."[59] Willie Colón named the band in which Héctor Lavoe secured his fame the Legal Alien Orchestra, emphasizing the hybrid status of Puerto Ricans as both unwanted outsiders *and* U.S. citizens. Yet

Colón always had more than Puerto Rico on his mind. Although his grandmother left the island in 1923 to come to New York, Colón and his parents were born in New York City. A Panamanian neighbor took care of Colón as a child, and he grew up on a block populated by Dominicans, Cubans, Venezuelans, Chicanos, and immigrants from several other Caribbean nations. Proud of having "white, black, and Indian" ancestry, Colón viewed salsa as a vehicle for creating a united front among Latinos. In a 1991 speech delivered at Yale University (where he served as a Chubb Fellow), Colón noted that the Puerto Rican flag was designed in New York and that the entire Latino community in the city had long participated in political mobilizations aimed at changing the governments of Cuba, the Dominican Republic, and Puerto Rico.[60]

Long-standing and deep-seated resentments about U.S. colonialism in Puerto Rico coupled with clear recognition of the sharp contrasts between the racial orders of the island and the mainland have positioned Puerto Ricans perfectly to disrupt and disturb the North American racial order. Yet the exact same anticolonial nationalism that fuels so much Puerto Rican subversion of racial binaries has often served to strengthen binary oppositions based on gender. Although Lolita Lebrón and other revolutionary activist women have played dramatic and well-publicized roles in the struggle for Puerto Rican independence, the nationalist movement itself has been permeated by misogynist practices, policies, and programs.[61] The association of specific songs and genres with Puerto Rican pride and pursuit of self-determination has tended to focus on male composers and performers. Iconic nationalist songs and slogans have often represented the nation through highly gendered allegories, and the policies and programs of nationalists have been pronatalist and patriarchal. Often the injuries suffered by Puerto Ricans of both genders have been represented as distinctly humiliating insults to the gendered privileges and power of Puerto Rican men. Arnoldo Cruz-Malavé points out that the abjection of Puerto Rico appears often in literary representations through images of violated male homosexuals.[62] The same cultural matrix that celebrates racial branching out and hybridity in respect to race often resists branching out and hybridity in respect to gender and sexuality.

In a characteristically brilliant discussion, Frances Aparicio notes how nationalist discourses have tended to belittle the cultural forms and practices most favored by women, including Spanish-language *salsa romantica* as well as interlingual and intercultural "crossover" performances blending dance music, house, and hip hop elements by the female performers La India, Lisette Melendez, Corrine, and Brenda K. Starr, and even male performers such as Marc Anthony and Huey Dunbar.[63] This "soft" salsa is often dismissed as less political than the "hard" salsa of the past with its overtly "political" lyrics. Yet Aparicio argues that these songs are permeated with a rich hybridity and an insistent refusal of simple binaries, both of which speak powerfully to the lives of Puerto Rican women, who, at least on some issues, might feel as much solidarity with women from Cuba or the Dominican Republic as they feel with men from Puerto Rico, if not more. Such women see their own intercultural everyday experiences and existences reflected best in performances that celebrate interethnic pan-Latina solidarity, that deploy musical devices from merengue, *montuno,* and *son* as well as salsa, that contain lyrics in both English and Spanish. Similarly, in her study of salsa in Cali, Colombia, Lise Waxer notes that while *salsa dura* songs often invoke pan-Latino solidarity in their lyrics, *salsa romantica* often do more to promote that solidarity in practice.

Aparicio explains that cultural expressions dismissed as apolitical because they do not invoke the traditional symbols and slogans of nationalism often contain tremendously important political meaning on the terrain of gender. She shows, for example, how Corrine's cover of Madonna's tropicalist hit song "La isla bonita," arranged by Afro-Haitian-American hip hop star Wyclef Jean, does not imitate Madonna's version but rather contests it, because Corrine "symbolically returns the songs to the voices, rhythms, and sounds of the cultural communities who were silenced and stereotyped in Madonna's composition."[64]

Just as Dominican merengue in the 1980s started to branch out to African and African American musical forms and started to reflect changes in gender roles as a result of the new realities of immigration in the transnational age, Puerto Rican music in New York has become more than *salsa dura,* no longer the sole province of men or, for that matter, Puerto Ricans. Yet the new realities do not replace old essentialist understandings of nationality with new essentialisms about the categories of "woman" and "transnationalism." Aparicio argues convincingly that La India's collaboration with the great Cuban singer Celia Cruz, for example, reveals unexpected affinities across generations and between the national origins of the two singers. It does not, however, obliterate or even occlude the profound differences that remain between the two singers regarding their respective nations' contributions to music and their political ideologies. Drawing on José Muñoz's important work on Latino/Latina "queer" performance, Aparicio furthermore demonstrates that La India's gesture of smoking a cigar during her performances or her and Dominican singer Yolanda Duke's tribute to Afro-Cuban singer La Lupe may do more to disturb the boundaries of gender and sexuality than they do to disturb the boundaries of nationality.[65]

The transnational dimensions of contemporary Puerto Rican musical production do not render the nation and its struggles obsolete. Under current conditions, the "nation" can be neither entirely embraced nor effectively avoided. For many cultures, this is a fundamentally new reality, but it has a long history among Puerto Ricans. As Juan Flores argues, "It was abroad, away from the island, and in the perception of others that the particular features and contours of the native culture came into view. This experiential paradox, the sense of moving closer because of physical and cultural distance, has recurred among so many Puerto Ricans."[66]

The creation of important parts of national culture in the homeland of the colonizer and in other nations that have been similarly exploited even though independent reveals the surprisingly transnational nature of nationalism and the distinctly national inflections of transnationalism. Ricardo Lemvo exemplified these dynamics in 1990 when he formed the band Makina Loca in Los Angeles to play Afro-Cuban salsa and Congolese music.[67] The flute, piano, and vocals in Lemvo's music are arranged by a Cuban, Jesús Alejandro, who started his career as a professional musician playing rock 'n' roll. Alejandro works with Puerto Rican band leader Edwin Bonilla, whose music sounds similar to Lemvo's.

Ricardo Lemvo was born in Kinshasa, in the Congo. The name he selected for his group constitutes an interlingual pun; "Makina Loca" translates as "Crazy Machine" in Spanish but as "Dancing in a Trance" in Kikongo. Lemvo sings in Portuguese, English, French, and Lingala as well as Spanish and Kikongo. Often treated critically as a novelty act (albeit an impressive one), the seemingly ungrounded and unbounded nature of Makina Loca in actuality reveals the long fetch of history and powerful waves propelling mutuality and symbiosis between two seemingly incommensurable national cultures. Puerto Rico and the Congo are far apart on the map but nonetheless oddly in dialogue with each other because of their experiences with imperialism.

The music of Lemvo's native Congo contained elements of Puerto Rico, Europe, America, and Africa long before he was born. Gary Stewart's history of popular music in the cities of Leopoldville and Brazzaville in the two Congos (the adjoining nations of the Congo Republic and the Democratic Republic of the Congo) illustrates the complications of the isomorphism of culture and place in the contemporary world. All places are crossroads, with many different currents flowing through them, but the Congo nations colonized by Belgium and France emerged within a particularly complicated nexus of national and transnational projects.

Henry Morton Stanley, an American born in Wales, and Pierre Savorgnan de Brazza, an Italian who had become a French citizen, explored the two Congos in the 1870s. France and Belgium took possession of different parts of the Congo as a result of agreements among European powers negotiated in Berlin in 1885. In the first third of the twentieth century, Congolese consumers preferred South American music to the culture of their colonizers, because the African-influenced music of the Western Hemisphere struck them as more familiar and pleasing than European music, as more grounded in the African idioms they knew. Greek immigrants, some of them born in Egypt to parents who had migrated from Cyprus, became the first Western music entrepreneurs in the region.[68]

Zachaire Elenga rapidly became the brightest light in Congolese popular music in the early 1950s. He developed a unique sound by replacing the D string on his guitar with another E string, creating a sound that he called Hawai'ian. Although his music bore little resemblance to music actually from Hawaii, the popularity of his playing led him to be known locally in the Congo as Jhimmy the Hawaiian.[69] Also on the scene was the Belgian guitarist Bill Alexandre, who had played music with the great Belgian-Romany virtuoso Django Rheinhardt in the 1930s. He turned to bebop after World War II, moving to the Congo in the early 1950s because the popularity of jukebox music from the United States eroded job op-

portunities for musicians who played live in Belgium and because
two Greek record company executives had asked him to set up a
recording studio in Leopoldville. The novelty of his shiny electric guitar and his skilled playing led the locals to call Alexandre
"Bill Indian," a reference to the handsome heroes of motion pictures from the new nation of India then popular in the city.[70] Yet
Jhimmy the Hawaiian was not from Hawai'i, and Bill Indian was
not from India.

By the late 1950s, another technically incorrect cognitive mapping proved important in the Congo. Unemployed youths who
smoked marijuana and watched cowboy movies from the United
States developed a slang hybrid of French and Lingala, which they
called Hindoubill. The name honored motion pictures from both
Bollywood (India) and Hollywood (the United States). The young
people who spoke Hindoubill created a counterculture based on
blending local realities with cinematic fantasies. They wore denim
jeans and checkered shirts, referred to their bicycles as horses, and
renamed their neighborhoods Texas, Dallas, and Santa Fe. Their
elaborate and energetic subculture permeated popular music. While
seemingly a completely passive response to the images of commercial culture sold by foreign media conglomerates, the Hindoubill
subculture injected a lively dynamism into Congolese popular culture and prefigured the imminent ascendance of anticolonial politics and culture in the years ahead.[71]

The complicated cultural politics of Congolese music exemplifies the problems with studying music in just one city or nation.
We need new kinds of cognitive mappings to account adequately
for the ways in which places shape musical production, distribution, and reception. Congolese culture emerged from complicated
dynamics, including Belgian and French imperialism, German di-
plomacy, the Greek diaspora in Cyprus, Egypt, and Africa, control
over Belgian popular music by U.S. jukebox manufacturers and
suppliers, motion pictures from India and the United States, and
African diasporic music from South America and the Caribbean,
including Puerto Rico. The synthesis that seems merely idiosyncratic in Makina Loca in reality represents long waves of cultural
fusion and fission forged in relations between colonizers and the
colonized around the globe.

In the face of direct colonization and economic exploitation,
military conquest, cultural marginality, and poverty, the Puerto

Rican culture created overseas and at home has taken a part of Puerto Rico to the rest of the world and in turn has absorbed back into Puerto Rico ideas and influences unavailable through other means. At a time when people in metropolitan centers mourn the loss of foundational certainty and the evaporating congruence of physical place and cultural space, Puerto Rican music has some important lessons to teach about how to survive, adapt, and innovate in an ever-changing world. In their negotiations with a world economy, Puerto Ricans have interacted freely with many cultures and paid a price for the terms of that interaction. But they have also survived and flourished by adapting, changing, and transforming without forgetting the conditions that have given rise to their struggles in the first place. When the Congolese expatriate Ricardo Lemvo plays salsa music with his band Makina Loca in Los Angeles, he participates in a long tradition even as he appears to be breaking it and adding something completely new.

In the decade after Héctor Lavoe's death, Puerto Rican music and musicians reached unprecedented commercial success. Dance-oriented albums by Ricky Martin and Jennifer Lopez topped the international best-seller charts, and both singers developed significant careers as actors on television, in films, and onstage. Singers Marc Anthony and La India secured extraordinary sales with contemporary blends of salsa, hip hop, and funk, while the careers of veteran salsa artists profited from the exposure they received from being featured in new motion picture soundtracks. Tito Puente appeared in a cameo role in *The Mambo Kings* (1992) and provided songs for that film's soundtrack album. Marc Anthony and Ray Barretto were featured on the soundtrack for *Carlito's Way* (1993). In hip hop, Joseph Cartagena, the product of a Puerto Rican and Cuban marriage, recorded under the name Fat Joe. He reached the top of the charts with the single "Floe Joe," from his first album, *Represent*. Fat Joe went on to collaborate with many of hip hop's best-known artists, including KRS-1, Foxy Brown, Raekwon, and LL Cool J.

Perhaps most important, Cartagena's South Bronx neighbor and friend Christopher Rios moved from homelessness and low-wage labor jobs to commercial and critical success under the stage name Big Punisher (aka Big Pun). A primarily anglophone rapper with novel and unique wordplay, imaginative English-language and interlingual rhymes, extraordinary breath control, and rhythmic brilliance, Rios won enormous respect from his peers. He went out of his way to link Puerto Ricans to the larger hip hop community as well. Big Pun's 2000 song "100%" pays tribute to Black hip hop icon Tupac Shakur but also mentions Marc Anthony and includes samples from the Puerto Rican national anthem and singing by Héctor Lavoe.[72] Rios continued to live in the South Bronx after he hit it big, even when he could easily have afforded to move out. He poured money into a variety of community institutions, including a youth center, a pool hall, and a barber shop.[73] Big Pun died of a heart attack in February 2000, at the age of twenty-eight. For all of his success as an entertainer, Rios could not overcome the combined effects of his obesity and considerable drug use. An enormous crowd gathered outside the funeral home in the South Bronx where services were held. Big Pun's wish was to have his body cremated. No one suggested that his body should be buried in Puerto Rico, but Big Pun had no desire to be buried in the Bronx.

From the perspective of many observers on the island, the popularity of Big Pun expressed the culture of New York and contained little significance for Puerto Rico. Their understanding of the national identity and aspirations of Puerto Ricans did not include the cultural fusions that young people of color fashioned across racial categories in New York. Big Pun performed hip hop rather than salsa, sang mostly in English rather than Spanish, highlighted the affinities between Puerto Ricans and Blacks, and could not be connected to the kind of cultural and political renaissance that accompanied the successes of Héctor Lavoe and Willie Colón in the 1970s and 1980s.

In the aftermath of Big Pun's death, however, controversy about him did erupt in New York City. Slightly more than a year after Rios's funeral, Dahu Bryson, a South Bronx record store owner, initiated a petition drive to change the name of Rogers Place between Westchester Avenue and 163rd Street to Big Pun Place. Bryson explained that the mural on the block portraying the image of the rapper had become a local shrine, that Big Pun's fans left flowers, lit candles, and messages honoring their departed hero at the site. The relevant local community governing board endorsed the idea, impressed by the outpouring of neighborhood sentiment reflected in Bryson's petition and moved by the dignified presentations made by young people at public meetings in support of the renaming. The local tabloid press, however, ridiculed the move, dredging up the sexist and misogynist content of some of Big Pun's lyrics in a manner that led the city council to reject the initiative on the grounds that Big Pun was not an appropriate representative of his community.[74]

If the career of Big Pun seems a point of rupture with the past from the perspective of many of the people who revered Héctor Lavoe, it also evidences the long fetch of history manifest in relentless waves of transnational and interracial antagonisms, alliances, identifications, and affiliations. Speaking for and from people who "laid in the slums" but "made a cake out of crumbs," Big Pun condemned police repression, economic inequality, and capital punishment. He implored the community to "call in order" and get "a chance to enhance broader." Despite all the hurts of history, Big Pun believed that his people could still succeed, telling his listeners that, for all their troubles, the things they desired were "right around the corner, baby, ours for the taking."[75] By turning complex contradictions into brilliantly creative cultural expressions that offer motivation and inspiration inside the community and beyond, Big Pun represented the concerns of Puerto Ricans and Nuyoricans perfectly. His views and actions on the terrains of gender privilege and intimate justice, however, tell another story.

Two years after Big Pun's death, his widow, Liza Rios, went public with the history of physical beatings and verbal abuse she had endured from her husband for years. She produced a DVD about her experiences that include footage of herself being pistol whipped by her husband. Attempting to make something constructive out of her contradictory feelings about her deceased partner, Rios tried to interest hip hop artists in participating in a tour that would pay tribute to the accomplishments of Big Pun, yet at the same time raise money for a foundation for battered women and children. The silence from usually talkative rappers was deafening, except from those who denied the allegations or condoned the things Big Pun was alleged to have done.[76] A Texas arts-based group dedicated to helping victims of gender and racial violence, Arte Sana, however, gave Liza Rios their Artista Activista Empowerment through the Arts Award in 2005.

The long fetch of history that propelled the advanced class and racial consciousness evident in Big Pun's lyrics also positioned him as masculine subject with extremely retrograde views about and actions toward women. His prominence as a rapper helped give legitimacy to those views and no doubt served to encourage some men listening to him to follow his example. At its best, hip hop can speak constructively to the most desperate and least powerful people in the ghetto, telling them that there are witnesses to the things they experience. At its worst, however, like many other forms of popular culture in U.S. society, hip hop envisions freedom as freedom from responsibility, empowerment as power over others. Its fantasies of ruthless gangsterism stand more as symptoms of prevailing social relations than as critiques of them.

Neither Héctor Lavoe nor Christopher Rios lived unblemished lives, yet they generated love from their fans. However, that response had less to do with them as individuals than with the ways in which their artistry helped their audiences understand themselves and their problems. As Puerto Ricans in New York, both artists influenced the cultural dialogue between the two locations. Their artistic triumphs and tragic deaths underscore the complexities of colonialism, nationalism, and transnationalism at the start of the twenty-first century. "Transnational diaspora life," as Juan Flores argues, "necessarily stretches the idea of national belonging by disengaging it from its presumed territorial and linguistic imperative, de-centering it in relation to any putative 'core' values or marks of greater or lesser 'authenticity.'"[77] Yet these realities, which seem to have arrived so suddenly, in truth, have long fetches of history behind them.

10. Techno

The Hidden History of Automation

[The] computer has given us the opportunity to tap into history in a way
we would never do before, and that gives us the opportunity to create
our own perspective of what we've been brought up with all our lives.
—**Derrick May**

The same historical dynamics elevating economies of scope over
economies of scale that led to the creation of Eden's Crush on *Pop
Stars* also helped produce the music known as Detroit techno. The
emergence of fully linked and integrated forms of production, distribution, and consumption created preconditions that enabled
some astute and creative music consumers to become music producers. The increasing differentiation among products and the
introduction of new ones encouraged the development of specific,
specialized, and even customized desires among consumers, desires
that the market could not meet, that could be fulfilled only by new
creative communities using consumer knowledge to create new
products.

In the 1970s and 1980s, Black teenagers from Detroit's deindustrialized neighborhoods used their bedrooms, basements,
and garages in creating the music that became known as Detroit
techno. The economic devastation wrought by deindustrialization
in Detroit destroyed almost all of the public venues where Black
teens had previously danced and listened to music. At the same
time, computer-generated automation and outsourcing led to fac-

tory shutdowns in mass-production industries. The teenage founders of techno, however, appropriated those very computer technologies to transform themselves from consumers into producers. They deployed computer sequencers and digital synthesizers to make a "new" recombinant music assembled from fragments of their tape and vinyl music collections. They used their knowledge as consumers to become producers of a specialized music that the industry's decision makers did not invent—a homemade hybrid that mixed hip hop rhythms, rock and funk guitar riffs, Eurodisco melodies and harmonies, electronic effects, and "break beats" at 120–130 beats per minute, created through turntable tricks, and all topped off by silly pseudosalacious adolescent lyrics about sex. By the 1990s, faster rhythms (170 beats per minute) and the low-frequency hums pioneered in "Miami Bass" hip hop by 2 Live Crew and others became important components of techno in the city.

"The music is just like Detroit," explains Derrick May, one of the genre's key founders, "a complete mistake. It's like George Clinton and Kraftwerk stuck in an elevator."[1] May's formulation references two seemingly incommensurate discourses: the "complete mistake" that Detroit seemed to be in the wake of deindustrialization and the imagined confusion that would result from popular artists associated with two very different market segments being stuck in the same elevator together.

George Clinton, born in North Carolina, raised in New Jersey, but best known as the key figure in Detroit's soul and funk efflorescence during the 1970s, led a group of more than forty musicians, who recorded together (in different combinations) under the names George Clinton, the Parliaments, Parliament, Funkadelic, P-Funk, Bootsy's Rubber Band, the Brides of Funkenstein, Parlet, and the P. Funk All-Stars, among others. Clinton garnered unexpected commercial success by cobbling together unlikely combinations of blues chords, pop hooks, dance rhythms, jazz improvisation, and performance gestures that blended remnants of 1960s-era Black Power imagery and counterculture idealism with Afro-futurism and 1970s consumption practices. The four musicians in Kraftwerk, on the other hand, came from Düsseldorf, Germany. They played only synthesizers and produced repetitious, stiff, cold, mechanical, and minimalist music that had an enormous popularity as art-rock music during the 1970s and 1980s. Kraftwerk's commitment to cybernetics was so thorough that eventually the group presented concerts in which the musicians did not appear at all, their places taken onstage by actual robots.[2]

Like the music made by both P-Funk and Kraftwerk, Detroit techno relies on a distinct aesthetic, social, and spatial logic emanating inescapably from the culture of containerization and the containerization of culture. Commercial imperatives as much as aesthetic inclination determined the contours of Clinton's artistry. The studio musicians in his band had an enormous repertoire of "hooks" garnered during years of session work that taught them to size up and seize on catchy sounds quickly. They developed their skills just as Charlie Parker and other jazz musicians had gained extensive knowledge of pop melodies and chord progressions when they apprenticed in "ten cents a dance" venues, playing one ninety-second pop tune after another, because that system made customers use up their dance tickets more quickly.

Clinton's incessant changes in the names and personnel in his band also stemmed from commercial considerations. His band the Parliaments reached the best-seller charts with "I Wanna Testify" and "All Your Goodies Are Gone" on the Revilot label in 1967. Revilot went bankrupt but still owned the name of the Parliaments. In order to keep recording and not violate Revilot's claims, Clinton formed Funkadelic. He turned the Parliaments' lead singers into backup singers and put the musicians up front. Then he regained the rights to the Parliaments name. Since this aggregation was a known and successful group, he started to put out new songs under a modified name, dropping *the* and the *s* to make them Parliament. Clinton found that having two names for the group gave him more options, more opportunities to be heard and hired, so he did not stop. He formed one ensemble called Brides of Funkenstein and another named the Bridesmaids. In addition to the names already mentioned, his group released records as the Bomb, the Uncut Funk, the Pee, the Horny Horns, and Bernie Worrell's Woo.[3] The constant changes in personnel and band names made it hard to know exactly who was playing on any particular Clinton production. He established clear precedents that paved the way for the compositions and performance identities of Detroit techno artists, who rarely record under their own names.

Techno artists have also inherited a certain studied indifference to the whims of the market from George Clinton and P-Funk. Bernie Worrell likes to talk about how the music tended to overwhelm everything else in the group P-Funk. Remembering one night when communication among the musicians was especially rich, Worrell recalls that he lost track of what song they were playing, of where the concert was being held, of what part of the evening's program they were playing at the time. He claims he looked up at the arena at one point only to notice that everyone had left the building. "Not just the audience had left," he observes, "*everybody* was gone. Even the security had left. But we were still playing."[4]

With similar indifference to commercial viability, techno functions as a version of what theorists of the Situationist International (and their journalistic interpreter Greil Marcus) call "detournement"—a repositioning and revaluing of aesthetic objects by assigning them new roles and meanings.[5] Mixing together low-prestige and seemingly incommensurable entities such as Kraftwerk, P-Funk, and the city of Detroit, creative consumer-based productions create new and original value from what others might view as discards and rejects.

In the 1980s, containerization had a devastating impact on industrial production centers like Detroit. It made outsourcing and offshore production feasible and profitable. The huge profits that globalization generated for transnational corporations and investors imposed enormous social costs and consequences on young people in industrial cities. Declines in the tax base and neoliberal abandonment of the social wage and welfare safety nets enacted a radical rupture with the past. For young people in Detroit, deindustrialization in that decade produced systematic economic and cultural disenfranchisement. Corporate directors and stockholders withdrew investments from the city's industrial infrastructure. Mortgage lenders, insurance agents, and bankers abandoned entire neighborhoods. Tax cuts for the wealthy (and the budget cuts they required) led to systematic reductions in state investments in the infrastructural resources most important in the lives of inner-city residents.[6]

Deindustrialization in Detroit produced deterritorialization. It transformed vibrant and lively urban neighborhoods into block after block of abandoned houses and storefronts. The deterioration of public transportation increased social isolation, and budget cuts undermined the services that citizens needed from firefighters and police officers. Cutbacks in youth service programs and the closing of small businesses left young people with few spaces for congregating, communicating, and collaborating on shared projects. Factory shutdowns and capital flight eliminated entry-level jobs, disrupted economic support networks, and left precious little funding for discretionary spending on activities like music and dance. As national television network programs publicized Detroit's dangers and decline as the emblematic example of a larger national problem, one local artist set up a Web site devoted to pictures of the city's abandoned factories, houses, and stores. He called his Web site "the fabulous ruins of Detroit."[7]

Techno music emerged from the deindustrialization of Detroit and the deterritorialization of its neighborhoods. Juan Atkins claims he drew his initial inspiration for the sounds of techno from the hum of traffic on the I-96 freeway late at night and from the drone of automated factories.[8] For some of the city's young people, home production of music has filled the spaces left by the dearth of opportunities for employment as well as consumption. The young people who have created techno have turned to art as a release from the monotony of the low-wage service jobs available to them in the postindustrial economy. Carl Craig worked in a copy shop and Derrick May worked in a video game arcade before they became professional musicians. When they turned to music, they made more creative kinds of "copies" and "games."[9] During the era when Black people worked mostly in agriculture and industry, they used bottleneck guitars, mouth harps, and electric guitars to imitate the sounds of steam whistles, railroad wheels, and assembly lines. In an information-based economy, the sounds of video games, motion picture scores, television and radio commercials, and multitrack recordings have become the "originals" on which copies are based. But just as blues musicians fused industrial sounds with the buzz tones and audial effects of acoustic instruments and the human voice, techno artists make a recombinant art out of the sounds they "steal" from the world around them.

With very few spaces for socializing available to them in their neighborhoods, inner-city Black youths in postindustrial Detroit in the 1980s began congregating in new venues. They ventured out to suburban malls, where they encountered "preppie" fashions and an astounding array of nonlocal music—the techno–electronic–art-rock music of Kraftwerk, the Eurodisco productions of Giorgio Moroder, Japan's Yellow Magic Orchestra, and Jamaican and British ska.[10] Yet deindustrialization in Detroit also accelerated the movement of working-class and professional African Americans to those few suburbs not completely closed to them by discriminatory realtors and mortgage lenders. Some of the key creators of Detroit techno lived far outside the city limits. Juan Atkins and Derrick May formed their Deep Space DJ collective, in part, because they lived in Belleville, some twenty-five miles southwest of Detroit, and could not initially break into the party scene on the east side of the city. Eventually, however, they founded a music club, Music Institute, in downtown Detroit.[11] Like other techno producers, Atkins and May took over newly available spaces in Detroit's increasingly empty downtown. The Women's City Club, a meeting place for women's civic organizations since the 1920s, went largely unused by the late 1980s. Techno artists revived the site by making its third floor the scene of what they called the Park Avenue Club, named for the street on which the building is located.[12]

At the same time that the long fetch of feminist women's activism in the city bequeathed to them a new space for performance and dance, the historical decline in work opportunities in nightclubs, social halls, and school dances drove techno artists to sell their music in the most misogynist of places—strip clubs. These seedy venues remained among the few commercial venues in the city that still needed a steady supply of music. The centrality of strip clubs to the commercial opportunities available to techno artists clearly influenced the generic conventions of techno: its beats, volume, and especially its lyrics, which often consist of seemingly endless repetition of demeaning slang expressions for parts of women's bodies.[13]

The sonic dimensions of strip club music that appear in Detroit techno have a long history in jazz, largely because of the venerable history of these establishments as sources of employment for unemployed and underemployed musicians. Sun Ra, for example, frequently told his drummers that he wanted them to play a sensuous beat mostly on the snare drums rather than the cymbals, because it gave the music what he called the "the burlesque sound."[14] In this case, the dynamics of deterritorialization and reterritorialization had a direct relationship to the sexualization of the commodity and to the sexism of the culture in which the commodity circulated. While many techno enthusiasts, including women, dismiss the genre's lyrical obsessions as playful fun, the music's spatial origins in strip clubs clearly influence the kinds of demeaning sexual and gender roles that it helps create and encourage.

On the other hand, this link between sexuality and space also entails the creation of communities capable of accepting more diverse understandings of sexuality. As techno became more popular during the 1980s, new venues opened up on the east side of Detroit and downtown. In these clubs, gay artists and patrons displayed a style of leadership that shaped techno in definitive ways, exerting a huge influence on all patrons regardless of their sexual identification. Legendary gay Detroit DJ Ken Collier occupied a central place in this culture. Techno artists and audiences still honor him today with a respect bordering on reverence. Collier served as the key role model for a generation of turntablists and producers. When he died from the complications caused by an undiagnosed (until too late) diabetic condition, techno enthusiast DJ-T1000 (Alan Oldham) eulogized Collier on the Internet as "the first person to champion Detroit techno" and as "a great champion of our music in the great black music tradition. When it was black and gay, before it became fashionable and suburban."[15] Of course, merely invoking this genealogy does not banish homophobia from the techno world, but it does demonstrate how recombinant artistic and spatial practices can create unexpected identifications and affiliations that have important possibilities for renegotiating social hierarchies and social identities.

Detroit techno artists responded to deterritorialization with reterritorialization, with a new sense of local space and place that reflected new cognitive mappings of the city mandated by deindustrialization in the 1980s and 1990s. They held raves in abandoned factories, such as the massive Packard Main plant on the city's east side. A new sense of temporality shaped the music as well. Raves appeared at unscheduled times in makeshift venues; knowledge of their existence spread by word of mouth, phone trees, and hand-lettered leaflets. Cut off from the past of Detroit, from Motown and P-Funk, from the era of civil rights and Black Power, young techno artists fearlessly embraced the city's present and future.

Juan Atkins, like Derrick May, demonstrated an advanced understanding of the new economy when he declared that his music owed more to the robots who have taken the places of workers on the Ford assembly line than it did to the legacy of Berry Gordy and Motown Records.[16] Yet Atkins's close friend Eddie "Flashin'"

Fowlkes, the DJ whose dexterity with turntables motivated Kevin Saunderson to try the form himself, incorporated the influences of Stevie Wonder and Marvin Gaye into his distinctive "techno soul" productions.[17] Despite their differences about Motown, Atkins and Fowlkes both used computers to monitor, audit, sequence, and control sounds—the same computers that made containerization possible by monitoring, auditing, sequencing, and controlling the loading and unloading of ships.

Yet the new spaces and new temporalities of techno are not completely new but rather recombinant permutations of past times and spaces. Carl Craig had played guitar before he was able to convince his parents to buy him a synthesizer and sequencer. He took pains to study the history of electronic music compositions by Pauline Oliveros, Wendy Carlos, and Morton Subotnick.[18] Juan Atkins played electric bass before he heard Parliament's brilliant deployment of keyboards and synthesizers, which inspired him to change instruments.[19] Derrick May identifies the soundtrack of Ridley Scott's 1982 science fiction motion picture *Blade Runner* as one of his first musical inspirations. Scored by synthesizer virtuoso Vangelis Papathanassiou, a Greek émigré living in France, *Blade Runner* led May to experiment with different forms of electronic musical equipment, from the Yamaha DX 100 digital synthesizer to the Ensoniq Mirage multisampling keyboard, from the Roland 808 and 909 drum machines to four-track tape recorders.[20]

The mass media presence in Detroit of the music of Vangelis, Eurodisco producer Giorgio Moroder, and Kraftwerk played an important role in the initial generation of techno music. Although they most often encountered these kinds of music at suburban shopping malls, inner-city techno creators heard more than novelty and difference when they listened to European art-rock music. The stiff mechanical sound and light melodies that Kraftwerk created in Düsseldorf, Germany, may not sound anything like North American rhythm and blues to most listeners, but in fact Kraftwerk's art originated in an effort to blend European harmonies and melodies with African American rhythm and blues. "We were fans of all American music: soul, the whole Tamla/Motown thing, and of course James Brown," Kraftwerk's Karl Bartos confides.[21] European musicians drawing on James Brown and Motown had direct affinities with George Clinton, underscoring the appropriateness rather than the inappropriateness of Derrick May's metaphor about Kraftwerk and Clinton caught in an elevator. Just as the members of Kraftwerk created a new and specialized taste by blending soul music from Detroit and other U.S. cities with the tradition of electronic and sound collages pioneered by Karlheinz Stockhausen, Detroit techno artists reappropriated the appropriation when they made Kraftwerk's music part of the new sounds of Detroit.

Detroit techno artists are not the only African Americans to embrace the music of Kraftwerk. The group's song "Numbers" rose to as high as number twenty-two on *Billboard*'s list of the top-forty best-selling rhythm-and-blues songs in 1981–82. It remained on the top-forty charts for fifteen weeks.[22] The group's 1981 song "Home Computer" played an important role in the development of "house" music in Chicago.[23] New York hip hop pioneer Afrika Bambaataa used parts of Kraftwerk's "Trans-Europe Express" and "Numbers" on his classic single "Planet Rock," and Luther Campbell and other practitioners of hip hop's Miami Bass style repeatedly sampled parts of Kraftwerk songs, especially the bass line from "Numbers."[24] The act of deterritorialization that makes electronic music from Düsseldorf popular in Detroit is also an act of reterritorialization, a homecoming for African American sounds vital to the practices of detournement in Europe by the members of Kraftwerk and others like them. In his extraordinary book about jazz artist Sun Ra, John Szwed points out that nearly all of the familiar elements in electronic music are variations of African American acoustic playing, that wah-wah pedals replicate the sounds of plunger mutes, that reverb, distortion, and multitonal effects originated in buzz tones and split tones, that phasing and delay are forms of call and response.[25]

Detroit techno reterritorializes the Motor City by using consumer competence and collective memory to create a cultural space that connects Detroit to Düsseldorf, that links street credibility in Detroit to global tours and performances. Yet the music that started in Detroit also came from many other places. Radio disc jockey Charles Johnson (known to his listeners as the Electrifying Mojo) played a key role in helping to bring the deterritorialized techno community into being through his broadcasts on station WGPR. Johnson grew up in Arkansas, began his radio career in the Philippines, and became a fan of techno at a party in Detroit in 1980 when DJ Darryl Shannon played a song that mixed Italian

Eurodisco sounds with Kraftwerk's "Robots." In 1981, station executives scolded Johnson for playing Kraftwerk's "Trans-Europe Express" on a station aimed at Black listeners, but the choice made perfect sense to Johnson. "I mean," he explained, "here's a band who's obviously from the same planet I'm from, right?"[26]

Producer and sound engineer Ade Mainor, known professionally as Mr. De', split his early childhood between Detroit and Panama City, Florida. He initially learned music from his gospel singer mother, who taught him to play the piano when he was six. Subsequently Mainor taught himself to play the guitar and became a break dancer. When he heard New York rapper Kurtis Blow's "The Breaks" in 1980, Mainor started "turntabling" (mixing and scratching with vinyl records) while programming synthesizers and drum machines. His music draws heavily on the Miami Bass sounds popularized by Luther Campbell and 2 Live Crew in Florida, but that also means he appropriates Campbell's appropriation of Afrika Bambaataa's appropriation of Kraftwerk's appropriation of Tamla/Motown records and James Brown!

As half of the team known as DJ Assault, Ade Mainor started mixing in the 170-beats-per-minute thumping bass that he loved in the music of Miami with the tape loops and computer sounds popularized by Derrick May and Juan Atkins. Because he could produce music so quickly, Mainor found he could stay ahead of the music industry, responding to trends in the clubs long before the major labels got wind of them. Distributing his music, however, was not so easy. "The distribution sucks," he explained to a reporter in 2001. "That's been our problem from the jump. That's the thing: the problem is that it's not a proven genre. I guess everybody knows that it's dance music and that it can sell, but it's not proven. Large labels and distributors can't understand it because it's not a guy standing in front of a keyboard looking weird, and it's not two guys standing in front of a car with an ass in front of them. So they're like, hold on, where does this thing fit?"[27] Mainor's music secured a huge following among Blacks in Detroit, but on the West Coast and in Europe his audiences were almost exclusively white. "Y'all don't know how to dance—it's funny as hell," he commented to a San Francisco journalist, adding, "It's hard to understand when you don't get the whole package. I wish I could just bring Detroit with me."[28] Mainor was not alone in his disappointment with the way music has traveled beyond Detroit.

When performing in the United Kingdom in 1989, Derrick May was horrified to learn that his music served as a focal point for a drug subculture among white youths.[29]

Today's city of Detroit may seem completely peripheral to the many different times and spaces that permeate Mainor's performances in Berlin and San Francisco, yet the physical space he inhabits makes a great deal of difference to his art. DJ Assault's *Off the Chain for the Y2K,* volume 6, album includes comedy skits replete with local references. In one of them, a voice claiming to be a Detroit schoolteacher on strike directs obscenities toward the school board and chants repeatedly, "No Contract? No Work!"[30] The commercial success of DJ Assault (Mainor and Craig Adams) depends in part on speed, on taking the sounds they hear at local venues and turning them into recordings. The oligopoly that runs the record industry is too big and bureaucratic to be that close to the streets, and as a result, Mr. De's music always has an edge, not only in Detroit, but in cities around the world where listeners want to hear the music that is current in Detroit. The music industry's stimulation of consumer desire for novelty and niche markets in this case has created a market that the industry cannot serve adequately but that talented consumers-turned-producers can. Although some of this time advantage seems certain to disappear as commercial music increasingly moves away from tapes and compact discs and positions itself to be downloaded from the Internet, Mainor and his fellow professionals will probably always derive market value from their sophisticated ability to negotiate the opportunities afforded by the multiplicity of temporalities and spaces endemic to the culture of containerization.

The success of techno also played a role in an unexpected event—the reindustrialization of at least one local business. Before techno became popular, the Archer Record pressing plant was the last manufacturer of its kind in the state of Michigan. The eclipse of vinyl records by compact discs devastated the record pressing industry and seemingly wrote just one more chapter in the long history of technological obsolescence and deindustrialization. The techno business provided a new market for vinyl, however, when turntable tricksters sought out the raw materials they needed to produce spontaneous and creative new mixtures, fusions, and hybrids. As a result, the Archer plant at the turn of the twenty-first century manufactured more vinyl records than it did during the

Motown era, with 85 percent of its sales due to techno and the other forms of dance music most closely related to it.[31]

The new commercial value that techno brought to local music in Detroit became evident to all when Detroit techno artist–composer Carl Craig persuaded city officials to turn over public parks in 2000 and 2001 for the Detroit Electronic Music Festival (DEMF). The event enabled artists active in the genre to showcase their talents for their friends and families in Detroit, to show off the skills that enabled them to secure high-paying jobs in Germany, Belgium, and England. To nearly everyone's surprise, 900,000 people showed up for the event in 2000, and it attracted 1.32 million in 2001. "People really was goin' wild there," observed Craig Adams, of the production team DJ Assault. "I was surprised that so many people was into it like they are."[32]

For an underground cultural practice that had received little media attention, that appeared on productions by small local labels without large public relations budgets, the drawing power techno displayed in the 2000 and 2001 DEMF events was simply astounding. This success, however, brought more contradictions. The Ford Motor Company (whose robots had interested Juan Atkins more than Berry Gordy's music) emerged as the sponsor of the 2001 event. Company officials succeeded in renaming the event "the Focus Detroit Electronic Music Festival" to publicize the automaker's line of Focus cars, a low-priced vehicle aimed largely at first-time car buyers. The company then advertised the Focus through television commercials that superimposed the words *Detroit techno* over scenes of auto assembly lines and records spinning on turntables.

For many techno artists and enthusiasts, the recognition and increased commercial visibility that the festival provided conflicted with the anticommercial practices that have made techno distinctly different from other music genres. Organized around the intelligent use of machines, techno music seems to flow *through* rather than *from* the artists associated with it. Detroit techno producers have gloried in anonymity, hiding their names behind pseudonyms and crafting their music in ways that deliberately make it difficult to establish both star personas for individuals and generic and brand equity for the form itself. In fact, the music known as Detroit techno never went by that name in Detroit until a British recording industry executive made it the title of a collection released on

Virgin Records in 1988. The album became a surprise hit in the United Kingdom, and the generic name stuck, even though practitioners and fans in Detroit still prefer a wide range of terms for it, including "booty music" and "ghetto tech."[33]

Techno artists deliberately blur their personal identities, releasing music under "corporate" names. Casual consumers buying techno productions by Model 500 or Infiniti have no way of knowing that the sole member of those "groups" is Juan Atkins, that "DJ Assault" is really Craig Adams *and* Ade Mainor, that the Detroit Escalator Company is only Neil Ollivierra, that Paperclip People, 69, and Innerzone Orchestra are all only Carl Craig, that Rhythim Is Rhythim is really Derrick May, that Tronic House, the Reese Project, E-Dancer, and Inter-City are simply Kevin Saunderson.[34] Carl Craig released seven full-length techno productions but only three under his own name.[35] Derrick May's music enjoyed enormous commercial success in Europe, but he steadfastly declined invitations to bring his work to major labels.[36]

Neil Ollivierra (the Detroit Escalator Company) wrote *Reality Slap,* a novel about his experiences in the early days of techno, but refused to publish it commercially, because he did not want his experiences with techno to revolve around personal gain.[37] He circulated the book by letting people make photocopies and by posting it for a time on a (now defunct) Web site. His novel connects the abstract sounds of techno music to the concrete and quotidian details of life in Detroit. "This is a city of slow motion," he writes. "Neglect breeds a return to earth . . . you can drive eight blocks and not see a single building that is not boarded up. There are dead storefronts, dead gas stations with long beds of dry grass poking up through the cracks in the concrete lots. There are whole factories and skyscrapers, filled with silent, dead rooms—all rotten drywood, rusted girders, broken windows and peeling paint. The dust is winning the war in Detroit."[38]

When the festival became a mass event, Carl Craig (among others) complained that the interests of large corporations, such as Ford Motor Company and the major recording labels, were antithetical to the interests of the techno scene. Shortly afterward, festival director Carol Marvin terminated Craig's involvement with the event. A local techno fan posted a letter on the World Wide Web complaining, "This time [they're] actually proposing that Ford Motor Company has had [some] sort of contribution to the creation of this music by footing the bill for huge ads in magazines such as *Spin,* boasting the phrase 'Detroit Techno' atop a photo of the Focus. What in the heck has the Ford Focus got to do with Detroit techno?"[39]

The answer to the fan's question about what the Ford Focus has to do with techno is both "everything" and "nothing." The new economy does special damage to the employment prospects of racial minorities, women, and young people. Between 1979 and 1984, 50 percent of Black males employed by manufacturers of durable goods in large industrial cities (including Detroit) along the Great Lakes lost their jobs.[40] Nationally, Black workers held nearly a third of the manufacturing jobs eliminated in 1990 and 1991.[41] Yet the new economy has also generated opportunities for a few of those displaced workers to create new social and cultural circuits and networks.

In some ways, Detroit techno gives in totally to the logic of containerization. For example, Craig Adams majored in marketing at Clark University, in Atlanta. Part of his success has stemmed from his ability to create music that fuses two previously distinct markets, to sell hip hop to "tech heads" and to expose the rap audience to "house" music. "I just happen to do two different things, and I kinda incorporate one into the other," Adams explains. "At raves, they really like it, because usually people that play fast music don't do a lot of tricks and scratches—they basically just mix records. But me, it's really like how you would see a hip-hop DJ with two of the same records, him going back and forth, repeatin' the same thing over and over again."[42] In other ways, however, techno breaks with the commercial logic of the fully integrated container system. The technology of "the look" and the relay system it inhabits have been deliberately left out of techno, much to the frustration of industry marketers. Charles Johnson, who has made himself a central player in Detroit techno as the disc jockey Electrifying Mojo, has never allowed himself to be photographed; in fact, his promotional "head shot" shows a face so covered by shadows that its features cannot be distinguished.[43]

Digital capitalism's ability to reshape the boundaries of reception and conception seems infinite. After all, the greatest goal of containerization was social rather than technical. It came into being specifically in order to break the power of waterfront workers and their unions, to supplant the social world of workers' control at the

point of production in factories with the supremacy of spending at
the point of consumption as the new center of the social world.[44]
Containerization is not innately efficient but merely profitable for
the people who control it. Its technologies could have been developed for many different purposes. Similarly, digital capitalism as
we know it has emerged as a system designed to increase profits
and, in Donald Lowe's formulation, to marginalize humans into
mere means, unable to pursue ethical ends.[45] But we can still ask
ourselves and others how production and consumption should be
organized and what role goods and commodities should play in the
lives of humans.

Detroit techno artists ask themselves those questions. They respond in their own way to the pervasive commodification of what
Donald Lowe calls "body practices"—social reproduction, gender
construction, and sexuality. They do so as entrepreneurs interested
in commercial success rather than as critical theorists. In order to
succeed commercially, however, they must understand some things
about the psychic and somatic needs of their audience. They live in
a world permeated by images of fragmentation and by a simulation
that continuously identifies new parts of the body as sites for eroticized commodification, that transmits the same messages to people
in nearly every corner of the globe. Yet the enormous scope, reach,
and regimentation of new technologies do not produce only uniform cultural expressions. On the contrary, the simultaneity and
hegemony of new machines, materials, and social relations also
generate new forms of expression based on the differences among
and between local circumstances and contexts.

The cultural forms that techno artists deploy originated in
the advertising agencies of New York's Madison Avenue. Techno
musicians perceive these forms, however, from the perspective of
Jefferson Avenue, one of the main thoroughfares in their home
town at the turn of the twenty-first century. Paradoxically, it is
their situated vantage point in a particular place at a particular
time that compels them to master a communications system based
on the unbounded and interchangeable nature of spaces and times.
In Lowe's formulation, society consists of not so much distinct social structures as a "combination and recombination" of structure,
discourse, cybernetic systems, and semiotics. Detroit techno music,
as a consequence, builds recreational and commercial experiences
from the material and social practices of society, from synthesized

sequences, cybernetic simulations, song fragments, and invocations of new forms of embodiment and disembodiment.[46]

Detroit techno music emerges out of the particular history of the industrial and postindustrial eras but invests itself in the possibilities of the future. It comes from specific spaces in one deindustrialized city but produces a new cognitive mapping that envisions and enacts new affiliations, alliances, and identifications. It helps us see how popular music has always generated alternative temporalities and spatialities, which we can understand by thinking about Detroit techno in the contexts of long waves of history, of the long fetches of percussive time and accordion spaces. Although the rise of Detroit techno marks a particular rupture in the history of industrial society, it grows out of what we might call the progressive history of percussive time—the history of "putting the drums up front" in U.S. popular music. This is a chronological, progressive, and developmental story, but it is one that emphasizes the creativity and contingency rather than the inevitability of historical change. This is a history of dance time, a history that pays attention to the ways in which famous dancers have encapsulated, highlighted, and brought to the fore what they learn from multitudes of unsung and unheralded dancers in taverns, auditoriums, churches, and recital halls all over the world. This is a history that might include names largely left out of Ken Burns's PBS series on jazz, such as the Whitman Sisters, the Four Step Brothers, Josephine Baker, Mae Barnes, Buck and Bubbles, Shorty Snowden, Big Bea, Stretch Jones, and Little Bea, not necessarily as transcendent original geniuses, but rather as interpreters of the collective creativity of their communities.

This history has to include the clash between European and African understandings of time, not to celebrate a story of idyllic reconciliation and cooperation between European Americans and African Americans (as Ken Burns does in *Jazz*), but rather to talk about how the growing presence and even predominance of African understandings of time in popular music have been productive of new conceptions of time, history, and human potential.

In his insightful interpretation of the rise of ragtime at the turn of the twentieth century, Christopher Small notes that ragtime was not so much a rhythm as it was an attitude about rhythm, an appreciation of syncopation, dialogue, and difference. The difference between the rhythmic concepts conveyed through ragtime's right-hand melodies and its left-hand bass accompaniment expanded the time of the present by making more than one thing happen at once. In addition, ragtime's additive rhythms (eighth notes divided into 3-3-2) evidenced a taste for multiple patterns speaking to one another, opening the door for more complex rhythmic innovations in the future.[47]

Jazz historians describe the 1920s and 1930s as the era that gave rise to Dixieland and swing music. A percussive history, however, would emphasize the movement during those decades from the fox-trot to the jitterbug and the Lindy Hop.[48] Such a story would feature the tap dancing of John "Bubbles" Sublette, who was dancing "four heavy beats to the bar and no cheating" fourteen years before the Count Basie band came east and popularized swing.[49] Charles "Honi" Coles considered it more difficult to dance four beats to the bar than two beats to the bar, because it required him to fill in his own ideas and to watch his balance. He compared the adjustment dancers had to make to 4/4 time to the challenge that instrumentalists faced when playing a slow ballad: they had more time to make embellishments, but the slower pace made their mistakes and shortcomings more evident as well.[50]

The swing bands of the 1930s opened up new possibilities on the guitar, drums, and bass. In 1932, Bennie Moten's music exemplified a growing shift to a different kind of rhythm and momentum for dancers by replacing the banjo with the guitar and substituting the string bass for the tuba.[51] By changing the voicing of the same chord with each beat, the Count Basie band's guitarist, Freddie Green, conveyed the impression of moving or "walking" while keeping steady time.[52] Trombonist Dennis Wilson remarked, "It's as if in the Bible they said 'Let There Be Time' and Freddie started playing."[53] Basie's drummer, Jo Jones, kept time on the top cymbal rather than the bass drum, enabling him to use the other drums to do more than mark the beat.[54] In the Duke Ellington Orchestra in the late 1930s, Jimmy Blanton played harmony and melody lines on the string bass while he pushed the beat subtly, making the double bass more melodic instead of following the prevailing pattern of playing the main chord tones on beats one and three.[55]

The development of electrical recording techniques in those years could be seen as more than a way to distribute music more effectively to a broader audience; they also marked a shift that enabled the bass and drums to replace the tuba and the banjo as the key sources of rhythm. The 1940s transition from swing to bop in this story would not focus on the privileging of chords over melody or on the eclipse of the big band by the small ensemble, but would instead highlight how string bass players and front line instrumentalists began to assume more responsibility for keeping time so that drummers could be free to experiment with polyrhythms and provide rhythmic accents for soloists.[56]

The distinctive creators of percussive time would not be the already-known virtuoso instrumentalists of modernist time but rather virtuoso "conversationalists," such as drummer Max Roach and dancers Earl "Groundhog" Basie and Baby Laurence. Roach usually reserved his collaborations with Baby Laurence for an "encore" in which the drummer and dancer would exchange rhythms through call and response.[57] Horace Tapscott took some of his time signatures from the rhythms that he encountered on Central Avenue, not just in the performances of other musicians, but in the pace of people carrying out their everyday chores and tasks. "When I'm walking down the street I might do something in five or I might do something in six that could run into five," he explained, adding, "I might see somebody walking and think what time is that. Every day, you see different patterns and rhythms going on, and it's just paying attention to what's around you."[58]

From the perspective of modernist time, Sun Ra's contributions to jazz might seem small. From the vantage point of percussive time, however, his attitudes toward rhythm make him an important part of a broader collective artistic effort to change the relationships between the drums and the rest of the orchestra, to put the drums up front. He objected to composers who wrote melodies but left it up to the musicians playing drums, bass, and piano to provide the rhythm. "For me," he explained, "the note is in my mind at the same time as the rhythm. My music is a music of precision. I know exactly the rhythm that must animate my music, and only this rhythm is valid."[59] His Arkestra once included as many as five drummers, not counting those playing the bells, congas, tympani, timbales, and other rhythm instruments that Sun Ra distributed to horn and reed players.[60] During the recording session that ultimately produced *Island of the Sun*, one of the band's regular drummers could not play the rhythm that Sun Ra wrote for him. The composer and band leader asked the drummer's female companion, a dancer, to play the part. She got it immediately.[61] When critics described his music as "far out," Sun Ra retorted, "There's humor in all my music. It always has rhythm. No matter how far out I may be, you can always dance to it."[62]

Seeing danceable rhythms as worthy ends inverts the hierarchies of virtuosity advanced in Ken Burns's *Jazz*. Pianist John Hicks explains, "People are always amazed, especially on piano, by technical displays. But working with guys like Little Milton, playing long slow shuffles and stuff, has always given me a certain feeling about keeping the blues in mind. A lot of people say, 'You've had classical training, haven't you?' I mean, okay, I did that, it's cool. But I don't think that is as important as the feeling that you get from some good old down-home swing."[63]

A genealogy of putting the drums up front would trace some of the roots of the fabulous rhythms and double drum and bass sounds of the Funk Brothers on Motown Records to hand-clapping patterns in sanctified churches and to the Afro-Caribbean rhythms of New Orleans. On "Baby Love" by the Supremes and on other Motown hits, the Funk Brothers played all four beats on the snare drum, not just the backbeats. This is in the style that John Boudreaux played in New Orleans on Prince Lala's "She Put the Hurt on Me." The infectious guitar riff featured on "Cleo's Back" by Junior Walker and the All-Stars originated years earlier in New Orleans when Mac Rebennack (Dr. John) played it on Miss Lavelle's "Teen Age Love."[64]

This history would have to acknowledge the rhythmic and sonic achievements of hip hop, techno, electronica, and other contemporary forms built around the sounds of drums, bass guitars, and the fat sonic booms of Roland TR-808 drum machines. In *Black Noise,* Tricia Rose emphasizes the roles played by rhythm and sound in hip hop. Citing Mark Dery and Bob Doerschuk's "new rules" of rap, "Keep it hot, keep the drums up front and boost that bass," Rose reveals how producers add effects to make the drums stand out, how they use buzz tones, distortion, and low frequency hums as sensory provocations and rhythmic accents, how they deliberately violate the rules of Western tonal harmony to take advantage of sounds that seem to clash.[65] Rose explains that while conventional music production practices favor mixing the drums smoothly with the other instruments, hip hop production practices isolate and augment drum sounds to make them stand out from the rest of the mix. Rose notes that some of the negative reactions hip hop receives come from the ways in which putting the drums up front confounds the dominant Euro-American progressive history of music. One letter writer to the *New York Times* challenged a review praising hip hop music by invoking this sense of historical progression. "Music began with rhythm, progressed to melody . . . reached its developmental culmination with harmony," the letter asserted, concluding erroneously, "Rap, despite its modern trappings is a regression."[66]

In an analysis that presents its own virtuosic performance, Robert Walser demonstrates how the rhythmic properties in Public Enemy's "Fight the Power" account for much of the song's affective power. He points to the eighth notes on the bass drum that begin each measure to define the beat, how the pickup to the second bar highlights the two-bar pattern, the ways in which the two and four backbeats on the snare drum are played on different drums featuring different pitches, placements, and positions in the stereo field, and how in the middle of each measure the first note of the eighth-note pattern is placed one-sixteenth notch ahead of the beat.[67] The history of percussive time could not be a history of modernist time, American space, or heroic subjectivity. Such a history would, however, broaden the circle of those credited with cultural creativity, mark a dialogic temporality that is not reducible to linear progressive history, and connect the sounds heard in America with the moral, spiritual, and political practices of Africa.

Filmmaker and photographer Brian Cross has created two exemplary demonstrations of percussive time under his pseudonym B+. His films *Keepintime* (2000) and *Brasilintime* (2006) explore the long fetch of history that has propelled the movement of drums and bass from the back of the bandstand to the front. In *Keepintime,* B+ stages a dialogue in rhythm onstage at Los Angeles' El Rey Theatre between legendary jazz and rhythm-and-blues drummers Roy Porter, Earl Palmer, Paul Humphrey, and James Gadson and three creative hip hop samplers and turntablists, Babu, Jrocc, and Cut Chemist, who have given new life to these old beats in their art. Playing together and feeding off one another's inspiration, the percussionists display rhythm not merely as accompaniment but also as a broad palette of colorful sounds and sensations characterized by extraordinary complexity.

Brasilintime moves this conversation between generations and genres to a new terrain beyond countries and continents. In 2002,

B+ visited Brazil looking for drummers, break beats, and percussive conversation. With the able assistance of guide and consultant DJ Nuts, the trip introduced B+ to a vast reservoir of recorded Afro-Brazilian beats and to a team of talented drummers, including the revered Joao Parahyba (aka Commanche) from the Trio Mocoto, Ivan "Mamao" Conti of Azymuth, and the great Wilson Das Neves. B+ had no guarantee that the Brazilian drummers would be eager to collaborate with hip hop performers, but any doubts he had disappeared when Joao Parahyba told him that he had been waiting his entire life for a project like this.

The North Americans were equally enthusiastic. James Gadson turned down a tour with the singer Beck to participate in the effort. Cut Chemist left a tour with Jurassic 5 to participate, and Jrocc and Babu spent twenty hours straight on airplanes riding from Japan to Brazil in order to join the project. Filmed onstage on November 25, 2002, in front of an enthusiastic audience of more than a thousand people, *Brasilintime* presents powerful evidence of previously invisible rhythmic affinities and affiliations linking people from very different parts of the African diaspora. The organic memories and mappings on display in the film do more than any written argument ever could to prove the virtues of supplementing linear chronological time with the unexpected reach and scope of percussive time.

Just as techno and turntablism enable us to imagine a compelling history of music revolving around the history of percussive time, techno's spatial imaginary also encourages us to ask how music creates audio spaces that influence the cognitive mapping and cultural morphology of physical places and spaces. One such counter-spatiality might emerge from an investigation of how the accordion historically has produced new social spaces.

Casual listeners might find little resemblance between the sounds of the accordion and the sounds of Detroit techno. Yet in many ways the relationships between postindustrial body practices and techno music resemble the relationship between the body practices of the industrial era and the music "synthesizer" dominant in its day—the accordion. Based on the principle of a vibrating reed found in ancient Chinese instruments, the piano accordion emerged out of the development of the button concertina and the button (box) diatonic accordion. Invented in Germany and Austria in the 1820s, the first commercial accordions imitated the sounds and structure of the harmonica. The piano accordion came into being in Vienna in 1863 and first appeared in the United States in San Francisco in 1909.[68]

Mass-produced, inexpensive diatonic accordions enabled a single player to mimic the sounds of several musicians and provide the volume that previously could be produced only by a small orchestra.[69] Created by the same automated technologies that killed jobs in so many industries in the nineteenth century, the accordion became a powerful mechanism for voicing the local, particular, and historical experiences of aggrieved groups. Diverse and dispersed communities created local styles that give this standardized instrument distinct local inflections. Mexican *norteño* musicians play the instrument differently from Czech polka players, the distinctive accordion voicing of Dominican merengue and Colombian–Venezuelan *vallenato* contrasts sharply with the dense swirling sounds of African American zydeco players or the rhythmic chanky chank style of Cajun players. On some occasions, accordion players move smoothly from one style to another. Narcisso Martinez, the "hurricane of the valley," released *norteño* records under his own name and, as mentioned in chapter 8, Polish-style polkas as the "Polski Kwartet" and Cajun music as "Louisiana Pete."[70] For some reason, all of his records enjoyed unusually strong popularity among Basque Americans.[71]

Like techno music in the twenty-first century, accordion playing during the twentieth century suffered from the stigma attached to mechanical means of reproducing sound. A *Far Side* cartoon codifies this legacy by contrasting one frame showing St. Peter issuing harps to new arrivals in heaven with a depiction of Satan passing out accordions to the souls who end up in hell.[72] Peter Bacho remembers that accordion playing was so common among young Filipinos in Seattle during his youth in the 1950s that his father jokingly complained about "accordioncy" as one of the key problems facing the community.[73] Art Pepper dramatizes his declining career in the 1950s by remembering he had been reduced to selling accordions door to door. A bumper sticker popular in the San Francisco Bay Area in the 1990s proclaimed, "Accordions don't play 'Lady of Spain,' people do!"

Yet, just as techno music has created new affinities between inner-city Blacks and suburban whites throughout the United

States, accordion music has produced its unique and generative spaces and social relations. While "Weird Al" Yankovic has made a career out of parody records based on the premise that it would be preposterous to combine rock music and the accordion, in lived social experience the accordion has been present at key moments in rock music history. The percussive sounds played by Augie Meyers on the Vox electric organ on the Sir Douglas Quintet's hits "She's about a Mover" in 1965 and "Mendocino" in 1968–69 may have seemed like original contributions to rock 'n' roll to most listeners.[74] But for Texans familiar with the life history of Meyers and the Sir Douglas Quintet's leader, Doug Sahm, as San Antonio musicians, the organ parts on those songs replicate the familiar sounds of *norteño* accordion playing by Mingo Saldivar and Santiago Jiménez. By the 1990s when the Sir Douglas Quintet could have coasted on the "oldies" circuit as a revival act, Sahm and Meyers teamed with *norteño* accordionist Flaco Jiménez (grandson and son of Santiago Jiménez Sr. and Jr.) and Freddy Fender (born Baldemar Huerta) to create the Tex-Mex Anglo-Chicano band Texas Tornados.

Similarly, the Rivieras' 1964 successful cover of Joe Jones's 1961 "California Sun" featured Otto Nuss imitating a rock drummer's "double beat" with his right hand on the organ, setting the pace for the lead and bass guitar players. As residents of South Bend, Indiana, the Rivieras had grown up hearing the accordion sounds of German, Czech, and Polish accordion players, and Nuss himself had been an accordion player before taking up the organ.[75] In the 1980s, the Chicano band Los Lobos produced several top-forty hits featuring the accordion playing of David Hidalgo. Their popularity brought something new to rock concerts when audience members, moved by the music of Los Lobos, moved their hands to mimic Hidalgo's movements on the accordion, playing "air accordion" instead of the ubiquitous "air guitar" at rock concerts. The indirect influence of *norteño* music on "She's about a Mover" and "Mendocino" and the influence of European polka playing on "California Sun" reveal the role of the accordion in creating spaces for interactions among diverse peoples and cultures. Tejano accordion player Steve Jordan has long mixed the melodies of the Afro-Latin funk band War with *corridos,* rancheras, and chords drawn from the guitar playing of Jimi Hendrix (among others) to fashion a popular, if inimitable, musical style.

The mass-production techniques that made the accordion possible might have led to the complete standardization of popular music. Yet, because players came to the instrument from different class positions, different ethnic cultures, and different musical traditions, they inflected a standardized mechanism with historically grounded local inflections. It is not simply that people retain the capacity for fantasy and self-expression in the face of depersonalization and dehumanization, but even more that the very mechanisms of domination provoke expressions of opposition, alterity, resistance, and transcendence. John Carlos Rowe credits capitalism with the great artistic achievement and lucrative practice of making an ideal out of the very kind of individualism that capitalist processes of production and consumption destroy. The system sells back to people in diluted form products that symbolize the life that has been stolen from them.[76] Yet this same process means that the mechanisms of domination suggest the sites of resistance, a suggestion that Detroit techno artists have embraced wholeheartedly.

Computer-based automation has a aura of inevitability about it in a society as technofilial as ours is, but the kinds of social uses to which it is put are still very much up for grabs, in life and commerce no less than in art. The successful job actions by dockworkers, truck drivers, and transport workers in Australia, North America, and Europe during the 1990s indicate that the battles over containerization are not quite over, especially at key points of distribution. The antisweatshop movement, "clean clothes" mobilizations against child labor, and IMPACT's campaign to force Philip Morris to drop "the Marlboro Man" from its advertising, all demonstrate that pressure at the point of consumption can also be an important weapon in elevating the interests of people over the extraction of profits. These oppositional social movements succeed precisely because they recognize the vulnerabilities in fully integrated systems of production, distribution, and consumption. Products made within systems of just-in-time production leave employers with little inventory and few fixed investments in plant and equipment, rendering them resistant to strikes at the point of production. Yet that system gives greater leverage to workers and consumers positioned at strategic points in the processes of distribution and consumption.

Cultural creations like *Pop Stars* certainly seem like harbingers of even more manipulative, intrusive, and calculated efforts in the years ahead. They threaten a radical restructuring of boundaries that people have long assumed must remain fixed and firm—boundaries between public and private, entertainment and sales, work and play. Every system has its contradictions, however, and the destruction of old forms of social relations can sometimes also be a stimulus toward the creation of new ones. As Donald Lowe explains in a discussion not motivated by knowledge of Detroit techno but nonetheless tremendously relevant to it,

> Resisting capital's marginalization of us as mere means, we create ourselves and others as ethical ends. Our resistances re-center us by up-ending the opposition between capital accumulation and bodily needs. Undertaking resistance as counter-practices, in the very process of attempting to change the world, we change ourselves and others.[77]

Nurturing and sustaining those forms of resistance in such a way as to point toward a different kind of organization of society are a tall order. Yet we live in an age of miracles, an age when unknowns become "pop stars," when ghetto youths turn to the newest technologies to voice long-standing grievances and desires, and when the accidental movement of plastic bath toys and stray running shoes inside ocean currents tells us a great deal about where we are and what time it is.

Epilogue
Long Waves after 9/11

You cannot sing a song and not change your condition. . . . I am talking about a culture that thinks it is important to exercise this part of your being. The part of your being that is tampered with when you run this sound through your body is a part of you that our culture thinks should be developed and cultivated, that you should be familiar with, that you should be able to get to as often as possible, and that if it is not developed, you are underdeveloped as a human being! If you go through your life and you don't meet this part of yourself, somehow the culture has failed you.

—Bernice Johnson Reagon

Ocean waves crashing on the shore, sound waves generated by instruments and voices, and waves of fads, fashion, style come and go quickly. Yet long waves of history expand time and space. They make the distant past part of the proximate present. They connect people and places across boundaries and barriers of all kinds.

Guitarist Tom Morello, of the punk metal groups Rage against the Machine and Audioslave, drew on the power of long waves in his remarks celebrating the induction of the political British punk band the Clash into the Rock 'n' Roll Hall of Fame in 2003. On the eve of the U.S.-led invasion of Iraq despite the largest peace mobilization in world history, Morello invoked the British band's motto, "The Future Is Unwritten," to declare that history was not yet over, that human will and human action could still influence the course of events.

Morello and many of his listeners knew that the justifications given for the war by George W. Bush and his administration were lies, that the Iraqi government did not possess operative weapons of mass destruction, and that Iraq had not been responsible for the attacks on the World Trade Center and the Pentagon on September 11, 2001. They knew that the plans for the war had been drawn up five years earlier by the neoconservative Committee for a New American Century as part of a project to secure a permanent military base for the United States in the Mideast, to commit the United States permanently to perpetual war as an instrument of empire. They knew that the Bush administration's fabrications merely served as pretexts to use the blood and bodies of Iraqis and Americans to achieve imperial ends.

In reminding listeners of the Clash's motto, Morello invited them to become active participants in shaping the course of the future. He drew on an alternative historical tradition, citing the slogan of a 1970s and 1980s British band that layered progressive lyrics over a mix of two- and three-chord punk rock, Jamaican reggae, and New Orleans rhythm and blues. As an African American guitarist who rose to fame in a Chicano punk band, a Harvard graduate who gave up an internship with a U.S. senator to pursue a career in popular music because he thought he could promote more social change in music than in politics, Morello situated himself within several different long waves of history. While imagining a future that has not yet been written, Morello spoke to the many histories that have never been written but instead sung, played, danced, and shouted.

The history that comes to us from official sources, however, has been written—over and over again. Historians, journalists, politicians, and even fiction writers have turned out reams of printed words about the past. Yet the written record is still inadequate and incomplete. Most written history presents the story of the past from the perspective of the victors. It reduces the infinitely diverse and plural activities of humans over centuries to a narrow succession of wars, elections, treaties, and scientific discoveries. It divides time into discrete centuries, decades, and historical periods and carves up the spaces of the earth into neat and clearly bounded national, regional, and municipal units.

The privileged moral geography of this kind of history is the nation-state, evading and obscuring the many other kinds of spatial organization that humans create. It views society from the top down, placing each of us in categories and identities that serve the needs of those in power. It scarcely mentions the calculated cruelty of elites, the recurrent crimes they commit, or the falsehoods they fabricate to justify their mistakes. The hurts of history experienced by exploited workers, displaced peasants, and demonized members of nonnormative groups are nowhere to be found in these narratives.

The dominant record of history has some utility. It conveys some real truths. It must be reckoned with, if for no other reason than the legitimacy it holds for many people. It is, however, only an impoverished rendering of a far richer reality. Despite all of the problems and pain, another history—and our as yet unwritten future—can still be authored by us, by serious people who believe that there is important work to do and that it is up to us to do it. That act of authorship will depend at least in part, however, on our ability to access and understand the parts of the past that are unwritten. One of the places we can find that past is in popular music, if we know how to look and listen for it.

A few months after Morello's speech at the Rock 'n' Roll Hall of Fame induction ceremony, a group of hip hop musicians turned to a song from the 1970s as a foundational source and a vehicle for accessing the long waves of history as we confront problems in the present. The Black Eyed Peas released "Where Is the Love?"—a complex multilayered piece that bears some resemblance to the Isley Brothers' "Footsteps in the Dark." The song mixes private desires with public issues in urging its listeners to look beyond surface realities to learn truths that are kept undercover.

The Black Eyed Peas' song references the 1972 rhythm-and-blues hit "Where Is the Love?" by Donny Hathaway and Roberta Flack. The lyrics of the original song speak about a private problem, about a person having an affair with a married woman who pledged to leave her partner as soon as she could get free. As the song unfolds, the singer realizes that the promise was a lie and asks sadly, "Where is the love you said you'd give to me?"[1] The Black Eyed Peas captured the affective power of the original song but channeled that power in a different direction. They fused this narrative of intimate personal betrayal to a broader societal betrayal, asking of the U.S. nation, "Where is the love?" at a time when "a war is goin' on but the reason's undercover."[2] The Black Eyed Peas' version of "Where Is the Love?" was a novelty in many ways. The song has offered one of the few publicly accessible antiwar messages in commercial culture since the onset of the war in Iraq. It uses the forms of sampling and oral recitation central to most hip hop recordings, but "Where Is the Love?" stands out because its lyrics explore public issues and, unlike many contemporary hip hop compositions, do not promote sexism, materialism, or egoism.

"Where Is the Love?" garnered extensive critical and commercial success. It culminated fifteen years of exploration and development by the group's two founders, William Jones (aka Will.I.Am) and Allan Pineda (aka apl.de.ap). This group came into being as one of the many unexpected consequences of the global shake-up in the relations linking production, distribution, consumption, management, labor, and land in the last third of the twentieth century. The effects of these dynamics drew the members of the Black Eyed Peas to Los Angeles from dispersed origins. In a highly segregated musical environment, the Black Eyes Peas—composed of three men (one Afro-Filipino, one Black, one Mexican) and one white woman—have become one of the most visible interracial acts. They met each other in a city where the incessant movement of populations across the globe, and across town, registers particularly strongly. In the wake of collective hardship, displacement, and loss, these movements have also created new opportunities for affiliation, identification, and alliance.

Allan Pineda moved to Los Angeles from the Philippines in 1989, when he was in the eighth grade. He makes it a point during performances to deliver raps in Tagalog, even though he knows most of his listeners do not understand that language. On arriving in Los Angeles, he joined the break-dancing crew Tribal Nation. Pineda then helped form a hip hop group, Atban Klann, with fellow eighth grader William Jones, an African American. Jones and Pineda soon recruited another into their band—the Mexican American Jaime Gomez (aka Taboo), who had been break-dancing with the Devine Tribal Brothers crew and performing hip hop with the Grass Roots. Pineda, Jones, and Gomez named their group the Black Eyed Peas.

The group displayed eclectic tastes in their first commercial releases, *Behind the Front,* in 1988, and *Bridging the Gap,* in 2000.

Macy Gray appeared as a guest artist on one of their recordings, and they gained local recognition from their propensity for having all three MCs rapping in front of live bands rather than using digital samples. The group did not achieve broad commercial success, however, until Pineda, Jones, and Gomez connected with two white pop music singers, Stacy Ferguson (aka Fergie), formerly with the group Wild Orchid, and Justin Timberlake, formerly with the "boy band" 'N Sync. Jones made the initial contact with Ferguson. He asked her to sing "Shut Up" on the *Elephunk* album. The collaboration went so well that she became a regular member of the group, completing their long search for a female voice. Jones met Timberlake at a club in Hollywood where they discovered a common enthusiasm for dancing in circles, old-school style. Jones showed Timberlake a version of the lyrics to "Where Is the Love?" and less than a week later, Timberlake presented Jones with the melodic chorus that provided the pop "hook" that secured crossover airplay on radio and helped make the song so memorable. The Black Eyed Peas decided to let Timberlake sing his melody on the recording, and they later joined with him to perform it in person as part of a massive tour headlined by Timberlake and Christina Aguilera. The tour helped introduce the song to affluent and mostly white pop audiences, propelling it onto the pop charts as a best-selling single, which, in turn, helped make *Elephunk* an extremely successful album.

The success of "Where Is the Love?" on the pop charts, however, did not translate into sales or credibility with hip hop audiences. The group's recognition from the pop charts and their association with Timberlake and Aguilera tempted many hard-core hip hop fans to dismiss the song as not hip hop at all but rather a pop song aimed at white listeners and buyers and a success because of that calculation. Calculation did, in fact, enter into the group's decision to work with Ferguson and Timberlake, but it was a calculation consistent with, rather than contrary to, the spirit, tradition, and aesthetic concerns of hip hop.

The emphasis placed on dancing in circles by the Black Eyed Peas in their performances paid tribute to their origins in late 1980s and early 1990s hip hop in Los Angeles. Their decision to mix rapping in front of live musicians with only occasional samples acknowledged and followed the example of the influential hip hop ensemble the Roots. Even their eclectic tastes in music and their decision to incorporate the pop sounds of Justin Timberlake and Fergie into their oeuvre had parallels with earlier efforts within hip hop, such as Afrika Bambaataa's samples from Kraftwerk's "Trans-Europe Express" and Run DMC's tribute to and collaboration with Aerosmith on "Walk This Way."

Yet it was politics more than aesthetics that motivated the Black Eyed Peas to add Fergie to the group, to collaborate with Timberlake, and to feature him prominently in their promotional video for "Where Is the Love?" Will.I.Am explained to Corey Moss of MTV News that putting Timberlake in the video was a deliberate choice. "I don't wanna get Dixied with it," he explained, referring to the campaign by the Clear Channel Radio conglomerate to ban the music of the Dixie Chicks and to incite listeners to boycott the group because the country music trio's Natalie Maines criticized President Bush in an offhand remark at a concert in England.

Clear Channel executives had contributed significant funds to the Bush electoral campaign in the 2000 election. The company then got the benefit of rulings by Bush appointees to the Federal Communications Commission, which added greatly to its profits. After the terrorist attacks on the World Trade Center and the Pentagon on September 11, 2001, Clear Channel executives ordered the stations in their chain to ban music that they considered inconsistent with the national interest. They defined that interest, however, as the popularity and political viability of the Bush administration and its procorporate policies. Clear Channel station managers targeted songs by Bruce Springsteen, Steve Earle, and others critical of inequality, militarism, and the lack of democracy in U.S. society.

When Maines told a British audience that the group was not proud of being from the same state as President Bush, the Clear Channel corporation attempted to destroy the Dixie Chicks' popularity. The conglomerate's disc jockeys fomented hostility to the group on the air in hopes of making them pariahs and ending their commercial appeal. In oddly ideological and noncapitalist fashion, Clear Channel executives were willing to betray their fiduciary responsibility to their stockholders by banning some of the very music that consumers liked most and that had enabled the company to secure considerable profits in the past.

Clear Channel's war on the Dixie Chicks exposed contradictions in the country music field. Throughout the 1990s, stations programming country music had courted advertisers interested in reaching suburban women over the age of thirty-five. Advertisers charged with selling Proctor and Gamble household products or cosmetic enhancements, such as the Crest Whitestrips dental whitening system, discovered that stations programming country music reached significant numbers of married adult females who made important household purchases. These women turned to country music because it had become a repository of melody in a popular music industry otherwise dominated by the rhythms of hip hop and the power chords of heavy metal but also because country music in the 1990s evidenced a new respect for women.[3]

The emergence of Garth Brooks as a male superstar in country music, a man who seemed to show intelligence, self-doubt, sentiment, and great respect for women in the lyrics of his songs, in combination with the popularity of Reba McIntyre, Deanna Carter, Lori Martin, and Faith Hill, signaled significant changes in the gender politics of country music. The Dixie Chicks, who played their own instruments skillfully and sang feisty lyrics about independent women in songs such as "Goodbye Earl," personified the new trends perfectly. Advertisers found that they could reach listeners on the 20 percent of radio stations in the United States that programmed a steady rotation of country music when the music on those stations featured "men singing love songs and apologies to women while sassy women are singing about dissing the men."[4]

Banning the Dixie Chicks and using country music stations to promote the military adventures of the Bush administration required more than censorship; it also entailed an effort to remasculinize commercial country music. Toby Keith's "Angry American: Courtesy of the Red White and Blue," a song written in response to the attacks on the World Trade Center and the Pentagon on September 11, 2001, served that purpose perfectly by grafting militarist masculine bravado onto family allegiances and obligations. In his spoken-word introduction to the song, Keith proclaims his love for his own father, who served in the military in the 1950s and lost his eye in a training combat mission. Keith notes that his father never complained about his injury and flew an American flag at the farm on which Keith was raised. In an effort to convert the women who like the Dixie Chicks into "security moms," Keith's lyrics begin with an address to "American girls and American guys" who always stand up and salute the flag, imploring them to fight back against the 9/11 attackers—even though none of the attackers came from Iraq or received significant support from Saddam Hussein. Asserting that "the big dog will fight when you rattle his cage," Keith addresses the enemy by warning, "We'll put a boot in your ass, it's the American way."

Keith's succinct phrasing eloquently expressed the view of the American way held by the Clear Channel corporation. Of course, the Dixie Chicks and their fans might have thought the American way includes the expressive freedoms of the Bill of Rights, especially the right to speak out against government malfeasance, something more precious than the right to "put a boot in your ass." Yet they did not have the power that the owners of monopoly conglomerates like Clear Channel had to frame public debate. Firms like Clear Channel were handed private control over the public airwaves by the 1996 Telecommunications Act, as we saw in chapter 1, and they then used that power to constrain open debate about the debacle in Iraq.

Promoted enthusiastically by Clear Channel stations, Keith's record was a major success. The company was less successful, however, in silencing the Dixie Chicks. The group's recordings have continued to sell well, and their concerts have drawn large and supportive crowds. The threat to the Dixie Chicks, however, greatly influenced the way that the Black Eyed Peas chose to promote "Where Is the Love?" Witnessing the treatment meted out to a group of white country music artists, to a group that had reached the top of the best-seller charts with a song about a battered woman who killed her husband by poisoning his food (his black eyed peas, coincidentally enough), the members of the hip hop group Black Eyed Peas understandably felt vulnerable to similar treatment. They knew that socially conscious Black hip hop performers Paris, Public Enemy, and KRS-1 (among others) had lost lucrative contracts with record labels when their lyrics attracted political criticism, as was discussed in chapter 7. In response, the Black Eyed Peas came up with a strategy to enable their music to be heard by millions. "It has to do with our own form of propaganda," Will.I.Am explained. "The media have their way of doing it. And we're going to inform the people what it is that we want them to know, how we think about life and how we live our life and what consumes our mind socially." Observing quite accurately that no current popular songs dealt with these kinds of issues, he proclaimed in 2003, "The world needs this song right now."[5]

By attaching themselves to the mass-market sex appeal of Fergie and Timberlake, the marketing power of the Timberlake–Aguilera tour, and the commercial appeal of Timberlake's catchy refrain, the Black Eyed Peas might seem to be collaborating with the very things that the song's lyrics criticize: the power of glamorous media images that make young people feel insignificant unless they imitate them, the propensity for people to make decisions on the basis of what the song's lyrics deem "visions of them dividends," and the pervasive selfish individualism in a society that mocks the values of fairness, equality, and love. It was not at all clear whether the Black Eyed Peas had appropriated the power of the mass market in order to promote the politics of fairness, equality, and love or whether they had mobilized popular desires for fairness, equality, and love in the service of augmenting the star power and market appeal of Justin Timberlake and Christina Aguilera. Was it more significant that the Black Eyed Peas used commercial culture to make a political statement or that oligopolistic corporations marketing commercial culture used the politics of the Black Eyed Peas to produce profits for their investors?

The massive success of "Where Is the Love?" does not answer these questions. We have no way of assessing the long- or short-term effects of the song's lyrics compared with its other dimensions as entertainment and marketing. Are the song's lyrics best understood as one part of a broader political moment or as merely a key component in differentiating one mass-marketed product from all the others? These are familiar questions in cultural studies. They can be answered only through concrete case studies, not through philosophical abstraction. All the evidence will never be fully accessible to any investigator or group of investigators. These are questions that need to be posed in terms of reasoned speculation as well as empirical inquiry. In the case of "Where Is the Love?" it is certainly significant that the song emerged at a time when the largest peace movement in the history of the world had failed to stop the U.S. war in Iraq, when government-sanctioned media mergers produced stultifying sameness on the radio and on television (because sameness does more to secure corporate synergy across media forms), at a time when hip hop's huge socially conscious and participatory do-it-yourself audience could find precious little with which to identify within mass-marketed music, and at a time when popular music artists were more quiescent and complicit with the corporate agenda than at any other time in recent memory. Clearly, the stage was set for a different kind of music within commercial culture, but the reasons for the song's success may have had as much to do with product differentiation as with politics.

Yet at a time when the most powerful forces in the U.S. political system have encouraged people to place their desires as consumers and accumulators above their responsibilities and obligations as community members and citizens, "Where Is the Love?" succeeded, at least in part, because it asked the right question, because it took the love-song format of top-forty radio and made it capable of speaking to broader social issues, much as the Isley Brothers had done twenty-five years earlier. The affective power and aesthetic appeal of "Where Is the Love?" draw on long traditions within popular culture and community life. The politicized art of aggrieved communities permeates the song, from its references to the traditions of hip hop and break dancing that emerged in inner cities in the wake of deindustrialization in the 1970s and 1980s to its poetic lyrics that reference a long history of folk music, protest songs, and speaking truth to power. The multicultural membership of the Black Eyed Peas appeals simultaneously to the legacy of race-based struggles for social justice in communities of color and to the kind of liberal and corporate multiculturalism that stages symbolic and largely empty representations of facile unity among antagonistic social groups to mask dramatic differences in opportunities and life chances.

Perhaps the most effective, and most problematic, element in the song's success comes from its ability to blend profound personal and political concerns in accessible vernacular language. The question "Where is the love?" connects diverse constituencies, allowing for many different moments of mutual recognition, affiliation, and alliance. It is not just that the musical content and personnel on the recording brought different constituencies into contact with one another, but also that the question "Where is the love?" brilliantly calls attention to what happened to most people in the United States over three decades of deindustrialization, privatization, militarism, economic polarization, and social disintegration. The song's lyrics connect desires for social justice with desires for what Black feminist Tricia Rose calls intimate justice. The lyrics attack the dominant system for its crimes against morality, mind, and spirit, not just for its failure to deliver the affluence it constantly promises. Perhaps most important, by blending musical styles, embodied identities, and unidentical but unantagonistic historical memories, the Black Eyed Peas' "Where Is the Love?" enacts the politics that it envisions. Safely disguised as a pop song asking the quintessential pop music question about love, the Black Eyed Peas' hit also remained on the fringes of the nation's political and commercial consciousness. Its main immediate breakthrough came in its marketing achievements, in giving "street" credibility (or at least the appearance of credibility) to Justin Timberlake and mainstream exposure (or at least the appearance of mainstream exposure) to the Black Eyed Peas.

"Where Is the Love?" contains no direct connection to "Footsteps in the Dark," but the two songs have many similarities. Both songs display the potential to link private desires with public issues. Both songs raise suspicions about how much we can know from surface appearances. Both songs express a desire to know and a fear of knowing at the same time. The conscious intentions of their creators matter a great deal, but the ultimate significance of the songs depends ultimately on their largely unintended effects, on the ways that listeners have understood them and deployed them in their own lives.

The histories of "Footsteps in the Dark" and "Where Is the Love?" alert us to the power of popular music to bring memories, perspectives, and critiques from the past into the present, but they also demonstrate the limits of commercial culture in arbitrating the social tensions generated by too little democracy and too much exploitation. "Where Is the Love?" and "Footsteps in the Dark" illustrate the promise and peril of popular music as social history. They resonate with the hidden histories that have informed the chapters of this book, histories of nationalist division and multicultural reconciliation, of commodification and exploitation, of colonialism and transnational migration, of urban renewal, deindustrialization, and corporate greed. They also carry within them the long fetch of history, legacies of struggle that animate and motivate people to desire and enact social change, that keep alive hopes for something better, even in the face of fears of impending catastrophe.

The multinational origins of the Black Eyed Peas and their groundedness in the civil rights traditions of abolition democracy in the United States raise another level of complexity in assessing their music. Like banda from Mexico, merengue from the Dominican Republic, and salsa from Puerto Rico, hip hop circulates in a global context. Music that reminds emigrants and exiles of home becomes popular in places far away. Songs that seem progressive and oppositional inside the United States nonetheless benefit from the monopoly power of U.S. media conglomerates. Cries for democracy inside the United States within this system can unwittingly suppress global democracy, because the apparatuses of communications industries amplify the voices of people inside the United States and mute those from outside.

At the same time, new technologies and new social relations shake up social identities. The model of digital capitalism that created the group Eden's Crush on the WB television program *Pop Stars* and the artistry and imagination at the heart of Detroit techno use the same technologies to move in different directions, but both reaffirm the centrality of consumption to the contemporary social world. The communities created by consumption practices become all the more appealing to people in the face of their pain, in response to the reckless and destructive practices that produce powerful and profound senses of "root shock" emanating from displacements of people in and across cities, nations, and continents. These disturbances provoke melancholy nostalgia for the music of the past but also serve to provoke the kinds of innovation exemplified by the Black Artist Group in St. Louis and the musical fusions forged by Ry Cooder and his fellow musicians on *Chávez Ravine*.

In the United States, the ever increasing reach and scope of global capitalism and the transformation of the nation-state into an ever compliant instrument of transnational corporate capital have deadly consequences for culture. They encourage the celebratory nationalism of Ken Burns's film *Jazz*, and they help produce moral panics like the one directed against inner-city youths that surfaced in the hip hop hearings. Yet this same spread and transformation can also pique interest in border crossers, masqueraders, and imposters, from both the past and the present, in people who find ways to enact a kind of agency despite the limiting identities that have been imposed on them. They bring to the surface previously occluded families of resemblance linking rap, reggae, and rara and at the same time reveal the long waves of history that might bring together groups pitted against one another in the United States.

Even the waves of the ocean seem to be taking on new identities now. In an evocative discussion, Allan Sekula proposes that present practices and processes of factory production and distribution have made the sea and the land exchange places. Stable sites of production such as factories, which used to be fixed and finite, have become fluid and mobile. Factories change their forms frequently as new technologies lead to the installation of new machines. Sometimes entire factories even slip away stealthily in the night, moving overseas in search of employees who will work for lower pay and laws that do less to protect workers and the environment. On the other hand, oceangoing ships, which formerly were mobile conduits for distributing goods, now resemble factories and warehouses. They carry interchangeable and uniform containers, each forty by eight by eight feet in dimension, over and over again on regular routes to shoreside cranes in fixed locations.[6] Spatial relations on land change rapidly and unpredictably in this system. Docks, piers, and waterfront neighborhoods become transformed into consumer shopping malls, and the work of unloading ocean cargo and sending it to destinations on land takes place in new switching centers hundreds of miles inland, centers such as Reno and Sparks in the high desert land of Nevada, hundreds of miles from the Pacific Ocean.

Yet long waves of history still shape the present. When the Isley Brothers sang about hearing "footsteps in the dark" on the *Go for Your Guns* album in 1977, they drew on the long fetch of history. Their success built on the history of music as an alternative academy, as a repository of social memory in the Black community, on their audience's shared social understanding of both the civil rights movement and its betrayal. By focusing on the affective dimensions of a failing love affair, "Footsteps in the Dark" marked its moment in time with a powerful allegory that still haunts us in the present.

In an album released in 1976, the Isley Brothers seemed to hear footsteps of a different sort. On *Harvest for the World*, the Isleys identify how systemic social injustice frustrates human desires for mutuality and happiness. The lyrics of their song "Harvest for the World" call on people to celebrate life and give thanks for their children, to recognize their commonalities as humans. Yet at the same time, the song identifies precisely those forces that divide people from one another. Its lyrics condemn greed, inequality, nationalism, and war. In this song, the Isley Brothers sing about how avarice tarnishes the love that is in every one of us. They condemn a nation "so concerned with gain" that it produces conditions in which "greater grows the pain." The final verse makes war against the war makers, rejecting those who "dress me up for battle when all I want is peace." It states that those who pay the price of combat are the ones who come home with the least. In a prophetic voice reminiscent of the Book of Revelation, the lyrics see entire nations turning into beasts, and they ask instead, "When will there be a harvest for the world?" The utopian hopes articulated in "Harvest for the World" contrasted sharply with the social realities of the 1970s. They remain sharply at odds with the social distribution of suffering and reward today. Yet asking "When will there be a harvest for the world?" is a good question. Like asking "Where is the love?" it is a question that assumes greater relevance and urgency every day.

At the turn of the twenty-first century, Ron Isley crafted a new identity for himself. In the midst of doing battle with the IRS over charges of hiding income, cashing his dead brother's royalty checks, and evading taxes, Isley released an album of pop songs written by composer Burt Bacharach, made appearances as the "character" Mr. Biggs on records by rhythm-and-blues singer (and accused felon) R. Kelly, did studio work with hip hop icons Nelly and Dr. Dre, and promoted a clothing line featuring fur coats and chinchilla bikinis.[7] Inhabiting the persona of a sharply dressed libertine longing for love, Ron Isley and the reconstituted Isley Brothers recorded the best-selling albums *Eternal* and *Body Kiss*. Still securing chart success in his midsixties, Isley is culminating an amazing career that has enabled him to function as a contemporary artist through six different decades. He has recorded with Snoop Dogg, R. Kelly, Mos Def, Nas, Ja Rule, Jay-Z, and Will.I.Am, of the Black Eyed Peas. Mr. Biggs embodies the hedonism and materialism that permeate so may hip hop videos and songs. His stage persona stands a long distance from "Footsteps in the Dark" and "Harvest for the World."

It may be impossible today for Ron Isley and his audience to continue to imagine a harvest for the world. The pursuit of personal gain and conspicuous consumption looms large in our era.

Perhaps like a large part of his audience, Ron Isley has lost hope for a harvest for the world or has become reduced to seeking momentary personal pleasure as reparation for all that has been lost over the past half-century. Yet the self-assertion and style that Mr. Biggs displays on the surface might still reflect an inner desire for something else, much in the same way that the zoot suit that Malcolm X wore in the 1940s was an outer manifestation of a desire for recognition and connection that eventually took political form.[8]

In an increasingly interdependent world it is difficult to see how any substantial problems can be solved only one nation at a time. Yet curiously, the nation-state does not recede in importance under these circumstances. Transnational capitalism does not create uniform working conditions, wages, and welfare systems but instead uses national borders as the vehicle for exploiting the comparative advantages that come from endless forms of differentiation. Struggles within nation-states as well as across them determine how people today ask the question the Isleys asked in the 1970s, about when (and if) there will be a harvest for the world. The diasporic affinities articulated within pan-African and pan-Asian popular music display strategies of cognitive mapping of great significance for those struggles.

All over the world today, people hear footsteps in the dark. They live with anxiety, insecurity, and dread. Some wonder with good reason if they will live to see another day. In the metropolitan centers of North America and Europe, the most powerful people and the most advanced institutions are "so concerned with gain" that, as the years come and go, "greater grows the pain." Committed to a kind of free-market fundamentalism that justifies plunder, exploitation, and war, our leaders insist that there is no alternative to the present system. They claim they have the long fetch of history behind them.

Yet we have some long waves of our own. The history of resistance is as old and as powerful as the history of oppression. Histories hidden in songs from around the nation and around the world tell us that another world is possible. The sound may be as faint as footsteps in the dark, but there is still time to seek a harvest for the world.

Acknowledgments

There's a Willie Nelson song that says we have only three days filled with tears and sorrow, but those days are "yesterday, today, and tomorrow." The harsh realities that haunt the writing of this book have made me all too aware of good reasons for tears and sorrow in this world. It is depressing to contemplate the depth, dimension, and duration of inequality and injustice.

It is not depressing, however, to know that everywhere around the world people are willing and able to stand up and speak up for justice, willing to help a fellow sojourner along the way. While writing this book I received the benefit of comments, criticism, corrections, and advice from many of these people. The errors that remain—and there are always errors of commission or omission in efforts to translate the rich and plural experiences of the social world into words on paper—are solely my own. The people to whom I owe great debts deserve to be thanked for their knowledge and their generosity in sharing it with me.

Musicians Johnny Otis, Ruben Guevara, Carlos Zialcita, Billy Peek, George Lewis, Vijay Iyer, Gregorio Landau, Ade Mainor, Oliver Lake, and the late Preston Love and Julius Hemphill explained their art to me and directed me toward the social worlds that produced them.

Indispensable tools and concepts came to me from the specialized work of musicologists. Rob Walser, Susan McClary, Christopher Small, Richard Leppert, Line Grenier, Jocelyne Guilbault, Jacqui

Malone, Steven Loza, and Deborah Wong helped me think in new ways and understand better how music functions as a social force.

Ivory Perry and Stan Weir made me aware that things that cannot be said can still be sung. Brian Cross and Marisela Norte showed me that there is more than one way to tell a story.

Generous academic colleagues have helped me by pointing out errors, omissions, and misinterpretations. They include Raul Fernandez, Deborah Pacini-Hernandez, Helena Simonett, Josh Kun, Frances Aparicio, Claudine Michel, Liza McAlister, Raphaella Nau, Barry Shank, and Charles McGovern.

Robin Kelley, Tricia Rose, David Roediger, and Melvin Oliver sing the songs of the unsung. Their work encourages and inspires me. Barbara Tomlinson always helps me remember why evidence matters and what ethical argument demands. At the University of Minnesota Press, Adam Brunner's careful reading and Richard Morrison's wise guidance have helped me immeasurably.

This book is dedicated to people who had little to do with it directly, people who hear footsteps in the dark and do something about them. I think everyone has important things to learn from fair housing activists and attorneys, from community groups seeking to end environmental racism and educational inequality, and from people who feel obligated to make peace in a world suffering from war. This book is dedicated specifically to Percy Green, a grassroots community activist in St. Louis who has been teaching us crucial lessons about the long fetch of history throughout his life. As long as people like Percy exist, the rest of us can hold on to hope.

Notes

Introduction

The epigraph to this chapter is drawn from Reverend C. L. Franklin, *Give Me This Mountain: Life History and Selected Sermons of the Reverend C. L. Franklin,* edited by Jeff Todd Titon (Urbana: University of Illinois Press, 1989), 89.

1. In the remix version of "It Was a Good Day," Ice Cube sampled Curtis Mayfield's "Let's Do It Again" as recorded by the Staple Singers and Parliament's "Sir Nose D'Voidoffunk," giving the song a totally different feel. On the same album, Ice Cube also sampled Evelyn Champagne King, who covered "Footsteps in the Dark."

2. For a sophisticated analysis of how fiction writers both revealed and occluded these conditions, see James Kyung-Jin Lee, *Urban Triage: Race and the Fictions of Multiculturalism* (Minneapolis: University of Minnesota Press, 2004).

3. Ice Cube, *The Predator,* liner notes, Priority Records P2-57185.

4. Hannah Arendt, *The Origins of Totalitarianism* (New York: Harvest Books, 1973), 462.

5. Gary Stewart, *Rhumba on the River: A History of the Popular Music of the Two Congos* (London and New York: Verso, 2000), 34; Joel Whitburn, *Joel Whitburn's Top Pop Singles, 1955–1986* (Menomonee Falls, Wisc.: Record Research, 1987), 142, 318.

6. Dr. John (Mac Rebennack), *Under a Hoodoo Moon: The Life of the Night Tripper,* with Jack Rummel (New York: St. Martin's, 1994), 46.

7. Ibid., 54.

8. George Lipsitz, *Dangerous Crossroads* (London: Verso, 1994), 124–26, 167; Zoila Mendoza, *Shaping Society through Dance: Mestizo*

Ritual Performance in the Peruvian Andes (Chicago: University of Chicago Press, 2000), 213.

9. Clyde Woods, *Development Arrested* (New York: Routledge, 1998).

10. Bill Dahl, "The Soulful Saxophone Sound of Gene 'Daddy G' Barge," *Living Blues* 31, no. 151, May–June 2000, 3, 27; John Soelder, "Bobby Womack Returns to His Gospel Roots?" *Cleveland Plain Dealer,* August 23, 1999.

11. Bob Shannon and John Javna, *Behind the Hits: Inside Stories of Classic Pop and Rock and Roll* (New York: Warner Books, 1988), 66; Fred Bronson, *The Billboard Book of Number One Hits* (New York: Billboard, 1988), 99.

12. Tony Mitchell, "Fightin' *da Faida:* The Italian Posses and Hip-Hop in Italy," in Tony Mitchell, ed., *Global Noise* (Middletown, Vt.: Wesleyan University Press, 2001), 207, 209.

13. Vernon Reid, "Brother from Another Planet," *Vibe* 1, no. 3, November 1993, 47.

14. Bronson, *The Billboard Book of Number One Hits,* 414.

15. Robert Farris Thompson, "Preface," in Raul Fernandez, *Latin Jazz: The Perfect Combination* (Washington, D.C.: Chronicle Books, 2002), 11.

16. See my discussion of 2 Live Crew and censorship in chapter 7, "The Hip Hop Hearings."

17. Dr. John, *Under a Hoodoo Moon,* 110.

18. David Ake, *Jazz Cultures* (Berkeley: University of California Press, 2002), 77–78.

19. Dr. John, *Under a Hoodoo Moon,* 187.

20. Ibid., 250.

1. Pop Stars

The epigraph to this chapter is quoted from Rupert Charles Lewis, *Walter Rodney's Intellectual and Political Thought* (Detroit: Wayne State University Press, 1998), 79; originally from Walter Rodney, *A Tribute to Walter Rodney: One Hundred Years of Development in Africa,* lectures given at the University of Hamburg, summer 1978 (Hamburg: Institut für Politische Wissenschaft der Universitat Hamburg).

1. Steven Flusty, *De-Coca-Colonization: Making the Globe from the Inside Out* (New York: Routledge, 2004), 156; C. C. Ebbesmeyer and W. J. Ingraham, "Shoe Spill in the North Pacific East," *Eos* 73 (1992): 361.

2. C. C. Ebbesmeyer and W. J. Ingraham, "Pacific Toy Spill Fuels Ocean Current Pathways Research," *Eos* 75 (1994): 425.

3. Gayle Wald, "'I Want It That Way': Teenybopper Music and the Girling of Boy Bands," *Genders* 35 (2002): 1–39; Judith Halberstam, *In a Queer Time and Place: Transgender Bodies, Subcultural Lives* (New York: New York University Press, 2005), 174–79.

4. Halberstam, *In a Queer Time and Place,* 177.

5. Sallie Hofmeister, "Company Town," *Los Angeles Times,* January 18, 2001, C6; Jim Ruttenberg, "AOL Combines TV Networks under a Chief," *New York Times,* March 7, 2001, C1; Kevin Downey, "Of Eden's Crush and Cross Media Synergies," *Medialife,* August 10, 2001, 1.

6. William K. Tabb, *The Amoral Elephant: Globalization and the Struggle for Social Justice in the Twenty-first Century* (New York: Monthly Review Press, 2001), 47, 169–70.

7. This is not to conclude that Eden's Crush did not present good music, that the producers, backup musicians, and group members were untalented. But it is to allege that such a heavy dependence on production values and promotion made it more difficult to discern in this music the virtuosity that appears in other genres of music.

8. Raymond Williams, *The Politics of Modernism: Against the New Conformists* (London: Verso, 1999), 132–33.

9. Sarah Banet-Weiser, *The Most Beautiful Girl in the World: Beauty Pageants and National Identity* (Berkeley: University of California Press, 1999).

10. "Ask Ivette's Dad," www.edenscrush.com/questions060601.html, accessed November 18, 2003.

11. Donald M. Lowe, *The Body in Late Capitalist USA* (Durham, N.C.: Duke University Press, 1995), 135.

12. Ibid., 166.

13. See George Lipsitz, *The Possessive Investment in Whiteness: How White People Profit from Identity Politics* (Philadelphia: Temple University Press, 1998), 108–13; Lowe, *The Body in Late Capitalist USA,* 165.

14. Lowe, *The Body in Late Capitalist USA,* 166.

15. Shari Waters, "Music for Teens," http://teenmusic.about.com/library/weekly/aa050801b.htm, accessed November 18, 2003.

16. Jenny Toomey, "Empire of the Air," in David Brackett, ed., *The Pop, Rock, and Soul Reader: Histories and Debates* (New York: Oxford University Press, 2005), 478.

17. David Brackett, "Public Policy and Pop Music History Collide," in Brackett, ed., *The Pop, Rock and Soul Reader,* 476.

18. Raymond Williams, *The Politics of Modernism: Against the New Conformists* (London: Verso, 1999), 120.

19. Dan Schiller, *Digital Capitalism: Networking the Global Market System* (Cambridge, Mass.: MIT Press, 2000), 1–2; Raymond Williams, *Television: Technology and Cultural Studies* (New York: Schocken Books, 1974).

20. Williams, *The Politics of Modernism,* 122.

21. Néstor García Canclini, "Cultural Reconversion," in George Yudice, Jean Franco, and Juan Flores, eds., *On Edge: The Crisis of Contemporary Latin American Culture* (Minneapolis: University of Minnesota Press, 1992), 33.

22. Williams, *The Politics of Modernism,* 132–33.

23. In a singularly important but unfortunately largely overlooked article, Joel Kovel explains how the constitution of the family as a privileged market site helps fuel this kind of cultural spectacle. "The point is not that people desire the administrative mode, it is rather that administration protects them against the desires they can not stand, while it serves out, in the form of diluted rationalization, a hint of the desire and power lost to them." Joel Kovel, "Rationalization and the Family," *Telos* 37 (1978): 19.

24. John Szwed, *Space Is the Place: The Lives and Times of Sun Ra* (New York: Da Capo, 1997), 151.

25. Ibid., 177.

26. Ibid., 155.

27. Brian Lowery, "New Faces of Synergy 2001," *Los Angeles Times,* Calendar section, March 11, 2001, 73.

28. Williams, *The Politics of Modernism,* 127.

29. Lowe, *The Body in Late Capitalist USA,* 11–12.

30. See George Lipsitz, "Consumer Spending as State Project: Yesterday's Solutions and Today's Problems," in Susan Strasser, Charles McGovern, and Matthias Judt, eds., *Getting and Spending: European and American Consumer Societies in the Twentieth Century* (Cambridge: Cambridge University Press, 1998), 127–47.

31. Schiller, *Digital Capitalism,* 8.

32. Ibid., 54.

33. Ibid.

34. Williams, *The Politics of Modernism,* 126.

35. Tabb, *The Amoral Elephant,* 167.

36. Schiller, *Digital Capitalism,* 123–24.

37. Williams, *The Politics of Modernism,* 134.

38. Bob Shannon and John Javna, *Behind the Hits: Inside Stories of Classic Pop and Rock and Roll* (New York: Warner Books, 1986), 113.

39. Joel Whitburn, *Joel Whitburn's Top Pop Singles, 1955–1986* (Menomonee Falls, Wisc.: Record Research, 1987), 23.

40. Dr. John (Mac Rebennack), *Under a Hoodoo Moon: The Life of the Night Tripper,* with Jack Rummel (New York: St. Martin's, 1994), 126.

41. Shannon and Javna, *Behind the Hits,* 76, 207.

42. Matthew Wheelock Stahl, "Reinventing Certainties: American Popular Music and Social Reproduction," Ph.D. dissertation, Department of Communication, University of California, San Diego, 2006.

2. Crossing Over

1. The Fugees' covers of 1970s songs "Killing Me Softly with His Song" and "No Woman, No Cry" conform to the pattern described in the

introduction in relation to hip hop references to the Isley Brothers' "Footsteps in the Dark" and Roberta Flack and Donny Hathaway's "Where Is the Love?"

2. Chris Wong Won of 2 Live Crew is a Chinese Trinidadian, Foxy Brown is Trinidadian and Asian, the families of Grandmaster Flash and Afrika Bambaataa came from Barbados, and Kool DJ Herc was born in Jamaica, as was Bushwick Bill (originally Richard Shaw) of the Geto Boys. See George Lipsitz, "The Lion and the Spider," *American Studies in a Moment of Danger* (Minneapolis: University of Minnesota Press, 2001).

3. Elizabeth McAlister, *Rara! Vodou, Power, and Performance in Haiti and Its Diaspora* (Berkeley: University of California Press, 2002), 191.

4. Sue Steward, "Compas, Carnival, and Voodoo," in Simon Broughton, Mark Ellingham, David Muddyman, and Richard Trillo, eds., *World Music: The Rough Guide* (London: Penguin, 1994), 498–502.

5. Gage Averill, *A Day for the Hunter, a Day for the Prey: Popular Music and Power in Haiti* (Chicago: University of Chicago Press, 1997), 133.

6. McAlister, *Rara!* 9. *Babylon* and *the Babylon System* are the Rastafarian terms for the site of their exile and captivity in Jamaica, for the Anglo-American–Creole capitalism, and for the police powers used to oppress Rastafarians.

7. Ibid., 192.

8. Ibid., 3–9.

9. Paula Ioanide's forthcoming work on the Louima beating brilliantly contextualizes this event within the broader psychosexual racist categories from which it emerged.

10. See chapter 9 as well as my discussion of Latin bugalu in *Dangerous Crossroads* (London: Verso, 1994).

11. Jim McCarthy and Ron Sansoe, *Voices of Latin Rock: The People and Events That Created This Sound* (Milwaukee: Hal Leonard, 2004), 72–73.

12. Douglas Henry Daniels, "Vodun and Jazz: 'Jelly Roll' Morton and Lester 'Pres' Young: Substance and Shadow," *Journal of Haitian Studies* 9, no. 1 (Spring 2003): 116, 118.

13. McAlister, *Rara!* 194.

14. *Haiti Progress,* English ed., March 22, 2000, 1–3.

15. Ibid., 3.

16. Paul Farmer, *The Uses of Haiti* (Monroe, Maine: Common Courage Press, 1994), 89–93.

17. David Nicholls, *From Dessalines to Duvalier: Race, Color, and National Independence in Haiti* (New Brunswick, N.J.: Rutgers University Press, 1996), 5.

18. Silvio Torres-Saillant and Ramona Hernandez, *The Dominican Americans* (Westport, Conn.: Greenwood Press, 1998), 14.

19. Gideon Granger to James Jackson, March 23, 1802, *American State Papers,* quoted in Stan Weir, "Early U.S. Labor Policy Revealed by Archives Find," *Random Lengths* 7, no. 12 (November 1986): 16.

20. Daniel C. Littlefield, "Black, John Brown, and a Theory of Manhood," in Paul Finkelman, ed., *His Soul Goes Marching On: Responses to John Brown and the Harper's Ferry Raid* (Charlottesville: University of Virginia Press, 1995), 87.

21. Farmer, *The Uses of Haiti,* 102.

22. Ibid., 107.

23. Michel-Rolph Trouillot, "Haiti's Nightmare and the Lessons of History," in Deidre McFayden, Pierre LaRamee, Mark Fried, and Fred Rosen, eds., *Haiti: Dangerous Crossroads* (Boston: South End Press, 1995), 129–30; Farmer, *The Uses of Haiti,* 113.

24. Trouillot, "Haiti's Nightmare and the Lessons of History," 129–30; Farmer, *The Uses of Haiti,* 51.

25. Trouillot, "Haiti's Nightmare and the Lessons of History," 125.

26. Gage Averill, "Haitian Dance Bands, 1915–1970: Class, Race, and Authenticity," *Latin American Music Review* 10, no. 2 (Fall–Winter 1989): 212, 222.

27. Averill, *A Day for the Hunter, a Day for the Prey,* 136–37.

28. Ibid, 139.

29. Claire Jean Kim, *Bitter Fruit: The Politics of Black-Korean Conflict in New York* (New Haven, Conn.: Yale University Press, 2001), 35.

30. Charley Rogulewski, "Fugees Take It Easy," *Rolling Stone On Line News,* August 25, 2005, www.rollingstone.com.

31. See Michael Dawson, *Behind the Mule: Race and Class in African American Politics* (Princeton, N.J.: Princeton University Press, 1994), for a profound rumination on this problem.

32. Timothy White, *Catch a Fire: The Life of Bob Marley* (New York: Henry Holt, 1993), 180.

33. See Robert A. Hill, "Dread History: Leonard P. Howell and Millenarian Visions in Early Rastafari Religions in Jamaica," *Epoche: Journal of the History of Religions at UCLA* (1981): 32–34.

34. Donald Clarke, ed., *The Penguin Encyclopedia of Popular Music,* 2nd ed., (London: Penguin, 1998), 690; Rose Ryan, "Aboriginal Music," in Marcus Breen, ed., *Our Place, Our Music: Aboriginal Music* (Canberra: Aboriginal Studies Press, 1989), 121; Bruce Weber, "Reggae Rhythms Speak to an Insular Tribe," *New York Times,* September 19, 2000, 1.

35. Carter Van Pelt, "Slyght of Hand," in Chris Potash, ed., *Reggae, Rasta, Revolution: Jamaican Music from Ska to Dub* (New York: Schirmer Books, 1997), 102.

36. Steve Barrow and Peter Dalton, *Reggae: The Rough Guide* (London: Rough Guides, 1997), 47–48.

37. Ibid., 160, 164, 339, 340.

38. Kevin O'Brien Chang and Wayne Chen, *Reggae Routes: The Story of Jamaican Music* (Philadelphia: Temple University Press, 1998), 98.

39. Chris Potash, "Introduction," in Potash, ed., *Reggae, Rasta, Revolution,* xxiv.

40. White, *Catch a Fire*, 150.

41. Barrow and Dalton, *Reggae,* 107–8.

42. White, *Catch a Fire,* 141.

43. Barrow and Dalton, *Reggae,* 35–36.

44. Chang and Cheng, *Reggae Routes,* 19, 210.

45. Barrow and Dalton, *Reggae,* 35–36.

46. Quoted in Potash, "Introduction," in Potash, ed., *Reggae, Rasta, Revolution,* xxiv.

47. Norman Stolzoff, *Wake the Town and Tell the People: Dancehall Culture in Jamaica* (Durham, N.C.: Duke University Press, 2000), 69.

48. Tom Stoddard, *Jazz on the Barbary Coast* (Berkeley: Heyday Books, 1998), 203–4.

49. Ibid., x.

50. Donald Clarke, ed., *The Penguin Encyclopedia of Popular Music,* 1st ed. (London: Penguin Books, 1990), 1220; Stoddard, *Jazz on the Barbary Coast,* 112.

51. E. Taylor Atkins, *Blue Nippon: Authenticating Jazz in Japan* (Durham, N.C.: Duke University Press, 2001), 87.

52. Robin Moore, *Nationalizing Blackness: AfroCubanismo and Artistic Revolution in Havana, 1920–1940* (Pittsburgh: University of Pittsburgh Press, 1997), 110, 259.

53. Ramiro Burr, *Tejano and Regional Mexican Music* (New York: Billboard, 1999), 52.

54. Lise Waxer, *The City of Musical Memory: Salsa, Record Grooves, and Popular Memory in Cali, Colombia* (Middletown, Vt.: Wesleyan University Press, 2002).

55. Rehan Hyder, *Brimful of Asia: Negotiating Ethnicity on the UK Music Scene* (Aldershot, England: Ashgate, 2004), 75.

56. Roque Bucton, "Interview with Eleanor Academia," *Padagudas ka den!* (Smash It), *World Kulintang Institute Newsletter* 1, no. 1 (Winter 1994): 6.

57. Interview with Eleanor Academia, by Daphne Barretto, July 23, 1995, in my possession.

58. Teresita Ybiernas, "On a Global Beat," *Filipinas* (June 1993): 36.

59. Devorah L. Knaff, "Bang a Gong," *Riverside Press-Enterprise,* January 23, 1998, AA16. http://members.tripod.com/eleanor_academia/blues_ea.htm.

60. Jane C. H. Park, "Cibo Matto's Stereotype A: Articulating Asian American Hip Pop," in Shilpa Davé, LeiLani Nishime, and Tasha G. Oren, eds., with foreword by Robert G. Lee, *East Main Street: Asian American Popular Culture* (New York: New York University Press, 2005), 293.

61. Hyder, *Brimful of Asia.*

62. Deborah Wong, *Speak It Louder: Asian Americans Making Music* (New York: Routledge, 2004).

63. Adelaida Reyes, *Songs of the Caged, Songs of the Free* (Philadelphia: Temple University Press, 1999), 89, 105, 154.

64. Ronnie Spector, *Be My Baby: How I Survived Mascara, Miniskirts and Madness or My Life as a Fabulous Ronette,* with Vince Waldron (New York: Harper, 1990), 34.

65. Oliver Wang, "Asian Americans and Hip Hop," *Asian Week,* November 12–18, 1998; Abigail Baker, "Poongmul, Hip Hop and Politics," *Yisei* 10, no. 1 (Winter 1996–97): 91.

66. Ellie M. Hisama, "Afro-Asian Hip Hop," *ISAM Newsletter* 32, no. 1 (Fall 2002).

3. Banda

1. Quoted by Rick Koster, *Louisiana Music* (Boston: Da Capo Press, 2002), 4–5.

2. Nathalie Petrowski, "A New Direction for a Quebec Star," *Canadian Composer* (September 1979): 26; Nathalie Petrowski, *"La Révolution Française," Disco-Mag* 1, no. 2 (1969): 41; P. V. "Les Québécois perdent la Révolution Française," *La Presse,* January 29, 1970, 14; Richard Tardif, "'Les Sinners' ils sont revenus," *Pop Eye,* December 1970, 14.

3. David Reyes and Tom Waldman, *Land of a Thousand Dances: Chicano Rock 'n' Roll from Southern California* (Albuquerque: University of New Mexico Press, 1998), 118–22.

4. Ramiro Burr, *Tejano and Regional Mexican Music* (New York: Billboard Books, 1999), 24, 26, 132–33.

5. Carlos Manuel Haro and Steven Loza, "The Evolution of Banda Music and the Current Banda Movement in Los Angeles," in Steven Loza, ed., *Selected Reports in Ethnomusicology,* vol. 10 (Los Angeles: Department of Ethnomusicology and Systematic Musicology, University of California, 1994), 60.

6. Claudia Puig, "Banda," *Los Angeles Times Magazine,* June 12, 1994, 24.

7. Eric Boehlert, "Banda Machos Takes Old Sound to New Heights," *Billboard* 105, no. 16, April 17, 1993, 1.

8. Christine Gonzales, "Banda Rides Wave of Hispanic Pride," *Wall Street Journal,* October 4, 1993, B1.

9. David G. Gutiérrez, "Ethnic Mexicans and the Transformation

of 'American' Social Space: Reflections on Recent History," in Marcelo Suárez-Orozco, ed., *Crossings: Mexican Immigration in Interdisciplinary Perspectives* (Cambridge, Mass.: Harvard University, David Rockefeller Center for Latin American Studies, 1998), 314–15, 320.

10. Ibid., 314.

11. Helena Simonett, *Banda: Mexican Musical Life across Borders* (Middletown, Conn.: Wesleyan University Press, 2001), 42–43, 45.

12. Puig, "Banda," 24; David E. Hayes-Bautista and Gregory Rodriguez, "Technobanda," *New Republic,* April 11, 1994, 10. The best banda researcher, Helena Simonett, has encouraged me to think about such stories as perhaps not necessarily true, as efforts to identify with listeners, a caution that I take seriously. Yet even if the story is not true, its identification with the desperation of undocumented immigrants is significant as a statement about the U.S. political climate of the 1990s.

13. Puig, "Banda," 26.

14. Hayes-Bautista and Rodriguez, "Technobanda," 10.

15. Puig, "Banda," 26.

16. George Sanchez, *Becoming Mexican American: Ethnicity, Culture, and Identity in Chicano Los Angeles* (New York: Oxford University Press, 1993), 177–89.

17. Matt Damsker, "*Corrido* for Don Pedro, an Unsung Folk Hero," *Los Angeles Times,* December 9, 1984, Calendar section, 86–87.

18. Reyes and Waldman, *Land of a Thousand Dances,* 45–48, 51, 53; Sanchez, *Becoming Mexican American,* 184, 233.

19. Haro and Loza, "The Evolution of Banda Music and the Current Banda Movement in Los Angeles," 61.

20. Ibid., 62, 63; Steven Loza, "Identity, Nationalism, and Aesthetics among Chicano/Mexicano Musicians in Los Angeles," in Loza, ed., *Selected Reports in Ethnomusicology,* vol. 10, 55.

21. Gonzales, "Banda Rides Wave of Hispanic Pride," B1.

22. Haro and Loza, "The Evolution of Banda Music and the Current Banda Movement in Los Angeles," 66.

23. Diane Seo, "Dancing Away from Trouble," *Los Angeles Times,* February 3, 1994, 1A.

24. Ruben Martinez, "The Shock of the New," *Los Angeles Times Magazine,* January 30, 1994, 12.

25. Simonett, *Banda,* 288.

26. Margy Rochlin, "Loud and Proud," *New York Times,* July 25, 1993, V5.

27. David Gutiérrez, *Walls and Mirrors: Mexican Americans, Mexican Immigrants, and the Politics of Ethnicity* (Berkeley: University of California Press, 1995).

28. Martinez, "The Shock of the New," 10.

29. Juan Flores, "Que Assimilated, Brother, yo soy assimilao: The Structuring of Puerto Rican Identity in the U.S.," *Journal of Ethnic Studies* 13, no. 1 (1985). See my discussion of merengue later in this book.

30. Martinez, "The Shock of the New," 12.

31. José Limón, "Texas–Mexican Popular Music and Dancing: Some Notes on History and Symbolic Process," *Latin American Music Review* 4 (1983): 238.

32. Seo, "Dancing Away from Trouble," A16.

33. Rochlin, "Loud and Proud," V5.

34. Ibid.

35. Hayes-Bautista and Rodriguez, "Technobanda," 10.

36. Boehlert, "Banda Machos Takes Old Sound to New Heights," 1.

37. José Limón, *Dancing with the Devil: Society and Cultural Poetics in Mexican-American South Texas* (Madison: University of Wisconsin Press, 1994), 164.

38. Deborah Pacini Hernandez, *Bachata: A Social History of a Dominican Popular Music* (Philadelphia: Temple University Press, 1995), 12–13; Robin D. G. Kelley, *Race Rebels: Culture, Politics, and the Black Working Class* (New York: Free Press, 1994), 183–227.

39. Simonett, *Banda,* 283.

40. Ibid., 300.

41. Michael Quintanilla, "Que Cool!" *Los Angeles Times,* June 16, 1993, E3.

42. Walden Bello, "Global Economic Counterrevolution: How Northern Economic Warfare Devastates the South," in Kevin Danaher, ed., *50 Years Is Enough: The Case against the International Monetary Fund and the World Bank* (Boston: South End, 1994), 19.

43. Carlos Fuentes, *A New Time for Mexico* (Berkeley: University of California Press, 1997), xiii.

44. Gutiérrez, *Walls and Mirrors.*

45. Timothy J. Dunn, *The Militarization of the U.S.–Mexico Border, 1978–1992* (Austin: University of Texas Press, 1996).

46. I thank Lisa Lowe for calling my attention to these disparities in her presentations in Los Angeles at the 1992 Centering Minority Discourse conference and the 1994 Modern Language Association conference in San Diego.

47. Haro and Loza, "The Evolution of Banda Music and the Current Banda Movement in Los Angeles," 69.

48. Julie Farrem, "Drywallers Protest in Loma Linda," *San Bernardino County Sun,* June 27, 1992, B8; Michael Flagg, "Southland Drywall Hangers Hold Out in Hope of Nailing Down a Union," *Los Angeles Times,* July 5, 1992, D5.

49. Flagg, "Southland Drywall Hangers Hold Out," D5.

50. Michael Flagg, "Unions Get a Wake-up Call as Drywallers

Achieve an Unlikely Victory," *Los Angeles Times,* November 8, 1992; Sandy Stokes, "INS Picking on Drywallers, Leader Claims," *Riverside Press-Enterprise,* March 22, 1994, B4.

51. Josh Kun, "What Is an MC If He Can't Rap to Banda? Making Music in Nuevo L.A.," in Raul Homero Villa and George J. Sanchez, eds., *Los Angeles and the Future of Urban Cultures* (Baltimore: Johns Hopkins University Press, 2005), 243–60.

52. Ibid.

4. Jazz

The epigraph to this chapter is drawn from Angels Carabi, "Toni Morrison Interview," *Belles Lettres: A Review of Books by Women* 10, no. 2 (1995): 40.

1. At least two people in show business have been named Darby Hicks, a Cajun singer and a dancer from Chicago, but the Darby Hicks of *this* story comes from the folklore of the streets—a character who sleeps with other men's wives and girlfriends, something like the "Jody" character in the folklore of U.S. military personnel in the mid-twentieth century. See Jeff Hanusch, "The Legend of Jody Ryder," *Living Blues* 163, May/June 2002, 21–22.

2. James Kyung-Jin Lee, *Urban Triage: Race and the Fictions of Multiculturalism* (Minneapolis: University of Minnesota Press, 2004), ix.

3. Douglas Henry Daniels, *Lester Leaps In: The Life and Times of Lester "Pres" Young* (Boston: Beacon Books, 2002), 69, 72, 101, 128.

4. Rich Koster, *Louisiana Music* (Boston: Da Capo Press, 2002), 17.

5. Richard Woodward, "Four Saxmen: One Great Voice," *New York Times* magazine, April 12, 1987, 47; David Ruben, "World Sax Quartet Swings to Its Own Beat," *San Francisco Chronicle* datebook, April 9, 1989, 47.

6. "Amazon.com Talks to Vijay Iyer," author interview, December 14, 2000, amazon.com/exec/obidos/show-interview/I-v-yerijay/002-2601507-4157631.

7. George Lipsitz, "Music, Migration, and Myth: The California Connection," *Reading California: Art, Image, and Identity, 1900–2000* (Berkeley: University of California Press and the Los Angeles County Museum of Art, 2000), 155–60.

8. Daniels, *Lester Leaps In,* 33.

9. Michael B. Bakan, "Way Out West on Central: Jazz in the African-American Community of Los Angeles before 1930," in Jacqueline Cogdell DjeDje and Eddie S. Meadows, eds., *California Soul: Music of African Americans in the West* (Berkeley: University of California Press, 1998), 27, 38; Rex Harris, *The Story of Jazz* (New York: Grosset and Dunlap, 1955), 70.

10. Burton Peretti, *The Creation of Jazz: Music, Race, and Culture in*

Urban America (Urbana: University of Illinois Press, 1994), 22, 41; Harris, *The Story of Jazz,* 70–71.

11. Peretti, *The Creation of Jazz,* 22, 41; Bakan, "Way Out West on Central," 24.

12. Harris, *The Story of Jazz,* 151–52.

13. Phil Pastras, *Dead Man Blues: Jelly Roll Morton Way Out West* (Berkeley: University of California Press, 2001), 112.

14. Farah Jasmine Griffin, *Who Set You Flowin? The African American Migration Narrative* (New York: Oxford University Press, 1995).

15. Quoted in George E. Lewis, "Experimental Music in Black and White: The AACM in New York, 1970–1985," *Current Musicology* 71–73 (Spring 2001–2): 143.

16. Susan McClary, *Conventional Wisdom: The Content of Musical Form* (Berkeley: University of California Press, 2000), 168.

17. Karen Bennett, "An Audience with Alodullah Ibrahim," *Musician,* March 1990, 41.

18. Penny Von Eschen, *Satchmo Blows Up the World: Jazz Ambassadors Play the Cold War* (Cambridge, Mass.: Harvard University Press, 2004), 154.

19. Eric Porter, *What Is This Thing Called Jazz? African American Musicians as Artists, Critics, and Activists* (Berkeley: University of California Press, 2002), 78.

20. John F. Szwed, *Crossovers: Essays on Race, Music and American Culture* (Philadelphia: University of Pennsylvania Press, 2005), 193.

21. James C. Hall, *Mercy, Mercy Me: African-American Culture and the American Sixties* (New York: Oxford University Press, 2001), 130.

22. Szwed, *Crossovers,* 194; Douglas Henry Daniels, "Vodun and Jazz: 'Jelly Roll' Morton and Lester 'Pres' Young: Substance and Shadow," *Journal of Haitian Studies* 9, no. 1 (Spring 2003): 112.

23. Von Eschen, *Satchmo Blows Up the World,* 170.

24. Ibid., 236.

25. Ibid., 34, 154.

26. Quoted in Daniels, *Lester Leaps In,* 34.

27. John F. Szwed, *Space Is the Place: The Lives and Times of Sun Ra* (New York: Da Capo Press, 1997), 236.

28. Horace Silver, *Let's Get to the Nitty Gritty: The Autobiography of Horace Silver* (Berkeley: University of California Press, 2006), 53.

29. Porter, *What Is This Thing Called Jazz?* 135.

30. Robin D. G. Kelley, "Dig They Freedom: Meditations on History and the Black Avant Garde," *Lenox Avenue* 3 (1997): 18.

31. Marshall and June Stearns, *Jazz Dance: The Story of American Vernacular Dance* (New York: Da Capo Press, 1994), 345.

32. Daniels, *Lester Leaps In,* 130.

33. Ralph Eastman, "'Pitchin' Up a Boogie': African-American Musicians, Nightlife, and Music Venues in Los Angeles, 1930–1945," in DjeDje and Meadows, eds., *California Soul*, 80.

34. Barney Hoskyns, *Waiting for the Sun: Strange Days, Weird Scenes, and the Sound of Los Angeles* (New York: St. Martin's Press, 1996), 8.

35. Robert Gordon, *Jazz West Coast* (London: Quartet Books, 1986), 16.

36. Clora Bryant, Buddy Collette, William Green, Steven Isoardi, Jack Kelson, Horace Tapscott, Gerald Wilson, and Marl Young: Central Avenue Sounds Editorial Committee, *Central Avenue Sounds: Jazz in Los Angeles* (Berkeley: University of California Press, 1998), 365.

37. Hoskyns, *Waiting for the Sun*, 8.

38. Daniels, *Lester Leaps In*, 383, 158–59; Silver, *Let's Get to the Nitty Gritty*, 49–50.

39. Steven L. Isoardi, *The Dark Tree: Jazz and the Community Arts in Los Angeles* (Berkeley: University of California Press, 2006), 9.

40. David Ake, *Jazz Cultures* (Berkeley: University of California Press, 2002), 71.

41. Mike Joyce, "Julius Hemphill, Making the Sax Sing," *Washington Post*, September 23, 1989, section C1, 2.

42. Darv Johnson, "Manuel 'Fess' Manetta's Home at 408–410 LeBoeuf Street," *Louisiana Weekly*, June 28–July 4, 2004, B2.

43. Stearns, *Jazz Dance*, 234.

44. Daniels, *Lester Leaps In*, 94.

45. Ian Carr, Digby Fairweather, and Brian Priestley, eds., *Jazz: The Rough Guide* (London: Rough Guides, 1995), 222.

46. Daniels, *Lester Leaps In*, 154, 158, 273.

47. Ake, *Jazz Cultures*, 71.

48. Koster, *Louisiana Music*, 78–79.

49. Scott DeVeaux, *The Birth of Bebop: A Social and Musical History* (Berkeley: University of California Press, 1997), 57.

50. Horace Boyer, *The Golden Age of Gospel* (Urbana: University of Illinois Press, 2000), 85; Tony Heilbut, *The Gospel Sound* (New York: Limelight, 1992), 81.

51. Horace Tapscott, *Songs of the Unsung: The Musical and Social Journey of Horace Tapscott* (Durham, N.C.: Duke University Press, 2001), 14.

52. Ibid., 129–30.

53. Preston Love, *A Thousand Honey Creeks Later: My Life in Music from Basie to Motown and Beyond* (Hanover, N.H.: University Press of New England/Wesleyan University Press, 1997), 161; Tapscott, *Songs of the Unsung*, 129–30.

54. Daniels, *Lester Leaps In*, 102.

55. James C. Hall, *Mercy, Mercy Me: African-American Culture and the American Sixties* (New York: Oxford University Press, 2001), 127.

56. Clovis E. Semmes, "The Dialectics of Cultural Survival and the Community Artist: Phil Cohran and the Afro-Arts Theater," *Journal of Black Studies* 24, no. 4 (June 1994): 449, 451, 452, 457, 458.

57. Tapscott, *Songs of the Unsung*, 1, 4, 27.

58. Ibid., 13. Doug Daniels tells me he thinks this also meant that people could touch the piano on the way in and out, as a kind of religious statement.

59. Tapscott, *Songs of the Unsung*, 18.

60. Gordon, *Jazz West Coast*, 38.

61. Tapscott, *Songs of the Unsung*, 29.

62. Ibid., 80.

63. Ibid., 106.

64. Ibid., 197.

65. Ibid., 89, 143, 148.

66. Ibid., 88.

67. Ibid.

68. Ibid., 90.

69. Ibid., 182.

70. Ibid.

71. Ibid., 200.

72. Love, *A Thousand Honey Creeks Later*, 57, 235, 144.

73. Szwed, *Space Is the Place*, 5.

74. Ibid., 6.

75. Ibid., 310.

76. Ibid., 264.

77. Christopher Small, *Music of the Common Tongue: Survival and Celebration in African American Music* (Hanover, N.H.: University Press of New England/Wesleyan University Press, 1998), 72.

78. Quoted in Porter, *What Is This Thing Called Jazz?* 310.

79. Lee, *Urban Triage*, 101.

80. Quoted in Porter, *What Is This Thing Called Jazz?* 307.

81. Vincent Harding, "Responsibilities of the Black Scholar to the Community," in Darlene Clark Hine, ed., *The State of Afro-American History: Past, Present, and Future* (Baton Rouge: Louisiana State University Press, 1986), 281.

82. Clora Bryant et al., *Central Avenue Sounds: Jazz in Los Angeles* (Berkeley: University of California Press, 1998), 356.

5. Weeds in a Vacant Lot

The epigraph to this chapter is drawn from C. L. Franklin, *Give Me This Mountain: Life History and Selected Sermons of the Reverend C. L.*

Franklin, edited by Jeff Todd Titon (Urbana: University of Illinois Press, 1989), 20.

1. John R. Logan and Harvey Molotch, *Urban Fortunes: The Political Economy of Place* (Berkeley: University of California Press, 1987), 182, 114, 168–69; Arelene Zarembka, *The Urban Housing Crisis: Social, Economic, and Legal Issues and Proposals* (Westport, Conn.: Greenwood, 1990), 104.

2. Mindy Thompson Fullilove, M.D., *Root Shock: How Tearing Up City Neighborhoods Hurts America and What We Can Do about It* (New York: Ballantine Books, 2004), 11, 20, 242.

3. Interview with Julius Hemphill, July 31, 1994, New York, N.Y.

4. Ibid. Vincent Terrell used the same metaphor to describe BAG when I interviewed him a few blocks from Hemphill's apartment the next day, August 1, 1994.

5. David Jackson, "Profile: Julius Hemphill, Oliver Lake," *Down Beat* 19, June 1975, 32.

6. Donald Clarke, "AACM," in Donald Clarke, ed., *The Penguin Encyclopedia of Popular Music* (London: Penguin Books, 1990), 1; Julius E. Thompson, *Dudley Randall, Broadside Press, and the Black Arts Movement in Detroit, 1960–1995* (Jefferson, N.C.: McFarland, 1999), 26.

7. Douglass S. Massey and Nancy A. Denton, *American Apartheid: Segregation and the Making of the Underclass* (Cambridge, Mass.: Harvard University Press, 1993), 204–5.

8. George Lipsitz, *A Life in the Struggle: Ivory Perry and the Culture of Opposition* (Philadelphia: Temple University Press, 1995), 146.

9. Charles J. Rolo, "This, Too, Is America," *Tomorrow* 4, May 1945, 63, quoted in Keneth Kinnamon and Michel Fabre, eds., *Conversations with Richard Wright* (Jackson: University Press of Mississippi, 1993), 67–68.

10. Quoted in Richard Woodward, "Four Saxmen, One Great Voice," *New York Times Magazine*, April 12, 1987, 72.

11. Ibid.

12. Ibid.

13. Harper Barnes, "Jazz Threads through Life of Oliver Lake," *St. Louis Post-Dispatch*, February 14, 1993, 3.

14. Woodward, "Four Saxmen, One Great Voice," 47; Harper Barnes, "Visit to St. Louis Stirs Memories of '60s for Julius Hemphill," *St. Louis Post-Dispatch*, April 9, 1989, 3E.

15. Woodward, "Four Saxmen, One Great Voice," 72.

16. David Ruben, "World Sax Quartet Swings to Its Own Beat," *San Francisco Chronicle*, Datebook, April 9, 1989, 48.

17. Fullilove, *Root Shock*, 29.

18. Darrel McWhorter, "Bowie in Line for Crown of St. Louis Trumpeters," *St. Louis Post-Dispatch*, February 3, 1992, D1.

19. Ibid., D3.

20. Interview with Oliver Lake, April 12, 1993, St. Louis, Mo.

21. Interview with Vincent Terrell, August 1, 1994, New York, N.Y.

22. Jack Schmidt, "Former Tenant Says Laclede Town Discriminated in Effort to Integrate," *St. Louis American,* letter to the editor, July 30–August 5, 1992, copy in author's possession.

23. Victor Turner, *Dramas, Fields and Metaphors* (Ithaca, N.Y.: Cornell University Press, 1975), 15.

24. Interview with Vincent Terrell, August 1, 1994, New York, N.Y.

25. Cathee Allen, "Dance—Black Artist Group," *Proud* 2, no. 6, June/July 1971, 31; Arts and Education Council of Greater St. Louis, Arts and Education Fund press release, May 14, 1968, Rockefeller Archives, Tarrytown, N.Y.

26. Interview with Vincent Terrell, August 1, 1994, New York, N.Y.

27. Interview with Julius Hemphill, July 31, 1994, New York, N.Y.

28. Ibid.

29. Summary of telephone conversations with Merrimon Cunninggim and Gene Schwik, conducted by Rockefeller personnel, September 16–18, 1969, Rockefeller Archives, Tarrytown, N.Y.

30. Mike Joyce, "Julius Hemphill, Making the Sax Sing," *Washington Post,* September 27, 1989, C2.

31. Cassandra Johnson, "Esoteric Expression," *Proud* 1, no. 6, June/July 1970, 21.

32. Jan Butterfield, "Oliver Jackson Interview," *Oliver Jackson* (Seattle: Seattle Art Museum, 1982), 7; Leah Ollman, "Oliver Jackson's Fluid Realm," *Los Angeles Times,* Orange County edition, Calendar section, November 27, 1991, 9.

33. Allen, "Dance—Black Artist Group," 31.

34. Paul A. Harris, "Living and Playing in the Present: Saxophonist Greg Osby Embraces Contemporary Black Pop Styles," *St. Louis Post-Dispatch,* September 29, 1991, 3G.

35. Lipsitz, *A Life in the Struggle.*

36. Arts and Education Council of Greater St. Louis, Arts and Education Fund, May 14, 1968, Rockefeller Archives, Tarrytown, N.Y.

37. Arts and Education Council of Greater St. Louis, Rockefeller Foundation, 1-2 200R, box 289, folder 2720, Rockefeller Archives, Tarrytown, N.Y.

38. Danforth Foundation summary of telephone conversations with Merrimon Cunniggim and Gene Schwik, September 16–18, 1969, Rockefeller Archives, Tarrytown, N.Y.

39. Interview with Vincent Terrell, August 1, 1994, New York, N.Y.

40. Herb Boyd, "World Saxophone Quartet: New Life After Julius," *Down Beat,* September 1996, 26.

41. Mike Joyce, "Julius Hemphill, Making the Sax Sing," *Washington Post*, September 27, 1989, C1–2.

42. Ruben, "World Sax Quartet Swings to Its Own Beat," 48.

43. Clifford Jay Safane, "The World Saxophone Quartet," *Down Beat* 46, October 1979, 29.

44. Barnes, "Jazz Threads through Life of Oliver Lake," 9.

45. Barnes, "Visit to St. Louis Stirs Memories of '60s for Julius Hemphill," 3E.

46. Barnes, "Jazz Threads through Life of Oliver Lake," 9.

47. Safane, "The World Saxophone Quartet," 28.

48. Néstor García Canclini, *Hybrid Cultures: Strategies for Entering and Leaving Modernity,* trans. Christopher L. Chiappari and Silvia L. Lopez (Minneapolis: University of Minnesota Press, 1995), 27.

49. Interview with Vincent Terrell, August 1, 1994, New York, N.Y.

50. Interview with Quincy Troupe, September 1, 1994, La Jolla, Calif.

51. Ry Cooder, *Chávez Ravine,* liner notes, 2, Nonesuch B0009353IW, 2005.

52. Elizabeth V. Spelman, *Fruits of Sorrow: Framing Our Attention to Suffering* (Boston: Beacon Press, 1997), 1.

53. Pachucos were Mexican American young people recognizable by distinct forms of dress, specific kinds of tattoos, and a particular kind of speech. See George Lipsitz, *Time Passages: Collective Memory and American Popular Culture* (Minneapolis: University of Minnesota Press, 1990), 137–40. For scholarship on pachucas, see Catherine Ramirez, "The Lady Zoot Suiter," forthcoming.

54. Eric Avila, *Popular Culture in the Age of White Flight: Fear and Fantasy in Suburban Los Angeles* (Berkeley: University of California Press, 2004).

55. Thomas Hines, "Housing, Baseball and Creeping Socialism," *Journal of Urban History* (February 1982): 140, gives the figure as $1,279,000. The transaction was complicated, and Hines and Poulson may not be describing exactly the same land. In either case there is reason to believe Hines's observation that the federal government lost four million dollars by having to return land cleared for public housing to the city.

56. Avila, *Popular Culture in the Age of White Flight,* 158.

57. George Lipsitz, "A Tale of Three Cities," *Journal of Sport and Social Issues* 8, no. 2 (1984): 1–18.

58. "Waimanalo Blues" is Pahanui's adaptation (via Country Comfort, from Oahu's windward side) of "Nanakulu Blues," by Liko Martin and Thor Wold, from Oahu's leeward coast.

59. Charles M. Lamb, *Housing Segregation in Suburban America*

since 1960 (Cambridge: Cambridge University Press), 2005; Evan McKenzie, *Privatopia: Homeowner Associations and the Rise of Residential Private Government* (New Haven, Conn.: Yale University Press, 1994), 29–78.

60. Tom Waldman and David Reyes, *Land of a Thousand Dances* (Albuquerque: University of New Mexico Press, 1998), 30.

61. Ibid., 15.

6. Merengue

1. I first became aware of *bachata* music through Deborah Pacini Hernandez, *Bachata: A Social History of Dominican Popular Music* (Philadelphia: Temple University Press, 1995), and Diasann McLane, "Islands of Stylin': Dominican Maleness and Popular Music in Washington Heights," presentation on the panel "Making Music Mix: Beyond the Boundary: Men, Race, and Culture," at New York University on February 25, 1995. My introduction to "Voy pa'lla" came from Patricia Pessar, *A Visa for a Dream: Dominicans in the United States* (Boston: Allyn and Bacon, 1995), 78. For the song itself, see Anthony Santos, *Greatest Hits,* Liters Entertainment Group, 2001.

2. Linda Basch, Nina Glick Schiller, and Christina Szanton Blanc, *Nations Unbound: Transnational Projects, Postcolonial Predicaments, and Deterritorialized Nation-States* (Amsterdam: Gordon Breach, 2000), 7.

3. Claire Jean Kim, *Bitter Fruit: The Politics of Black-Korean Conflict in New York* (New Haven, Conn.: Yale University Press, 2001), 35.

4. James Ferguson, *Dominican Republic: Beyond the Lighthouse* (London: Latin American Bureau, 1992), 75.

5. Pessar, *A Visa for a Dream,* 24.

6. Ninna Nyberg Sorenson, "Narrating Identity across Dominican Worlds," in Michael Peter Smith and Luis Eduardo Guarnizo, eds., *Transnationalism from Below* (New Brunswick, N.J.: Transaction Publishers, 1998), 242, 263.

7. John Gennari, "Passing for Italian," *Transition* 6, no. 4 (Winter 1996): 40.

8. Pessar, *A Visa for a Dream,* 72.

9. Mike Davis, *Magical Urbanism: Latinos Reinvent the U.S. Big City* (London: Verso, 2000), 84, quoting *New York Times,* July 19, 1998.

10. Luis E. Guarnizo, "Los Dominicanyorks: The Making of a Binational Society," in Mary Romero, Pierette Hondagneu-Sotelo, and Vilma Ortiz, eds., *Challenging Fronteras: Structuring Latina and Latino Lives in the U.S.* (New York: Routledge, 1997), 165–66.

11. I thank Rob Walser for explaining these rhythmic devices to me.

12. Jorge Duany, "Ethnicity, Identity, and Music: An Anthropological Analysis of Dominican *Merengue,*" in Gerard H. Behague, ed., *Music*

and Ethnicity: The Caribbean and South America (New Brunswick, N.J.: Transaction Publishers, 1994), 66; Martha Davis, "Music and Black Ethnicity in the Dominican Republic," in Behague, ed., *Music and Ethnicity,* 135; Deborah Pacini [Hernandez], "Social Identity and Class in *Bachata,* an Emerging Dominican Popular Music," *Latin American Music Review* 10, no. 1 (June 1989): 69; Mark Holston, "The Women of *Merengue,*" *Americas* 42, no. 3 (May–June 1990): 54; Paul Austerlitz, *Merengue: Dominican Music and Dominican Identity* (Philadelphia: Temple University Press, 1997), 31.

13. Pacini Hernandez, *Bachata,* 40.

14. Ibid., 43; Austerlitz, *Merengue,* 60. See also Ernesto Sagas, *Race and Politics in the Dominican Republic* (Gainesville: University Press of Florida, 2000), 64.

15. Austerlitz, *Merengue,* 71.

16. Ibid., 39.

17. Pacini Hernandez, *Bachata,* 42, 130.

18. Ferguson, *Dominican Republic,* 83.

19. Paul Farmer, *The Uses of Haiti* (Monroe, Maine: Common Courage Press, 1994), 103.

20. Ibid.

21. Austerlitz, *Merengue,* 66.

22. Pacini Hernandez, *Bachata,* 131.

23. Duany, "Ethnicity, Identity, and Music," 66–69; David Nicholls, *From Dessalines to Duvalier: Race, Color, and Independence in Haiti* (New Brunswick, N.J.: Rutgers University Press, 1996), xxiii.

24. Martha Ellen Davis, "Dominican Folk Dance and the Shaping of National Identity," in Susanna Sloat, ed., *Caribbean Dance from Abakua to Zouk: How Movement Shapes Identity* (Gainesville: University Press of Florida, 2002), 132.

25. Nicholls, *From Dessalines to Duvalier,* 5, 33, 78.

26. Sagas, *Race and Politics in the Dominican Republic,* 34.

27. Nicholls, *From Dessalines to Duvalier,* 7.

28. Sagas, *Race and Politics in the Dominican Republic,* 56.

29. Leonardo Padura Fuentes, *Faces of Salsa: A Spoken History of the Music,* translated by Stephen J. Clark (Washington, D.C.: Smithsonian Books, 2003), 42.

30. Pacini Hernandez, *Bachata,* 82, 122.

31. Fuentes, *Faces of Salsa,* 110.

32. Sassen cited in Kim, *Bitter Fruit,* 35.

33. Silvio Torres-Saillant and Ramona Hernandez, *The Dominican Americans* (Westport, Conn.: Greenwood Press, 1998), 25.

34. Ibid., 27.

35. Ferguson, *The Dominican Republic,* 18.

36. Eric Paul Roorda, *The Dictator Next Door* (Durham, N.C.: Duke University Press, 1998), especially 48–62. Roorda argues that U.S. officials merely tolerated Trujillo when they could find no acceptable alternative. Yet even Trujillo's generosity toward the State Department does not conceal the significant help he received from the United States. For a more critical, and in my view more accurate, interpretation, see Bernardo Vega, *Trujillo y las fuerzas armadas norteamericanas* (Santo Domingo: Fundación Cultural Dominicana, 1992). See also Ferguson, *Dominican Republic*, 23–24.

37. Ferguson, *Dominican Republic*, 25–38; Torres-Saillant and Hernandez, *The Dominican Americans*, 39–40.

38. Saskia Sassen, "Why Immigration?" *NACLA Report on the Americas* 26, no. 1 (July 1992): 15; Sherri Grasmuck and Patricia R. Pessar, *Between Two Islands: Dominican International Migration* (Berkeley: University of California Press, 1991), 19–23.

39. Ferguson, *Dominican Republic*, 77.

40. Guarnizo, "Los Dominicanyorks," 165, 168.

41. Pacini Hernandez, *Bachata*, 63. In 1980, 77.6 percent of Dominicans in the United States resided in New York; 8.4 percent, in New Jersey. Grasmuck and Pessar, *Between Two Islands*, 23. For information about the 1960s, see Peter Manuel, "The Soul of the Barrio," *NACLA Report on the Americas* 28, no. 2 (September–October 1994): 28.

42. Pessar, *A Visa for a Dream*, 5.

43. Grasmuck and Pessar, *Between Two Islands*, 162–98.

44. Guarnizo, "Los Dominicanyorks," 164.

45. Davis, *Magical Urbanism*, 108; Pessar, *A Visa for a Dream*, 41.

46. Davis, *Magical Urbanism*, 108.

47. Pessar, *A Visa for a Dream*, 17.

48. Davis, "Dominican Folk Dance and the Shaping of National, Identity," 149.

49. Ramon H. Rivera-Severa, "A Dominican York in Andhra," in Sloat, ed., *Caribbean Dance from Abakua to Zouk*, 153, 158–59.

50. Karen Juanita Carrillo, "Kicking the Black Out of DR?" *New York Amsterdam News*, July 27–August 2, 2006, 2.

51. Pessar, *A Visa for a Dream*, 49–51.

52. Juan Flores, "Que Assimilated, Brother, yo soy assimilao: The Structuring of Puerto Rican Identity in the U.S.," *Journal of Ethnic Studies* 13, no. 3 (1986): 11.

53. Fuentes, *Faces of Salsa*, 53–57.

54. Austerlitz, *Merengue*, 130.

55. Ibid., 93.

56. Fuentes, *Faces of Salsa*, 141.

57. Sue Steward and Jan Fairley, "*Merengue* Mania," in Simon Brough-

ton, Mark Ellingham, David Muddyman, and Richard Trillo, eds., *World Music: The Rough Guide* (London: The Rough Guides, 1994), 496, 497; Philip Sweeny, *The Virgin Directory of World Music* (New York: Henry Holt, 1991), 208; Fuentes, *Faces of Salsa,* 142.

58. Duany, "Ethnicity, Identity, and Music," 79; Pacini [Hernandez], "Social Identity and Class in *Bachata,*" 83; Deborah Pacini Hernandez, "*Bachata:* From the Margins to the Mainstream," *Popular Music* 11, no. 3, 1992, 359.

59. Ferguson, *Dominican Republic,* 82. A survey in Samana in the 1980s found that 50 percent of respondents spoke English. See Torres-Saillant and Hernandez, *The Dominican Americans,* 13.

60. Neil Leonard III, "*Merengue* Messiah," *Rhythm Music Magazine,* May–June 1994, 21–23.

61. Pacini Hernandez, "*Bachata:* From the Margins to the Mainstream," 359–60.

62. Steward and Fairley, "*Merengue* Mania," 497.

63. Gary Stewart, *Rhumba on the River* (London: Verso, 2004), 215.

64. Paul Austerlitz, "From Transplant to Transnational Circuit: *Merengue* in New York," in Ray Allen and Lois Wilcken, eds., *Island Sounds in the Global City: Caribbean Popular Music and Identity in New York* (Urbana: University of Illinois Press, 2001), 49.

65. Davis, "Dominican Folk Dance and the Shaping of National Identity," 133.

66. Gage Averill, "Haitian Dance Bands, 1915–1970: Class, Race, and Authenticity," *Latin American Music Review* 10, no. 2 (Fall–Winter 1989): 222.

67. Fuentes, *Faces of Salsa,* 147.

68. Pessar, *A Visa for a Dream,* 9.

69. Ferguson, *Dominican Republic,* 79.

70. Fuentes, *Faces of Salsa,* 160.

71. Duany, "Ethnicity, Identity, and Music," 87–90.

72. Austerlitz, "From Transplant to Transnational Circuit," 51.

73. Steward and Fairley, "*Merengue* Mania," 496.

74. Quoted in Austerlitz, "From Transplant to Transnational Circuit," 51.

75. Austerlitz, *Merengue,* 117.

76. Daisann McLane, "*Bachata* in New York," oral presentation, author's notes, New York University, February 25, 1995.

77. Holston, "The Women of *Merengue,*" 54–55.

78. Deborah Pacini Hernandez, "Race, Ethnicity, and the Production of Latina/o Popular Music," in Andreas Gebesmair and Alfred Smudits, eds., *Popular Music Within and Beyond the Transnational Music Industry* (Aldershot, UK: Ashgate Publishing, 2002).

79. Jenny Holland, "The Name's Patrick, and He's a Merengue Star," *New York Times,* July 30, 2000, City section, 10.

80. Joyce Millen, Alec Irwin, and Jim Yong Kim, "Introduction: What Is Growing? What Is Dying?" in Jim Yong Kim, Joyce V. Millen, Alec Irwin, and John Gershman, eds., *Dying for Growth: Global Inequality and the Health of the Poor* (Monroe, Maine: Common Courage Press, 2000), 5.

81. Brook Schoepf, Claude Schoepf, and Joyce Millen, "Theoretical Therapies: Remote Remedies: SAPs and the Political Ecology of Poverty and Health in Africa," in Kim, Millen, Irwin, and Gershman, eds., *Dying for Growth,* 120–21.

82. Kemala Kempadoo, ed., *Sun, Sex, and Gold: Tourism and Sex Work in the Caribbean* (Lanham, Md.: Rowman and Littlefield, 1999); Lisa Law, *Sex Work in Southeast Asia: The Place of Desire in a Time of AIDS* (New York: Routledge, 2000).

83. Charles Kernaghen, "Sweatshop Blues: Companies Love Misery," *Dollars and Sense* 22 (1998): 18.

7. The Hip Hop Hearings

1. Toni Morrison, *Song of Solomon* (New York: Alfred A. Knopf, 1977), 59–60.

2. Ibid., 237–38.

3. Subcommittee on Commerce, Consumer Protection, and Competitiveness of the Committee on Energy and Commerce, *Music Lyrics and Interstate Commerce,* H.R. hearing 112, 103rd Cong., 2nd sess., February 11, 1994, 5.

4. Ibid., 6.

5. Ibid., 5.

6. Subcommittee on Commerce, Consumer Protection, and Competitiveness of the Committee on Energy and Commerce, *Music Lyrics and Interstate Commerce,* February 11, 1994, 24.

7. Ibid., 31.

8. Reginold Bundy, "The Great Divide," *Pittsburgh Courier,* January 13, 1996, A1, A3.

9. On the alleged mental deficiencies of minorities, see Charles Murray and Richard Herrnstein, *The Bell Curve: Intelligence, Class Structure and American Life* (New York: Free Press, 1994). On their cultural deficiencies, see Dinesh D'Souza, *The End of Racism* (New York: Free Press, 1996).

10. Holly Sklar, *Chaos or Community: Seeking Solutions Not Scapegoats* (Boston: South End Press, 1995), 69.

11. Noel J. Kent, "A Stacked Deck," *Explorations in Ethnic Studies* 14, no. 1 (January 1991): 12, 13; Richard Rothstein, "Musical Chairs as

Economic Policy," in Don Hazen, ed., *Inside the L.A. Riots* (New York: Institute for Alternative Journalism, 1992), 143.

12. William Chafe, *The Unfinished Journey* (New York: Oxford University Press, 1986), 442; Kent, "A Stacked Deck," 11.

13. Richard Child Hill and Cynthia Negry, "Deindustrialization and Racial Minorities in the Great Lakes Region, USA," in D. Stanley Eitzen and Maxine Baca Zinn, eds., *The Reshaping of America: Social Consequences of the Changing Economy* (Englewood Cliffs, N.J.: Prentice-Hall, 1989), 168–78.

14. Melvin L. Oliver and Thomas M. Shapiro, *Black Wealth/White Wealth: A New Perspective on Racial Inequality* (New York: Routledge, 1995), 158.

15. For a detailed account of the extent and significance of censorship efforts aimed at the gangster film, see the brilliant dissertation by L. Jonathan Munby, "Screening Crime in the USA, 1929–1958: From Hays Code to HUAC: From Little Caesar to Touch of Evil," Ph.D. dissertation, University of Minnesota, 1995, especially 46–52.

16. In *Inventing the Public Enemy: The Gangster in American Culture, 1918–1934* (Chicago: University of Chicago Press, 1996), David E. Ruth presents an important discussion of gangster films that delineates the centrality of misogyny, material acquisitions, and style to that genre. This discussion holds some important parallels to the internal properties of the "gangster" image and ideal that emerges within gangsta rap as well.

17. See, for example, Nayan Shah, *Contagious Divides: Epidemics and Race in San Francisco's Chinatown* (Berkeley: University of California Press, 2001); Roderick Ferguson, *Aberrations in Black: Toward a Queer of Color Critique* (Minneapolis: University of Minnesota Press, 2004).

18. Brian Neve, *Film and Politics in America: A Social Tradition* (London: Routledge, 1992), 12.

19. Leola Johnson, "Silencing Gangsta Rap: Class and Race Agendas in the Campaign against Hardcore Rap Lyrics," *Temple Political and Civil Rights Law Review* 3, no. 19 (Fall 1993–Spring 1994): 25.

20. After leaving the bureau Milt Ahlerich became director of security for the National Football League, charged with the responsibility of keeping players from associating with criminals, illegal drugs, and steroids and engaging in sexual assaults and fights. The record, in this case, speaks for itself. The record of criminal activity by NFL players on his watch indicates that the zeal Ahlerich displayed in trying to suppress *imaginary* violence in gangsta rap did not carry over to effective policing of *actual* violence and other violations of the law by the athletes paid large sums of money by Ahlerich's millionaire employer–owners in the NFL.

21. Quoted in Houston A. Baker, "Handling 'Crisis': Great Books, Rap Music, and the End of Western Homogeneity" (Reflections on the Humanities in America), *Callalloo* 13 (1990): 177.

22. Dave Marsh, *Louie Louie: The History and Mythology of the World's Most Famous Rock 'n' Roll Song* (Ann Arbor: University of Michigan Press, 2004). See also Todd Snider's album *East Nashville Skyline*, Oh Boy Records OBR031, 2004.

23. Jon Wiener, *Gimme Some Truth: The John Lennon FBI Files* (Berkeley: University of California Press, 1999), 114.

24. Tricia Rose, *Black Noise: Rap Music and Black Culture in Contemporary America* (Hanover, N.H.: University Press of New England/Wesleyan University Press, 1994), 128.

25. Johnson, "Silencing Gangsta Rap," 29–30.

26. Dave March and Phyllis Pollack, "Wanted for Attitude," *Village Voice*, October 10, 1989, 33–37, quoted in Rose, *Black Noise*, 129.

27. Chuck Phillips, "The 'Batman' Who Took On Rap," *Los Angeles Times*, June 18, 1990, F1.

28. Chuck Phillips, "The Anatomy of a Crusade," *Los Angeles Times*, June 18, 1990, F4.

29. Associated Press, "Rap Group Members Arrested over 'Nasty Lyrics," *St. Paul Pioneer Press*, June 11, 1990, 2.

30. Amy Binder, "Constructing Racial Rhetoric: Media Depictions of Harm in Heavy Metal and Rap Music," *American Sociological Review* 58 (December 1993): 753; Phillips, "The Anatomy of a Crusade," F4.

31. Chuck Phillips, "Boss Apparently OKs Crew's Use of 'U.S.A.,'" *Los Angeles Times*, June 26, 1990, F10.

32. Robin D. G. Kelley, *Race Rebels* (New York: Free Press, 1994), 190; Rose, *Black Noise*, 183.

33. Johnson, "Silencing Gangsta Rap," 31; Rose, *Black Noise*, 183.

34. Quoted in Johnson, "Silencing Gangsta Rap," 33.

35. Dave Marsh, "The Censorship Zone," *Rock & Rap Confidential* 100, August 1992, 5.

36. Ibid., 7.

37. Johnson, "Silencing Gangsta Rap," 33.

38. Rose, *Black Noise*, 184.

39. Eric Taylor, "Gangsta Rap Is Deferring the Dream," *Los Angeles Times*, March 7, 1994, F3.

40. Johnson, "Silencing Gangsta Rap," 34.

41. Ibid.

42. Subcommittee on Commerce, Consumer Protection, and Competitiveness, Committee on Energy and Commerce, *Music Lyrics and Interstate Commerce*, February 11, 1994, 4.

43. Ibid., 5–6.

44. Subcommittee on Commerce, Consumer Protection, and Competitiveness, Committee on Energy and Commerce, *Music Lyrics and Interstate Commerce,* H.R. hearing 112, 103rd Cong., 2nd sess., May 5, 1994, 75.

45. Marlene Cimons, "Outrage over Lyrics Unites Unlikely Pair," *Los Angeles Times,* July 5, 1995, A1.

46. Dave Marsh, "Cops 'n' Gangstas," *Nation,* June 26, 1995, 908.

47. Jesse Jackson, "A Call to Bold Action," in Hazen, ed., *Inside the L.A. Riots,* 149.

48. Marsh, "The Censorship Zone," 7.

49. Steve Eddy, "Warwick Blames Pot on Someone Else," *Orange County Register,* February 27, 2003, Show section, 2.

50. Joshua Green, "The Bookie of Virtue," *Washington Monthly,* June 2003.

51. Mark Landler, "Label Tied to Time Warner Sues a Critic of Rap Lyrics," *New York Times,* August 16, 1995, C5; Jeffrey Trachtenberg, "Interscope Records Sues Activist Critic, Alleging Distribution Pact Interference," *Wall Street Journal,* August 16, 1995, B8; Chuck Phillips, "Interscope Files Lawsuit against Rap Music Critic," *Los Angeles Times,* August 16, 1995, D1; Dave Marsh, "We Told You So," *Rock & Rap Confidential* 127, September 1995, 7.

52. Kelley, *Race Rebels,* 190.

53. Dave Marsh, "Doug and the Slugs," *Rock & Rap Confidential* 125, July 1995, 4.

54. Edna Gunderson, "Rap against Time Warner," *USA Today,* October 2, 1995, 4D.

55. Dave Marsh, "Cracked Rear View," *Rock & Rap Confidential* 125, July 1995, 2.

56. Subcommittee on Commerce, Consumer Protection, and Competitiveness of the Committee on Energy and Commerce, *Music Lyrics and Interstate Commerce,* February 11, 1994, 21.

57. Kelley, *Race Rebels,* 192.

58. Maxine Waters, "Testimony before the Senate Banking Committee," in Hazen, ed., *Inside the L.A. Riots,* 26.

59. Bernard D. Headley, "'Black on Black Crime: The Myth and the Reality," *Crime and Social Justice* 20 (Fall–Winter 1983): 53.

60. Judith R. Blau and Peter M. Blau, "The Cost of Inequality: Metropolitan Structure and Violent Crime," *American Sociological Review* 47 (February 1982): 114, 126.

61. Gunderson, "Rap against Time Warner," 4D.

62. Subcommittee on Commerce, Consumer Protection, and Competitiveness of the Committee on Energy and Commerce, House of Representatives, February 11, 1994, 65.

63. Ibid., 38–39.

64. Tricia Rose, "Rap Music and the Demonization of Young Black Males," *USA Today Magazine*, May 1994, 35–36.

65. Kelley, *Race Rebels*, 210.

66. Michael Eric Dyson, *Between God and Gangsta Rap: Bearing Witness to Black Culture* (New York: Oxford University Press, 1996), 185.

67. James Baldwin, *Tell Me How Long This Train's Been Gone* (New York: Vintage, 1968), 204.

68. Sister Souljah, *No Disrespect* (New York: Times Books/Random House, 1994).

69. Subcommittee on Commerce, Consumer Protection, and Competitiveness of the Committee on Energy and Commerce, House of Representatives, May 5, 1994, 65–66.

70. Ibid., 65.

71. Robert Warshow, *The Immediate Experience* (New York: Atheneum, 1971), 64.

72. Lee Ballinger, "Sean 'P. Diddy' Combs and the Sweatshops: Making a Dollar out of 15 Cents," *Counterpunch*, October 31, 2003, 1; Earl Ofari Hutchinson, "P. Diddy and Hip Hop's Tattered Garments," *Hutchinson Report*, October 31, 2003, 1.

73. Susan Keith, "The Deal: Kellwood Buys Phat Fashions," *St. Louis Business Journal*, December 10, 2004, 1.

74. Tracie Rozhon, "Can Urban Fashion Be Def in Des Moines," *New York Times*, August 24, 2003, Business section, 9.

75. Ballinger, "Sean P. Diddy Combs and the Sweatshops," 1.

76. Amecia Taylor, "Mixing Hip Hop and Social Conscientiousness," *Louisiana Weekly*, August 15–21, 2005, B5.

77. Morrison, *Song of Solomon*, 237–38.

8. Masquerades and Mixtures

1. Deborah Wong, *Speak It Louder: Asian Americans Making Music* (New York: Routledge, 2004), 89–113; Adelaida Reyes, *Songs of the Caged, Songs of the Free* (Philadelphia: Temple University Press, 1999).

2. Reyes, *Songs of the Caged, Songs of the Free*, 126.

3. Seth Mydans, "Miss Saigon, U.S.A.," *New York Times*, September 19, 1993, V10; "Dalena," September 6, 2005, www.vietscape.com/music/singers/dalena/biography.html.

4. Phil Pastras, *Dead Man Blues: Jelly Roll Morton Way Out West* (Berkeley: University of California Press, 2001), 10.

5. Ibid., 19.

6. Burton W. Peretti, *The Creation of Jazz: Music, Race, and Culture in Urban America* (Urbana: University of Illinois Press, 1994), 194.

7. R. J. Smith, "The Many Faces of Korla Pandit," *Los Angeles Magazine,* June 2001.

8. Mark Poepsel, *True Hollywood Story: How One Columbia Man Became a Music-Making Legend,* KOMU radio program, Columbia, Missouri, aired July 14, 2002; Smith, "The Many Faces of Korla Pandit."

9. Tom Gary, "A Place Called Center Street," *Living Blues* 184, May–June 2006, 86–87.

10. Smith, "The Many Faces of Korla Pandit," 4–5; Poepsel, *True Hollywood Story.*

11. Smith, "The Many Faces of Korla Pandit," 12.

12. George Yoshida, *Reminiscing in Swingtime: Japanese Americans in American Popular Music, 1925–1960* (Los Angeles: National Japanese American Historical Society, 1997), 226–27.

13. W. E. B. Du Bois, *Black Reconstruction in America* (New York: Touchstone, 1995), 52.

14. Albert Memmi, *Racism* (Minneapolis: University of Minnesota Press, 2000), 7.

15. Pauline Tuner Strong and Barril Van Winkle, "'Indian Blood': Reflections on the Reckoning and Reconfiguring of a Native North American Identity," *Cultural Anthropology* 11, no. 4 (November 1996): 551.

16. Carolyn Cooper, *Noises in the Blood: Orality, Gender, and the "Vulgar" Body of Jamaican Popular Culture* (Durham, N.C.: Duke University Press, 1995), 4. Jamaican dramatist Dennis Scott's 1974 play *An Echo in the Bone* may have influenced Reid's 1983 novel. See also Joseph Roach, *Cities of the Dead: Circum Atlantic Performance* (New York: Columbia University Press, 1996).

17. As we saw in chapter 4, Vincent Harding has warned against reducing the struggle to merely desegregating the ranks of the pain inflictors of this world; Charlotta Bass has argued against settling for "dark faces in high places."

18. Timothy Beneke, "Curriculum for a New California," *Express* 21, no. 50, September 17, 1999, 10.

19. Chris Iijima, "Pontifications on the Distinction between Grains of Sand and Yellow Pearls," in Steve Louie and Glenn Omatsu, eds., *Asian Americans: The Movement and the Moment* (Los Angeles: UCLA Asian American Studies Center Press, 2001), 7.

20. Roberta Hill Whiteman (now Roberta Hill), "Preguntas," in *Philadelphia Flowers: Poems by Roberta Hill Whiteman* (Duluth, Minn.: Holy Cow Press, 1996), 89.

21. Ibid., 91.

22. Elizabeth McAlister, *Rara! Vodou Power, and Performance in Haiti and Its Diaspora* (Berkeley: University of California Press, 2002),

49; Sterling Stuckey, *Slave Culture: Nationalist Theory and the Foundations of Black America* (New York: Oxford University Press, 1987).

23. Helena Simonett, *Banda: Mexican Musical Life across Borders* (Middletown, Conn.: Wesleyan University Press, 2001), 57.

24. Rachel Buff, *Immigration and the Political Economy of Home: West Indian Brooklyn and American Indian Minneapolis, 1945–1992* (Berkeley: University of California Press, 2001), 147–70.

25. W. E. B. Du Bois, *The Souls of Black Folk* (New York: Fawcett Publications, 1961), 181, 183–84.

26. Frederick Douglass, *Narrative of the Life of Frederick Douglass, an American Slave* (Middlesex: Harmondsworth, 1982), 57–58.

27. L. Frank, *Acorn Soup* (Berkeley, Calif.: Heyday Books, 1999), 10.

28. Nellie Wong, "The Art and Politics of Asian American Women," in Fred Ho, ed., *Legacy to Liberation: Politics and Culture of Revolutionary Asian Pacific America,* with Carolyn Antonio, Diane Fujino, and Steve Yip (San Francisco: Big Red Media, AK Press, 2000), 235.

29. Lorna Dee Cervantes, "Visions of Mexico While Attending a Writing Symposium in Port Townsend, Washington," in *Emplumada* (Pittsburgh: University of Pittsburgh Press, 1981), 45.

30. Farah Jasmine Griffin, *"Who Set You Flowin'?" The African American Migration Narrative* (New York: Oxford University Press, 1995).

31. Quoted in M. Jacqui Alexander, "Erotic Autonomy as a Politics of Decolonization: An Anatomy of Feminist and State Practice in the Bahamas Tourist Economy," in M. Jacqui Alexander and Chandra Talpade Mohanty, eds., *Feminist Genealogies, Colonial Legacies, Democratic Futures* (New York: Routledge, 1997), 63.

32. Lori Andrews, *Black Power, White Blood: The Life and Times of Johnny Spain* (Philadelphia: Temple University Press, 1999).

33. George Lipsitz, *American Studies in a Moment of Danger* (Minneapolis: University of Minnesota Press, 2001), 10–12. Figures like these are of special interest as well to neoliberal opponents of movements for racial justice.

34. Mary Katherine Aldin and Mark Humphrey, "Lowell Fulson," *Living Blues* 115, June 1994, 11.

35. Burton Peretti, *The Creation of Jazz: Music, Race, and Culture in Urban America* (Urbana: University of Illinois Press, 1994), 42.

36. Dr. John (Mac Rebennack) *Under a Hoodoo Moon: The Life of the Night Tripper* (New York: St. Martin's, 1994), 44–45.

37. James Brown, *James Brown: The Godfather of Soul,* with Bruce Tucker (New York: Thunder's Mouth Press, 1997), 2.

38. David Parker and Miri Song, "Introduction: Rethinking 'Mixed Race,'" in David Parker and Miri Song, eds., *Rethinking "Mixed Race"* (London: Pluto Press, 2001), 1.

39. Nicole Davis, "Racefile," *Color Lines Action* 4, no. 2, Summer 2001, 1.

40. David A. Hollinger, *Postethnic America* (New York: Basic Books, 1995), 166.

41. George J. Sanchez, "'Y tú, ¿qué?' (Y2K): Latino History in the New Millennium," in Marcelo M. Suárez-Orozco and Mariela M. Páez, eds., *Latinos: Remaking America* (Berkeley: University of California Press, 2002), 54.

42. France Winddance Twine, *Racism in a Racial Democracy: The Maintenance of White Supremacy in Brazil* (New Brunswick, N.J.: Rutgers University Press, 1998).

43. Davis, "Racefile."

44. Alexandra Harmon, "Wanted: More Histories of Indian Identity," in Philip J. Deloria and Neal Salisbury, eds., *A Companion to American Indian History* (Malden, Mass.: Blackwell, 2002), 261.

45. Luis Alberto Urrea, *Nobody's Son: Notes from an American Life* (Tucson: University of Arizona Press, 1998), 15.

46. Maryse Conde, "Pan-Africanism, Feminism, and Culture," in Sidney Lemelle and Robin D. G. Kelley, eds., *Imagining Home: Class, Culture, and Nationalism in the African Diaspora* (London: Verso, 1994), 60.

47. Grace Lee Boggs, *Living for Change: An Autobiography* (Minneapolis: University of Minnesota Press, 1998).

48. Nabeel Abraham, "Arab Americans," in Mari Jo Buhle, Paul Buhle, and Dan Georgakus, eds., *Encyclopedia of the American Left*, 2nd ed. (New York: Oxford University Press, 1998), 58.

49. E. San Juan, "Filipinos," in Buhle, Buhle, and Georgakus, eds., *Encyclopedia of the American Left*, 225.

50. Beatrice Griffith, *American Me* (Cambridge, Mass.: Houghton Mifflin, 1948), 321.

51. Yuri Kochiyama, *Discover Your Mission: Selected Speeches and Writings of Yuri Kochiyama* (Los Angeles: UCLA Asian American Studies Center), 1998.

52. Richard White, "On the Beaches," *London Review of Books*, March 21, 2002, 26.

53. Gary Nash, "The Hidden History of Mestizo America," *Journal of American History* 82, no. 3 (December 1995).

54. Timothy White, *Catch a Fire: The Life of Bob Marley* (New York: Henry Holt, 1998), 15–16, 114–15.

55. Julie Quiroz, "Poetry Is a Political Act: An Interview with June Jordan," *Color Lines* 1, no. 3, Winter 1999, 29–30.

56. Michael Silverstone, *Winona LaDuke: Restoring Land and Culture in Native America* (New York: Feminist Press at the City University of New York, 2001), 17, 20, 22, 23.

57. Karl Marx, "The German Ideology," in Robert C. Tucker, ed., *The Marx–Engels Reader* (New York: W. W. Norton, 1978), 193.

58. Gayatri Spivak, *Outside in the Teaching Machine* (New York: Routledge, 1993), 3–4. Spivak's argument prefigured Lisa Lowe's deployment of multiplicity. See Lisa Lowe, "Heterogeneity, Hybridity, and Multiplicity: Marking Asian American Differences," *Diaspora* 1, no. 1 (1991): 28.

59. Sharon O'Brien, *Willa Cather: The Emerging Voice* (New York: Oxford University Press, 1987), 136–37, 205–6.

60. Quoted in Kim Lacy Rodgers, *Righteous Lives* (New York: New York University Press, 1993), 111–12.

61. Juan Flores, "Que Assimilated, Brother, yo soy assimilao: The Structuring of Puerto Rican Identity in the U.S.," *Journal of Ethnic Studies* 13, no. 3 (n.d.): 1–16.

62. Babs Gonzales [Lee Brown], *I, Paid My Dues: Good Times . . . No Bread, a Story of Jazz* (East Orange, N.J.: Expubidence Publishing, 1967), 14.

63. Ibid., 14–15.

64. Sabu starred in *The Elephant Boy* (1937) and went on to star in movies connected to the jungle, *Drums* (1938), *Jungle Book* (1942), and *Jungle Hell* (1955), and in a dose of interchangeable orientalism *The Thief of Baghdad* (1940) and *Arabian Nights* (1942). Vijay Prashad, *The Karma of Brown Folk* (Minneapolis: University of Minnesota Press, 2000), 28.

65. Gonzales, *I, Paid My Dues,* 20–21. Confounding U.S. national racial categories by referring to acceptance of nonwhite foreigners in places U.S. Blacks could not go is an old trope. Booker T. Washington used it in *Up from Slavery.* James Weldon Johnson deployed an anecdote about getting better treatment on a railroad car by speaking Spanish. Malcolm X used it as well.

66. Ibid., 138.

67. Aurora Levins Morales, "Child of the Americas," in Roberto Santiago, ed., *Boricuas: Influential Puerto Rican Writings—an Anthology* (New York: One World, 1995), 79.

9. Salsa

1. A New York dance promoter gave Héctor Pérez the name Héctor Lavoe. Leonardo Padura Fuentes, *Faces of Salsa: A Spoken History of the Music* (Washington: Smithsonian Books, 2003), 6; Donald Clarke, ed., *The Penguin Encyclopedia of Popular Music* (New York: Vintage, 1999), 731.

2. Wilson A. Valentín Escobar, *"El hombre que respiro debajo de agua*: Trans-*Boricua* Memories, Identities, and Nationalisms Performed

through the Death of Héctor Lavoe," in Lise Waxer, ed., *Situating Salsa: Global Markets and Local Meaning in Latin Popular Music* (New York: Routledge, 2002), 161–63. Valentín Escobar's brilliant study places him in the company of Frances Aparicio, Deborah Pacini Hernandez, Lise Waxer, and Jocelyne Guilbault as a leading interpreter and analyst of the ways in which popular music registers broader changes in social identities for people and nations.

3. Joanne Silver, "9 Artists Explore Their Own Puerto Rico," *Boston Sunday-Herald*, May 19, 1991, 51.

4. Ronald Fernandez, Serafín Méndez Méndez, and Gail Cueto, "Jones Act," in Ronald Fernandez, Serafín Méndez Méndez, and Gail Cueto, *Puerto Rico Past and Present: An Encyclopedia* (Westport, Conn.: Greenwood Press, 1998), 178–79.

5. Ronald Fernandez, Serafín Méndez Méndez, and Gail Cueto, "Coastwise Shipping Laws," in Fernandez, Méndez, and Cueto, *Puerto Rico Past and Present*, 78–79.

6. Frances Negrón-Muntaner, *Boricua Pop: Puerto Ricans and the Latinization of American Culture* (New York: New York University Press, 2004), 19.

7. Linda Basch, Nina Glick Schiller, and Christina Szanton Blanc, *Nations Unbound: Transnational Projects, Postcolonial Predicaments and Deterritorialized Nation States* (Amsterdam: Overseas Publishers Association, 1994), 7.

8. Juan Flores, *From Bomba to Hip Hop: Puerto Rican Culture and Latino Identity* (New York: Columbia University Press, 2000), 51.

9. José Torres, "A Letter to a Child Like Me," *Parade Magazine,* February 24, 1991, reprinted in Roberto Santiago, ed., *Boricuas: Influential Puerto Rican Writings—an Anthology* (New York: Ballantine Books, 1995), 15.

10. José Luis González, "The 'Lamento borincano,'" in Santiago, ed., *Boricuas,* 49.

11. See Juan Flores, "Que Assimilated, Brother, yo soy assimilao: The Structuring of Puerto Rican Identity in the U.S.," *Journal of Ethnic Studies* 13, no. 1 (1985).

12. Ruth Glasser, "*Buscando ambiente*: Puerto Rican Musicians in New York," in Ray Allen and Lois Wilcken, eds., *Island Sounds in the Global City* (Urbana: University of Illinois Press, 2001), 11.

13. Ibid.

14. Flores, *From Bomba to Hip Hop*, 67.

15. Juan Flores, "The Diaspora Strikes Back: Reflections on Cultural Remittances," *NACLA Report on the Americas* 39, no. 3 (November–December 2005): 21–25.

16. Lise Waxer, *The City of Musical Memory: Salsa, Record Grooves,*

and Popular Culture in Cali, Colombia (Middletown, Conn.: Wesleyan University Press, 2002), 65.

17. Ibid., 64.

18. Laura Briggs, *Reproducing Empire: Race, Sex, Science, and U.S. Imperialism in Puerto Rico* (Berkeley: University of California Press, 2002), 81–84.

19. Negrón-Muntaner, *Boricua Pop*, 19.

20. Ruth Glasser, *My Music Is My Flag: Puerto Rican Musicians and Their New York Communities, 1917–1940* (Berkeley: University of California Press, 1995), 56, 57.

21. Reid Badger, *A Life in Ragtime* (New York: Oxford University Press, 1995), 145.

22. Glasser, *My Music Is My Flag*, 60.

23. I thank Raul Fernandez for calling these relationships to my attention.

24. Badger, *A Life in Ragtime*, 145, 158, 171; Glasser, *My Music Is My Flag*, 57, 62, 63.

25. Sue Steward, *Musica! The Rhythm of Latin America* (San Francisco: Chronicle Books, 1999), 47.

26. Glasser, *My Music Is My Flag*, 76.

27. Glasser, *"Buscando ambiente,"* 14–15.

28. Ruth Glasser, "The Backstage View: Musicians Piece Together a Living," *Centro de estudios puertorriqueños bulletin* 3, no. 2 (1991): 27, 40.

29. Iris Lopez and David Forbes, "Celebrando Hawaii Style: The Puerto Rican Centennial in Hawaii," *Centro News* 6, no. 2 (Spring 2000): 6.

30. Peter Bloch, *La-Le-Lo-Lai: Puerto Rican Music and Its Performers* (New York: Plus Ultra, 1973), 45.

31. Ibid., 46.

32. Thanks to Raul Fernandez for communicating these insights to me in a personal communication, April 21, 2006.

33. Peter Manuel, "Puerto Rican Music and Cultural Identity: Creative Appropriation of Cuban Sources from Danza to Salsa," *Ethnomusicology* 38, no. 2 (Spring–Summer 1994): 69.

34. Steward, *Musica!* 50.

35. Flores, *From Bomba to Hip Hop*, 106.

36. George Lipsitz, *Dangerous Crossroads* (London: Verso, 1994), 82.

37. Juan Flores, "'It's a Street Thing!' An Interview with Charlie Chase," *Callalloo* 15, no. 4 (1992): 999–1000.

38. Flores, *From Bomba to Hip-Hop*, 118.

39. Manuel, "Puerto Rican Music and Cultural Identity Creative Appropriation of Cuban Sources from Danza to Salsa," 260, 261, 265, 272.

40. Padura Fuentes, *Faces of Salsa*, 79.

41. Waxer, *The City of Musical Memory*, 72–73.

42. Manu Dibango, *Three Kilos of Coffee: An Autobiography* (Chicago: University of Chicago Press, 1994), 91.

43. Waxer, *The City of Musical Memory*.

44. Ibid., 78, 81, 109–10.

45. Ibid., 116.

46. See Flores, "Que Assimilated, Brother, yo soy assimilao."

47. Negrón-Muntaner, *Boricua Pop*, 4.

48. Bloch, *La-Le-Lo-Lai*, 47.

49. Flores, *From Bomba to Hip-Hop*, 10.

50. Flores, "Que Assimilated, Brother, yo soy assimilao," 8.

51. Piri Thomas, *Down These Mean Streets* (New York: Knopf, 1967).

52. Flores, "Que Assimilated, Brother, yo soy asimilao," 8, 11.

53. Fernandez, Méndez, and Cueto, *Puerto Rico Past and Present*, 45.

54. Ibid., 8.

55. Ibid., 51–52.

56. Lopez and Forbes, "Celebrando Hawaii Style," 6.

57. Laura Briggs, *Reproducing Empire* (Berkeley: University of California Press, 2002), 91; Fernandez, Méndez, and Cueto, *Puerto Rico Past and Present*, 222.

58. Shifra M. Goldman, *Dimensions of the Americas: Art and Social Change in Latin America and the United States* (Chicago: University of Chicago Press, 1994), 437.

59. Flores, *From Bomba to Hip Hop*, 179.

60. Padura Fuentes, *Faces of Salsa*, 29, 35.

61. Briggs, *Producing Empire*.

62. Arnoldo Cruz-Malavé, "'What a Tangled Web!': Masculinity, Abjection, and the Foundations of Puerto Rican Literature in the United States," in Daniel Balderston and Donna Guy, eds., *Sex and Sexuality in Latin America* (New York: New York University Press, 1997), 18.

63. Frances Aparicio, "*La Lupe, La India*, and *Celia*: Toward a Feminist Genealogy of Salsa Music," in Waxer, ed., *Situating Salsa*, 135–60.

64. Ibid., 145.

65. Ibid., 147.

66. Juan Flores, "Cortijo's Revenge: New Mappings of Puerto Rican Culture," in George Yudice, Jean Franco, and Juan Flores, eds., *On Edge* (Minneapolis: University of Minnesota Press, 1992), 197.

67. Isabelle Leymaire, *Cuban Fire: The Story of Salsa and Latin Jazz* (London: Continuum Books, 2002), 296.

68. Gary Stewart, *Rhumba on the River* (London: Verso, 2004), 6, 10, 13, 23.

69. Ibid., 34.

70. Ibid., 44.

71. Ibid., 78–80.

72. Raquel Rivera, *New York Ricans from the Hip Hop Zone* (New York: Palgrave Macmillan, 2003), 171–76.

73. Ibid., 175.

74. Ibid., 178–82.

75. Big Punisher, "Capital Punishment," on *Capital Punishment,* Relativity B00000K3HL.

76. Elizabeth M. Berry, "Love Hurts: Rap's Black Eye," *Vibe,* March 2005.

77. Flores, "The Diaspora Strikes Back."

10. Techno

The epigraph to this chapter is drawn from Timothy D. Taylor, *Strange Sounds: Music, Technology and Culture* (New York: Routledge, 2001), 41.

1. Dan Sicko, *Techno Rebels: The Renegades of Electronic Funk* (New York: Billboard Books, 1999), 26.

2. Mark Prendergast, *The Ambient Century: From Matter to Trance, the Evolution of Sound in the Electronic Age* (London: Bloomsbury Publishing, 2000), 297.

3. W. A. Brower, "George Clinton: Ultimate Liberator of Constipated Notions," in David Brackett, ed., *The Pop, Rock, and Soul Reader: Histories and Debates* (New York: Oxford University Press, 2005), 263.

4. Transcription of comment in televised interview with Bernie Worrell, on VH1's *Behind the Music* presentation of "Legends: George Clinton."

5. Greil Marcus, *Lipstick Traces* (Cambridge, Mass.: Harvard University Press, 1989).

6. For an analysis of the history that made Detroit so susceptible to deindustrialization, see Thomas Sugrue, *The Origins of the Urban Crisis: Race and Inequality in Postwar Detroit* (Princeton, N.J.: Princeton University Press, 1996).

7. Sicko, *Techno Rebels,* 62.

8. Vladimir Bogdanov, Chris Woodstra, Stephen Thomas Erlewine, and John Bush, eds., *All Music Guide to Electronica* (Ann Arbor, Mich: All Media Guide, 2001), 28.

9. Ibid., 106, 322.

10. Donald Clarke, ed., *The Penguin Encyclopedia of Popular Music* (London: Penguin Books, 1998), 1277–78; Sicko, *Techno Rebels,* 32.

11. Bogdanov et al., eds., *All Music Guide to Electronica,* 27; Sicko, *Techno Rebels,* 55–57.

12. Sicko, *Techno Rebels,* 35.

13. See, for example, Mr. De', *Electronic Funkysh*t*, Electrofunk Records Catalog #EF-2001-1, 2000.

14. John F. Szwed, *Space Is the Place: The Lives and Times of Sun Ra* (New York: Da Capo Press, 1997), 144. Szwed notes that Sun Ra called this "the Calumet City sound," named after the Chicago suburb well known for its strip clubs and burlesque shows. Chicano musician and producer Ruben Guevara has told me that he started playing music for burlesque shows as a teenager and that he has on occasion tried to orchestrate horns and drums to evoke the sounds he remembers from those engagements.

15. Sicko, *Techno Rebels*, 56.

16. Clarke, ed., *The Penguin Encyclopedia of Popular Music*, 1277.

17. Tim Barr, *Techno: The Rough Guide* (London: Rough Guides, 2000), 127.

18. Bogdanov et al., eds., *All Music Guide to Electronica*, 106.

19. Ibid., 27.

20. Prendergast, *The Ambient Century*, 381.

21. Sicko, *Techno Rebels*, 26.

22. Joel Whitburn, ed., *Top R&B Singles, 1942–1988* (Menomonee Falls, Wisc.: Record Research, 1989), 247.

23. Sicko, *Techno Rebels*, 24.

24. Darren Keast, "Bass Time Continuum," *Urb* 82, March 2001, 113; Sicko, *Techno Rebels*, 73.

25. Szwed, *Space Is the Place*, 236–37.

26. Sicko, *Techno Rebels*, 52, 87, 88.

27. Amanda Nowinski, "Got Back?" *San Francisco Bay Guardian*, April 11, 2001, 51.

28. Ibid.

29. Prendergast, *The Ambient Century*, 382.

30. Jay Babcock, "Paid in Full," *LA Weekly*, December 1–7, 2000.

31. Sicko, *Techno Rebels*, 186–87.

32. Babcock, "Paid in Full."

33. Sicko, *Techno Rebels*, 97–99.

34. Bogdanov et al., eds., *All Music Guide to Electronica*, 27, 106, 129, 332, 445.

35. Ibid., 106.

36. Ibid., 322.

37. Ibid., 129.

38. Neil Ollivierra, *Reality Slap*, in author's possession.

39. Tamara Palmer, "Forward: Techno Hailstorm," *Urb* 11, no. 87, September 2001, 52–53.

40. Richard Child Hill and Cynthia Negry, "Deindustrialization and Racial Minorities in the Great Lakes Region, USA," in D. Stanley Eitzen

and Maxine Baca Zinn, eds., *The Reshaping of America: Social Consequences of the Changing Economy* (Englewood Cliffs, N.J.: Prentice-Hall, 1989), 168–78.

41. Barbara Ransby, "The Black Poor and the Politics of Expendability," in Louis Kushnick and James Jennings, eds., *A New Introduction to Poverty: The Role of Race, Power, and Politics* (New York: New York University Press, 1999), 321.

42. Babcock, "Paid in Full."

43. Sicko, *Techno Rebels*, 89.

44. See Stan Weir, *Singlejack Solidarity* (Minneapolis: University of Minnesota Press, 2004).

45. Donald M. Lowe, *The Body in Late Capitalist USA* (Durham, N.C.: Duke University Press, 1995), 176.

46. Ibid., 89, 174.

47. Christopher Small, *Music of the Common Tongue: Survival and Celebration in African American Music* (Hanover, N.H.: University Press of New England/Wesleyan University Press, 1998), 269.

48. Marshall and June Stearns, *Jazz Dance: The Story of American Vernacular Dance* (New York: Da Capo Press, 1994), 1.

49. Ibid., 215.

50. Ibid., 216.

51. Ibid., 325.

52. Preston Love, *A Thousand Honey Creeks Later: My Life in Music from Basie to Motown and Beyond* (Hanover, N.H.: University Press of New England/Wesleyan University Press, 1997), 209, 226.

53. Donald E. Clarke, *The Penguin Encyclopedia of Popular Music,* 2nd ed. (London: Penguin, 1989), 520.

54. Ibid., 664.

55. Ibid., 122. Thanks to Rob Walser for clarifying this for me.

56. Lewis Erenberg, *Swingin' the Dream: Big Band Jazz and the Rebirth of American Culture* (Chicago: University of Chicago Press, 1998), 229.

57. Jacqui Malone, *Steppin' on the Blues* (Urbana: University of Illinois Press, 1996), 95, quoted in John Mowitt, *Percussion: Drumming, Beating, Striking* (Durham, N.C.: Duke University Press, 2002), 88.

58. Horace Tapscott, *Songs of the Unsung: The Musical and Social Journey of Horace Tapscott* (Durham, N.C.: Duke University Press, 2001), 178–79.

59. Szwed, *Space Is the Place,* 235.

60. Ibid., 143.

61. Ibid., 113.

62. Ibid., 236.

63. Karen Bennett, "The Pleasure of His Accompany," *Musician,* June 1991, 26.

64. Dr. John (Mac Rebennack), *Under a Hoodoo Moon: The Life of the Night Tripper,* with Jack Rummel (New York: St. Martin's, 1994), 83–84.

65. Tricia Rose, *Black Noise: Rap Music and Black Culture in Contemporary America* (Hanover, N.H.: University Press of New England/Wesleyan University Press, 1994), 75–76, 81.

66. Ibid., 81.

67. Robert Walser, "Rhythm, Rhyme and Rhetoric in the Music of Public Enemy," *Ethnomusicology* 39, no. 2 (Spring–Summer 1995): 195, 200.

68. Victor Greene, *A Passion for Polka: Old-Time Ethnic Music in America* (Berkeley: University of California Press, 1992), 123.

69. Carlos Guerra, "Accordion Menace . . . Just Say Mo'!" in Juan Tejada and Avelardo Valdez, eds., *Puro Conjunto: An Album in Words and Pictures* (Austin, Tex.: CMAS Press, 2001), 116–17.

70. Joe Nick Patoski, "Uno, Dos, One, Two, Tres, Quatro . . . ," *Journal of Texas Music History* 1, no. 1 (Spring 2001): 13.

71. Greene, *A Passion for Polka,* 147.

72. Ibid., 115.

73. Peter Bacho, *Dark Blue Suit* (Seattle: University of Washington Press, 1997), 18.

74. The *New York Times* obituary of Doug Sahm on November 22, 1999, spelled the keyboard player's name as "Augie Meyer," but on his recordings the name is spelled "Meyers."

75. David Hoekstra, "Rivieras Bask in 'Sun,'" *Chicago Sun-Times,* December 3, 2000, 13D.

76. John Carlos Rowe, *The New American Studies* (Minneapolis: University of Minnesota Press, 2002), 119.

77. Lowe, *The Body in Late-Capitalist USA,* 176.

Epilogue

The epigraph to this chapter is drawn from *The Songs Are Free,* available on Mystic Fire Videos #76204, 1991, originally presented on *Moyers on America.*

1. Atlantic Records 28798, Joel Whitburn, Top R&B Singles, 1942–88, 151, 183.

2. *Elephunk,* A&M Records, B00009V7RF.

3. Neil Strauss, "The Country Music Country Radio Ignores," *New York Times,* March 24, 2002, sec. 2, 1.

4. Ibid.

5. Corey Moss, "Vow Timberlake Clip Won't Get Dixie Chicks Treatment," *MTV News,* May 13, 2003, 1.

6. Allan Sekula, "Freeway to China (Version 2 to Liverpool)," *Public Culture* 12, no. 2 (2000): 411.

7. Shaheem Reid, "Ron Isley Challenges Diddy's Rat Pack Plans Line of Chinchilla Bikinis," *MTV News*, January 26, 2004, 1.

8. See Robin D. G. Kelley, "The Riddle of the Zoot," in Robin D. G. Kelley, *Race Rebels: Culture, Politics, and the Black Working Class* (New York: Free Press, 1994).

Index

Abyssinian Baptist Church
(Harlem), 168
Academia, Eleanor, 48, 49
Accordion time, 258–62
Acosta, Maria, 150
Adams, Craig, 248, 249, 250
Adams, Eric, 36
Addis Ababa, Ethiopia, 41
Ademambo, Jean, 44
"Adventure," 48
*Adventures in Music with Korla
Pandit,* 188
African Americans: audience, x;
social conditions, x
Africa Unite, 41
Afro Arts Theatre (Chicago), 97
Aguilera, Christina, 14, 267, 271
Ahlerich, Milt, 164, 165
AIDS, 211
Akwid, 76, 77
Albizu Campos, Pedro, 228
Aleman, Oscar, 90
Alexandre, Bill ("Bill Indian"),
232–33
Alienation, 16
"All Your Goodies Are Gone,"
240

Alma Latina, 221
American Civilization, 179
American Idol, 2, 17
American Indian Movement (AIM),
131, 202
American Woodman Marching
Drum and Bugle Corps, 112
America Online, 7–9, 97
America's Most Wanted, 17
"And the Trees Still Stand," 96
Anderson, Gary, xix
Andy, Horace, 44
"Angry American: Courtesy of the
Red, White, and Blue," 269
Anishinaabeg (Ojibwe) people,
203
Anthony, Marc, 150, 230, 234, 235
Anthony, Wendell, 168
Antonio Morel y Su Orquesta, 137
Apache Indian (Steve Kapur), 47
Aparicio, Frances, 229–31
"A pedir su mano," 147
Apess, William, 202
Apl.de.ap (Allan Pineda), 266–67
Apollo Theatre, 96
Archer Record Pressing Plant,
248–49

Archies, 23
Arendt, Hannah, xiv–xv
Arieto, 147
Arismendi, José (Petán), 136
Aristide, Jean-Bertrand, 30, 32, 33, 39, 42
Armstrong, Louis, 54, 84, 95
Arte Sana, 236
Artist's Workshop (Detroit), 110
Artistic Heritage Ensemble (Chicago), 97
Arts and Education Council (St. Louis), 116
Arvelo, Pepito, 221
Arzivu, Ersi, 126
Asian American Latinos, 197
Asian American movement, 193–94
Asian–Black interactions, 44, 46; in Africa, 46; in Asia, 46; in California, 48–49, 130; in Cuba, 47; in Jamaica, 44–45; in Latin America, 47; in New York, 45, 51–52; in the Philippines and the Filipino diaspora, 48; and popular music, 49, 186–90, 266–73; in Trinidad, 47; in the United Kingdom, 47, 50
Asian Dub Foundation, 50
Asian Immigrant Women Advocates, 209–10
Asian–Latino interactions, 50, 51, 266–73
As Nasty as They Want to Be, xxiii, 165, 166, 169, 170
Association for the Advancement of Creative Musicians, 110, 114
AT&T, 19
Atban Klann, 266
Atkins, Cholly, 96
Atkins, Juan, 242, 243, 244, 245, 247, 249

Audio Home Recording Act, 169
Audioslave, 263
Auguste, Annette, 36
Austerlitz, Paul, 137
Avila, Eric, 127–28
Axe, xxiv, xxv
Ayoshi, Toshiko, 90
Azusa Street Revival, xxii

Babu, 257, 258
"Baby Love," 256
Bach, J. S., 83, 84
Bacharach, Burt, 276
Bachata, 67, 135, 139, 146, 149, 150
Bachata Rosa, 146
Bacho, Peter, 259
Backstreet Boys, 3, 14, 15, 22, 23, 24
Badu, Erykah, 41
Baez, Josefina, 143
Baha Men, xxiii, xxiv
Bajuni, 46
Baker, Houston, 85
Baker, Josephine, 90, 125, 253
Baker, Laverne, 46, 223
Baker Boys, 90
Bakhtin, Mikhail, xi
Balaguer, Joaquín, 139, 141
Baldwin, James, 177
Banda, xvi, 54–78, 186
Banda El Recodo, 76, 77
Banda Machos, 57, 61, 64, 73
Banda R-15, 64
Banda Sinaloense, 61
Banda Superbandidos, 64
Banet-Weiser, Sarah, 10
Baraka, Amiri, 114
Barge, Gene, xix, xx
Bar mitzvah, xxi
Barnes, Mae, 253
Barretto, Ray, 234
Basch, Linda, 133

Basie, Count (Bill), 95, 96, 103, 254
Basie, Earl (Groundhog), 93, 255
Bass, Charlotta, 105
Bass, Fontella, 114, 124
Bass, Martha, 114
Bataan, Joe, 33, 34, 48, 223, 224
Bateman, Jaime, 225–26
Bauza, Mario, 90
Baxter, Les, 17
Beanie Babies, 24
Bearden, Romare, 93
"Beast, The," 31, 32
Beatles, the, 23, 146
Beaubrun, Lolo, 30
Bechet, Sidney, 90
Beck, 258
Beethoven, Ludwig van, 84
Beiderbecke, Leon "Bix," 21
Bello, Walden, 70
Bellson, Louie, 188
Beltrán, Graciela, 67
Bennett, William, 170, 171
Berea Presbyterian Church
    (St. Louis), 115
Berger, Jerry, 115
Bernal, Gil, 126
Bernstein, Betty, 203
Bernstein, Helen, 203
Berry, Richard, 130, 131
Best of the Wailers, The, 45
Betances, Eunice, 150
Betances, Ramón Emeterio, 228
Bethel, Marion, 196
Between God and Gangsta Rap,
    177
Bhangra, 50
Big Bea, 253
Big Brother, 17
Bigga Haitian (Charles Dorismond),
    30, 36
Big Maybelle, 96
Big Pun (Christopher Rios),
    234–37

Biko, Steven, 35
Billboard, 48, 246
Binasuan, 195
Black Artist Group, 108–25, 274
Black Arts movement, xvi, 120
Black Congressional Caucus, 156,
    178
Black Consciousness movement, 35
Black Eyed Peas, 265–67, 270,
    271, 272, 273, 276
Black Indians, 196, 197
Black Latinos, 197
Black–Latino interaction, 89,
    130, 227–28; in jazz, 89, 186,
    206–8; in rock 'n' roll, 130–31
Black Noise, 176, 256
Black Panther Party, 168, 196
Blacks, The, 116
Black Wealth, White Wealth, 161
Black Women's Forum, 178
Blade Runner, 245
Blades, Ruben, 224
Blake, Eubie, 220
Blakey, Art, 17, 90
Blanc, Christina Szanton, 133
Blanton, Jimmy, 254
Blind Lemon Jefferson, 96
Blount, Herman "Sonny," 104
Blow, Kurtis, 247
Blowfly, xxii, xxiii, xxiv
"Blow Your Whistle," xxii
Blue Devils, 93
Blues music, xviii
Bluiett, Hamiet, 85, 109, 112–14,
    118, 121, 124, 125
Bo Diddley (Ellas McDaniel), xxi,
    223
Bo Diddley (jazz singer), 46
Body Count, 167, 168
Boggs, Grace Lee, 202
Bollywood, 233
Bolton, Michael, 64
Bomba, 215–16, 224

Bonds, Margaret, 222
Book of Virtues, 171
Boo Yaa Tribe, 49
Boney M, 32
Booker, Beryl, 92
Booker, James, xvii
Bop Marley Studio, 41
Border Patrol, 71, 72
Boricua Pop, 211
Bosch, Juan, 139, 141
Bosques, Emma, 224
Bostic, Earl, 96
"Bottle, The," 223
Boudreau, John, 256
Boukman Eksperyans, 30, 35, 36, 39, 40
Bowen, Patty, 92
Bowie, Lester, 113–14, 124
Boy bands, 3–7
Boy Scouts, 38
Bradford, Bobby, 93
Branching out, 205–6, 227–28
Brasilintime, 257–58
Braun, Carol Mosely, 168, 176
Brazza, Savorgnan de, 232
Brazzaville (Congo), xvii, 232
"Breaks, The," 247
Brinquito, 62
Brooks, Garth, 269
Brown, Anthony, 49
Brown, Arthur, 109
Brown, Foxy (Inga Marchand), 47, 234
Brown, James, 197–98, 245, 247
Brown, John, 38
Brown, Lee, xvii, 206–8
Brown, Vinnie, 173
Brown, Walter, 96
Bryant, Clora, 92, 93, 106
Bryson, Dahu, 235
Buchanan, Pat, 120, 172
Buck and Bubbles, 253
Buck and the Preacher, xi

Buckner, Reginald, 85
Buena Vista Social Club, 126
Burgos, Julia de, 228
Burke, Solomon, xx, 114
Burlesque sound, 243–44
Burning Spear, 90
Burns, Ken, 82–106, 253, 256, 274
Bush, George H. W., 39, 167, 175
Bush, George W., 39, 264, 268, 269
Bushwick Bill, 174
Bus Riders Union, 209–10
Butler, Judith, 184
Butts, Calvin, 168
Byrd, Robbie Tapscott, 94

Caballito, 6
Cachi cachi music, 228
Cagney, James, 93, 162
Calderón, Gilberto (Joe Cuba), 222
Calhoun, John C., 37
"California Sun," 260
Calypso, 216
Camarillo, Sully, 64
Campbell, Buck, 46
Campbell, Luther, xiii, 166, 246, 247
Canclini, Nestor Garcia, 123
"Can I Kill It?" ix
Cantinflas (Mario Moreno), 59
Capers, Valerie, 92
Cape Verde, xix, xx, 197
Capone, Al, 41
Carey, Mutt, 85, 86
Carey, Zeke, xxii
Carlito's Way, 234
Carlos, Wendy, 245
Carnegie Hall, 217
Carnival, The, 33
Carr, Leroy, 96
Carrero, Jaime, 212
Carrion, Enrico, 114
Carter, Benny, 93
Carter, Betty, 92

Carter, Deanna, 269
Carter, Jack, 46
Casey, Harry, xxii, xxiv
Casimira, 57, 61, 65
Castellanos, Sergio, 66
Castle, Irene, 217
Castle, Vernon, 217
Castro, Fidel, 223
Castro Sisters, 47
Cather, Willa, 204, 205
Catholic Church, 38, 40, 41, 147,
    162–63
Censorship, 21–22
Central African Republic, 147
Central Avenue (Los Angeles),
    93–94, 99, 106, 255
Central Park (New York), 31
Cervantes, Lorna Dee, 196
Chambers, Jordan, 113
Chancy, Myriam, 26
Chandu the Magician, 188
Channel One Studios, 44
Chantelle, 149
Charlebois, Robert, 55
Charleston (dance), 95
Chase, Charley (Carlos Mandes),
    223
Chauvin, Louis, 197
Chávez, César, 202
Chavez Ravine, 107, 125–32, 274
Cheeks, Judy, 185
Cheeks, Julius, 185
Cherry, Don, 95
Chess Records, 114
Cheve Simbi, 29
Chic, 223
Chicano movement, 193
Chicha music, xviii, 57
"Chikki Chikki Ahh Ahh," 21
"Child of the Americas," 210
Chile, 125, 194
Chin, Clive, 44
Chin, Leonard, 44

Chin, Vincent "Randy," 44
China, 40, 46, 47, 90
"Chinito chinito," 51, 127
Chomsky, Noam, 43
Christ in Concrete, xxi
Chuck D, 173
Cibo Matto, 49
Circle Coffee House (St. Louis),
    115–16
Clanton, Jimmy, 130
Clapton, Eric, 175
Clara Ward Singers, 114
Clash, the, 263
Clay, Sonny, 46
Clayton, Buck, 46, 90
Clear Channel, 15, 268, 270
"Cleo's Back," 256
Clinton, George, xxi, 104, 239,
    240, 245–46
Club Alabam, 106
Club Dos Amantes, 64
Club Invasion Musical, 66
Club Rendez-Vous, 32
Coates, Buster, 103
Cocolos, 146
Coen, August, 220
Cohran, Frankie, 97
Cohran, Phil, 96–97, 114
COINTELPRO, 120
Cole, Carolyn Kozo, 126
Coleman, Ornette, xxv, 94, 95
Coles, Honi, 254
College Inn (Boulder, Colorado),
    103
Collette, Buddy, 99
Collier, Ken, 244
Collins, Cardiss, 156, 168, 176
Collins, Lee, 186
Colo, Papo, 228
Colombia, 47, 57, 224
Colón, Johnny, 223
Colón, Willie, 211, 224, 228–29,
    235

Coloured Stone, xvii
Colton, George R., 140
Coltrane, John, 90, 96
Columbia/Sony, 97
Combined Law Enforcement Association of Texas (CLEAT), 167
Combs, Sean, 180. *See also* P. Diddy
Commagere, Juliet and Carla, 126
Commodity relations, 1
Communist Party (USA), 163
Compton's Most Wanted, ix
Concepción, César, 216
Conde, Maryse, 201
Congress of Industrial Organizations, 60
Conjunto Clásico, 224
Connerly, Ward, 198
Connor, Eugene "Bull," xiii
"Consejo a las mujeres," 145
Containerization, 2–25, 252, 275
Conti, Ivan "Mamao," 258
Cooder, Ry, 107, 125–32, 274
Cooper, Carolyn, 191
"Cop Killer," 167, 168, 169, 170
Cops, 17
Corday Perfume, 17
Cornelius, Don, 174
Cornershop, 50
Correas, 63
Corrine, 230
Cortijo, Rafael, 216, 224
Cosby, Bill, 43
Costa Rica, 90
"Cowboy," 30, 32, 33
Craig, Carl, 242, 245, 249
Crawley, Wilton, 94, 95
Cross, Brian (B+), 257–58
Cruz, Celia, 14, 33, 34, 224, 231
Cruz, Emilio, 109, 121
Cruz, Miriam, 150
Cruz-Malave, Arnoldo, 229
Crystal Caverns (Washington, D.C.), 121

Cuarto, 63
Cuba, 30, 34, 40, 43, 46, 47, 126, 138, 149, 213, 221, 222, 223, 224, 230
Cuba, Joe, 222, 223
Cuff, Dana, 126
Cuff Links, 23
Cultural remittances, 216
Cumbia, 62
Cut Chemist, 257, 258

Daddy G and the Church Street Five, xix, xx
Daddy Grace, xix, xx
Dafora, Asadata, 89
Daifallah, Nagi, 202
Dakar Festival, 89
Dale, Dick, 130
Dalena, 185
Dancing banda, 62–63
Danforth Foundation, 116, 119, 120
Daniels, Douglas Henry, 35
Dante, Ron, 23
Danza Azteca, 195
Dark Latin Groove, 150
Dash, Damon, 180
Das Neves, Wilson, 258
Daulne, Anita, 197
Daulne, Maria, 197
Davis, Jefferson, 98
Davis, Martha Ellen, 143
Davis, Mike, 126
Davis, Miles, 113, 114, 125
Dead Prez, 52, 180
Death Row Records, 172
DeBeeson, Beryl, 188
"Dede Priscilla," 147
Deep Space DJ Collective (Detroit), 243
Def Jam Records, 175
De Graca, Marcelino Manoel, xix. *See also* Daddy Grace

Deindustrialization, 120–21, 160–61, 241–43

Dekker, Desmond, 45

Delgado, Maceo Hernandez, 51

Del Rosario, Felix, 137

Denny, Martin, 17

Department of Defense, 18

DePoe, Peterm, 131. *See also* Lost Walking Bear

Dery, Mark, 256

DeSanto, Sugar Pie (Umpeylia Marasema Balinton), 47

Desdoumes, Mamie, 35

Detroit, xvi, 110, 120, 165, 168; techno and deindustrialization, 238–53

Detroit Electronic Music Festival, 249

Detroit Emeralds, xvii

Detroit NAACP, 158

Detroit techno, xv, 186, 249–50, 262

Devine Tribal Brothers, 266

De Zes Winden, 121

Diallo, Amadou, 35, 36

Dias, Luis, 143

Dibango, Manu, 225

Diblo, 147

Dick Tracy, 179

di Donato, Pietro, xxi

Diggs, Pancho, 206

Digital capitalism, 1–25; appetites and competition, 10–13, 16; containerization, 1–3; corporate synergy, 7–9; in jazz, 97–98; race as commodity, 14–15; state involvement, 15–16, 18–19; subject positions, 20–22; techno, 250–53; time and space, 18–20

DiMucci, Dion, xx, xxi

Dion and the Belmonts, xx

Disco, xxii

Dislocation, 16

Disney Channel, 15

Disney Studios, 188

Disney World, 15

Disposable Heroes of Hiphoprisy, 175

Dixie Chicks, 268–70

Dixon, Floyd, 96

DJ Assault, 247, 248, 249

DJ Nuts, 258

DJ Rekha, 49

DJ Rhetmattic, 49

DJ-T1000 (Alan Oldham), 244

Doctor John, the Night Tripper, xxiv, xxv, 23, 256. *See also* Rebennack, Mac

Dodds, Baby, 91–92

Doerschuk, Bob, 256

Dole, Robert, 170, 171, 174

Dolphy, Eric, 94

Dominicanish, 143

Dominican Republic, 14, 30, 34, 36, 40, 57, 124; Cibao, 135, 136; diaspora, 134–35, 142–43; gender, 149–50; Hatillo Palma, Monte Cristi, 143; history, 140–42 merengue and migration, 133–53; race, 138–39, 143–49; Sabana Iglesias, 134; Santo Domingo de Guzmán, 134, 141; Trujillo dictatorship, 136–39, 141

Don and Dewey, 130, 131

Don and Juan, xvi

"Don't Call Me Red," 128–29

Dorismond, Andre, 36, 40

Dorismond, Charles (Bigga Haitian), 30, 36

Dorismond, Marie Rose, 36

Dorismond, Patrick, 35, 36

Dorsey, Tommy, 89, 189, 220

Douglas, Anselm, xxiv

Douglass, Frederick, 168, 196

Down These Mean Streets, 227

Dragonaires, 44
Drayton, William (Flava Flav), 179
Dr. Dre, 276
Drifters, 223
Drywall Strike (California), 74–77
Du Bois, W. E. B., 190, 195–96
Duchesne, Miguel Ángel, 89, 220
Duke, Yolanda, 231
Duke Records, 96
Dukwallas, 46
Duluc, Jose, 143
Dunbar, Huey, 230
Dunbar, Sly, 44
Dunham, Katherine, 116, 125
Duran, Blas, 145
Durham, Eddie, 197
Durham, Jimmie, 191
Dusen, Frank, 87
Dusseldorf, Germany, 239, 245, 246
Duvalier, François, 29, 38
Duvalier, Jean-Claude, 29, 39
Duy, Pham, 50
Dyson, Michael Eric, 176, 177

Earle, Steve, 268
Earth, Wind, and Fire, 97
Ebbesmeyer, Curtis, 1
Echo, Eulalia, 35
Eckstine, Billy, 93, 113
Eclectic, The, 35
Eden's Crush, xv, 7–8, 10–14, 22, 23, 24, 238, 274
Edison, Harry, 208
"El africano," 145
El Chicano, 55
"El costo de la vida," 147
"Eleanor Rigby," 146
Electrifying Mojo (Charles Johnson), 246, 250
Elenga, Zachaire (Jhimmy the Hawaiian), 232
Elephunk, 267

El General, 33
El Gran Combo, 224
"El jardinero," 145
El judio maravilloso, 222
Ellington, Duke, 84, 89, 113, 220, 254
Elliott, Robert Malinke, 109, 121, 124
Ellis, Alton, 44
El Peladillo, 59
El Rey Theatre (Los Angeles), 257
El zapateado, 62
Enriquez, Joceyln, 49
"Equal Rights," 35
Eric B. and Rakim, 182
Esaki, John, 51
Escudero, Ralph, 220
Espinosa, Bobby, 55
"Estase Enamorada," 150
Ethington, Phil, 126
Eurodisco, 32, 239, 242, 245, 247
Europe, James Reese, 89, 217–20
Evers, Medgar, 158
"Every Ghetto, Every City," 40
Exotica, 17

"Faith in Trujillo," 136
Fania All-Stars, 225
Fania Records, 145
Fanon, Frantz, 133
Far East Sound (Jamaica), 45
Farmer, James, 158
Farsi, 46
Far Side, 259
Father Divine, xx
Fat Joe (Joseph Cartagena), 234
Fausto, Fidel, 58
FCC, 60
Federal Bureau of Investigation (FBI), 120, 130, 131, 164, 170
Fefita La Grande, 149
Fender, Freddy (Baldemar Huerta), 260

Fernández Reyna, Leonel, 134
Fergie (Stacy Ferguson), 267, 268, 270
"Fight the Power," ix, 143. *See also* Isley Brothers
"Fight the Power" (Public Enemy), 257
Filipino Agricultural Workers Organizing Committee, 202
Finch, Rick, xxii, xxiv
Fitts, Burton, 60
Five Sisters Café (St. Louis), 112
Flack, Roberta, 27, 265
Flamingos, xxii
"Flash Light," xxi
Flatbush, 30
Flores, Imelda, 66
Flores, Joan Milke, 167
Flores, Juan, 65, 144, 154, 205, 213, 216, 227, 231
Flores, Pedro, 224
Flynn, Errol, 207
"Footsteps in the Dark," viii, xii, xiii, xiv, xxv, 27, 265, 273, 276, 277. *See also* Isley Brothers
Ford, Frankie, xvii
Ford, John, 205
Ford, Peter, 21
Fordham Road, xx
Ford Motor Company, 249; Ford Focus, 449–50
Forrest, Jimmy, 112–13
4:40, 146
Four Step Brothers, 253
Four Tops, 96
Fowlkes, Eddie "Flashin'," 244–45
Frank, L., 196
Frankie Ford and the Thunderbirds, xvii
Frankiphone, 97
Franklin, Reverend C. L., vii, 107
Franti, Michael, 175
Fraternal Order of Police, 167

"Freedom," ix. *See also* Isley Brothers
Freedom Alliance, 167
Freeman, Charles, 166
French revolution, 37
Frolic presto, 96
"F—— the Police," 164, 165, 166, 169, 170
Fugees, the, 26, 27, 28, 29, 31, 32, 33, 35, 36, 41, 42, 43, 45, 48
Fulanito, 150
Fullilove, Mindy Thompson, 108
Fulson, Lowell, 130, 197
Fumarola, Piero, xxi
Fumio, Nanri, 46
Fun-da-mental, 50
Funkadelic, 240
Funk Brothers, 256
"Funky Town," xxiii
Furia musical, 58

Gabriel, Ana, 47
Gabriel, Juan, 76
Gadson, James, 257, 258
Gaillard, Slim, 95
Gambling, xxiv, xxv
Gang fighting, 6
Ganja, 45, 203
Garcia, Jesus, 59
Garcia, Louis "King," 89, 220
Garibaldi, Giuseppe, x
Garifuna, 197
Garment Workers Center, 181
Garofalo, Janeane, 43
Garvey, Marcus, 90
Gary U.S. Bonds (Gary Anderson), xix
Gateway Symphony, 113
Gaye, Marvin, 113, 245
Geffrard, Fabre-Nicholas, 138
Gender, 3; banda music, 68; beauty as commodity, 10–14; contradictions, 24; ; in country music,

269–71; girls' culture, 4–6;
in hip hop, 41, 166, 235–37;
in jazz, 92; as marketing cate-
gory, 3–7; migration, 144;
passing, 208; queer responses,
5–7, 244; in salsa, 229–31; in
techno, 243–44, 49–50
General Motors, 97
Genet, Jean, 116
German soldiers in Haiti, 37
Geto Boys, 174
"Ghetto Bastard," 32
Ghost Dance, 195
Gibbs, Marla, 101
Gig, xxiv
Gillespie, Dizzy, 89, 90, 91, 103, 113
Gillette Company, 21
Gilroy, Paul, 85
Gilmore, Ruth Wilson, 186
Giuliani, Rudolph, 36
Go for Your Guns (album), ix, 275
"Go for Your Guns" (song), ix
"Going Back to the Island," xxiii
Gómez, Francisco, 76, 77
Gómez, Sergio, 76, 77
Gonzales, Jose Luis, 214
Gonzalez, Anita, 186
Gonzalez, Babs, 207. See also
Brown, Lee
González, Pedro, 60
Goodman, Benny, 89, 93, 220
Gordy, Berry, xi, 244, 249
Gorinstein, Joseph, 39
Goytisolo, Fermin, xxii
Grace, Charles Manuel, xix. See
also Daddy Grace
"Grand Larceny," 173
Grass dance, 195
Grass Roots (Los Angeles), 266
Gray, Howard Seymour, 188
Gray, Macy, 267
"Great Sebastien, the" (Tom
Wong), 44

Green, Freddie, 103, 254
Green, Percy, 115, 119, 120
Greenberg, Steve, xxiii
Griffin, Farah Jasmine, 88, 196
Grillo, Frank (Machito), 90, 222
Grupo de Acción Dominico-
Haitiano, 144
"Guantanamera," 33
Guantanamo Naval Base, 30
"Guavaberry," 146
Guerra, Juan Luis, 145, 146, 147,
148
Guerrero, Lalo, 126, 127
Guillen, Liz, 199
Gurley, Ossie, xxiv
Guy, François, 55
"Gypsy Woman," 48

Haiti, 26–40; Aristide, 32–33, 39;
Duvalier dictatorship, 29–30,
38; immigrants in U.S., 26–27,
29, 30, 32–33, 35–36; rara,
31; revolutionary history, 34,
36–38, world-transcending
citizenship, 39–41, 47, 90,
125, 136, 137, 138, 139, 140,
143–44, 145, 147, 149, 195, 211
Haitian Flag Day, 38
Halberstam, Judith, 5–7, 24
Hampton, Lionel, 85, 92, 100
Hancock, Hunter, 60
Hansa Carrier, 1
Harleston, David, 175
Harlow, Larry (Lawrence Ira
Kahn), 222
Harmon, Alexandra, 200
Harrar, George, 119
Harris, Don, 130
Harris, Rebert, 96
"Harvest for the World," ix, 275,
276. See also Isley Brothers
Harvest for the World, 275–76
Harvey Danger, 49

Hatfield, Bobby, 130
Hathaway, Donnie, 265
Hatori, Miho, 49
Hawai'i, 14, 46, 48, 126, 129,
    130, 131, 147; Puerto Ricans
    in, 217, 221, 226, 227, 228
Hawaiian Gentlemen, 227
Hawes, Hampton, 94
Hayward, William, 217
Hegamin, Bill, 46
Hemphill, Julius, 88, 94, 107–25
Henderson, Fletcher, 89, 220
Hendrix, Jimi, 40, 260
Hernandez, Brenda Zoe, 149
Hernandez, Deborah Pacini,
    150
Hernandez, Joe, 55
Hernández, Raphael, 89, 213–20,
    221, 222, 224, 226
Hernandez, Victoria, 220
Herrera, L'il Julian, 209
Hershensohn, Bruce, 172
Hibbler, Al, 106
Hicks, Darby, 79–80, 106
Hicks, John, 256
Hidalgo, David, 126, 260
Hidalgo, Juan Carlos, 59
High Voltage, 49
Hill, Andrew, 102
Hill, Bob, 46
Hill, Faith, 269
Hill, Lauryn, 26, 27, 28, 40, 41,
    43, 177, 180
Hill, Roberta, 194
Hindoubill, 233
Hines, David, 114
Hines, Earl "Fatha," 95
Hip hop, 26–29, 31, 32, 36,
    154–83, 186, 226; gangsta rap,
    164, 176–77; gender, 235–37;
    materialism and marketing,
    180–82; moral panic about,
    156–83; police brutality,

167–68; social conditions,
    159–61, 174–75
Hmong, 49
Ho, Fred, 52
Holley, James, 168
Hollinger, David, 198–99
Hollywood Holiday, 188
Holt, John, 44
"Home Computer," 246
Home Invasion, 168
"Home Is Where the Hatred Is,"
    77–78
Honda, xxiv
Honda, Yuka, 49
Hopkins, Lightnin', 112
Hornweb, 121
Hot End (Fort Worth, Texas),
    112
House Resolution 4437, 77, 143
House UnAmerican Activities
    Committee, 129, 163, 164
Houston, 96, 98–99
Howard Stern Show, The, 17
Huerta, Delores, 202
Huey Smith and the Clowns, xvii
Hugg, Dick, 60
Hughes, Howard, 128
Hull, Cordell, 137
Humes, Helen, 197
Humphrey, Paul, 257
Hunt, Guy, 170
Hussein, Saddam, 270
Hyder, Rehan, 50

Ibrahim, Abdulla, 89
Ice Cube, ix, xii, xiii, xiv, 27, 64,
    166, 170
Ice-T, 167, 168, 170, 173
Iha, James, 49
Iijima, Chris, 193
Il trovatore, 96
Ilocano, 48
"I'm Your Pusher," 173

Immigration and Naturalization
Service, 71
Immigration Reform and Control
Act (1986), 142
Immigration to the U.S., 26, 50,
53; Dominicans, 133–53; Hai-
tian, 26–36; hostility to, 63,
70–74, 77–78; Mexican, 53–78;
Vietnamese, 50, 184–85
"Incident at Neshabur," 34, 35
Inheritance, 177
International Monetary Fund, 27,
70, 142
International Sweethearts of
Rhythm, 96
Internet, 18–21
Intimate justice, xii, 272. *See also*
Rose, Tricia
Iraq War, 43, 263–71
Isaacs, Gregory, 44
"I Shot the Sheriff," 175
Island of the Sun, 255
Isley, Ron, 276, 277
Isley Brothers, viii–xi, xiv, xxv, 27,
143, 265, 275
Itchy Fingers, 121
I-Threes, 44
Itliong, Larry, 202
"Itsy Bitsy Teenie Weenie Yellow
Polka Dot Bikini," 69
"It's Your Thing," ix. *See also* Isley
Brothers
"It Was a Good Day," ix, xii, 27.
See also Ice Cube
Ivette's dad, 10–12
"I Wanna Testify," 240
Iyer, Vijay, 49, 86

Jackson, Mahalia, 96
Jackson, Michael, 24
Jackson, Oliver, 109, 116, 118, 121,
124
Jackson Five, 22, 24

James, C. L. R., 179
James, Harry, 220
Jamez Chang, 49, 51–52
J&N Records, 150
Jang, Jon, 49, 102
Japan, 46, 49, 179, 242, 258
Japanese Americans, 189
Jara, Carmen, 67
Ja Rule, 276
"Java," 45
Jay-Z, 41, 180, 276
Jazz, 79–106; democracy, 104–6;
modernism, 85–86, 88; ra-
cial power, 93–94, 98–103,
110–12, 114–17, 119–20,
122; speech, 94–95, 118; as
symbol of modernity, 83–84;
as symbol of U.S. space, 94,
118–25; time, 254–58; virtuos-
ity, 91, 95–96, 108–25, 186;
world-transcending citizenship
through, 89–89
Jazz (television series), xvi, 80–92,
253, 256, 274
Jean, Wyclef, 26, 27, 28, 29, 30, 31,
33, 34, 35, 36, 41, 42, 43, 181
Jean-Baptiste, Nemours, 40, 147
Jefferson, Blind Lemon, 197
Jefferson, Thomas, 37
Jerry Byrnes and the Loafers, xvii
Jerry Springer Show, The, 17
Jetty, Boukman, 40
Jhimmy the Hawaiian (Zachaire
Elenga) xvii, 232
Jibaro, 215, 224
Jiménez, Flaco, 126, 260
Jiménez, Manuel "Canario," 215,
216
Jimenéz, Santiago, 260
Jimenez, Santiago, Jr., 260
Jimmy Jam and Terry Lewis, 21
"John Sinclair," 165
Johnson, Bessie, 186

Johnson, Bill, 86
Johnson, Budd, 90
Johnson, Leola, 169
Johnson, Lyndon, xiii, 120, 141
Jolson, Al, xx
Jones, Jo, 93, 103, 254
Jones, Joe, 260
Jones, Kipper, ix
Jones, Quincy, 48
Jones, Stretch, 253
Jones Act, 212
Jordan, June, 203
Jordan, Steve, 260
Jrocc, 257, 258
"Jump Lester Jump," 35
Junior Walker and the All-Stars, 256
Junkanoo, xxii
Juvenile Style, 76

Kalapati, 195
Kansas City Bar (Tijuana, Mexico), 87
Kaufman, Philip, xxi
KBUE-FM, 59
KC and the Sunshine Band, xxii, xxiii, xxiv
KC and the Sunshine Junkanoo Band, xxii
Keith, Toby, 269
Kelley, Robin D. G., 176, 194
Kellner, Jamie, 8
Kellwood Corporation, 180
Kelly, R., 276
KELW, 60
"Kem pa sote" (My Heart Does Not Leap, I Am Not Afraid), 35
Kenya, 40, 47, 90
Kenyatta, Jomo, 90
Keppard, Freddie, 87
Key Kool, 49
Keys, Alicia, 41
Khaled, Cheb, 44

Kikongo, 231
"Killing Me Softly with His Song," 27
Kim, Jo Jo Hoo, 44
King, B. B., 130
King, Evelyn "Champagne," ix
King, Martin Luther, Jr., 38, 121, 158, 159, 168
King, Maurice, 96
King, Porter, 35
King, Rodney, xiii, 166
King, Saunders, 34
King Kino, 30, 32, 33
"King Porter Stomp," 35
Kingsmen, 130, 164
Kirk, Rahsaan Roland, 95, 101
Kirschner, Don, 23
Kitano, Harry (Harry Lee), 189–90
KLAX, 55–56, 58, 59, 60, 64
KLOK, 57
KLSX, 56
Knapp, Captain Harry, 140
Knopf Publishing, 97
Kochiyama, Yuri, 202
Kolner Saxophone Mafia, 121
Kong, Leslie, 45
Konpa music, 145, 147, 148
Korean Immigrant Worker Advocates, 209–10
Kraftwerk, 239, 241, 242, 245–47, 268
Kreyòl, 33, 39
KRS-1, 177, 234, 270
Krupa, Gene, 17
Kuchipudi, 143
Kun, Josh, 76
Kweli, Talib, 180
Kykotsmovi, Arizona, 44

La Anacoana, 47
"La bamba," 33–34
Laboe, Art, 60
"La chica de las caderas," 67

"La culebra," 77
LaDuke, Winona, 203
"Lady of Spain," 259
La Equis, 55, 58, 66
La Gran Manzana, 149
"La herradura," 65
La India, 230, 231, 234
"La isla bonita," 230
Lake, Oliver, 109, 110, 112, 114, 118, 121, 122, 124, 125
Lake Art Quartet, 115
Lakou, 40
La Lupe, 231
"Lamento borincano," 213, 214, 215, 226
"Land of a Thousand Dances," 69
Lanes, Jack, 87
Langford's night spot, 95
La Opinion, 58
Lapassade, George, xxi
La Révolucion Française, 55
Las Chicas del Can, 149–50
L.A. 17 to 30 (program), 178
Lashley, Lester, 93
"Las nubes," 55
La social vancería, 226
Lastie, David, xxv
Lastie, Melvin, xxv
Latin bugalu, 33, 223, 227
La Tongolele, 225
Laurence, Baby, 255
Lavalas, 30, 32, 36, 39
Lavoe, Héctor, 211, 213, 228, 234, 235, 237
La Voz del Yuna, 136
La Voz Dominicana, 136
"La yola," 148
Lazo, Ralph, 202
Lebrón, Lolita, 229
Lee, Bruce, 52
Lee, Byron, 44, 45
Lee, James Kyung-Jin, 82, 105
Lee Sisters, 47

Leflore, Floyd, 109
Leflore, Shirley, 109
"Le Freak," 223
Legal Alien Orchestra, 228
Lemvo, Ricardo, 231–34
Lennon, John, 165
Leonard, Harlan, 79
LeProtti, Sid, 46
Lescot, Elie, 139
"Lester Leaps In," 35
L'etat, 39
Lewis, John, 158
Lewis, Terry, 21
Liberman Broadcasting Corporation, 58
Lignazi, Lea, 147
Limón, José, 66, 67
Lin, Jeff, 49
Lincoln, Abby, 92
Linebaugh, Peter, vii
Lipps Inc., xxiii
Liston, Melba, 92
Little Bea, 253
Little Joe and the Latinaires, 55
Little Joe y la familia, 55
Little Saigon, 184
Little Willie G, 126, 127
Live with Regis and Kelly, 7–8
LL Cool J, 41, 234
"Loco cha cha," 130
Lombo, Ana Marie, 13
Long Tongues, 121
Lonidier, Fred, 76
Lopez, Jennifer, 14, 234
Lord Creator, 33
Los Angeles, 21; banda music in, 54–78; jazz music in, 83, 86, 87, 93, 99, 100; L.A. Police Protective League, 167; L.A. Unified School District, 58; public library, 126; urban renewal and local memory, 120, 125–32, 164, 166, 174, 181,

187–89, 202, 207, 208, 231, 257, 267
Los Angeles riots, xiii, 72, 166, 172, 174
"Los chucos suaves," 127
Los drywaleros, 76
Los Illegales, 150
Los Lobos, 260
"Lost Ones," 41
Lost Walking Bear, 131
Los Vecinos, 149
Lotus, 34
"Louie Louie," 130, 131, 164
Louima, Abner, 32
Louisiana Pete, 208, 259
L'Ouverture, Toussaint, 34, 37
Love, Preston, 96, 103
"Love Like Sisters," 124
Lowe, Donald, 12–13, 18, 252, 262
Loy, Herman Chin, 44
Loza, Steven, 63
Luke Skywalker, 166
Lumbee people, 197
L'wa, 29, 39
Lyle, K. Curtis, 109
Lymon, Frankie, 24, 223

Maceo: Demon Drummer of East LA, 51
Machado, Gerardo, 34
Machito (Frank Grillo), 90, 222
Machito and His Afro-Cubans, 222
Madison, Joseph, 158–59, 169, 170
Madonna, 230
Mahogany, xi
Maines, Natalie, 268
Mainor, Ade (Mr. De), 247, 248
Makeba, Miriam, 224
Makina Loca, 231, 232, 234
Making the Band, 2, 7
Malcolm X, 168, 202
"Mal de amor," 147

Maldonado, Adel, 228
Mambo Kings, The, 234
"Mamie's Blues," 35
Manetta, Fess, 95
Manfred Schulze's Blaster Quintet, 121
Manhattans, the, xvii
Manning, Frank, 66
Manzanar Relocation Center, 202
Marcus, Greil, 241
Mardi Gras Indians, 205
Maresca, Ernie, xx, xxi
María, Angélica, 67
Mariscal, Griselda, 6
Marlborough Projects, 27
Marley, Bob, 27, 28, 29, 30, 32, 36, 39, 41, 43, 44, 45, 51, 52, 203
Marley, Rita, 43
Marley, Rohan, 28
Marley, Stephen, 27, 28
Marsalis, Wynton, 82–84, 89, 98, 102, 103, 104–5
Marsh, Dave, 172
Marshall, William, 101
Marti, José, 33
Martin, Lori, 269
Martin, Ricky, 234
Martinez, Bob, 166
Martinez, Narcisso, 208, 259
Martínez, Rubén, 126
Mashia, Allan, 182
Maurice's Gold Coast Lounge (St. Louis), 115
May, Derrick, 238, 239, 242, 245, 247, 248
Mayfield, Curtis, xi, 33
Maytals, 45
Mbira, 97
McAlister, Elizabeth, 31
McCartney, Paul, 146
McClary, Susan, 89
McCoy, Neal, 47
McCracken, Tommy, 197

McGhee, Dorothy, 93
McGhee, Howard, 93
MCI, 18
McIntyre, Reba, 269
MC Lyte, 177
McShann, Jay, 96
McWilliams, Freddie, 46
Medley, Bill, 130
Melendez, Lisette, 230
"Mellow Loving," 185
Melodians, 45
Memphis Minnie, xvi
Mendez, Alfredo (Alfred Mendel-
    sohn), 222
"Mendocino," 260
Mento, 216
Menudo, 3
Mercury, Freddie (Farrokh
    Bulsara), 47
Merengue, xvi, 40, 57, 133–53,
    186, 230
"Messin' with the Kid," 124
Meyers, Augie, 260
Mexican American Legal Defense
    Fund, 199
Mexico, 19, 34, 54–78, 124, 213,
    214, 222, 225; Acapulco, 193;
    Chiapas, 71; Colima, 63, 67;
    El Maguey, Guanajuato, 75;
    Gaumuchli, 47; Guerrero, 63;
    Jalisco, 60, 61, 63; Michoacan,
    59, 60, 63, 76; Nayarit, 60,
    65; Oaxaca, 63; Puebla, 63;
    Sinaloa, 47, 60, 61, 63; Ti-
    juana, 87; Veracruz, 34, 193;
    Zacatecas, 63
Miami bass, 239, 247
Michel, Pras, 26, 31
Mickey and the Invaders, 55
Mickey Mouse Club, 15
Milburn, Amos, 96
Miles, Tiya, 196
Miley, Bubber, 94

Millinder, Lucky, 96
Mingus, Charles, 47, 90, 93, 99,
    197
Misajon, Maile, 13, 14
Miseducation of Lauryn Hill,
    The, 27, 40, 41, 42
"Misere," 96
Miss Lavelle, 256
Mitchell, Roscoe, 93
Mixed-race identities, xvi,
    190–200; activists, 202–3
M-19 (Colombian guerrilla force),
    225
Monkees, 23
Montuno, 230
Moody, James, 208
Morales, Aurora Levins, 210
Moran, Anderson, 35, 36
More, Benny, 77
Morello, Tom, 263–65
Morgan, Derrick, 45
Moroder, Giorgio, 242, 245
Morris, Chester (Morris Carnov-
    sky), 163
Morrison, Toni, 79, 154–56, 182,
    196
Morton, Jelly Roll, 35, 87, 96, 186
Mosby, Curtis, 106
Mos Def, 180, 276
Moss, Corey, 268
Most Beautiful Girl in the World,
    The, 10
Moten, Bennie, 254
Motown, 96, 244, 245, 248, 256
Mountain Brothers, 49
Mozart, Wolfgang Amadeus, 84
Mr. Biggs (Ron Isley), 276
MTV News, 268
Munby, Jonathan, 162
Muñoz, Carlos, 193
Muñoz, José, 231
Muñoz Marín, Luis, 214, 222,
    226, 228

Murray, Albert, 85
Murray, David, 121
Murphy, Rick, 185
Musica antillana, 225
Music Institute (Detroit), 243
Musicland stores, 166
"Muy Fifi," 127
My Ántonia, 204
Myron, Aaron, xxi, xxiii

Nanny Town, 192
Nas, 276
National Association for the Advancement of Colored People (NAACP), 168
National Association of Black Police Officers, 167
National Education Association, 172
National Labor Committee, 180
National Labor Relations Board, 75
National Political Congress of Black Women, 157, 168, 171
National Urban League, 168, 182
Nations Unbound, 134
Native Americans, 131, 194
Natty Dread, 27
Naughty by Nature, 31–32, 36, 173
Negritude, 201
Negron-Muntaner, Frances, 211, 214–15, 226
Negroni, Joe, 223
Nelly, 276
Nelson, Oliver, 96
Ncruda, Pablo, 146
Nesmith, Michael, 23
New Edition, 3, 22, 24
New Kids on the Block, 3, 22, 24
New Orleans, xvii, xxiv, 83, 86, 87, 91, 95, 103, 197, 205, 256
Newton Street Police Station (Los Angeles), 94
New York, 14, 47, 83, 89, 103, 124, 125, 133, 142, 147, 150, 214, 224
New York Band, the, 148–49
New York Mets, xxiv
Nicholas, Albert, 90
Nico, 147
"Night Chicago Died, The," 69
"Night Train," 113, 124. See also Forrest, Jimmy
Nike running shoes, 1
9/11, 263–78
98 Degrees, 14
Nixon, Hammie, 197
No Disrespect, 177
No Fixed Address, 44
"No hay manera," 76, 77
"No me empuje," 139
Normark, Don, 126
Norteno music, 259, 260
North, Oliver, 167, 170
North American Free Trade Agreement, 63, 71, 72
"No Woman, No Cry," 2, 28, 31, 32, 40
'N Sync, 3, 14, 15, 22, 24, 267
Nueva canción, 146
"Numbers," 246
Nuss, Otto, 260
NWA, 164, 165, 166, 170, 171

Odets, Clifford, 163, 179
Office of Economic Opportunity, 116
Off the Chain for the Y2K, vol. 6, 248
"Ojala que llueva café," 146, 148
Oliver, Melvin, 43, 161
Oliveros, Pauline, 245
Olugbala, Knm, 52
Olugbala, Mutulu, 52
O'Malley, Walter, 128
"Once There Was a Holding Corporation Called America," 90

One Hundred Blacks in Law Enforcement, 36
"100%," 235
Opel, Jackie, 44
Oracle of the Black Swan, 49
Organization of Afro-American Unity, 202
Orgullo Maldito, 66
Orquesta Generalissimo Trujillo, 136
Orquesta San Jose, 136
Ortiz, Nancy, 221
Ory, Kid, 87
Osby, Greg, 118
Otis, Johnny, 21, 48, 60, 96, 208
"Our Latin Thing," 225

Pablo, Augustus, 44
Pacheco, Johnny, 144, 224
Pachuco Boogie Boys, 126
Pahanui, James "Bla," 129
Paiute Indians, 131
Palace Theatre, 7
Palmer, Earl, xxv, 257
Palmieri, Charlie, 222
Palmieri, Eddie, 222
Pan Afrikan People's Arkestra, 100, 110
Pandit, Korla, 187–89, 190, 191, 207, 208
Pansori, 52
Papa Celestin's Original Tuxedo Jazz Orchestra, 95
Papathanassiou, Vangelis. *See also Vangelis,* 245
Paradise, 49
Parahyba, Joao (Comanche), 258
Paris (Bay Area rapper), 168, 270
Park Avenue Club (Detroit), 243
Parker, David, 198
Parker, Charlie, 84, 89, 113, 240
Parker, Ray, Jr., 48
Parks, Rosa, 158

Parliament(s), xxi, 239, 240, 245
Parsi, 47
Parsons, Lucy, 203
Partido Popular Democratico (PR), 214
Pascoe, Peggy, 177
Passing and racial masquerade, 186
"Pata Pata," 224
Pataki, George, 168
PBS, xvi
P. Diddy (Sean Combs), 41, 180, 182
Peacock Records, 96
Pearlman, Louis, 21
Peña, Manuel, 220
Penn, Sean, 43
Pennsylvania commonwealth secretary, 172
"Penny Lane," 146
Pentecostal religion, xix, xxii, xxv, 29
People's Art Center, 116
Pepper, Art, 259
Pequot people, 203
Perfume Set to Music, 17
Perry, Darthard, 120
Perry, Ivory, 115, 119, 120
Pessar, Patricia, 142, 144
Petit, Buddy, 87
P-Funk, 104, 239, 241, 244
Phantoms, 30, 32, 39
Pharaohs, the, 97
Phat Farm, 181
Phat Fashions, 180
Philippe, Guy, 39
Phillips, Esther, 77–78
Pietri, Pedro, 228
Pilipino Cultural Nights, 195
Pinedo, Nelson, 224
Pink Floyd, 146
Pittsburgh Courier, 159
"Planet Rock," 246
Plantation Club (St. Louis), 113

Plena, 215–16, 224
Plessy v. Ferguson, 38
Poitier, Sydney, xi
Pokemon Cards, 24
Police, 114
Police brutality, 170, 174–75
Polish soldiers in Haiti, 37
Polka, 62, 259
Polski Kwartet, 208, 259
Pons, Antoinetta, 225
Poongmul, 52
"Poor Man's Shangri-la," 127
Poor People's March, 159
Pop Stars, 7–15, 17, 22, 23, 238, 261
Popular Culture in the Age of White Flight, 127
Porter, Roy, 257
Poulson, Norris, 128
Poverty, 160, 174
Powers, Bill, 46
Powers, Gene, 46
Preacher's Son, The, 29
"Preciosa," 226
Predator, The, xiii, xiv
"Preguntas," 194
Prejean, Sister Helen, 43
"Pretty Woman," 9
"Pride, The," ix. *See also* Isley Brothers
Prince Buster, 45
Prince Lala, 256
Priority Records, 164
Product differentiation, 13
Professor Longhair (Roeland Roy Byrd), 95–96
Proposition 187 (California), 72, 73, 74, 75, 78
Prospect Park, 31
Proyecto Akwid, 76, 77
Proyecto Uno, 150
Pruitt-Igoe Housing Project (St. Louis), 116

Psalm 150, xx
"Pua 'Olena," 227
Public Enemy, 173, 177, 179, 257, 270
Puente, Tito, 34, 90, 224, 234
Puerto Rico, 14, 47, 48, 89–90, 124, 134, 138, 142, 143, 148, 149, 150, 185; migration to the mainland, 212; history of U.S. colonialism, 212–13; race, 213–15, 217–23

Q-Bert (Robert Quitevis), 49, 51
"Quarter to Three, A," xix, xx, xxiv
Quayle, Dan, 167, 172
"Quebecois," 55
Quebradita, 61, 63, 64, 65, 66, 67, 68, 69, 76
Queen, 47
Queen Latifah, 177
Queer fandom, 6–7
Queer time, 6–7, 24
Quezada, Jocelyn, 149
Quezada, Millie, 145, 149
Quisqueya, 147

Race Rebels, 176
Raekwon, 234
Rage against the Machine, 263
Ragtime, 254
Rai music, xviii, 26, 27, 32, 149
Rainy, Ma, 96
Raposo, Bony, 143
Rara, 30–31, 195
Rastafarianism, 29, 30, 39, 44, 203
Reagon, Bernice Johnson, 263
Real World, The, 17
Rebennack, Mac, xvii, xxiv, 256. *See also* Doctor John
Redbone, 131
Redd, Ernest S., 187

Redd, John Roland, xvii, 187–89, 190, 206
Redd, Speck, 188
Reddiker, Marcus, vii
"Redemption Song," 52
Refugee Project, 40, 43
Reggae, 32, 33, 44, 45, 149
Reid, Clarence, xxii, xxiii, xxiv
Reid, Vernon, xxi
Reid, Vic, 192, 195
Reinhardt, Django, 90, 232
"Remember Rockefeller at Attica," 90
Remittances, 58, 134
Reno, Janet, 165, 166
"Rescue Me," 114
Revilot Records, 240
Rhythm Rockers, 129, 130, 131
Ricardo, Ricky, xvii
Rich, Buddy, 17
Righteous Brothers, 130, 131
Rillera, Barry, 129, 131
Rillera, Nancy, 130
Rillera, Rick, 129
Rimsky-Korsakov, Nikolai, 189
Rios, Lisa, 236–37
Rivera, Ismael, 224
Rivera, Mon, 215
Riviera Club (St. Louis), 113
Rivieras, 260
Roach, Max, 17, 93, 254
Roberto Clemente Park, 30
Roberts, Dorothy, 43
Robertson, Pat, 172
Robey, Don, 96
Robinson, Edward G. (Emmanuel Goldenberg), 162, 163
"Robots," 247
Rocawear, 180
Rockefeller Drug Laws, 181
Rockefeller Foundation, 116, 119, 120
Rocker, John, 52

Rock 'n' Roll Hall of Fame, 263, 265
Rockolas, 225
Rodney, Walter, 1
Rodriguez, Chino, 47
Rodríguez, Pete, 223
Rodriguez, Silvio, 146
Roediger, David, 108
Rolando, Juan, 187–89. See also Pandit, Korla; Redd, John
Rolling Stones, 146
Rosalva, 67
Rose, Tricia, xii, 176, 256, 272
Ross, Diana, 24, 96
Rowe, John Carlos, 261
Rugrats, The, xxiv
Run–DMC, 180, 268
Rutlin, Ajule, 109

Sabrina the Teenage Witch, 8
Sabu, 189, 207
Sahm, Doug, 260
Sahra, 44
Salas, Rudy, 126
Sales, Grover, 85
Salinas, Carlos, 71
Salisbury, George, 103
Salsa, xvi, 57, 186, 211–237; in Colombia, 225–26; in Hawai'i, 227; salsa dura, 230; salsa romantica, 230
Sanchez, George, 199
"Sangre de indio," 61
San Juan, Puerto Rico: municipal band, 218; concert in, 215
Santamaría, Mongo, 90
Santana, Carlos, 34
Santería drumming, xxii
Santiago, Herman, 223
Santos, Anthony, 133, 135
Santos, Daniel, 224
Sarandon, Susan, 43
Sassen, Saskia, 140

Saunderson, Kevin, 245
"Save the Last Dance for Me," 223
Sawahil, 46
"Say Man," 223
Scherzinger, Nicole, 13, 14
Schiller, Nina Glick, 133
Schwarzenegger, Arnold, 171, 175
Score, The, 26, 27, 28, 31, 32, 33, 40, 41, 42, 45, 48
Scot-Heron, Gil, 77–78
Scott, Hazel, 92
Scott Air Force Base, 112
S-Curve Records, xxiii
Seaga, Edward, 44
Sean Jean Clothing, 180
Second Baptist Church (Columbia, Missouri), 187
Sekula, Allan, 275
Seoul Brothers, 49
Sepia Club (Des Moines), 188
Sesma, Chico, 130
Seventh Heaven, 7
Seventieth Precinct Police Station (New York), 32
Shades of LA, 126
Shadows, the, xvii
Shaft, xi
Shakur, Tupac, 235
Shange, Ntozake, 109, 121, 124
Shankar, Ravi, 90
Shannon, Darryl, 246
Shannon, Patrick, 150, 185
Shapiro, Thomas, 161
Shaw, Charles "Bobo," 109
Shea Stadium, xxiv
Sheldon Auditorium (St. Louis), 117
"She's about a Mover," 260
"She's Put the Hurt on Me," 256
Shievers, Frank, 46
Shirley and Lee, xvii
Shonen Knife, 49
Shrine Auditorium, 93
Sicot, Weber, 40

Siegals, Charley, 95
Simmons, Russell, 180, 181, 182
Simone, Nina, 41, 92
Simonett, Helena, 54, 68
Sinatra, Frank, 96
Singh, Ram, 207–8. *See also* Brown, Lee
Sir Douglas Quintet, 260
"Si saliera petroleo," 147
Sissle, Noble, 89, 220
Sister Souljah, 167, 177
Situationist International, 241
"Skokiaan," 137
Skyliners, xvii
Sleet, Frank, 103
Slim and Slam, 95
Small, Christopher, 104, 253
Smashing Pumpkins, 49
Smith, Bessie, 92, 96
Smith, Jerome, 205
Snoop Dogg, 276
Snowden, Shorty, 253
So Anne (Annette August), 36
SOB's (New York), 147
Soca, 149
Some Time in New York City, 165
Son, 230
Song, Miri, 198
"Song of India," 189
Song of Solomon, 154–56, 182–83
Songs of the Unsung, 98, 102
Son jarocho, 34
Sonora Matancera, 224
Sosa, Annette Ramos, 149
Sosa, Ivette, 13, 14
"Soul Makossa," 225
Soul Train, 143, 174
Soul Vibrations, 147
"Sound Your Funky Horn," xxii, xxiv
Southard, Harry, 99
Southeast Textiles, 180
Southern Railway, xix

Spain, Johnny, 196
Spearhead, 175
Spears, Britney, 15
Speck Redd Plays, 188
Spector, Ronnie, 51
Speech and jazz, 94–95
Spelman, Elizabeth, 126
Spice Girls, 24
Spikes, Reb, 46
Spirit of Haiti, 26
Springsteen, Bruce, 268
Stafford, Jo, 96
Stahl, Matthew, 23
Stanley, Earl, 197
Stanley, Henry Morton, 232
Starr, Brenda K., 230
Starr, Maurice, 22
"Star-Spangled Banner," 32
Stearns, Clifford, 169, 170
Stern, Howard, 56
Stetson hats, 63
Stewart, Gary, 232
Stewart, Slam, 95
St. Louis, Missouri, 109–25, 178; police department, 120; symphony, 114
St. Louis Jimmy, xvi
Stockhausen, Karlheinz, 246
Strachwitz, Chris, 126
Straight Out of Compton, 164, 165
Strata (Detroit), 110
Strategic anti-essentialism, 204
St. Raymond's Cemetery (Bronx), 211
Studio Museum of Harlem, 121
Subculture, 20–21
Sublette, John "Bubbles," 254
Subotnick, Morton, 245
Sugar and Sweet, xvii
Sun Ra, 92, 97, 100, 103–4, 243, 246, 255–56. *See also* Blount, Herman "Sonny"
Superfly, xi

Supremes, 256
Survivor, 17
SweatX, 181
"Sweets for My Sweet," 223
Szwed, John, 246

Taboo (Jaime Gomez), 266–67
Tabou Combo, 29, 36, 39
Taburello, xxi
Taiko, 51
Taino Indians, 147, 214
"T'Ain't Nobody's Business," 103
Takaki, Walter, 51
Tapscott, Horace, 92, 94, 96, 98–103, 255
Tapscott, Mary Lou Malone, 94
Tarantella, xxi
Taveras, Alexandra, 145, 149
Taveras, Fafa, 139
Taverez, Rosanna, 13, 14
Taylor, Billy, 85
Taylor, Eric (writer), 54
Taylor, Eric (attorney), 168
Techno, 238–62
Techno Banda, 61
"Teen Age Love," 256
Tejanos, 63
Telecommunications Act (1996), 15
Televisa, 58
Tell Me How Long This Train's Been Gone, 177
"Te lo pido por favor," 76
Temptations, 96
Terminator, 171, 175
Terrell, Vincent, 109, 114, 116, 117, 120, 121, 124, 125
Terry, Clark, 114
Texas Tornadoes, 260
Thee Midnighters, 126
"They Trespass on the Land of the Sacred Sioux," 90
Third Army Brigade (Colombia), 225

"3rd Base, Dodger Stadium," 129
Thomas, Pirri, 227
Thomas, Rufus, 114
Thompson, Carroll, 44
Thompson, Jack, 165, 166, 167, 170
Thompson, Robert Farris, xxii, 109
Thompson, Sir Charles, 187
Thompson Twins, xvi
Thousand Honey Creeks Later, A, 103
"Three Cool Cats," 127
369th Infantry "Hellfighters," 217–20
Thrill, Werner, 39
Tierra, 126
"Till There Was You," 146
Timberlake, Justin, 267, 268, 271
Time for Beany, 188
Time Warner, 7–9, 22, 24, 97, 167, 168, 170, 172
Tin Tan, 225
Tinikling, 195
Tio Lorenzo, 197
Tipico guitar, 40
Tit for Tat Club, 44
Tizol, Francisco, 220
Tizol, Juan, 220
Tizol, Manuel, 218
TK Records, xxii, xxiii
Torres, Celso, 67
Torres, Mark, 144
Tosh, Peter, 35
Toshiba, 21
Tosti, Don, 51, 126, 127
"Toussaint L'Ouverture," 34, 35
Touzet, Rene, 130
Toyosaburo, Yamaguchi "Shanghai," 46
"Trans Europe Express," 246, 268
Trans World Stores, 166
Tranzlator Crew, 26, 29
Treaty of Guadalupe-Hidalgo, 71
Tribal Nation, 266

Trio Borinquen, 90, 215, 221
Trio Mocoto, 258
Trio Quisqueya, 221
Troupe, Quincy, 109, 121, 124, 125
Trujillo, Rafael, 34, 136–39, 141
"Trujillo Is Great and Immortal," 136
Tsaba, 137
Tucker, C. Delores, 154, 158, 159, 168, 170, 171–72, 175
Turks and Caicos, 146
Turner, Tina, 112, 114
Turner, Victor, 115
"Tweedle Dee," 223
2 Live Crew, xxiii, xxiv, 165, 166, 239, 247
"Two Shades of Soul," 102
2 Sides II a Book, 35

"Uhuru Africa," 90
Underground Musicians Association (UGMA), 101
"Un Indio quiere llolar" 61
Union of God's Musicians and Artists Ascension (UGMAA), 101
United Farm Workers (UFW) union, 202
United House of Prayer for All People, xx, xxiii
Universal City Walk (Los Angeles), 77
Urban renewal, xvi, 107–25
Urrea, Luis Alberto, 200
U.S. Marine Corps, 166

Valdes, Carlos "Patato" 90
Valoy, Cuco, 139, 145, 149
"Vaqueros nortenos," 65
Vaquero style, 62
Varela, Chuey, 126
Vargas, Wilfrido, 145, 148, 149
Vasquez, Anthony, 35, 36

Vasquez, Lolly, 130
Vasquez, Pat, 130
Vaughan, Sarah, 92
Vegas Brothers, 130
Velasquez, Karen, 69
Ventura, Johnny, 139
Vera Cruz, Philip, 202
Verdi, Giuseppe, 96
Viacom, 15
Vicioso, Tony, 143
Victoria Quartet, 222
Vidal, Hernan, 194
Vietnamese Americans, 50, 184
Vietnam War, 50, 120
Vigneault, Gilles, 55
Viloria, Angel, 147
Vinson, Eddie "Cleanhead," 96
VIPs, 55
"Visa para un sueno," 148
"Viva tirado," 5
Voodoo Queens, 50
Vodou, 35, 194
"Voy Pa'lla," 133, 135

Wailer, Bunny, 45
Wald, Gayle, 5–6
Waley, Wade, 87
Walker, T-Bone, 197
"Walk This Way," 268
Wall of Respect (St. Louis), 116
Walser, Rob, 257
Waltz, 62
"Wanderer, The," xx, xxi, xxiv
Wanderers, The, xxi
War, 260
Warner Music Group, 7–8
Warshow, Robert, 179
Warwick, Dionne, 171
Washington, Dinah, 92
Washington Philharmonic Orchestra, 121
Waters, Maxine, 175, 178
Waters, Muddy, 112

Watson, Johnny "Guitar," 96
Watts Writers Workshop, 110, 121
Waxer, Lisa, 47, 225, 230
WB network, 7, 8, 274
Weatherford, Teddy, 46
Webb, Chick, 90
Webster, Ben, 208
"Weed King, The," 125
Welcome to Haiti: Creole 101, 33
Weston, Randy, 90
"We Venerate Trujillo," 136
Whaley, Earl, 46
"Where Is the Love?" 265–66,
    270, 271, 272, 273
Whitby, Ontario, xxiv
White, Maurice, 97
White Earth Reservation, 203
Whiteman, Paul, 89, 220
Witherspoon, Jimmy, 103
Whitman Sisters, 253
"Who Let the Dogs Out?" xxiii,
    xxiv
Whyteshadows, 49
Wild Orchid, 267
Wilkinson, Frank, 127, 128–29
Will.I.Am (William Jones),
    266–68, 270, 276
Williams, Hank, xx
Williams, Mary Lou, 89, 92
Williams, Raymond, 9, 12–13, 15,
    16, 18, 22
Williams, Reggie, 165
Williams, Roger, 188
Williams, Tex, xvi
Wilson, Dennis, 254
Wilson, Gerald, 55
Wilson, Pete, 58, 72
Wilson, Philip, 114
Wilson, Woodrow, 140
Winfrey, Oprah, 43
Womack, Bobby, xx
Women's City Club (Detroit), 243
Wonder, Stevie, 245

Wong, Dickie, 44
Wong, Francis, 49
Wong, Nelly, 196
Wong, Tom ("the Great Sebastien"),
    44
Woods, Clyde, xviii–xix
Woodson, Carter G., 41
World Bank, 27, 70, 142
World Kulintang Institute, 49
World Saxophone Quartet (WSQ),
    121–22
Worrell, Bernie, 240–41
Wounded Knee, 131, 202
Wretched of the Earth, The, 133
Wright, Richard, 111–12, 114

Yankovic, "Weird Al," 260
Yaqui people, 197
Yellow Magic Orchestra, 242
"Yo soy latino," 222
Young, Lee, 86
Young, Lester, 84, 85, 94, 95, 96,
    103
Young Communist League, 93
Youth, 1–25, 154–83, 238–243

Zap Mama, 197
Zapatista uprising, 71
Zayas, Doreen Ann, 149
Zoot suit riots, 127
Zouk, 147, 149

George Lipsitz is professor of black studies and sociology at the University of California, Santa Barbara. He is the author of several books, including *American Studies in a Moment of Danger* and *Time Passages,* both published by the University of Minnesota Press.